BRITISH RAILWAYS
LOCOMOTIVES & COACHING STOCK
2000

The Complete Guide to all
Locomotives & Coaching Stock
Vehicles which run on
Britain's Mainline Railways

Peter Fox, Nei Webster & Peter Hall

ISBN 1 902336 13 5

© 2000. Platform 5 Publishing Ltd., 3 Wyvern House, Sark Road, Sheffield,
S2 4HG, England.

CONTENTS

READERS' COMMENTS

With such a wealth of information as contained in this book, it is inevitable a few inaccuracies may be found. The authors will therefore be pleased to receive notification from readers of any such inaccuracies, and also of any additional information to supplement our records and thus enhance future editions.

Please send comments to: Editorial Department, Platform 5 Publishing Ltd., 3 Wyvern House, Sark Road, Sheffield, S2 4HG, England. Fax: 0114 255 2471. Note: Our e-mail address is likely to change shortly. Please see advertisements in "Today's Railways" and "Rail Express".

Special Note: Readers are advised the authors and staff of Platform 5 regret they are unable to answer ANY specific locomotive and rolling stock queries (concerning either the UK or elsewhere) other than through the 'Q & A' section in the Platform 5 magazine *Today's Railways*.

UPDATES

A comprehensive update to *British Railways Locomotives & Coaching Stock* is published every month in the Platform 5 magazine, *Today's Railways*, which also contains news and rolling stock information on the railways of Britain, Ireland and Continental Europe. Rolling Stock updates will also be found in other magazines specialising mainly in British matters, such as *Rail Express*. For further details of *Today's Railways*, please see the advertisements elsewhere within this book.

Information in this edition is intended to illustrate the actual situation on Britain's railways, rather than necessarily agree with TOPS, RSL and other computer records. Information is updated to 1st January 2000.

ORGANISATION & OPERATION OF BRITAIN'S RAILWAY SYSTEM

INFRASTRUCTURE & OPERATION

Britain's national railway infrastructure (i.e. the track, signalling, stations and associated power supply equipment) is owned by a public company – Railtrack PLC. Many stations and maintenance depots are leased to and operated by Train Operating Companies (TOCs), but some larger stations remain under Railtrack control. The only exception is the infrastructure on the Isle of Wight, which is nationally owned and is leased to the Island Line franchisee.

Trains are operated by TOCs over the Railtrack network, regulated by access agreements between the parties involved. In general, TOCs are responsible for the provision and maintenance of the locomotives, rolling stock and staff necessary for the direct operation of services, whilst Railtrack is responsible for the provision and maintenance of the infrastructure and also for staff needed to regulate the operation of services.

DOMESTIC PASSENGER TRAIN OPERATORS

The large majority of passenger trains are operated by the TOCs on fixed term franchises. Franchise expiry dates are shown in parentheses in the list of franchisees below:

Franchise	Franchisee	Trading Name
Anglia Railways	GB Railways Ltd. (until 4 April 2004)	Anglia Railways
Cardiff Railway	Prism Rail PLC (until 12 April 2004)	Cardiff Railways
Central Trains	National Express Group PLC (until 1 April 2004)	Central Trains
Chiltern Railways	M40 Trains Ltd. (until 20 July 2003)	Chiltern Railways
Cross Country	Virgin Rail Group Ltd. (until 4 January 2012)	Virgin Trains
Gatwick Express	National Express Group PLC (until 27 April 2011)	Gatwick Express
Great Eastern Railway	First Group PLC (until 4 April 2004)	First Great Eastern
Great Western Trains	First Group PLC (until 3 February 2006)	First Great Western
InterCity East Coast	GNER Holdings Ltd. (until 4 April 2004)	Great North Eastern Railway
InterCity West Coast	Virgin Rail Group Ltd. (until 8 March 2012)	Virgin Trains

Island Line	Stagecoach Holdings PLC (until 12 October 2001)	Island Line
LTS Rail	Prism Rail PLC (until 25 May 2011)	LTS Rail
Merseyrail Electrics	MTL Rail Ltd. (until 18 March 2004)	Merseyrail Electrics
Midland Main Line	National Express Group PLC (until 27 April 2006)	Midland Mainline
Network South Central	Connex Rail Ltd. (until 25 May 2003)	Connex South Central
North London Railways	National Express Group PLC (until 1 September 2004)	Silverlink Train Services
North West Regional Railways	First Group PLC (until 1 April 2004)	First North Western
Regional Railways North East	MTL Rail Ltd. (until 1 April 2004)	Northern Spirit
Scotrail	National Express Group PLC (until 30 March 2004)	ScotRail
South Eastern	Connex Rail Ltd. (until 12 October 2011)	Connex South Eastern
South Wales & West	Prism Rail PLC (until 12 April 2004)	Wales & West Passenger Trains
South West	Stagecoach Holdings PLC (until 3 February 2003)	South West Trains
Thames	Victory Railways Holdings Ltd. (until 12 April 2004)	Thames Trains
Thameslink	GOVIA Ltd. (until 1 April 2004)	Thameslink Rail
West Anglia Great Northern	Prism Rail PLC (until 4 April 2004)	WAGN

The above companies may also operate other services under 'Open Access' arrangements.

The following operate non-franchised services only:

Operator	Trading Name	Route
British Airports Authority	Heathrow Express	London Paddington–Heathrow Airport
West Coast Railway	West Coast Railway	Fort William–Mallaig

INTERNATIONAL PASSENGER OPERATIONS

Eurostar (UK) operates international passenger-only services between the United Kingdom and continental Europe, jointly with French National Railways (SNCF) and Belgian National Railways (SNCB/NMBS). Eurostar (UK) is a subsidiary of London & Continental Railways, which is jointly owned by National Express Group PLC and the British Airways.

In addition, a service for the conveyance of accompanied road vehicles through the Channel Tunnel is provided by the tunnel operating company, Eurotunnel.

FREIGHT TRAIN OPERATIONS

Freight train services are operated under 'Open Access' arrangements by the following operators:

English Welsh & Scottish Railway Ltd. (EWS)
Freightliner Ltd.
Direct Rail Services Ltd. (DRS)
Mendip Rail Ltd.

1. LOCOMOTIVES

USING THIS SECTION – LAYOUT OF INFORMATION

Locomotives are listed in numerical order of class number, and then in numerical order of individual locomotives – using current numbers as allocated by the Rolling Stock Library (RSL). The only exceptions are locomotives numbered in the 89xxx series (see page 11), which are listed under their previous class numbers. Where numbers actually carried are different to those officially allocated, these are noted in class headings where appropriate. Each locomotive entry is laid out as in one of the following examples:

Shunting Locomotives

RSL No.	Detail	Livery	Owner	Pool	Depot	Location
08388	a	**B**	E	WSSE	OC	*Old Oak Common TMD*

Official names carried are appended in a table following each class as appropriate.

Main Line Locomotives

RSL No.	Detail	Livery	Owner	Pool	Depot	Name
47777	x	**RX**	E	WHDP	CD	Restored

In cases where a two column format is used, official names carried are appended in a table following each class as appropriate.

CLASS HEADINGS

Principal details and dimensions are quoted for each class in metric and/or imperial units as considered appropriate bearing in mind common UK usage. Abbreviations used are shown in Section 6.9.

All dimensions and weights are quoted for locomotives in an 'as new' condition with all necessary supplies (e.g. oil, water and sand) on board. Dimensions are quoted in the order Length – Width – Height. Lengths quoted are over buffers or couplings as appropriate. All dimensions quoted are maxima (Electric locomotives – with pantograph lowered). Where two different wheel diameter dimensions are shown, the first refers to powered wheels and the second refers to non-powered wheels.

DETAIL DIFFERENCES

Only detail differences which currently affect the areas and types of train which locomotives may work are shown. All other detail differences are specifically excluded. Where such differences occur within a class or part class, they are shown in the 'Detail' column alongside the individual locomotive number. Standard abbreviations used are:

a	Train air brake equipment only.
b	Buckeye couplers.
c	Scharfenberg couplers.

j	RCH jumper cables for operating with Propelling Control Vehicles.
k	Swinghead automatic knuckle couplers.
p	Train air, vacuum and electro-pneumatic brakes.
r	Radio Electronic Token Block (RETB) equipment.
s	Slow Speed Control equipment.
v	Train vacuum brake only.
x	Train air and vacuum brakes ('Dual brakes').
+	Additional fuel tank capacity.

In all cases use of the above abbreviations indicates the equipment indicated is normally operable. Meaning of non-standard abbreviations and symbols is detailed in individual class headings.

LIVERY CODES

Livery codes are used to denote the various liveries carried. It is impossible in a publication of this size to list every livery variation which currently exists. In particular items ignored for the purposes of this publication include:

- Minor colour variations.
- Omission of logos.
- All numbering, lettering and branding.

Descriptions quoted are thus a general guide only. Logos as appropriate for each livery are normally deemed to be carried. A complete list of livery codes used appears in Section 6.1.

OWNER CODES

Owner codes are used to denote the owners of locomotives listed. A complete list of owner codes used appears in Section 6.2.

POOL CODES

Locomotives are split into operational groups ('pools') for diagramming and maintenance purposes. The official codes used to denote these pools are shown in this publication. A complete list of locomotive pool codes used appears in Section 6.3.

DEPOT & LOCATION CODES

Depot codes are used in this to denote the normal maintenance base of each operational locomotive (except Freightliner operated locomotives). However, maintenance may be carried out at other locations and may also be carried out by mobile maintenance teams.

The codes FD, FE and FS are used for locomotives operated by Freightliner. This company does not operate a depot based maintenance system for its locomotives, instead using mobile maintenance teams to carry out day-to-day maintenance, with heavier repairs being performed by contractors.

Location codes are used to denote the current actual location of stored vehicles. A location code will always be followed by (S) to denote stored.

A complete list of depot and location codes used appears in Section 6.6.

A complete list of the abbreviations used to denote different types of depots appears in Section 6.7.

SHUNTING LOCOMOTIVE LOCATIONS

The actual location of operational shunting locomotives, updated to reports received as at 1st January 2000, is included as a guide to readers as to where these locomotives may be found. Whilst some locomotives remain at certain locations for some considerable length of time, others may move around far more frequently. Readers must appreciate the listing of a locomotive at a location is no absolute guarantee the locomotive concerned (or any other locomotive) will remain present on a subsequent date.

NAMES

Only names carried with official sanction are listed in this publication. As far as possible names are shown in UPPER/lower case characters as actually shown on the name carried on the locomotive. Inscriptions carried on crests and/or plates additional to the main nameplate are not shown. Names known to be carried on one side only are suffixed [1] (e.g. Back Tor[1]).

GENERAL INFORMATION

CLASSIFICATION AND NUMBERING

All locomotives are classified and allocated numbers under the TOPS numbering system, introduced in 1972. This comprises a two-digit class number followed by a three-digit serial number. Where the actual number carried by a locomotive differs from the allocated number, or where an additional number is carried to the allocated number, this is shown by a note in the class heading.

For diesel locomotives, class numbers offer an indication of engine horsepower as shown in the table below.

Class No. Range	Engine hp
01–14	0–799
15–20	800–1000
21–31	1001–1499
32–39	1500–1999
40–54, 57	2000–2999
55–56, 58–69	3000+

For electric locomotives class numbers are allocated in ascending numerical order under the following scheme:

Class 70–80   direct current and d.c./diesel dual system locomotives.
Class 81 onwards   alternating current and a.c./d.c. dual system locos.

Numbers in the 89xxx series (except 89001) are allocated by the Rolling Stock Library to locomotives which have been de-registered but subsequently re-registered for use on the Railtrack network and whose original number has already been re-used. Such numbers are normally only carried inside locomotive cabs and are carried externally in normal circumstances.

Although the TOPS system is expected to be phased-out during 2000, the existing numbering scheme is likely to continue unchanged for the foreseeable future.

WHEEL ARRANGEMENT

For main line locomotives the system whereby the number of driven axles on a bogie or frame is denoted by a letter (A = 1, B = 2, C = 3 etc.) and the number of non-powered axles is denoted by a number is used. The use of the letter 'o' after a letter indicates each axle is individually powered, whilst the + symbol indicates bogies are inter-coupled.

For shunting locomotives, the Whyte notation is used. In this notation the number of leading wheels are given, followed by the number of driving wheels and then the trailing wheels.

HAULAGE CAPABILITY OF DIESEL LOCOMOTIVES

The haulage capability of a diesel locomotive depends upon three basic factors:

1. Adhesive weight. The greater the weight on the driving wheels, the greater the adhesion and more tractive power can be applied before wheelslip occurs.

2. The characteristics of its transmission. To start a train the locomotive has to exert a pull at standstill. A direct drive diesel engine cannot do this, hence the need for transmission. This may be mechanical, hydraulic or electric. The present British Standard for locomotives is electric transmission. Here the diesel engine drives a generator or alternator and the current produced is fed to the traction motors. The force produced by each driven wheel depends on the current in its traction motor. In other words, the larger the current, the harder it pulls. As the locomotive speed increases, the current in the traction motor falls, hence the *Maximum Tractive Effort* is the maximum force at its wheels the locomotive can exert at a standstill. The electrical equipment cannot take such high currents for long without overheating. Hence the *Continuous Tractive Effort* is quoted which represents the current which the equipment can take continuously.

3. The power of its engine. Not all power reaches the rail, as electrical machines are approximately 90% efficient. As the electrical energy passes through two such machines (the generator or alternator and the traction motors), the *Power at Rail* is approximately 81% (90% of 90%) of the engine power, less a further amount used for auxiliary equipment such as radiator fans, traction motor blowers, air compressors, battery charging, cab heating, Electric Train Supply (ETS) etc. The power of the locomotive is proportional to the tractive effort times the speed. Hence when on full power there is a speed corresponding to the continuous tractive effort.

HAULAGE CAPABILITY OF ELECTRIC LOCOMOTIVES

Unlike a diesel locomotive, an electric locomotive does not develop it power on board and its performance is determined only by two factors, namely its weight and the characteristics of its electrical equipment. Whereas a diesel locomotive tends to be a constant power machine, the power of an electric locomotive varies considerably. Up to a certain speed it can produce virtually a constant tractive effort. Hence power rises with speed according to the formula given in section three above, until a maximum speed is reached at which tractive effort falls, such that the power also falls. Hence the power at the speed corresponding to the maximum tractive effort is lower than the maximum speed.

BRAKE FORCE

The brake force is a measure of the braking power of a locomotive. This is shown on the locomotive data panels so operating staff can ensure sufficient brake power is available on freight trains.

ELECTRIC TRAIN SUPPLY (ETS)

A number of locomotives are equipped to provide a supply of electricity to the train being hauled to power auxiliaries such as heating, cooling fans, air conditioning and kitchen equipment. ETS is provided from the locomotive by means of a separate alternator, except in the case of Class 33 which have a d.c. generator. The ETS index of a locomotive is a measure of the electrical power available for train supply.

Similarly, most loco-hauled coaches also have an ETS index, which in this case is a measure of the power required to operate equipment mounted in the coach. The sum of the ETS indices of all the hauled vehicles in a train must not exceed the ETS index of the locomotive.

ETS is commonly (but incorrectly) known as ETH (Electric Train Heating), which is a throwback to the days before loco-hauled coaches were equipped with other electrically powered auxiliary equipment.

ROUTE AVAILABILITY (RA)

This is a measure of a railway vehicle's axle load. The higher the axle load of a vehicle, the higher the RA number on a scale from 1 to 10. Each Railtrack route has a RA number and in general no vehicle with a higher RA number may travel on that route without special clearance. A map showing route availability on all routes is published on the Railtrack internet web site.

MULTIPLE & PUSH-PULL WORKING

Multiple working between vehicles (i.e. two or more powered vehicles being driven from one cab) is facilitated by jumper cables connecting the vehicles. However, not all types are compatible with each other, and a number of different systems are in use, each system being incompatible with any other.

Association Of American Railroads (AAR) System: Classes 59, 66, and 67.
Blue Star Coupling Code: Classes 20, 25, 31, 33, and 37. Locomotives 47971, 47972 and 47976.
Green Circle Coupling Code: Class 47 (not all equipped).
Orange Square Coupling Code: Class 50.
Red Diamond Coupling Code: Classes 56 and 58.
SR System: Classes 33/1, 73 and various 750 V d.c. EMUs.
Within Own Class only: Classes 43 and 60.

Class 47 locos 47701–47717 use a time-division multiplex (TDM) system for push-pull working which utilises the existing Railway Clearing House (RCH) jumper cables fitted to coaching stock vehicles. Previously these cables had only been used to control train lighting and public address systems.

A number of other locomotives are equipped with a more modern TDM system for push-pull working which also facilitates multiple working.

1.1. DIESEL LOCOMOTIVES

Note: All diesel locomotives authorised to operate under their own power on the Railtrack network are listed in this section. Diesel locomotives authorised to operate solely on the Eurotunnel network are listed in section 1.5.

CLASS 01/5   BARCLAY   0-6-0

Built: 1984 by Andrew Barclay, Kilmarnock for the Ministry of Defence Army Department. Registered for use on the Railtrack network in 1999.
Engine: Rolls Royce CV12TCE of 445 kW (600 hp) at ? rpm.

Transmission: Hydraulic.	**Maximum Tractive Effort:**
Continuous Tractive Effort:	**Train Brakes:** Air.
Brake Force: 46 t.	**Dimensions:** 9.45 x ? x ? m.
Weight: 61.0 t.	**Wheel Diameter:**
Design Speed: 28.5 mph.	**Maximum Speed:** 10 mph.
Fuel Capacity: 1590 litres.	**RA:** 7.
Train Supply: Not equipped.	**Multiple Working:** Not equipped.

Non standard livery/numbering:
• 01505/506 are in Army Department green livery.

01505	**0**	MD	MBDL	KN	*Defence Munitions, Kineton*
01506	**0**	MD	MBDL	KN	*Defence Munitions, Kineton*

CLASS 01/5   HUNSLET-BARCLAY   0-6-0

Built: 1971 by The Hunslet Engine Company, Leeds for the National Coal Board (Western Area). Subsequently sold to Hunslet-Barclay, Kilmarnock and rebuilt prior to sale to The Felixstowe Dock and Railway Company in 1999.
Engine: Caterpillar 3412C DITA of 475 kW (640 hp) at ? rpm.
Transmission: Hydraulic. Twin Disc 13800 series torque converter coupled to a Hunslet final drive.
Maximum Tractive Effort: 180 kN (40365 lbf).
Continuous Tractive Effort: 235 kN (52700 lbf) at ?? mph.
Train Brakes: Air.

Brake Force: 48 t.	**Dimensions:** 3.95 x 2.51 x 3.80 m.
Weight: 64.3 t.	**Wheel Diameter:** 1143 mm.
Design Speed: 15 mph.	**Maximum Speed:** 15 mph.
Fuel Capacity: 930 litres.	**RA:** 7
Train Supply: Not equipped.	**Multiple Working:** Not equipped.

Non standard livery/numbering:
• 01531 is in Felixstowe Dock and Railway Company livery of blue with a green stripe picked out in white. Also carries number H4323.

01531	**0**	FX	MBDL	FX	*Felixstowe South Container Terminal*

Name: 01531   COLONEL TOMLINE

CLASS 03   BR/GARDNER   0-6-0

Built: 1962 by BR at Swindon Works.
Engine: Gardner 8L3 of 152 kW (204 hp) at 1200 rpm.
Transmission: Mechanical. Fluidrive type 23 hydraulic coupling to Wilson-Drewry CA5R7 gearbox with SCG type RF11 final drive.
Maximum Tractive Effort: 68 kN (15300 lbf).
Continuous Tractive Effort: 68 kN (15300 lbf) at 3.75 mph.
Train Brakes: Air & vacuum.

Brake Force: 13 t.	**Dimensions:** 7.93 x 2.59 x 3.73 m.
Weight: 31.3 t.	**Wheel Diameter:** 1092 mm.
Design Speed: 28.5 mph.	**Maximum Speed:** 28.5 mph.
Fuel Capacity: 1364 litres.	**RA:** 1.
Train Supply: Not equipped.	**Multiple Working:** Not equipped.

03179   **WN**   WN   HQXX   HE   *Hornsey T&RSMD*

Name: 03179   CLIVE

CLASS 08   BR/ENGLISH ELECTRIC   0-6-0

Built: 1955–62 by BR at Crewe, Darlington, Derby, Doncaster or Horwich Works.
Engine: English Electric 6KT of 298 kW (400 hp) at 680 rpm.
Main Generator: English Electric 801.
Traction Motors: Two English Electric 506.
Maximum Tractive Effort: 156 kN (35000 lbf).
Continuous Tractive Effort: 49 kN (11100 lbf) at 8.8 mph.

Power At Rail: 194 kW (260 hp).	**Train Brakes:** Air & vacuum.
Brake Force: 19 t.	**Dimensions:** 8.92 x 2.59 x 3.89 m.
Weight: 49.6–50.4 t.	**Wheel Diameter:** 1372 mm.
Design Speed: 20 mph.	**Maximum Speed:** 15 mph.
Fuel Capacity: 3037 litres.	**RA:** 5.
Train Supply: Not equipped.	**Multiple Working:** Not equipped.

Non-standard liveries/numbering:
- 08375/519/730/788/867 are BR style black.
- 08397 is as **F**, but with BR Railfreight General yellow & red logos.
- 08414 is as **DG**, but with BR & Railfreight Distribution logos and large bodyside numbers. Also carries number D3529.
- 08454/887/934 are in Virgin Trains 'Pitstop' livery of black with a large black & white chequered flag on the bodyside.
- 08460 is light grey with black underframe, cab doors, window surrounds and roof. Also carries number D3575.
- 08500 is red, lined out in black and white. Also carries a large number '1' on the bodyside.
- 08527 is light grey with a black roof, blue bodyside stripe and 'Ilford Level 5' branding.
- 08593 is Great Eastern Railway style blue. Also carries number D3760.
- 08596/724 are in RFS(E) livery of blue with silver lining.
- 08601 is London Midland & Scottish Railway style black.
- 08616 is Great Western Railway style green with cast numberplates 3783.

- 08617 is in Virgin Trains 'Pitstop' livery of black with a large red and black bodyside flag.
- 08642 is London & South Western Railway style black. Also carries number D3809.
- 08649 is grey with blue, white and red stripes and WTL logo. Also carries number D3816.
- 08682 is dark blue with a grey roof.
- 08689 is as **DG**, but with BR Railfreight General yellow & red logos and large bodyside numbers.
- 08715 is 'Dayglo' orange.
- 08721 is as **B**, but with a red and yellow stripe.
- 08743/903 are in Enron Teesside Operations livery of Trafalgar blue with a red lower body stripe.
- 08785 is silver grey.
- 08793 is LNER style apple green.
- 08801 carries number 801.
- 08805 is London Midland & Scottish Railway style maroon. Also carries number 3973.
- 08830 carries number D3998.
- 08870 is in RMS Locotech livery of blue and red. Also carries RMS No. 024.
- 08879 is green and black with Railfreight Distribution logos.
- 08883 is Caledonian Railway style blue.
- 08907 is London & North Western Railway style black.
- 08928 is as **FR**, with large bodyside numbers and light blue solebar.
- 08938 is grey and red.

Note: † – Equipped with remote control.

Class 08/0. Standard Design.

08077		**RF**	P	DFLS	FS	Southampton Maritime FLT
08308	a	**CP**	RT	HASS	IS	Inverness CARMD
08331		**GN**	RF	RFSH	EC	Craigentinny T&RSMD
08375		**0**	RT	DFLS	FS	Ipswich SD
08388	a	**FP**	E	WNZX	ZB(S)	
08389	a	**B**	EF	WSXX	OC(S)	
08393	a	**FE**	EF	WSSE	OC	London International Freight Terminal
08397	a	**0**	E	WSWM	BS	Padeswood Hall Cement Works
08401	a	**DG**	E	WSYH	IM	Immingham TMD
08402	a	**DG**	E	WSWS	EH	Avonmouth
08405	a	**DG**	E	WSYH	IM	Immingham TMD
08410	a	**GL**	GW	HJSL	LA	Laira T&RSMD
08411	a	**B**	E	WSSC	ML	Ayr SD
08413	a	**DG**	EF	WNZX	ZB(S)	
08414	a	**0**	E	WSWX	OC(S)	
08417	a	**B**	SO	XYPS	MD	Merehead
08418	a	**F**	E	WSYH	IM	Tinsley Yard
08419	a	**B**	E	WHZX	ZC(S)	
08428	a	**B**	E	WSYH	IM	Doncaster TMD
08441	a	**B**	E	WSSC	ML	Ayr SD
08442	a	**F**	E	WSYH	IM	Immingham Reception Sidings
08445	a	**B**	E	WNZX	ZB(S)	
08448	a	**B**	E	WNZX	BS(S)	

08449	a	B	E	WNZX	TT(S)	
08451		B	VW	HFSN	WN	*Willesden TMD*
08454		0	VW	HFSN	WN	*Wembley CSD*
08460	a	0	E	WSNW	AN	*Warrington Yards*
08466	a	E	E	WSAW	CF	*Allied Steel & Wire, Cardiff*
08472	a	BR	RF	RFSH	EC	*Craigentinny T&RSMD*
08473	v	B	E	WNZX	LR(S)	
08480	a	G	E	WSWS	EH	*Eastleigh Yards*
08481		B	E	WSSW	CF	*Margam SD*
08482	a	DG	E	WSSE	OC	*Euston Downside CARMD*
08483	a	DG	GW	HJXX	PM	*St. Phlips Marsh T&RSMD*
08484	a	DG	RC	KWSW	ZN	*Railcare Wolverton*
08485	a	B	EF	WSNW	AN	*Warrington Yards*
08489	a	F	E	WSXX	WA(S)	
08492	a	B	E	WSSC	ML	*Millerhill Yard*
08493	a	B	E	WSWX	CF(S)	
08495		B	E	WSYH	IM	*Worksop Yards*
08499	a	F	E	WSXX	KY(S)	
08500		0	E	WSWS	EH	*Bristol Barton Hill T&RSMD*
08506	a	B	E	WSXX	CF(S)	
08509	a	F	E	WSXX	TI(S)	
08510	a	B	E	WSYH	IM	*Goole Docks*
08511	a	E	E	WSEM	TO	*Toton TMD*
08512	a	F	E	WSYH	IM	*Doncaster Belmont Yard*
08514	a	B	E	WSYH	IM	*Worksop Yards*
08515	a	B	E	WNZX	GD(S)	
08516	a	DG	E	WSEM	TO	*Peterborough SD*
08517	a	B	E	WNZX	SF(S)	
08519	a	0	E	WNZX	ZB(S)	
08523		ML	E	WSXX	CD(S)	
08525		F	MA	HISL	NL	*Neville Hill (InterCity) T&RSMD*
08526		E	E	WSSE	OC	*Dagenham Dock Up Sidings*
08527		0	AD	KCSI	ZI	*Adtranz, Ilford*
08528		DG	E	WSEM	TO	*Toton TMD*
08529		B	E	WSYH	IM	*Tinsley Yard*
08530		DG	P	DFLS	FS	*Felixstowe North FLT*
08531	a	DG	P	DFLS	FS	*Tilbury FLT*
08534		DG	E	WSSC	ML	*Motherwell T&RSMD*
08535		DG	EF	WSWM	BS	*Bescot TMD*
08536		B	MA	HISE	DY(S)	
08538		DG	E	WSEM	TO	*Peterborough West Yard*
08540		DG	E	WSWM	BS	*Bescot Yard*
08541		DG	E	WSWX	OC(S)	
08542		F	E	WSWM	BS	*Bescot Yard*
08543		DG	E	WSWM	BS	*Bescot TMD*
08561	a	B	E	WSNW	AN	*Carnforth Bottom End Sidings*
08567		B	E	WSWM	BS	*Wolverhampton Steel Terminal*
08568	a	B	RC	KGSS	ZH	*Railcare, Glasgow*
08569		E	EF	WSEM	TO	*Peterborough West Yard*
08571	a	B	RF	XYPS	MD	*Whatley Quarry*
08573		U	AD	KCSI	ZI	*Adtranz, Ilford*

08575		**B**	P	DFLS	FS	*Southampton Maritime FLT*
08576		**B**	E	WSWX	CF(S)	
08577		**B**	E	WSNE	TE	*Tyne Yard*
08578		**RG**	E	WSNW	AN	*Edge Hill Tuebrook Sidings*
08580		**B**	E	WSWM	BS	*Northampton Castle Yard*
08581		**BR**	E	WNZX	ZB(S)	
08582	a	**DG**	E	WSNE	TE	*Thornaby T&RSMD*
08585		**B**	P	DFLS	FS	*Crewe Basford Hall Yard*
08586	a	**F**	E	WNZX	AY(S)	
08587		**B**	E	WSYH	IM	*Doncaster TMD*
08588		**BR**	MA	HISL	NL	*Neville Hill (InterCity) T&RSMD*
08593		**0**	E	WSSE	OC	*Ipswich Upper Yard*
08594		**B**	E	WNZX	TT(S)	
08596	†	**0**	RF	RFSH	ZB	*RFS(E), Doncaster*
08597		**B**	E	WSYH	IM	*Hull King George Dock*
08599		**B**	E	WSNW	AN	*Allerton T&RSMD*
08601		**0**	E	WSXX	AN(S)	
08605		**B**	E	WSYH	IM	*Neville Hill DMU/EMU T&RSMD*
08607		**B**	E	WNZX	TT(S)	
08609		**B**	E	WNZX	ZB(S)	
08610		**B**	E	WNZX	ZB(S)	
08611		**V**	VW	HFSL	LO	*Longsight CARMD*
08616		**0**	MA	HGSS	TS	*Soho T&RSMD*
08617		**0**	VW	HFSN	WN	*Willesden T&RSMD*
08618		**B**	E	WNZX	GD(S)	
08619		**B**	E	WNZX	ZB(S)	
08622		**B**	E	WNZX	ML(S)	
08623		**B**	E	WSWM	BS	*Bescot Yard*
08624		**B**	P	DFLS	FS	*Coatbridge FLT*
08625		**B**	E	WNZX	CF(S)	
08628		**B**	E	WSWX	SY(S)	
08629		**RP**	RC	KWSW	ZN	*Railcare, Wolverton*
08630		**E**	E	WSSC	ML	*Deanside Transit, Hillingdon*
08631		**N**	FR	HSSN	NC	*Norwich Crown Point T&RSMD*
08632		**B**	E	WSYH	IM	*Immingham T&RSMD*
08633		**RX**	E	WSNE	TE	*Tyne Yard SD*
08634		**B**	E	WNZX	SF(S)	
08635		**B**	E	WSSE	OC	*Dagenham Dock Up Sidings*
08641		**DG**	GW	HJSL	LA	*Laira T&RSMD*
08642		**0**	P	DFLS	FS	*Felixstowe North FLT*
08643		**DG**	GW	HJXX	PM	*St. Philips Marsh T&RSMD*
08644		**IM**	GW	HJSL	LA	*Penzance*
08645		**DG**	GW	HJSL	LA	*Laira T&RSMD*
08646		**F**	E	WSWS	EH	*Eastleigh Yards*
08648		**DG**	GW	HJSL	LA	*Laira T&RSMD*
08649		**0**	AM	KESE	ZG	*Alstom, Eastleigh*
08651		**DG**	E	WSAW	CF	*Cardiff Canton TMD*
08653		**FE**	EF	WSWS	EH	*Avonmouth Bulk Terminal*
08655		**F**	EF	WSYH	IM	*Knottingley T&RSMD*
08661	a	**F**	EF	WSYX	AN(S)	
08662		**B**	E	WSYH	IM	*Goole Docks*

08663	a	DG	GW	HJSL	LA	Laira T&RSMD
08664		E	E	WSWS	EH	Eastleigh T&RSMD
08665		B	E	WSYH	IM	Immingham T&RSMD
08666		B	E	WSYX	AN(S)	
08670	a	B	E	WSSC	ML	Motherwell T&RSMD
08673		IM	E	WSYX	AN(S)	
08675		F	E	WSXX	ML(S)	
08676		B	E	WSYH	IM	Immingham Mineral Quay
08677		B	E	WNZX	ZB(S)	
08682		0	AD	KDSD	ZF	Adtranz, Doncaster
08683		B	E	WSAW	CF	Cardiff Canton T&RSMD
08685		B	E	WSSC	ML	Polmadie T&RSMD
08689	a	0	E	WSYH	IM	Ferrybridge T&RSMD
08690		MA	MA	HISE	DY	Derby Etches Park
08691		G	FL	DFLS	FS	Trafford Park FLT
08693		B	E	WNZX	SP(S)	
08694	a	B	EF	WSSE	OC	Old Oak Common T&RSMD
08695	a	E	E	WSWM	BS	Bescot TMD
08696	a	V	VW	HFSL	LO	Liverpool Downside CSD
08697		B	MA	HISE	DY	Derby Etches Park T&RSMD
08698	a	E	E	WSWM	BS	Oxley T&RSMD
08700	a	B	E	WNZX	SF(S)	
08701	a	RX	E	WSNW	AN	Warrington Yards
08702		B	E	WSXX	ZB(S)	
08703	a	B	EF	WSNW	AN	Guide Bridge Brookside Sidings
08706		B	E	WSEM	TO	Toton TMD
08709		B	E	WSNW	AN	Carlisle Kingmoor Yard
08711		RX	E	WSSE	OC	Stratford TMD
08713	a	B	E	WNZX	ZB(S)	
08714		RX	E	WSEM	TO	Peterborough SD
08715	v	0	E	WSXX	SF(S)	
08718		B	E	WNZX	AY(S)	
08720	a	E	E	WSSC	ML	Motherwell T&RSMD
08721		0	VW	HFSL	LO	Longsight CARMD
08723		B	E	WNZX	TT(S)	
08724		0	RF	XYPS	MD	Whatley Quarry
08730		0	RC	KGSS	ZH	Railcare, Glasgow
08731		B	E	WNZX	ML(S)	
08733		B	E	WNZX	SP(S)	
08734		B	E	WNZX	CF(S)	
08735		DG	E	WSXX	FW(S)	
08737	a	FE	EF	WSNW	AN	Warrington Yards
08738		E	E	WSWM	BS	Crewe Diesel TMD
08739		B	EF	WSXX	AN(S)	
08740		F	E	WSXX	SF(S)	
08742		RX	E	WSWM	BS	Longport Sidings
08743		0	EN	MBDL	BL	ICI, Billingham
08745		FE	P	DFLS	FS	Crewe Diesel Depot
08746		DG	E	WSXX	DR(S)	
08750		B	E	WNZX	SF(S)	
08751		F	EF	WSXX	ZB(S)	

08752		CE	E	WSYH	IM	*Tinsley Yard*
08754		B	RT	MBDL	ZB(S)	
08755		B	E	WNZX	ZB(S)	
08756		DG	E	WSXX	CF(S)	
08757		E	E	WSEM	TO	*Toton TMD*
08758		B	E	WSXX	SF(S)	
08762		B	RT	MBDL	ZB(S)	
08765		DG	E	WSWM	BS	*Saltley SD*
08768		B	E	WSSC	ML	*Motherwell T&RSMD*
08770	a	DG	E	WSSW	CF	*Margam Knuckle Sidings*
08773		B	E	WNZX	TO(S)	
08775		E	E	WSSE	OC	*Wembley Yards*
08776	a	DG	E	WSEM	TO	*Toton TMD*
08780		B	GW	HJSE	LE	*Landore T&RSMD*
08782	a	B	E	WSXX	KY(S)	
08783		B	E	WSYH	AN	*Doncaster Belmont Yard*
08784		B	EF	WSNW	AN	*Trafford Park Freight Terminal*
08785	a	O	P	DFLS	FS	*Crewe Basford Hall Yard*
08786	a	DG	E	WSWS	EH	*Tavistock Junction*
08788		O	RT	HASS	IS	*Inverness T&RSMD*
08790		B	VW	HFSL	LO	*Longsight Diesel T&RSMD*
08792		T	E	WSAW	CF	*Allied Steel & Wire, Cardiff*
08793	a	O	E	WNZX	ZB(S)	
08795		IM	GW	HJSE	LE	*Landore T&RSMD*
08798		B	E	WSWS	EH	*Tavistock Junction*
08799		B	EF	WSSE	OC	*Wembley Yards*
08801		B	E	WSAW	CF	*Allied Steel & Wire, Cardiff*
08802		RX	E	WSWM	BS	*Dee Marsh Sidings*
08804		B	E	WSWS	EH	*Reading West Yard*
08805		O	MA	HGSS	TS	*Tyseley T&RSMD*
08806	a	F	E	WSNE	TE	*Tyne Yard*
08807		BR	E	WSSC	ML	*Killoch Disposal Point*
08810	a	AR	AR	HSSN	NC	*Norwich Crown Point T&RSMD*
08813	a	DG	E	WSNE	TE	*Thornaby T&RSMD*
08815		B	E	WSYX	AN(S)	
08817		BR	E	WSXX	AN(S)	
08818		B	HN	HNRL	BH(S)	
08819		DG	E	WSXX	CF(S)	
08822		GL	GW	HJSE	LE	*St. Philips Marsh T&RSMD*
08823	a	B	AD	KDSD	ZF	*Adtranz, Doncaster*
08824	a	F	E	WSYH	IM	*Scunthorpe Yard*
08825	a	B	EF	WSXX	ZB(S)	
08826	a	B	E	WNZX	ML(S)	
08827		B	E	WSSC	ML	*Motherwell T&RSMD*
08828	a	E	E	WSAW	CF	*Allied Steel & Wire, Cardiff*
08829	a	B	E	WNZX	TT(S)	
08830		G	CA	HLSV	CP	*L&NWR Crewe Carriage Depot*
08834		FD	RF	RFSH	BN	*Bounds Green T&RSMD*
08836		I	GW	HJXX	OO	*Old Oak Common HST Depot*
08837		DG	EF	WSNW	AN	*Allerton T&RSMD*
08842		B	EF	WSNW	AN	*Trafford Park Freight Terminal*

08844		**B**	EF	WSXX	ZB(S)	
08847		**B**	AM	KESE	ZG	*Alstom, Eastleigh*
08853	a	**B**	RF	RFSH	BN	*Bounds Green T&RSMD*
08854		**E**	E	WSSW	CF	*Margam SD*
08855		**B**	E	WNZX	ZB(S)	
08856		**B**	EF	WSWS	EH	*Westbury*
08865		**B**	E	WSXX	PQ(S)	
08866		**B**	E	WSWM	BS	*Dee Marsh Sidings*
08867		**0**	E	WSXX	DE(S)	
08868		**B**	HN	HNRL	CP	*The Railway Age, Crewe*
08869		**G**	AR	HSSN	NC(S)	
08870		**0**	RL	MBDL	DE	*Brunner-Mond, Northwich*
08872		**DG**	EF	WSSE	OC	*Wembley Yards*
08873		**RX**	E	WNZX	ZB(S)	
08874		**SL**	RT	MBDL	BY	*Bletchley T&RSMD*
08877		**DG**	E	WSXX	SP(S)	
08879		**0**	EF	WSYH	IM	*Doncaster TMD*
08880		**B**	E	WSXX	AN(S)	
08881		**DG**	E	WSSC	ML	*Ayr SD*
08882		**B**	E	WSSC	ML	*Inverness Milburn Yard*
08883		**0**	E	WSSC	ML	*Perth WRD*
08884		**B**	E	WSWM	BS	*Saltley SD*
08886	†	**E**	E	WSYH	IM	*Immingham T&RSMD*
08887	a	**0**	VW	HFSN	PC	*Polmadie T&RSMD*
08888		**E**	E	WSWM	BS	*Daventry International Freight Terminal*
08890		**DG**	E	WSSE	OC	*Willesden South West Sidings*
08891		**B**	P	DFLS	FS	*Garston FLT*
08892		**GN**	RF	RFSH	BN	*Bounds Green T&SMD*
08893		**DG**	E	WSYX	ZB(S)	
08894		**B**	E	WSXX	AN(S)	
08895		**B**	E	WNZX	MG(S)	
08896		**E**	E	WSWS	EH	*Bristol Barton Hill T&RSMD*
08897		**E**	E	WSWM	BS	*Rugby Up Sidings*
08899		**MM**	MA	HISE	DY	*Derby Etches Park*
08900		**DG**	E	WSSW	CF	*Margam SD*
08901		**B**	E	WSYX	ZB(S)	
08902		**B**	EF	WSXX	AN(S)	
08903		**0**	EN	MBDL	BL	*ICI, Billingham*
08904		**B**	E	WSWS	EH	*Didcot Yard*
08905		**B**	EF	WSWM	BS	*Hams Hall Freight Terminal*
08906		**B**	E	WSXX	ML(S)	
08907		**0**	EF	WSWM	BS	*Crewe Diesel Depot*
08908		**MM**	MA	HISL	NL	*Neville Hill (InterCity) T&RSMD*
08909		**ML**	E	WSXX	AN(S)	
08910		**B**	E	WSSC	ML	*Aberdeen Guild Street Yard*
08911		**DG**	E	WSNW	AN	*Wigan Springs Branch CRDC*
08912		**B**	E	WSNW	AN	*Carlisle Currock*
08913		**DG**	EF	WSSE	OC	*Temple Mills Yard*
08914		**B**	E	WSXX	ZB(S)	
08915		**F**	E	WSNW	AN	*Peak Forest Sorting Sidings*
08918		**DG**	E	WSSE	OC	*Wembley Yards*

08919	**RX**	E	WSSE	OC	*Dagenham Dock Up Sidings*
08920	**F**	E	WSWM	BS	*Wolverhampton Steel Terminal*
08921	† **E**	E	WSAW	CF	*Allied Steel & Wire, Cardiff*
08922	**DG**	E	WSNW	AN	*Carlisle High Wapping Sidings*
08924	**DG**	E	WSXX	ZB(S)	
08925	**B**	E	WSNW	AN	*Allerton T&RSMD*
08926	**DG**	EF	WSXX	AN(S)	
08927	**B**	E	WSYH	IM	*Immingham T&RSMD*
08928	**0**	AR	HSSN	NC(S)	
08931	**B**	E	WSYX	ZB(S)	
08932	**B**	E	WSXX	CF(S)	
08933	**E**	E	WSSC	ML	*Motherwell T&RSMD*
08934	a **0**	VW	HFSN	WN	*Willesden T&RSMD*
08938	**0**	E	WNZX	SP(S)	
08939	**B**	EF	WSWM	BS	*Crewe Diesel Depot*
08940	**B**	E	WSYX	AN(S)	
08941	**B**	E	WSWS	EH	*St. Blazey T&RSMD*
08942	**B**	E	WSXX	ZB(S)	
08944	**DG**	E	WNZX	ZB(S)	
08946	**FE**	EF	WSWM	BS	*Saltley SD*
08947	**B**	E	WSWS	EH	*Westbury*
08948	c **EP**	EU	GPSS	OC	*North Pole International T&RSMD*
08950	**IM**	MA	HISL	NL	*Neville Hill (InterCity) T&RSMD*
08951	**DG**	EF	WSWS	EH	*Didcot Yard*
08952	**B**	E	WNZX	SP(S)	
08953	**DG**	E	WSWS	EH	*St. Blazey T&RSMD*
08954	**T**	E	WSYH	DR	*York Yard North*
08955	**T**	E	WSAW	CF	*Allied Steel & Wire, Cardiff*
08956	**B**	SO	CDJD	DY	*Serco Railtest, Derby*
08957	**E**	E	WSXX	CF(S)	
08958	**B**	E	WSXX	SF(S)	

Class 08/9. Reduced height cab. Details as Class 08/0 except:

Converted: 1985–87 by BR at Landore depot.
Dimensions: 8.92 x 2.59 x 3.60 m.

08993	**E**	E	WSSW	CF	*Cardiff Canton TMD*
08994	a **E**	E	WSSW	CF	*Margam SD*
08995	a **E**	E	WSSW	CF	*Margam SD*

Names:

08578	Lybert Dickinson	08874	Catherine
08629	BRML WOLVERTON LEVEL 5	08879	Sheffield Childrens Hospital
08649	G.H. Stratton	08896	STEPHEN DENT
08682	Lionheart	08903	John W Antill
08701	The Sorter	08919	Steep Holm
08714	Cambridge	08950	Neville Hill 1st
08743	Bryan Turner	08993	ASHBURNHAM
08790	M.A. SMITH	08994	GWENDRAETH
08869	The Canary	08995	KIDWELLY

CLASS 09   BR/ENGLISH ELECTRIC   0-6-0

Built: 1959–62 by BR at Darlington or Horwich Works.
Engine: English Electric 6KT of 298 kW (400 hp) at 680 rpm.
Main Generator: English Electric 801.
Traction Motors: English Electric 506.
Maximum Tractive Effort: 111 kN (25000 lbf).
Continuous Tractive Effort: 39 kN (8800 lbf) at 11.6 mph.
Power At Rail: 201 kW (269 hp).   **Train Brakes:** Air & vacuum.
Brake Force: 19 t.   **Dimensions:** 8.92 x 2.59 x 3.89 m.
Weight: 50 t.   **Wheel Diameter:** 1372 mm.
Design Speed: 27 mph.   **Maximium Speed:** 27 mph.
Fuel Capacity: 3037 litres.   **RA:** 5.
Train Supply: Not equipped.   **Multiple Working:** Not equipped.

Class 09/0. Standard Design.

09001	E	E	WSWS	EH	Fowey
09003	E	E	WSSW	CF	Margam SD
09004	B	SC	HWSU	SU(S)	
09005	DG	E	WSYH	IM	Healey Mills Yard
09006	ML	E	WSSE	OC	Hither Green TMD
09007	ML	E	WSYH	IM	Doncaster TMD
09008	E	E	WSWS	EH	Plymouth Station
09009	E	E	WSSE	OC	Sheerness Dockyard
09010	DG	E	WSSE	OC	Parkeston Yard
09011	DG	EF	WSSE	OC	Hither Green TMD
09012	DG	E	WSSE	OC	Hoo Junction
09013	DG	E	WSSW	CF	Margam SD
09014	DG	E	WSYH	IM	Doncaster TMD
09015	DG	E	WSSW	CF	Sudbrook Pumping Station
09016	DG	E	WSWS	EH	Eastleigh Yards
09017	E	E	WSSW	CF	Cardiff Canton TMD
09018	E	E	WSSE	OC	Wembley Yards
09019	ML	E	WSSE	OC	Hither Green TMD
09020	B	E	WSXX	ZB(S)	
09021	E	EF	WSWM	BS	Bescot Yard
09022	E	EF	WSXX	AN(S)	
09023	E	E	WSNE	TE	Allerton T&RSMD
09024	ML	E	WSSE	OC	Hoo Junction
09025	CX	SC	HWSU	BI	Brighton T&RSMD
09026	G	SC	HWSU	BI	Brighton T&RSMD

Names:
09009	Three Bridges C.E.D.
09012	Dick Hardy
09026	William Pearson

Class 09/1. Converted from Class 08/0. 110 V electrical equipment. Details as Class 09/0 except:

Built: 1960–61 by BR at Crewe, Derby or Horwich Works. Converted 1992–93 by RFS Industries, Kilnhurst.

09101		**DG**	E	WSWS	EH	*Swindon Cocklebury Yard*
09102		**DG**	E	WSSW	CF	*Cardiff Canton TMD*
09103		**DG**	E	WSSC	ML	*Mossend Yard*
09104		**DG**	E	WSSC	ML	*Mossend Yard*
09105		**DG**	E	WSSW	CF	*Cardiff Canton TMD*
09106		**DG**	E	WSNE	TE	*Tees Yard*
09107		**DG**	E	WSSW	CF	*Cardiff Canton TMD*

Class 09/2. Converted from Class 08/0. 90 V electrical equipment. Details as Class 09/0 except:

Built: 1958–60 by BR at Crewe or Derby Works. Converted 1992 by RFS Industries, Kilnhurst.

09201	a	**DG**	E	WSYH	IM	*Knottingley T&RSMD*
09202		**DG**	E	WSSC	ML	*Aberdeen Guild Street Yard*
09203		**DG**	E	WSSW	CF	*Newport Alexandra Dock Junction*
09204		**DG**	E	WSNE	TE	*Tees Yard*
09205		**DG**	E	WSSC	ML	*Millerhill Yard*

CLASS 20   ENGLISH ELECTRIC   Bo-Bo

Built: 1957–68 by English Electric Company at Vulcan Foundry, Newton le Willows or by Robert Stephenson & Hawthorn at Darlington.
Engine: English Electric 8SVT Mk. II of 746 kW (1000 hp) at 850 rpm.
Main Generator: English Electric 819/3C.
Traction Motors: English Electric 526/5D or 526/8D.
Maximum Tractive Effort: 187 kN (42000 lbf).
Continuous Tractive Effort: 111 kN (25000 lbf) at 11 mph.
Power At Rail: 574 kW (770 hp).   **Train Brakes:** Air & vacuum.
Brake Force: 35 t.   **Dimensions:** 14.25 x 2.67 x 3.86 m.
Weight: 73.4–73.5 t.   **Wheel Diameter:** 1092 mm.
Design Speed: 75mph.   **Maximum Speed:** 60 mph.
Fuel Capacity: 1727 litres.   **RA:** 5.
Train Supply: Not equipped.   **Multiple Working:** Blue Star.

Class 20/0. Standard Design.

20007	s	**B**	DR	XHSS	ZB(S)	20121	s	**B**	DR	XHSS	ZB(S)
20032	s	**B**	DR	XHSS	ZB(S)	20165		**FQ**	E	WNZX	BS(S)
20059	s	**FQ**	E	WNXX	MG(S)	20168	s	**B**	E	WNXX	MG(S)
20072	s	**B**	DR	XHSS	ZB(S)	20177	s	**B**	E	WNYX	TT(S)
20119		**B**	E	WNYX	TT(S)						

Class 20/3. Direct Rail Services refurbished locos. Details as Class 20/0 except:

Refurbished: 1995–96 by Brush Traction at Loughborough (20301–305) or 1997–98 by RFS(E) at Doncaster (20306–315).
Train Brakes: Air.   **Max. Speed:** 75 mph.
Brake Force: 31 t.   **Fuel Capacity:** 2900 (+ 4909) litres.
Multiple Working: Blue Star (20301–305 at non-driving end only).

20301	+	**DR**	DR	XHSD	KD	20309	+	**DR**	DR	XHSD	KD
20302		**DR**	DR	XHSD	KD	20310	+	**DR**	DR	XHSD	KD
20303	+	**DR**	DR	XHSD	KD	20311	+	**DR**	DR	XHSD	KD
20304		**DR**	DR	XHSD	KD	20312	+	**DR**	DR	XHSD	KD
20305		**DR**	DR	XHSD	KD	20313	+	**DR**	DR	XHSD	KD
20306	+	**DR**	DR	XHSD	KD	20314	+	**DR**	DR	XHSD	KD
20307	+	**DR**	DR	XHSD	KD	20315	+	**DR**	DR	XHSD	KD
20308	+	**DR**	DR	XHSD	KD						

Name:
20301   FURNESS RAILWAY 150

Class 20/9. Direct Rail Services (former Hunslet-Barclay) refurbished locos. Details as Class 20/0 except:

Refurbished: 1989 by Hunslet-Barclay at Kilmarnock.
Train Brakes: Air.   **Fuel Capacity:** 1727 (+ 4727) litres.

20901		**DR**	DR	XHSD	NATO	20904		**HB**	DR	XHSD	KD
20902	+	**DR**	DR	XHSD	NATO	20905	+	**HB**	DR	XHSD	KD
20903	+	**DR**	DR	XHSD	NATO	20906		**DR**	DR	XHSD	KD

CLASS 25   BR/BEYER PEACOCK/SULZER   Bo-Bo

Built: 1965 by Beyer Peacock at Gorton.
Engine: Sulzer 6LDA28-B of 930 kW (1250 hp) at 750 rpm.
Main Generator: AEI RTB15656.   **Traction Motors:** AEI 253AY.
Max. Tractive Effort: 200 kN (45000 lbf).
Cont. TE: 93 kN (20800 lbf) at 17.1 mph.
Power At Rail: 708 kW (949 hp).
Brake Force: 38 t.
Weight: 71.45 t.
Design Speed: 90 mph.
Fuel Capacity: 2270 litres.
Train Supply: Not equipped.
Train Brakes: Air & vacuum.
Dimensions: 15.39 x 2.73 x 3.86 m.
Wheel Diameter: 1143 mm.
Maximum Speed: 60 mph.
RA: 5.
Multiple Working: Blue Star.

Class 25/3. GEC Series 3 Control Equipment.

| 25278 | **G** | NY | MBDL | NY | SYBILIA |

CLASS 31   BRUSH/ENGLISH ELECTRIC   A1A-A1A

Built: 1958–62 by Brush Traction at Loughborough.
Engine: English Electric 12SVT of 1100 kW (1470 hp) at 850 rpm.
Main Generator: Brush TG160-48.   **Traction Motors:** Brush TM73-68.
Maximum Tractive Effort: 160 or * 190 kN (35900 or * 42800 lbf).
Cont. TE: 83 kN (18700 lbf) at 23.5 mph. (* 99 kN (22250 lbf) at 19.7 mph.).
Power At Rail: 872 kW (1170 hp).
Brake Force: 49 t.
Weight: 106.7–111 t.
Design Speed: 90 (* 80) mph.
Fuel Capacity: 2409 litres.
Train Supply: Not equipped.
Train Brakes: Air & vacuum.
Dimensions: 17.30 x 2.67 x 3.87 m.
Wheel Diameter: 1092/1003 mm.
Maximum Speed: 60 mph.
RA: 5 or 6 (See below).
Multiple Working: Blue Star.
Non-standard livery/numbering:
• 31110 carries number D5528.

Class 31/1. Standard Design. RA: 5.

31102	**CE**	E	WNZX	CG(S)		31196	**CE**	E	WNZX	SF(S)
31110	**G**	E	WMAN	OC		31200	**FC**	E	WNZX	CW(S)
31112	* **TC**	E	WNZX	BS(S)		31201	**FC**	E	WNZX	WA(S)
31113	**CE**	E	WNXX	OC(S)		31203	**CE**	E	WMAN	OC
31119	**CE**	E	WNYX	CL(S)		31207	**CE**	E	WMAN	OC
31132	**FO**	E	WNZX	BS(S)		31224	**CE**	E	WNZX	CL(S)
31142	**CE**	E	WNZX	TO(S)		31232	**CE**	E	WNZX	BS(S)
31144	**CE**	E	WNYX	CL(S)		31233	**CE**	E	WNYX	OC(S)
31146	**CE**	E	WNZX	WA(S)		31235	**CE**	E	WNZX	CL(S)
31154	**CE**	E	WNYX	OC(S)		31237	**CE**	E	WNZX	BS(S)
31155	**FA**	E	WNZX	BS(S)		31248	**FO**	E	WNZX	BS(S)
31158	**CE**	E	WNZX	BS(S)		31252	**FO**	E	WNZX	PB(S)
31164	**FO**	E	WNZX	BS(S)		31270	**F**	E	WNZX	CL(S)
31171	**FO**	E	WNZX	BS(S)		31273	**CE**	E	WNZX	HM(S)
31178	**CE**	E	WNZX	BS(S)		31275	**FC**	E	WNZX	CS(S)
31185	**CE**	E	WNZX	BS(S)		31283	**B**	E	WNZX	SF(S)

31285	**CE**	E	WNYX	CL(S)		31317	**FO**	E	WNZX	BS(S)
31296	**FA**	E	WNZX	CP(S)		31319	**FC**	E	WNZX	BS(S)
31299	**FO**	E	WNZX	SF(S)		31320	**B**	E	WNZX	SF(S)
31306	**CE**	E	WNXX	OC(S)		31327	**FQ**	E	WNYX	CL(S)
31308	**CE**	E	WNXX	OC(S)						

Names:
31110   TRACTION magazine
31233   Severn Valley Railway

Class 31/4. Electric Train Supply equipment. Details as Class 31/1 except:

Maximum Speed: 90 mph.   **RA:** 6.
Train Supply: Electric, but not operational (e – Electric, index 66).

31402	**B**	E	WNZX	BS(S)		31434	**B**	E	WNZX	HM(S)
31405	**IM**	E	WNZX	DR(S)		31442	**B**	E	WNZX	CW(S)
31407	**ML**	E	WNZX	BS(S)		31444	**CE**	E	WNZX	SP(S)
31408	**B**	E	WNZX	SP(S)		31452 e	**FR**	FR	SDFR	TM
31410	**RR**	E	WNZX	CS(S)		31455	**RR**	E	WNZX	SP(S)
31411	**DG**	E	WNZX	BS(S)		31459 e	**FR**	FR	SDFR	TM
31417	**DG**	E	WNZX	BS(S)		31460	**B**	E	WNZX	BS(S)
31420 e	**IM**	E	WMAN	OC		31465	**RR**	E	WNXX	OC(S)
31421	**RR**	E	WNZX	CW(S)		31466 e	**E**	E	WMAN	OC
31427	**B**	E	WNXX	OC(S)		31468 e	**FR**	FR	SDFR	TM
31432	**B**	E	WNZX	SP(S)						

Names:
31452   MINOTAUR
31459   CERBERUS
31468   HYDRA

Class 31/1 ("31/5"). Electric Train Supply equipment fitted, but isolated. Details as Class 31/1 except:

Maximum Speed: 60 mph.   **RA:** 6.
Train Supply: Electric, isolated.

31512	**CE**	E	WNZX	BS(S)		31541	**CE**	E	WNYX	OC(S)
31514	**CE**	E	WNXX	OC(S)		31545	**B**	E	WNZX	BS(S)
31519	**CE**	E	WNZX	SP(S)		31546	**CE**	E	WNZX	BS(S)
31530	**CE**	E	WNWX	HM(S)		31554	**CE**	E	WNXX	WA(S)
31533	**CE**	E	WNZX	BS(S)		31556	**CE**	E	WNYX	CL(S)
31538	**B**	E	WNYX	CL(S)						

Class 31/6. Electric Train Supply through wiring and controls. Details as Class 31/1 except:

Maximum Speed: 90 mph.   **Train Supply:** Electric through wired.

No.	Former No.					
31601	(31186)	**FR**	FR	SDFR	TM	BLETCHLEY PARK 'STATION X'
31602	(31191)	**FR**	FR	SDFR	TM	CHIMAERA

CLASS 33   BRCW/SULZER   Bo-Bo

Built: 1960–62 by the Birmingham Railway Carriage & Wagon Company at Smethwick.
Engine: Sulzer 8LDA28 of 1160 kW (1550 hp) at 750 rpm.
Main Generator: Crompton Parkinson CG391B1.
Traction Motors: Crompton Parkinson C171C2.
Maximum Tractive Effort: 200 kN (45000 lbf).
Continuous Tractive Effort: 116 kN (26000 lbf) at 17.5 mph.
Power At Rail: 906 kW (1215 hp).   **Train Brakes:** Air & vacuum.
Brake Force: 35 t.   **Dimensions:** 15.47 x 2.82 x 3.86 m.
Weight: 77.7 t.   **Wheel Diameter:** 1092 mm.
Design Speed: 85 mph.   **Max. Speed:** 60 (* 75, † 85) mph.
Fuel Capacity: 3410 litres.   **RA:** 6.
Train Supply: Electric, not operational (e – index 48 (750 V dc only).
Multiple Working: Blue Star.
Non-standard livery/numbering:
• 33051 also carries number 6569.
• 33109 also carries number D6525.
• 33116 also carries number D6535.
• 33208 carries number D6593.

Class 33/0. Standard Design.

33019	**CE**	E	WNYX	ML(S)	
33021	e†	**R**	WF	SDFR	TM	Eastleigh
33025	*	**CE**	E	WSAC	ML	
33026		**CE**	E	WNYX	EH(S)	
33030	*	**E**	E	WSAC	ML	
33038		**B**	E	WHZX	SF(S)	
33046		**CE**	E	WNYX	EH(S)	
33051		**B**	E	WNYX	EH(S)	Shakespeare Cliff

Class 33/1. Blue Star & BR Southern Region Multiple Working Equipment. Details as Class 33/0 except:

Train Brakes: Air, vacuum & electro-pneumatic.
Weight: 78.5 t.   **Multiple Working:** Blue Star & SR System.

33103	be†	**G**	CM	CTLO	TM	
33109	be†	**B**	HT	MBDL	RL	Captain Bill Smith RNR
33116	b	**B**	E	WNXX	OC(S)	

Class 33/2. Narrow body profile. Details as Class 33/0 except:

Weight: 77.5 t.   **Dimensions:** 15.47 x 2.64 x 3.86 m.

33202		**CE**	E	WNXX	OC(S)	
33205		**FD**	E	WNZX	OC(S)	
33208	e*	**G**	HT	MBDL	RL	

CLASS 37   ENGLISH ELECTRIC TYPE 3   Co-Co

Built: 1960–65 by English Electric Company at Vulcan Foundry, Newton le Willows or by Robert Stephenson & Hawthorn at Darlington.
Engine: English Electric 12CSVT of 1300 kW (1750 hp) at 850 rpm.
Main Generator: English Electric 822/10G.
Traction Motors: English Electric 538/A.
Maximum Tractive Effort: 245 kN (55500 lbf).
Continuous Tractive Effort: 156 kN (35000 lbf) at 13.6 mph.
Power At Rail: 932 kW (1250 hp).   **Train Brakes:** Air & vacuum.
Brake Force: 50 t.   **Dimensions:** 18.75 x 2.74 x 3.94 or 3.99 m.
Weight: 102.8–108.4 t.   **Wheel Diameter:** 1092 mm.
Design Speed: 90 mph.   **Maximum Speed:** 80 mph.
Fuel Capacity: 4046 (+ 7678) litres.   **RA:** 5.
Train Supply: Not equipped.   **Multiple Working:** Blue Star.
Notes: 37073/074/131–298/358/370–384/401–431/610–679/682–698/800–899 have roof mounted horns and are 3.99 m. high. The remainder have nose mounted horns and are 3.94 m. high.
§   Sandite laying equipment (with standard size Sandite hopper).
$ Sandite laying equipment (with large size Sandite hopper).
Non-standard liveries/numbering:
· 37101 is officially numbered 37345, but it is doubtful it has ever carried this number.
· 37116 is as **B**, but with Transrail markings.
· 37131 also carries number 6831.
· 37330 is blue with yellow cabs and black window surrounds.
· 37350 also carries number D6700.
· 37351 carries number 37002 on one side only.
· 37403 carries number D6607.

Class 37/0. Standard Design. Details as above.

No.	Note	Livery		Pool	Loc.	No.	Note	Livery		Pool	Loc.
37010	a	CE	E	WKMF	SNCF	37057	+	E	E	WKBN	TO
37012		CE	E	WNYX	SP(S)	37058	a+	CE	E	WKMF	SNCF
37013	+	ML	E	WNXX	TL(S)	37059	a+	FD	E	WNXX	IM(S)
37019	+	FD	E	WNZX	HM(S)	37065	+	ML	E	WKBN	TO
37023		ML	E	WNXX	OC(S)	37068	+	FD	E	WNZX	IM(S)
37025		BL	E	WNZX	TO(S)	37069	a+	CE	E	WKMF	SNCF
37026	+	FD	E	WNZX	SP(S)	37071	a+	CE	E	WKMF	SNCF
37029		B	RV	MBDL	CP	37073	a+	T	E	WKMF	SNCF
37037	a	F	E	WKMF	SNCF	37074	a+	ML	E	WKMF	SNCF
37040		E	E	WKBN	TO	37077	a	ML	E	WKMF	SNCF
37042	+	E	E	WKBN	TO	37078	+	FM	E	WNZX	SP(S)
37043	§	TC	E	WKMS	BS	37079	+	FD	E	WNZX	ZH(S)
37045	+	F	E	WNZX	TT(S)	37083	+	CE	E	WNZX	ID(S)
37046	a	CE	E	WKMF	SNCF	37087		CE	E	WNYX	CW(S)
37047	+	ML	E	WKBN	TO	37088		TC	E	WNZX	SP(S)
37048		MG	E	WNZX	TT(S)	37092		CE	E	WNZX	TT(S)
37051		E	E	WKBN	TO	37095	+	CE	E	WNZX	ZB(S)
37054		CE	E	WNYX	ML(S)	37097		CE	E	WNYX	MH(S)
37055	+	ML	E	WKBN	TO	37098	+	CE	E	WNYX	OC(S)

37100	a	T	E	WKMF	SNCF	37212	+	T	E	WNYX	EH(S)
37101	+	FD	E	WHZX	IM(S)	37213	+	FC	E	WNZX	TT(S)
37104		CE	E	WNZX	ID(S)	37214	+	T	E	WNZX	BS(S)
37106	+	CE	E	WNZX	SP(S)	37216	r+	ML	E	WKBN	TO
37109	a	E	E	WKBN	TO	37217	+	B	E	WNZX	AY(S)
37110	+	F	E	WNZX	ID(S)	37218	+	F	E	WNZX	ID(S)
37114	+	E	E	WKBN	TO	37219		ML	E	WKBN	TO
37116	+	O	E	WKBN	TO	37220	+	E	E	WKBN	TO
37131	+§	F	E	WNXX	CF(S)	37221	a	T	E	WKMF	SNCF
37133	a§	CE	E	WKMF	SNCF	37222	+	MG	E	WNZX	CF(S)
37137		MG	E	WNZX	TT(S)	37223	+	FC	E	WNZX	ID(S)
37139	+	FC	E	WNZX	TE(S)	37225	+	F	E	WNXX	CF(S)
37140		CE	E	WNZX	SP(S)	37227	+	MG	E	WNXX	OC(S)
37141		CE	E	WNZX	CG(S)	37229	+§	FC	E	WNXX	TO(S)
37142		CE	E	WNZX	CW(S)	37230	+§	TC	E	WKMS	BS
37144		FA	E	WNZX	ID(S)	37232		TC	E	WNZX	SP(S)
37146	a	CE	E	WKMF	SNCF	37235	+	F	E	WNZX	DR(S)
37152	§	IS	E	WNXX	ML(S)	37238	a+	F	E	WKMF	SNCF
37153	§	TC	E	WNYX	SP(S)	37240	+	CE	E	WNZX	BS(S)
37154	+§	T	E	WNYX	SP(S)	37241		MG	E	WNZX	TT(S)
37156		T	E	WNZX	SP(S)	37242	+§	ML	E	WNYX	SP(S)
37162	+	DG	E	WKMF	SNCF	37244	+	F	E	WNZX	SP(S)
37165	a+	TC	E	WNXX	TO(S)	37245		CE	E	WNZX	SP(S)
37170	a	TC	E	WKMF	SNCF	37248	+	ML	E	WKBN	TO
37174	a	E	E	WKBN	TO	37250	a+	T	E	WKMF	SNCF
37175	a	CE	E	WNXX	OC(S)	37252		FD	E	WNYX	DR(S)
37178	+§	F	E	WNXX	EH(S)	37254	+	CE	E	WNZX	ZH(S)
37184		CE	E	WNZX	BS(S)	37255	+§	CE	E	WNYX	SP(S)
37185	+	CE	E	WNXX	CF(S)	37261	a+	FD	E	WKMF	SNCF
37188		TC	E	WNZX	TT(S)	37262	+§	DG	E	WNXX	CF(S)
37191	a	CE	E	WNZX	SP(S)	37263	§	CE	E	WNXX	EH(S)
37194	+	MG	E	WNZX	OC(S)	37264		CE	E	WNXX	CF(S)
37196	a§	CE	E	WKMF	SNCF	37274	+	ML	E	WKBN	TO
37198	+	ML	E	WNXX	TO(S)	37275	+	B	E	WNXX	TO(S)
37201		TC	E	WNZX	BS(S)	37278	+	FC	E	WNZX	TT(S)
37203		ML	E	WKBN	TO	37293	+	ML	E	WKMF	SNCF
37209		BL	E	WNZX	DR(S)	37294	a+	CE	E	WKMF	SNCF
37211		CE	E	WNYX	TE(S)	37298	a+	E	E	WKMF	SNCF

Names:

37023	Stratford TMD Quality Approved
37051	Merehead
37057	Viking
37114	City of Worcester
37116	Sister Dora
37185	Lea & Perrins
37194	British International Freight Association
37248	Midland Railway Centre
37262	Dounreay[1]
37275	Oor Wullie

Class 37/3. Re-geared (CP7) bogies. Details as Class 37/0 except:

Maximum Tractive Effort: 250 kN (56180 lbf).
Continuous Tractive Effort: 184 kN (41250 lbf) at 11.4 mph.
Design Speed: 80 mph.
Notes: 37334 has standard bogies, but has not officially been reclassified 37/0.

37330	+	**0**	E	WNZX	TT(S)		37359	**FP**	E	WNYX	TE(S)
37331		**FM**	E	WNYX	DR(S)		37370	**E**	E	WKBN	TO
37332	+	**FC**	E	WNZX	OC(S)		37372	**ML**	E	WKBN	TO
37334	a+	**F**	E	WNXX	IM(S)		37375	+	**ML**	E	WKBN	TO
37335	+	**F**	E	WNZX	IM(S)		37376	a+	**F**	E	WKMF	SNCF
37340	+	**FD**	E	WNZX	IM(S)		37377	+	**CE**	E	WKBN	TO
37341	+	**F**	E	WNYX	TE(S)		37379	r	**ML**	E	WKBN	TO
37343		**CE**	E	WNZX	TT(S)		37380		**MG**	E	WNYX	CD(S)
37344	+	**FD**	E	WNYX	IM(S)		37381	+	**FD**	E	WNZX	FH(S)
37350	+	**G**	E	WNXX	TE(S)		37382		**FP**	E	WNZX	IM(S)
37351	+	**TC**	E	WNXX	TE(S)		37383	+	**ML**	E	WNXX	IM(S)
37358	+	**F**	E	WNXX	IM(S)		37384	+§	**CE**	E	WNYX	SP(S)

Names:
37350   NATIONAL RAILWAY MUSEUM
37379   Ipswich WRD Quality Approved

Class 37/4. Refurbished with train supply equipment. Main generator replaced by alternator. Re-geared (CP7) bogies. Details as class 37/0 except:

Main Alternator: Brush BA1005A.   **Power At Rail:** 935 kW (1254 hp).
Maximum Tractive Effort: 256 kN (57440 lbf).
Continuous Tractive Effort: 184 kN (41250 lbf) at 11.4 mph.
Weight: 107 t.   **Design Speed:** 80 mph.
Fuel Capacity: 7678 litres.   **Train Supply:** Electric, index 38.

37401	r	**E**	E	WKCD	CD	Mary Queen of Scots
37402		**F**	E	WNXX	CD(S)	Bont Y Bermo
37403	ar	**G**	E	WKMB	ML	Ben Cruachan
37404		**T**	E	WNXX	CD(S)	
37405	r	**E**	E	WKMB	ML	
37406	r	**T**	E	WKMB	ML	The Saltire Society
37407		**T**	E	WKCN	TO	Blackpool Tower
37408	a	**E**	E	WKCD	CD	Loch Rannoch
37409	r	**T**	E	WKMB	ML	Loch Awe
37410	r	**T**	E	WKMB	ML	Aluminium 100
37411	r	**E**	E	WKMB	ML	Ty Hafan
37412		**T**	E	WKCN	TO	Driver John Elliott
37413	r	**E**	E	WKMB	ML	The Scottish Railway Preservation Society
37414		**RR**	E	WKCN	TO	Cathays C & W Works 1846-1993
37415		**E**	E	WKCD	CD	
37416	r	**E**	E	WKMB	ML	
37417	a	**E**	E	WNXX	CF(S)	
37418	r	**E**	E	WKMB	ML	East Lancashire Railway
37419	r	**E**	E	WKMB	ML	
37420		**RR**	E	WKCN	TO	The Scottish Hosteller
37421		**E**	E	WKCD	CD	

▲ 08617 is owned by Virgin West Coast and wears a variation of the company's 'Pitstop' livery for shunting locomotives. It is seen here at Willesden TMD on 13th August 1998.
Hugh Ballantyne

▼ Rarely photographed is 08903 'John W Antill', owned by Enron Teesside Operations Ltd. This loco and sister 08743 are normally used at ICI Billingham, where this photograph was taken in January 1999.
Terry Bye

▲ A regular coaching stock shunt takes place at Brighton to release locomotives which have arrived at the East Sussex terminus on Virgin Cross Country services. Here, Connex liveried 09025 carries out such a shunt after the arrival of 1O30, 06.20 ex-Preston, on 20th July 1999.   **Bob Sweet**

▼ 33021 'Eastleigh' passes Paddock Wood at the head of a 13.20 Tonbridge–Maidstone West special service on 28th August 1999.   **David Brown**

Three Class 20 locomotives owned by Direct Rail Services are on hire to NATO for use in Kosovo. 20901 is pictured here en route to Kosovo, being turned on the turntable at Budapest Ferencváros depot after fuelling on 21st September 1999.

Ferenc Joó

Prior to the transfer of Class 150/2 DMUs to the route, Silverlink Train Services hired Class 31 locomotives from Fragonset Railways to work passenger services between Bedford and Bletchley. 31468 headed 2N27, 18.50 Bletchley–Bedford, on 17th October 1998.

Anthony Underwood

▲ 37429 approaches Conwy with 1G11, 13.54 Holyhead–Birmingham New Street on 28th May 1999. Locomotive hauled First North Western trains are scheduled to be replaced by Class 175 DMUs during Spring 2000. **Les Nixon**

▼ 37798 stands at the head of a train of ballast wagons in Didcot Yard on 14th September 1998. **Stephen Widdowson**

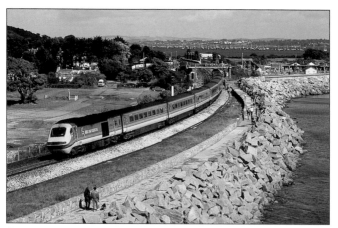

▲ Whilst on hire to Virgin Cross Country, 43066 heads the Midland Mainline HST set forming 1V38, 06.05 Leeds–Newquay on 12th September 1998.

Russell Ayre

▼ Class 46, D172 'Ixion', at Newcastle upon Tyne after arriving with the 07.09 Bristol Temple Meads–Newcastle upon Tyne railtour, 'The Severn-Tyne', on 27th May 1995.   **Richard Bolsover**

▲ 47152 powers through on the centre road at Doncaster station with 4L85, 10.34 Leeds FLT–Felixstowe North FLT on 24th July 1999. **Peter Fox**

▼ 47814 'Totnes Castle' leaves Chester with 1A46, 09.19 Holyhead–London Euston on 6th July 1999. This Virgin West Coast train is a regular duty for a Class 47/4 hired from Virgin Cross Country. **Paul Shannon**

▲ 50017 has been repainted in 'LMS Coronation Scot' style for use by VSOE. It is seen here leaving Crewe with an empty coaching stock train bound for Wolverhampton on 25th September 1999. **Brian Denton**

▼ Saturday railtour work for D9000 'ROYAL SCOTS GREY' in 1999 was rare due to regular use by Virgin Cross Country on summer-only scheduled services. Prior to the start of the summer timetable, the loco appeared on a London King's Cross–Bradford Forster Square charter on 22nd May, which was photographed at Whitehall Junction (Leeds). **Les Nixon**

56084 crosses the viaduct at Todmorden with 7Z83, 15.21 Healey Mills–Fidlers Ferry 'merry-go-round' coal train on 29th July 1999.

Anthony Underwood

▲ 57004 'Freightliner Quality' runs light past Stratford station on 1st May 1999.
Kevin Conkey

▼ 58033 passes South Moreton with 6S65, 15.19 Eastleigh–Mossend EWS 'Enterprise' service on 23rd July 1999.
Anthony Underwood

▲ 59101 'Village of Whatley' at Merehead T&RSMD on 28th June 1998.
Stephen Widdowson

▼ 60088 'Buachaille Etive Mor' heads a train of Railtrack wagons forming 6C10, 10.09 Penmaenmawr–Carnforth, near Chester on 16th July 1999.　**Paul Shannon**

▲ 66005 just south of Beighton with 6V67, 15.26 Wakefield–Cardiff Tidal Sidings conveying empty steel-carrying wagons on 19th April 1999. **Peter Fox**

▼ Class 71, E5001, part of the National Collection, has very occasional outings on the Railtrack network. On 20th April 1996 it headed 1Z33, 14.10 Brighton–Eastbourne excursion, seen here near Berwick. **Brian Denton**

Now in the course of delivery are 30 GM/Alstom Class 67 locomotives for EWS mail and charter services. The first to arrive from the builder's factory in Spain was 67003, which was photographed just after unloading on 7th October 1999.

Bob Sweet

▲ 86256 'Pebble Mill' was repainted into Virgin Trains livery just as this edition closed for press, but still sported InterCity colours when photographed approaching Carlisle on 24th May 1998 with 1S59, 12.06 London Paddington–Glasgow Central. **Kevin Conkey**

▼ 87022 at Birmingham New Street with 1A48, 13.19 Wolverhampton–London Euston on 8th August 1998. **Stephen Widdowson**

▲ 89001 propels 1A17, 11.05 Leeds–London King's Cross into Doncaster station on 24th July 1999. **Peter Fox**

▼ 90019 passes Low Gill whilst working 1V04, Glasgow Central–Bristol Temple Meads Rail Express Systems' service on 30th May 1997. This train has now been replaced by a working from the new Shieldmuir Royal Mail Terminal. **Dave McAlone**

▲ 91022 'Double Trigger' pauses at Edinburgh Haymarket with 1E18, 16.00 Glasgow Central– London King's Cross on 19th October 1999. **Peter Fox**

▼ A test run comprising containers loaded with ballast passes Wreay on 16th July 1998 worked by 92003 'Beethoven'. **Kevin Conkey**

37422		**RR**	E	WNXX	CF(S)	Robert F. Fairlie Locomotive Engineer 1831-1885
37423		**T**	E	WNXX	ML(S)	Sir Murray Morrison 1873-1948 Pioneer of the British Aluminium Industry
37424	r	**T**	E	WKMB	ML	
37425	ar	**RR**	E	WKMB	ML	Sir Robert McAlpine/Concrete Bob
37426		**E**	E	WKCD	CD	
37427	r	**E**	E	WKMB	ML	
37428	r	**GS**	E	WKMB	ML	
37429		**RR**	E	WKCD	CD	Eisteddfod Genedlaethol
37430	ar	**T**	E	WKMB	ML	Cwmbrân
37431		**IM**	E	WNYX	SP(S)	

Class 37/5. Refurbished without train supply equipment. Main generator replaced by alternator. Re-geared (CP7) bogies. Details as Class 37/4 except:

Maximum Tractive Effort: 248 kN (55590 lbf).
RA: 5 ($ 6).
Weight: 106.1–107.3 ($ 110.0) t.   **Train Supply:** Not equipped.

37503	§	**E**	E	WKBN	TO		37516	s	**LH**	E	WKBN	TO
37505		**T**	E	WNXX	AY(S)		37517	ars	**LH**	E	WKMB	ML
37509		**F**	E	WKBN	TO		37518		**FM**	E	WNXX	SF(S)
37510	a	**IS**	E	WKMF	SNCF		37519	§	**FM**	E	WNXX	EH(S)
37513	as	**LH**	E	WKMF	SNCF		37520	r$	**E**	E	WKMB	ML
37515	as	**FM**	E	WKMF	SNCF		37521	$	**E**	E	WKBN	TO

Names:
37505   British Steel Workington
37521   English China Clays

Class 37/6. Refurbished for Nightstar services. Main generator replaced by alternator, re-geared bogies and UIC jumpers. Details as class 37/5 except:

Maximum Speed: 80 († 90) mph.   **Train Brake:** Air.
Train Supply: Not equipped, but electric through wired.
Multiple Working: TDM († plus Blue Star).

37601		**EP**	EU	GPSV	OC		37607	†	**DR**	DR	XHSD	KD
37602		**EP**	EU	GPSV	OC		37608	†	**DR**	DR	XHSD	KD
37603		**EP**	EU	GPSV	OC		37609	†	**DR**	DR	XHSD	KD
37604		**EP**	EU	GPSV	OC		37610	†	**DR**	DR	XHSD	KD
37605		**EP**	EU	GPSV	OC		37611	†	**DR**	DR	XHSD	KD
37606		**EP**	EU	DFLT	OC		37612	†	**DR**	DR	XHSD	KD

Class 37/5 (Continued).

37667	rs$	**E**	E	WKMB	ML		37676		**F**	E	WNXX	AY(S)
37668	s$	**E**	E	WKBN	TO		37677	§	**F**	E	WNXX	TO(S)
37669	$	**E**	E	WKBN	TO		37678	a	**F**	E	WNXX	DR(S)
37670	r$	**E**	E	WKMB	ML		37679	a	**F**	E	WNXX	BS(S)
37671	a	**T**	E	WKMF	SNCF		37680	§	**FA**	E	WNXX	SF(S)
37672	as	**T**	E	WKMF	SNCF		37682	r$	**E**	E	WKMS	BS
37673	$	**T**	E	WKMS	BS		37683	a	**T**	E	WKMF	SNCF
37674	r$	**T**	E	WKMS	BS		37684	r$	**E**	E	WKMB	ML
37675	s$	**T**	E	WKMS	BS		37685	a	**IS**	E	WKMF	SNCF

37686	a	FA	E	WKMF	SNCF
37688	§	E	E	WKBN	TO
37689	$	F	E	WKMS	BS
37692	s	FC	E	WNXX	AY(S)
37693	as	T	E	WKMF	SNCF

37694	$	E	E	WKBN	TO
37695	s$	E	E	WKBN	TO
37696	as	T	E	WKMF	SNCF
37697	s	E	E	WNXX	TO(S)
37698	s$	LH	E	WKBN	TO

Names:

37667	Meldon Quarry Centenary
37674	St. Blaise Church 1445-1995
37682	Hartlepool Pipe Mill
37684	Peak National Park
37692	The Lass O' Ballochmyle

Class 37/7. Refurbished locos. Main generator replaced by alternator. Re-geared (CP7) bogies. Ballast weights added. Details as class 37/5 except:

Main Alternator: GEC G564AZ (37796–803) Brush BA1005A (others).
Maximum Tractive Effort: 276 kN (62000 lbf).
Fuel Capacity: 7678 (* 4046) litres.
Weight: 120 t.　　　　　　　　　　　**RA:** 7.

37701	as	T	E	WNXX	OC(S)
37702	s	T	E	WKGN	TO
37703		E	E	WKGN	TO
37704	s	E	E	WKGN	TO
37705		MG	E	WNXX	ML(S)
37706		E	E	WKGN	TO
37707		E	E	WKGN	TO
37708	a	FP	E	WKMF	SNCF
37709		MG	E	WKGN	TO
37710		LH	E	WKGN	TO
37711		FM	E	WNXX	OC(S)
37712	a	E	E	WKGN	TO
37713		LH	E	WKGN	TO
37714	a	E	E	WKGN	TO
37715		MG	E	WNXX	CF(S)
37716		E	E	WKGN	TO
37717		E	E	WKGN	TO
37718		E	E	WKGN	TO
37719	a	FP	E	WNXX	OC(S)
37796	as	FC	E	WKMF	SNCF
37797	as	E	E	WKGN	TO
37798		ML	E	WKGN	TO

37799	s	T	E	WKGN	TO
37800	a	MG	E	WKMF	SNCF
37801	s	E	E	WKGN	TO
37802	s	T	E	WNXX	OC(S)
37803	a	ML	E	WKMF	SNCF
37883		E	E	WKGN	TO
37884		LH	E	WKGN	TO
37885		E	E	WKGN	TO
37886		E	E	WKGN	TO
37887	s	T	E	WNXX	IM(S)
37888	*	F	E	WKGN	TO
37889		T	E	WNXX	CD(S)
37890	a	MG	E	WKMF	SNCF
37891	a	MG	E	WKMF	SNCF
37892		MG	E	WKGN	TO
37893		E	E	WKGN	TO
37894	as	FC	E	WKMF	SNCF
37895	as	E	E	WKGN	TO
37896	s	T	E	WKGN	TO
37897	s	T	E	WKGN	TO
37898	s	T	E	WNXX	CF(S)
37899	s	E	E	WKGN	TO

Names:

37702	Taff Merthyr
37715	British Petroleum
37717	Berwick Middle School, Railsafe Trophy Winners 1998
37799	Sir Dyfed/County of Dyfed
37884	Gartcosh
37892	Ripple Lane[1]
37898	Cwmbargoed DP

Class 37/9. Refurbished locos. New power unit. Main generator replaced by alternator. Ballast weights added. Details as Class 37/4 except:

Engine: Mirrlees MB275T of 1340 kW (1800 hp) at 1000 rpm (‡ Ruston RK270T of 1340 kW (1800 hp) at 900 rpm).
Train supply: Not equipped.
Main Alternator: Brush BA1005A (‡ GEC G564AZ).
Maximum Tractive Effort: 279 kN (62680 lbf).
Continuous Tractive Effort: 184 kN (41250 lbf) at 11.4 mph.
Weight: 120 t.   **RA:** 7.

37901	T	E	WNYX	CF(S)	Mirrlees Pioneer
37902	FM	E	WNYX	IM(S)	
37903	FM	E	WNYX	CD(S)	
37904	FM	E	WNYX	CF(S)	
37905 ‡s	FM	E	WNYX	IM(S)	
37906 ‡s	T	E	WNYX	OC(S)	

CLASS 43   BREL/PAXMAN   Bo-Bo

Built: 1976–82 by BREL at Crewe Works.
Engine: Paxman Valenta 12RP200L of 1680 kW (2250 hp) at 1500 rpm († Paxman 12VP185 of 2010 kW (2700 hp) at 1800 rpm).
Main Alternator: Brush BA1001B.
Traction Motors: Brush TMH68–46 or GEC G417AZ, frame mounted.
Maximum Tractive Effort: 80 kN (17980 lbf).
Continuous Tractive Effort: 46 kN (10340 lbf) at 64.5 mph.
Power At Rail: 1320 kW (1770 hp).   **Train Brakes:** Air.
Brake Force: 35 t.   **Dimensions:** 17.79 x 2.71 x 3.88 m.
Weight: 70 t.   **Wheel Diameter:** 1020 mm.
Design Speed: 125 mph.   **Maximum Speed:** 125 mph.
Fuel Capacity: 4500 litres.   **RA:** 5.
Train Supply: Three-phase electric.
Multiple Working: Within class, jumpers at non-driving end only.

43002	GW	A	IWRP	PM	Techni?uest
43003	GW	A	IWRP	PM	
43004	GW	A	IWRP	PM	Borough of Swindon
43005	GW	A	IWRP	PM	
43006	IS	A	IWCP	LA	
43007	IS	A	IWCP	LA	
43008	V	A	IWCP	LA	
43009	GW	A	IWRP	PM	
43010	GW	A	IWRP	PM	
43011	GW	A	SCXL	ZC(S)	Reader 125
43012	GW	A	IWRP	PM	
43013	V	P	ICCP	LA	
43014	V	P	ICCP	LA	
43015	GW	A	IWRP	PM	
43016	GW	A	IWRP	PM	
43017	GW	A	IWRP	LA	
43018	WO	A	IWRP	LA	The Red Cross

43019	GW	A	IWRP	LA	Dinas Abertawe/City of Swansea
43020	GW	A	IWRP	LA	John Grooms
43021	GW	A	IWRP	LA	
43022	GW	A	IWRP	LA	
43023	GW	A	IWRP	LA	County of Cornwall
43024	GW	A	IWRP	LA	
43025	GW	A	IWRP	LA	Exeter
43026	GW	A	IWRP	LA	City of Westminster
43027	GW	A	IWRP	LA	Glorious Devon
43028	GW	A	IWRP	LA	
43029	IS	A	ICCP	LA	
43030	GW	A	IWRP	PM	
43031	WO	A	IWRP	PM	
43032	GW	A	IWRP	PM	The Royal Regiment of Wales
43033	GW	A	IWRP	PM	
43034	GW	A	IWRP	PM	The Black Horse
43035	GW	A	IWRP	PM	
43036	GW	A	IWRP	PM	
43037	GW	A	IWRP	PM	
43038	GN	A	IECP	EC	
43039	GN	A	IECP	EC	
43040	GW	A	IWRP	PM	
43041	GW	A	IWRP	LA	City of Discovery
43042	GW	A	IWRP	LA	
43043	MM	P	IMLP	NL	LEICESTERSHIRE COUNTY CRICKET CLUB
43044	MM	P	IMLP	NL	Borough of Kettering
43045	MM	P	IMLP	NL	
43046	MM	P	IMLP	NL	Royal Philharmonic
43047 †	MM	P	IMLP	NL	
43048	MM	P	IMLP	NL	
43049	MM	P	IMLP	NL	Neville Hill
43050	MM	P	IMLP	NL	
43051	MM	P	IMLP	NL	
43052	MM	P	IMLP	NL	
43053	MM	P	IMLP	NL	Leeds United
43054	MM	P	IMLP	NL	
43055	MM	P	IMLP	NL	Sheffield Star
43056	MM	P	IMLP	NL	
43057	MM	P	IMLP	NL	
43058	MM	P	IMLP	NL	MIDLAND PRIDE
43059 †	MM	P	IMLP	NL	
43060	MM	P	IMLP	NL	County of Leicestershire
43061	MM	P	IMLP	NL	
43062	V	P	ICCP	LA	
43063	V	P	ICCP	LA	
43064	MM	P	IMLP	NL	
43065	V	P	ICCP	LA	
43066	MM	P	IMLP	NL	Nottingham Playhouse
43067	V	P	ICCP	LA	
43068	V	P	ICCP	LA	

43069		V	P	ICCP	LA	
43070		V	P	ICCP	LA	
43071		IS	P	ICCP	LA	Forward Birmingham
43072		MM	P	IMLP	NL	Derby Etches Park
43073		MM	P	IMLP	NL	
43074	†	MM	P	IMLP	NL	BBC EAST MIDLANDS TODAY
43075	†	MM	P	IMLP	NL	
43076		MM	P	IMLP	NL	THE MASTER CUTLER 1947-1997
43077		MM	P	IMLP	NL	
43078		IS	P	ICCP	LA	Golowan Festival Penzance
43079		IS	P	ICCP	LA	
43080		V	P	ICCP	LA	
43081		MM	P	IMLP	NL	
43082		MM	P	IMLP	NL	DERBYSHIRE FIRST
43083		MM	P	IMLP	NL	
43084		V	P	ICCP	LA	County of Derbyshire
43085		MM	P	IMLP	NL	
43086		V	P	ICCP	LA	
43087		IS	P	ICCP	LA	
43088		V	P	ICCP	LA	
43089		V	P	ICCP	LA	
43090		V	P	ICCP	LA	
43091		V	P	ICCP	LA	
43092		V	P	ICCP	LA	Institution of Mechanical Engineers 150th Anniversary 1847–1997
43093		V	P	ICCP	LA	Lady in Red
43094		IS	P	ICCP	LA	
43095		GN	A	IECP	EC	
43096		GN	A	IECP	EC	The Great Racer
43097		IS	P	ICCP	LA	
43098		V	P	ICCP	LA	railwaychildren
43099		V	P	ICCP	LA	
43100		V	P	ICCP	LA	Blackpool Rock
43101		V	P	ICCP	LA	The Irish Mail Trên Post Gwyddelig
43102		V	P	ICCP	LA	
43103		V	P	ICCP	LA	
43104		IS	A	SCXL	LA(S)	County of Cleveland
43105		GN	A	IECP	EC	
43106		GN	A	IECP	EC	
43107		GN	A	IECP	EC	
43108		GN	A	IECP	EC	
43109		GN	A	IECP	EC	
43110		GN	A	IECP	EC	
43111		GN	A	IECP	EC	
43112		GN	A	IECP	EC	
43113		GN	A	IECP	EC	
43114		GN	A	IECP	EC	
43115		GN	A	IECP	EC	
43116		GN	A	IECP	EC	
43117		GN	A	IECP	EC	
43118		GN	A	IECP	EC	

43119		GN	A	IECP	EC	
43120		GN	A	IECP	EC	
43121		V	P	ICCP	LA	
43122		IS	P	ICCP	LA	South Yorkshire Metropolitan County
43123		V	P	ICCP	LA	
43124		GW	A	IWRP	PM	
43125		GW	A	IWRP	PM	Merchant Venturer
43126		GW	A	IWRP	PM	City of Bristol
43127		GW	A	IWRP	PM	
43128		GW	A	IWRP	PM	
43129		GW	A	IWRP	PM	
43130		GW	A	IWRP	PM	Sulis Minerva
43131		GW	A	IWRP	PM	Sir Felix Pole
43132		GW	A	IWRP	PM	
43133		GW	A	IWRP	PM	
43134		GW	A	IWRP	PM	County of Somerset
43135		GW	A	IWRP	PM	
43136		GW	A	IWRP	PM	
43137		GW	A	IWRP	PM	Newton Abbot 150
43138		GW	A	IWRP	PM	
43139		GW	A	IWRP	PM	
43140		GW	A	IWRP	PM	
43141		GW	A	IWRP	PM	
43142		GW	A	IWRP	PM	
43143		GW	A	IWRP	PM	
43144		GW	A	IWRP	PM	
43145		GW	A	IWRP	PM	
43146		GW	A	IWRP	PM	
43147		GW	A	IWRP	PM	
43148		GW	A	IWRP	PM	
43149		GW	A	IWRP	PM	B.B.C. Wales Today
43150		GW	A	IWRP	PM	Bristol Evening Post
43151		GW	A	IWRP	PM	
43152		GW	A	IWRP	PM	
43153		V	P	ICCP	LA	THE ENGLISH RIVIERA TORQUAY PAIGNTON BRIXHAM INTERCITY
43154		V	P	ICCP	LA	
43155		V	P	ICCP	LA	City of Aberdeen
43156		IS	P	ICCP	LA	
43157		V	P	ICCP	LA	HMS Penzance
43158		V	P	ICCP	LA	
43159		IS	P	ICCP	LA	
43160		V	P	ICCP	LA	
43161		V	P	ICCP	LA	Reading Evening Post
43162		V	P	ICCP	LA	
43163		GW	A	IWRP	LA	
43164		GW	A	IWRP	LA	
43165		GW	A	IWRP	LA	
43166		IS	A	ICCP	LA	
43167	†	GN	A	IECP	EC	

43168	†	**GW**	A	IWRP	LA
43169	†	**GW**	A	IWRP	LA	The National Trust
43170	†	**GW**	A	IWRP	LA	Edward Paxman
43171		**GW**	A	IWRP	LA	
43172		**GW**	A	IWRP	LA	
43174		**GW**	A	IWRP	LA	Bristol-Bordeaux
43175	†	**GW**	A	IWRP	LA	
43176		**GW**	A	IWRP	LA	
43177	†	**GW**	A	IWRP	LA	University of Exeter
43178		**V**	A	IWCP	LA	
43179	†	**GW**	A	IWRP	LA	Pride of Laira
43180		**V**	P	ICCP	LA	City of Newcastle upon Tyne
43181		**GW**	A	IWRP	LA	Devonport Royal Dockyard 1693-1993
43182		**GW**	A	IWRP	LA	
43183		**GW**	A	IWRP	LA	
43184		**V**	A	IWCP	LA	
43185		**GW**	A	IWRP	LA	Great Western
43186		**GW**	A	IWRP	LA	Sir Francis Drake
43187		**GW**	A	IWRP	LA	
43188		**GW**	A	IWRP	LA	City of Plymouth
43189		**GW**	A	IWRP	LA	RAILWAY HERITAGE TRUST
43190		**GW**	A	IWRP	LA	
43191	†	**GW**	A	IWRP	LA	Seahawk
43192		**GW**	A	IWRP	LA	City of Truro
43193		**IS**	P	ICCP	LA	Plymouth SPIRIT OF DISCOVERY
43194		**V**	P	ICCP	LA	
43195		**IS**	P	ICCP	LA	British Red Cross 125th Birthday 1995
43196		**IS**	P	ICCP	LA	The Newspaper Society Founded 1836
43197		**IS**	P	ICCP	LA	Railway Magazine Centenary 1897-1997
43198		**IS**	P	ICCP	LA	

CLASS 46   BR/SULZER   1Co-Co1

Built: 1963 by BR at Derby Locomotive Works.
Engine: Sulzer 12LDA28B of 1860 kW (2500 hp) at 750 rpm.
Main Generator: Brush TG160-60.   **Traction Motors:** Brush TM73-68 Mk3.
Maximum Tractive Effort: 245 kN (55000 lbf).
Continuous Tractive Effort: 141 kN (31600 lbf) at 22.3 mph.
Power At Rail: 1460 kW (1960 hp).   **Train Brakes:** Air & vacuum.
Brake Force: 63 t.   **Dimensions:** 20.70 x 2.78 x 3.92 m.
Weight: 140 t.   **Wheel Diameter:** 914/1143 mm.
Design Speed: 90 mph.   **Maximum Speed:** 75 mph.
Fuel Capacity: 3591 litres.   **RA:** 7.
Train Supply: Not equipped.   **Multiple Working:** Not equipped.
Non-standard livery/numbering:
• 46035 carries number D172. Official RSL number is 89472.

46035	**G**	CN	MBDL	CQ	Ixion

CLASS 47 BR/BRUSH/SULZER Co-Co

Built: 1963–67 by Brush Traction, at Loughborough or by BR at Crewe Works.
Engine: Sulzer 12LDA28C of 1920 kW (2580 hp) at 750 rpm.
Main Generator: Brush TG160-60 Mk4 or TM172-50 Mk1.
Traction Motors: Brush TM64-68 Mk1 or Mk1A.
Maximum Tractive Effort: 267 kN (60000 lbf).
Continuous Tractive Effort: 133 kN (30000 lbf) at 26 mph.
Power At Rail: 1550 kW (2080 hp). **Train Brakes:** Air.
Brake Force: 61 t. **Dimensions:** 19.38 x 2.79 x 3.9 m.
Weight: 111.5–120.6 t. **Wheel Diameter:** 1143 mm.
Design Speed: 95 mph. **Maximum Speed:** 75 (‡ 95) mph.
Fuel Capacity: 3273 (+ 5550; † 4410 litres).
Train Supply: Not equipped.
Multiple Working: Green Circle (n – not equipped).
Non-standard liveries/numbering:
• 47016 also carries number 1546.
• 47114 is two-tone green with Freightliner logos.
• 47145 is dark blue with Railfreight Distribution logos.
• 47484 is Great Western Railway style green, with cast numberplates.
• 47515 is livery **IM** on one side and all-over white on the other side.
• 47519 also carries number D1102.
• 47803 is yellow and white with a red stripe.
• 47972 is in British Railways Board Central Services livery of red and grey.

Class 47/0 (Dual braked) or Class 47/2 (Air braked). Standard Design. Details as above.

47004	xn	**G**	E	WNZX	OC(S)	Old Oak Common Traction & Rolling Stock Depot
47016	xn	**FO**	E	WNZX	SP(S)	ATLAS[1]
47033	+	**FE**	EF	WNXX	BS(S)	The Royal Logistic Corps
47049	+	**FE**	EF	WNZX	SP(S)	
47051	+	**FE**	EF	WNZX	SP(S)	
47052		**FF**	P	DFLT	FD	
47053	+	**FE**	EF	WNYX	HM(S)	
47095	+	**FE**	EF	WNYX	AN(S)	
47114	+	**O**	FL	DFLM	FD	Freightlinerbulk
47125	+	**FE**	EF	WNZX	CW(S)	
47145	+	**O**	EF	WNXX	CD(S)	Merddin Emrys
47146	+	**FE**	EF	WNYX	CG(S)	
47150	+	**FL**	FL	DFLM	FD	
47152	+	**FF**	FL	DFLT	FD	
47156	+	**FD**	E	WNZX	CW(S)	
47157	+	**FF**	P	DFLM	FD	Johnson Stevens Agencies
47186	+	**FE**	EF	WNYX	HM(S)	
47188	+	**FE**	EF	WNYX	CD(S)	
47193	xn	**FL**	P	DHLT	CD(S)	
47194	+	**FD**	EF	WNXX	SF(S)	
47197	n	**FF**	P	DFFT	FD	
47200	+	**FE**	EF	WNXX	HM(S)	

47201	+	FE	EF	WNYX	HM(S)	
47205	+	FF	FL	DFLM	FD	
47206	n	FF	P	DFLT	FD	The Morris Dancer
47207	+	FF	P	DFLM	FD	The Felixstowe Partnership
47209	+	FF	P	DFLM	FD	
47210	+	FD	EF	WNZX	SP(S)	
47211	+	FD	EF	WNYX	EH(S)	
47212	xn†	FF	P	DFLT	FD	
47213	+	FD	EF	WNXX	HM(S)	
47217	+	FE	EF	WNXX	BS(S)	
47218	+	FE	EF	WNYX	HM(S)	
47219	+	FE	EF	WNZX	HM(S)	
47221	xn†	FP	E	WNXX	LB(S)	
47223	xn†	F	E	WNYX	CW(S)	
47224	xn†	F	FL	DFLT	FD	
47225	n	FF	P	DFLT	FD	
47226	+	FD	EF	WNZX	HM(S)	
47228	+	FE	EF	WNYX	HM(S)	
47229	+	FD	EF	WNYX	HM(S)	
47234	+	FF	P	DFLM	FD	
47236	+	FE	EF	WNZX	SF(S)	
47237	+	FE	EF	WNYX	HM(S)	
47238	xn	FD	E	WNZX	BS(S)	
47241	+	FE	EF	WNXX	HM(S)	
47245	+	FE	EF	WNZX	DR(S)	
47256	xn	FD	E	WNZX	DR(S)	
47258	+	FL	FL	DFLM	FD	Forth Ports Tilbury
47270	n	FF	P	DFFT	FD	Cory Brothers 1842-1992
47276	†	F	EF	WNXX	SP(S)	
47277	xn†	FD	E	WNZX	IM(S)	
47279	+	FF	P	DFLM	FD	
47280	+	FD	EF	WNZX	HM(S)	
47281	+	FD	EF	WNZX	SP(S)	
47283	n	FF	FL	DHLT	CW(S)	
47285	+	FE	EF	WNZX	TO(S)	
47286	+	FE	EF	WNXX	BS(S)	Port of Liverpool
47287	+	F	FL	DFLM	FD	
47289	+	FF	P	DFLM	FD	
47290	+	FF	FL	DHLT	CW(S)	
47292	+	F	P	DFLM	FD	
47293	+	FE	EF	WNZX	HM(S)	
47294	ns†	FD	E	WNZX	TT(S)	
47295	n†	F	FL	DFFT	FD	
47296	xn	FF	P	DFLT	FD	
47297	+	FE	EF	WNXX	BS(S)	Cobra RAILFREIGHT
47298	+	FD	EF	WNZX	HM(S)	

Class 47/3 (Dual braked) or Class 47/2 (Air braked). Details as Class 47/0 except: **Weight:** 113.7 t.

| 47300 | xn | CE | E | WNXX | BS(S) | |
| 47301 | + | FF | P | DHLT | CW(S) | Freightliner Birmingham |

47302	+	FF	FL	DFLM	FD	
47303	+	FF	P	DFLM	FD	Freightliner Cleveland
47304	+	FD	EF	WNZX	TO(S)	
47305	n	FF	P	DHLT	CW(S)	
47306	+	FE	EF	WNZX	CD(S)	The Sapper
47307	+	FE	EF	WNZX	HM(S)	
47308		FF	FL	DHLT	CW(S)	
47309	+	FF	FL	DFFT	FD	European Rail Operator of The Year
47310	+	FE	EF	WNZX	HM(S)	
47312	+	FE	EF	WNXX	CG(S)	
47313	+	FD	EF	WNZX	HM(S)	
47314	+	FD	EF	WNZX	HM(S)	
47315	xns	CE	E	WNXX	SY(S)	
47316	+	FE	EF	WNXX	TO(S)	
47318	xn	FO	E	WNZX	BS(S)	
47319	xn†	FP	E	WNZX	IM(S)	
47323	+	FF	P	DFLM	FD	
47326	+	FE	EF	WNZX	CD(S)	Saltley Depot Quality Approved
47328	+	FD	EF	WNXX	CW(S)	
47330	+	FF	FL	DFLM	FD	
47331	xns	CE	E	WNXX	CD(S)	
47334	n	FF	P	DFLT	FD	P & O Nedlloyd
47335	+	FD	EF	WNZX	HM(S)	
47337	+	FF	FL	DHLT	CW(S)	
47338	+	FE	EF	WNXX	CD(S)	
47339	n	FF	P	DHLT	CW(S)	
47341	xn	CE	E	WNZX	TT(S)	
47344	+	FE	EF	WNXX	SF(S)	
47345	xn	FF	P	DFLT	FD	
47348	‡+	FE	EF	WHCN	CD	St. Christopher's Railway Home
47349	xn	FF	P	DFLT	FD	
47351	+	FE	EF	WNZX	SP(S)	
47352	xn	CE	E	WNZX	FH(S)	
47353	xn	FF	FL	DHLT	CW(S)	
47354		FF	FL	DFLT	FD	
47355	+	FD	EF	WNYX	HM(S)	
47357	xn	CE	E	WNYX	BS(S)	
47358	+	FF	P	DFLM	FD	
47360	+	FE	EF	WNXX	HM(S)	
47361	+	FF	P	DFLM	FD	Wilton Endeavour
47362	+	FD	EF	WNXX	BS(S)	
47363	+	F	EF	WNXX	SP(S)	
47365	+	FE	EF	WNYX	CF(S)	Diamond Jubilee
47367	+	FF	P	DFLM	FD	
47368	xn	F	E	WNYX	SF(S)	Andrew A Hodgkinson
47370	+	FF	P	DFLM	FD	
47371	xn	FF	P	DFLT	FD	
47372	xn	FF	FL	DFLT	FD	
47375	+	FE	EF	WNYX	HM(S)	
47376	xn	FF	P	DHLT	CD(S)	Freightliner 1995
47377	n	FF	P	DFLT	FD	

Class 47/4. Electric Train Supply equipment. Details as Class 47/0 except:

Weight: 120.4–125.1 t.
Fuel Capacity: 3273 (+ 5887) litres.
Train Supply: Electric, index 66.
Multiple Working: Not equipped (m – Green Circle; † – Blue Star).

Maximum Speed: 95 (* 75, † 100) mph.
RA: 7.

47462	x*	RG	E	WNYX	TT(S)
47467	x*	BL	E	WNZX	SP(S)
47471	x	I	E	WNYX	CW(S)
47474	x	RG	E	WHCN	CD	Sir Rowland Hill
47475	x*	RX	E	WNXX	HM(S)
47476	x	RG	E	WHCN	CD	Night Mail
47478	x*	B	E	WNYX	BS(S)
47481	x	BL	E	WNYX	CW(S)
47484	x*	O	E	WNXX	CD(S)
47488	x	G	FR	SDFR	TM
47489		RG	E	WNZX	BS(S)
47492	x*	RX	E	WNXX	OC(S)
47501	x	RG	E	WNXX	CD(S)	Craftsman[1]
47513	x*	BL	E	WNYX	CG(S)
47515	x	O	E	WNYX	CW(S)
47519	x+*	G	E	WNXX	CD(S)
47522	x*	RG	E	WNZX	SP(S)
47523	*	IM	E	WNZX	SP(S)
47524	x*	RX	E	WNYX	CW(S)
47525	x*	FE	E	WNYX	CG(S)
47526	x*	BL	E	WNYX	CW(S)
47528	x*	IM	E	WNYX	DR(S)
47530	x*	RX	E	WNYX	CW(S)
47532	x*	RX	E	WNYX	CW(S)
47535	x*	RX	E	WNXX	OC(S)
47536	x*	RX	E	WNYX	CD(S)
47539		RX	E	WNYX	CW(S)
47540	xm*	CE	E	WNYX	CW(S)	The Institution of Civil Engineers
47547		N	E	WNZX	CW(S)
47550	x*	IM	E	WNYX	IM(S)
47565	x	RX	E	WHDT	CD	Responsive
47566	x*	RX	E	WNYX	CW(S)
47574	x*	RG	E	WNXX	CD(S)
47575	x	RG	E	WHCN	CD	City of Hereford
47576	x*	RX	E	WNYX	CW(S)
47584	x	RX	E	WHCN	CD	THE LOCOMOTIVE & CARRIAGE INSTITUTION 1911
47596	x	RX	E	WNXX	CD(S)
47624	xj*	RX	E	WNYX	AN(S)
47627	x	R	E	WHCN	CD
47628	j*	RX	E	WNZX	CW(S)
47634	x	RG	E	WHCN	CD	Holbeck
47635	xj	RG	E	WHCN	CD
47640	j	RG	E	WHCN	CD	University of Strathclyde

Class 47/7. Electric Train Supply and Push & Pull equipment (RCH System).
Details as Class 47/4 except:

Weight: 118.7 t.   **Fuel Capacity:** 5887 litres.

47701	x	**FR**	WF	SDFR	ZA(S)	Waverley
47702	x	**V**	E	ILRA	TO	County of Suffolk
47703	x	**FR**	FR	SDFR	TM	
47704	*	**RX**	E	WNZX	CD(S)	
47705	x	**LW**	RV	MBDL	CP	GUY FAWKES
47707	x	**RX**	E	WNYX	CW(S)	Holyrood
47709	x	**FR**	FR	SDFR	TM	
47710	x	**FR**	FR	SDFR	TM	
47711	x	**V**	E	ILRA	TO	County of Hertfordshire
47712	x	**WL**	FR	SDFR	TM	
47714	x	**RX**	E	WNYX	CW(S)	
47715	*	**N**	E	WNYX	CW(S)	
47716	x*	**RX**	E	WNYX	CW(S)	
47717	x	**RG**	E	WNYX	CW(S)	

Class 47/7. Electric Train Supply equipment and RCH Jumper Cables. Details
as Class 47/4 except:

Weight: 118.7 t.   **Fuel Capacity:** 5887 litres.

47721		**RX**	E	WHDP	CD	Saint Bede
47722		**RX**	E	WHDM	CD	The Queen Mother
47725		**RX**	E	WHDM	CD	The Railway Mission
47726		**RX**	E	WHDM	CD	Manchester Airport Progress
47727		**RX**	E	WHDP	CD	Duke of Edinburgh's Award
47732	x	**RX**	E	WHDP	CD	Restormel
47733		**RX**	E	WHDM	CD	Eastern Star
47734		**RX**	E	WHDM	CD	Crewe Diesel Depot Quality Approved
47736		**RX**	E	WHDP	CD	Cambridge Traction & Rolling Stock Depot
47737		**RX**	E	WHDM	CD	Resurgent
47738		**RX**	E	WHDP	CD	Bristol Barton Hill
47739		**RX**	E	WHDM	CD	Resourceful
47741		**RX**	E	WHDP	CD	Resilient
47742		**RX**	E	WHDM	CD	The Enterprising Scot
47744		**E**	E	WHDP	CD	
47745	x	**RX**	E	WHDP	CD	Royal London Society for the Blind
47746		**RX**	E	WHDP	CD	The Bobby
47747		**RX**	E	WHDP	CD	Res Publica
47749		**RX**	E	WHDM	CD	Atlantic College
47750		**RX**	E	WHDM	CD	Royal Mail Cheltenham
47756		**RX**	E	WHDC	ML	Royal Mail Tyneside
47757		**RX**	E	WHDP	CD	Restitution
47758		**E**	E	WHDP	CD	Regency Rail Cruises
47759		**RX**	E	WHDP	CD	
47760		**E**	E	WHDC	ML	Ribblehead Viaduct

47761		RX	E	WHDP	CD	
47762	x	RX	E	WHDP	CD	
47763		RX	E	WHDP	CD	
47764		RX	E	WHDM	CD	Resounding
47765	x	RX	E	WHDP	CD	Ressaldar
47766	x	RX	E	WHDP	CD	Resolute
47767		RX	E	WHDM	CD	Saint Columba
47768	x	RX	E	WHDP	CD	Resonant
47769		RX	E	ILRA	TO	Resolve
47770		RX	E	WHDP	CD	Reserved
47771		RX	E	WHDP	CD	Heaton Traincare Depot
47772	x	RX	E	WHDP	CD	
47773		RX	E	WHDC	ML	Reservist
47774	x	RX	E	WHDP	CD	Poste Restante
47775		RX	E	WHDT	CD	Respite
47776	x	RX	E	WHDP	CD	Respected
47777	x	RX	E	WHDM	CD	Restored
47778		RX	E	WHDP	CD	Irresistible
47779		RX	E	WNXX	CD(S)	
47780		RX	E	WHDP	CD	
47781		RX	E	WHDP	CD	Isle of Iona
47782		RX	E	WHDP	CD	
47783		RX	E	WHDM	CD	Saint Peter
47784		RX	E	WHDP	CD	Condover Hall
47785		E	E	WHDP	CD	Fiona Castle
47786		E	E	WHDP	CD	Roy Castle OBE
47787		RX	E	WHDM	CD	Victim Support
47788		RX	E	WHDP	CD	Captain Peter Manisty RN
47789		RX	E	WHDP	CD	Lindisfarne
47790		RX	E	WHDC	ML	Dewi Sant/Saint David
47791		RX	E	WHDC	ML	
47792		RX	E	WHDP	CD	Saint Cuthbert
47793		RX	E	WHDM	CD	Saint Augustine

Class 47/7. Electric Train Supply equipment. Locos dedicated for Royal Train & (occasional) Charter Train use. Details as Class 47/4 except:

Weight: 118.7 t.   **Fuel Capacity:** 5887 litres.

47798	RP	E	WHDA	CD	Prince William
47799	RP	E	WHDA	CD	Prince Henry

Class 47/4 ("47/8" & "47/9") Continued.

47802	+*	IS	E	WNZX	CG(S)	
47803	+*	O	E	WNYX	SF(S)	
47805	+	IS	P	ILRA	TO	
47806	+	V	P	ILRA	TO	
47807	+	V	P	ILRA	TO	The Lion of Vienna
47810	+	IS	P	ILRA	TO	PORTERBROOK
47811	+	GL	P	IWLA	LE	
47812	+	IS	P	ILRA	TO	
47813	+	GL	P	IWLA	LE	S.S. Great Britain
47814	+	V	P	ILRA	TO	Totnes Castle

47815	+	**GL**	P	IWLA	LE	
47816	+	**GL**	P	IWLA	LE	Bristol Bath Road
						Quality Approved
47817	+	**V**	P	ILRA	TO	The Institution of Mechanical
						Engineers
47818	+	**V**	P	ILRA	TO	
47822	+	**V**	P	ILRA	TO	Pride of Shrewsbury
47825	+	**IS**	P	IANA	NC	Thomas Telford
47826	+	**IS**	P	ILRA	TO	
47827	+	**V**	P	ILRA	TO	
47828	+	**IS**	P	ILRA	TO	
47829	+	**V**	P	ILRA	TO	
47830	+	**GL**	P	IWLA	LE	
47831	+	**IS**	P	ILRA	TO	Bolton Wanderer
47832	+	**GL**	P	IWLA	LE	
47839	+	**IS**	P	ILRA	TO	
47840	+	**IS**	P	ILRA	TO	NORTH STAR
47841	+	**V**	P	ILRA	TO	Spirit of Chester
47843	+	**IS**	P	ILRA	TO	
47844	+	**V**	P	ILRA	TO	
47845	+	**V**	P	ILRA	TO	County of Kent
47846	+	**GL**	P	IWLA	LE	THOR
47847	+	**IS**	P	ILRA	TO	
47848	+	**IS**	P	ILRA	TO	
47849	+	**IS**	P	ILRA	TO	
47851	+	**IS**	P	ILRA	TO	
47853	+	**V**	P	ILRA	TO	
47854	+	**IS**	P	ILRA	TO	Women's Royal Voluntary Service
47971	x†	**BL**	E	WNYX	ZC(S)	Robin Hood
47972	†	**0**	E	WNYX	CD(S)	
47976	x†	**CE**	E	WNZX	SP(S)	

Class 47/3 ("47/9") Continued.

| 47981 | xs | **CE** | E | WNZX | SP(S) |

CLASS 50   ENGLISH ELECTRIC   Co-Co

Built: 1967–68 by English Electric at Vulcan Foundry, Newton-le-Willows.
Engine: English Electric 16CVST of 2010 kW (2700 hp) at 850 rpm.
Main Generator: English Electric 840/4B.
Traction Motors: English Electric 538/5A.
Maximum Tractive Effort: 216 kN (48500 lbf).
Continuous Tractive Effort: 147 kN (33000 lbf) at 23.5 mph.
Power At Rail: 1540 kW (2070 hp).   **Train Brakes:** Air & vacuum.
Brake Force: 59 t.   **Dimensions:** 20.88 x 2.78 x 3.96 m.
Weight: 116.9 t.   **Wheel Diameter:** 1092 mm.
Design Speed: 105 mph.   **Maximum Speed:** 90 (* 100) mph.
Fuel Capacity: 4796 litres.   **RA:** 6.
Train Supply: Electric, index 66.   **Multiple Working:** Orange Square.
Non-standard livery/numbering:
• 50017 is 'LMS Coronation Scot' style maroon with four gold bands.
• 50044 carries number D444.

50017	*	**0**	JK	MBDL	CQ	
50031		**BL**	50	MBDL	KR	Hood
50044		**B**	50	MBDL	KR	
50050		**BL**	HS	DNLL	NC	Fearless

CLASS 55   ENGLISH ELECTRIC   Co-Co

Built: 1961 by English Electric at Vulcan Foundry, Newton-le-Willows.
Engine: Two Napier-Deltic D18-25 of 1230 kW (1650 hp) each at 1500 rpm.
Main Generators: Two English Electric 829.
Traction Motors: English Electric 538/A.
Maximum Tractive Effort: 222 kN (50000 lbf).
Continuous Tractive Effort: 136 kN (30500 lbf) at 32.5 mph.
Power At Rail: 1969 kW (2640 hp).   **Train Brakes:** Air & vacuum.
Brake Force: 51 t.   **Dimensions:** 21.18 x 2.68 x 3.94 m.
Weight: 104.7 t.   **Wheel Diameter:** 1092 mm.
Design Speed: 100 mph.   **Maximum Speed:** 100 mph.
Fuel Capacity: 3755 litres.   **RA:** 5.
Train Supply: Electric, index 66.   **Multiple Working:** Not equipped.
Non-standard livery/numbering:
• 55009 carries number D9009. Official RSL number is 89509.
• 55016 is in Porterbrook Leasing livery of purple with grey lower body skirt, white window surrounds and white stripe. Carries number 9016. Official RSL number is 89516.
• Official RSL number of 55019 is 89519.
• 55022 carries number D9000. Official RSL number is 89500.

55009	**G**	DP	MBDL	CP	ALYCIDON
55016	**0**	90	DNLL	SY	GORDON HIGHLANDER
55019	**B**	DP	MBDL	CP	ROYAL HIGHLAND FUSILIER
55022	**G**	90	DNLL	NC	ROYAL SCOTS GREY

CLASS 56   BRUSH/BR/PAXMAN   Co-Co

Built: 1976–84 by Electroputere at Craiova, Romania (as sub contractors for Brush) or BREL at Doncaster or Crewe Works.
Engine: Ruston Paxman 16RK3CT of 2460 kW (3250 hp) at 900 rpm.
Main Alternator: Brush BA1101A.
Traction Motors: Brush TM73-62.
Maximum Tractive Effort: 275 kN (61800 lbf).
Continuous Tractive Effort: 240 kN (53950 lbf) at 16.8 mph.
Power At Rail: 1790 kW (2400 hp).   **Train Brakes:** Air.
Brake Force: 60 t.   **Dimensions:** 19.36 x 2.79 x 3.9 m.
Weight: 125.2 t.   **Wheel Diameter:** 1143 mm.
Design Speed: 80 mph.   **Maximum Speed:** 80 mph.
Fuel Capacity: 5228 litres.   **RA:** 7.
Train Supply: Not equipped.   **Multiple Working:** Red Diamond.
Note: All equipped with Slow Speed Control.
Non-standard livery/numbering:
• 56063 is as **F**, but with the light grey replaced by a darker grey.

56003	**LH**	E	WNXX	DR(S)	
56004	**B**	E	WNXX	DR(S)	
56006	**B**	E	WNXX	OC(S)	
56007	**T**	E	WGAN	IM	
56008	**B**	E	WNZX	IM(S)	
56010	**T**	E	WNXX	DR(S)	
56011	**E**	E	WGAN	IM	
56012	**FC**	E	WNZX	IM(S)	
56013	**FC**	E	WNZX	TT(S)	
56014	**FC**	E	WNZX	IM(S)	
56018	**E**	E	WGAN	IM	
56019	**FQ**	E	WNXX	IM(S)	
56021	**LH**	E	WNXX	IM(S)	
56022	**T**	E	WNXX	IM(S)	
56023	**FC**	E	WNZX	TT(S)	
56025	**T**	E	WGAN	IM	
56027	**LH**	E	WGAN	IM	
56029	**T**	E	WGAN	IM	
56031	**CE**	E	WNXX	TE(S)	
56032	**E**	E	WGAN	IM	
56033	**T**	E	WGAN	IM	Shotton Paper Mill
56034	**LH**	E	WNXX	TO(S)	Castell Ogwr/Ogmore Castle
56035	**LH**	E	WNZX	SP(S)	
56036	**TC**	E	WGAN	IM	
56037	**E**	E	WGAN	IM	
56038	**E**	E	WGAN	IM	
56039	**LH**	E	WNXX	TE(S)	
56040	**T**	E	WGAN	IM	Oystermouth
56041	**E**	E	WGAN	IM	
56043	**FM**	E	WGAN	IM	
56044	**T**	E	WGAN	IM	Cardiff Canton

56045	LH	E	WNXX	IM(S)	British Steel Shelton
56046	CE	E	WNXX	DR(S)	
56047	TC	E	WNXX	DR(S)	
56048	CE	E	WGAN	IM	
56049	TC	E	WGAN	IM	
56050	LH	E	WNXX	TO(S)	British Steel Teesside
56051	E	E	WGAN	IM	
56052	T	E	WNXX	DR(S)	The Cardiff Rod Mill
56053	T	E	WNXX	DR(S)	Sir Morgannwg Ganol/ County of Mid Glamorgan
56054	T	E	WGAN	IM	British Steel Llanwern
56055	LH	E	WGAN	IM	
56056	T	E	WGAN	IM	
56057	E	E	WNXX	IM(S)	British Fuels
56058	E	E	WGAN	IM	
56059	E	E	WGAN	IM	
56060	E	E	WGAN	IM	
56061	FM	E	WNXX	TO(S)	
56062	E	E	WGAN	IM	
56063	O	E	WGAN	IM	
56064	T	E	WGAN	IM	
56065	E	E	WGAN	IM	
56066	T	E	WNXX	CF(S)	
56067	E	E	WGAN	IM	
56068	E	E	WGAN	IM	
56069	E	E	WGAN	IM	Wolverhampton Steel Terminal
56070	T	E	WGAN	IM	
56071	E	E	WGAN	IM	
56072	T	E	WGAN	IM	
56073	T	E	WGAN	IM	Tremorfa Steelworks
56074	LH	E	WGAN	IM	Kellingley Colliery
56075	F	E	WNXX	TO(S)	
56076	T	E	WGAN	IM	
56077	LH	E	WGAN	IM	Thorpe Marsh Power Station
56078	F	E	WGAN	IM	
56079	T	E	WGAN	IM	
56080	F	E	WNXX	IM(S)	Selby Coalfield
56081	E	E	WGAN	IM	
56082	F	E	WNXX	IM(S)	
56083	LH	E	WGAN	IM	
56084	LH	E	WGAN	IM	
56085	LH	E	WGAN	IM	
56086	T	E	WNXX	IM(S)	The Magistrates' Association
56087	E	E	WGAN	IM	ABP Port of Hull
56088	E	E	WGAN	IM	
56089	E	E	WGAN	IM	
56090	LH	E	WGAN	IM	
56091	E	E	WGAN	IM	Stanton
56092	T	E	WNZX	SP(S)	
56093	T	E	WNXX	DR(S)	
56094	E	E	WGAN	IM	Eggborough Power Station

56095	E	E	WGAN	IM	
56096	E	E	WGAN	IM	
56097	FM	E	WNZX	SP(S)	
56098	F	E	WGAN	IM	
56099	T	E	WNXX	DR(S)	Fiddlers Ferry Power Station
56100	LH	E	WGAN	IM	
56101	T	E	WGAN	IM	Mutual Improvement
56102	LH	E	WGAN	IM	
56103	E	E	WGAN	IM	STORA
56104	FC	E	WNXX	IM(S)	
56105	E	E	WGAN	IM	
56106	LH	E	WGAN	IM	
56107	LH	E	WGAN	IM	
56108	F	E	WNXX	TE(S)	
56109	LH	E	WGAN	IM	
56110	LH	E	WGAN	IM	Croft[1]
56111	LH	E	WGAN	IM	
56112	LH	E	WGAN	IM	Stainless Pioneer
56113	E	E	WGAN	IM	
56114	E	E	WGAN	IM	
56115	E	E	WGAN	IM	
56116	LH	E	WGAN	IM	
56117	E	E	WGAN	IM	
56118	LH	E	WNXX	IM(S)	
56119	E	E	WGAN	IM	
56120	E	E	WGAN	IM	
56121	T	E	WNYX	CU(S)	
56123	T	E	WNXX	IM(S)	Drax Power Station
56124	T	E	WNXX	KY(S)	
56125	F	E	WNXX	IM(S)	
56127	T	E	WGAN	IM	
56128	T	E	WNXX	IM(S)	
56129	T	E	WNXX	IM(S)	
56130	LH	E	WNXX	TO(S)	Wardley Opencast
56131	F	E	WNXX	TO(S)	Ellington Colliery
56132	T	E	WGAN	IM	
56133	F	E	WNXX	TO(S)	Crewe Locomotive Works
56134	FC	E	WGAN	IM	Blyth Power
56135	F	E	WNXX	IM(S)	Port of Tyne Authority

CLASS 57   BRUSH/GM   Co-Co

Built: 1965 by Brush Traction at Loughborough as Class 47. Rebuilt 1997–2000 by Brush Traction at Loughborough.
Engine: General Motors 645-12E3 of 1860 kW (2500 hp) at 900 rpm.
Main Alternator: Brush BA1101A.
Traction Motors: Brush TM68-46.
Maximum Tractive Effort: 244.5 kN (55000 lbf).
Continuous Tractive Effort: 140 kN (31500 lbf) at ?? mph.
Power at Rail: 1507 kW (2025 hp).   **Train Brakes:** Air.
Brake Force: 80 t.   **Dimensions:** 19.38 x 2.79 x 3.9 m.
Weight: 120.6 t.   **Wheel Diameter:** 1143 mm.
Design Speed: 75 mph.   **Maximum Speed:** 75 mph.
Fuel Capacity: 3273 (+ 5550 litres).   **RA:** 6
Train Supply: Not equipped.   **Multiple Working:** Not equipped.
Note: 57010–012 were still in the process of rebuilding as at 1st January 2000.

No.	Former No.					
57001	(47356)	FL	P	DFHZ	FD	Freightliner Pioneer
57002	(47322)	FL	P	DFHZ	FD	Freightliner Phoenix
57003	(47317)	FL	P	DFHZ	FD	Freightliner Evolution
57004	(47347)	FL	P	DFHZ	FD	Freightliner Quality
57005	(47350)	FL	P	DFHZ	FD	Freightliner Excellence
57006	(47187)	FL	P	DFHZ	FD	Freightliner Reliance
57007	(47332)	FL	P	DFHZ	FD	Freightliner Bond
57008	(47060)	FL	P	DFHZ	FD	Freightliner Explorer
57009	(47079)	FL	P	DFHZ	FD	Freightliner Venturer
57010	(47231)	FL	P	DFHZ	FD	Freightliner Crusader
57011	(47329)	FL	P	DFHZ	FD	Freightliner Challenger
57012	(47204) +	FL	P	DFHZ	FD	Freightliner Envoy

CLASS 58   BREL/PAXMAN   Co-Co

Built: 1983–87 by BREL at Doncaster Works.
Engine: Ruston Paxman 12RK3ACT of 2460 kW (3300 hp) at 1000 rpm.
Main Alternator: Brush BA1101B.   **Traction Motors:** Brush TM73-62.
Maximum Tractive Effort: 275 kN (61800 lbf).
Continuous Tractive Effort: 240 kN (53950 lbf) at 17.4 mph.
Power At Rail: 1780 kW (2387 hp).   **Train Brakes:** Air.
Brake Force: 62 t.   **Dimensions:** 19.13 x 2.72 x 3.93 m.
Weight: 130 t.   **Wheel Diameter:** 1120 mm.
Design Speed: 80 mph.   **Maximum Speed:** 80 mph.
Fuel Capacity: 4214 litres.   **RA:** 7.
Train Supply: Not equipped.   **Multiple Working:** Red Diamond.
Note: All equipped with Slow Speed Control.

58001	MG	E	WNXX	KY(S)	
58002	ML	E	WFAN	TO	Daw Mill Colliery
58003	MG	E	WNXX	TO(S)	Markham Colliery
58004	MG	E	WNXX	DR(S)	
58005	ML	E	WFAN	TO	Ironbridge Power Station

58006	MG	E	WFAN	TO	
58007	MG	E	WFAN	TO	Drakelow Power Station
58008	ML	E	WNXX	TO(S)	
58009	MG	E	WFAN	TO	
58010	MG	E	WNXX	SF(S)	
58011	MG	E	WNXX	SF(S)	Worksop Depot
58012	MG	E	WNXX	DR(S)	
58013	ML	E	WFAN	TO	
58014	ML	E	WFAN	TO	Didcot Power Station
58015	MG	E	WNXX	DR(S)	
58016	E	E	WFAN	TO	
58017	MG	E	WNXX	DR(S)	Eastleigh Depot
58018	MG	E	WNXX	SF(S)	High Marnham Power Station
58019	MG	E	WFAN	TO	Shirebrook Colliery
58020	MG	E	WFAN	TO	Doncaster Works
58021	ML	E	WFAN	TO	Hither Green Depot
58022	MG	E	WNXX	DR(S)	
58023	ML	E	WNXX	DR(S)	Peterborough Depot
58024	E	E	WFAN	TO	
58025	MG	E	WFAN	TO	
58026	MG	E	WFAN	TO	
58027	MG	E	WNXX	DR(S)	
58028	MG	E	WNXX	TO(S)	
58029	MG	E	WFAN	TO	
58030	E	E	WFAN	TO	
58031	MG	E	WFAN	TO	
58032	ML	E	WFAN	TO	Thoresby Colliery
58033	E	E	WFAN	TO	
58034	MG	E	WNXX	DR(S)	Bassetlaw
58035	MG	E	WNXX	DR(S)	
58036	ML	E	WFAN	TO	
58037	E	E	WFAN	TO	
58038	ML	E	WNXX	TO(S)	
58039	E	E	WNXX	TO(S)	
58040	MG	E	WNXX	SF(S)	Cottam Power Station
58041	MG	E	WFAN	TO	Ratcliffe Power Station
58042	ML	E	WFAN	TO	Petrolea
58043	MG	E	WFAN	TO	
58044	MG	E	WNXX	DR(S)	Oxcroft Opencast
58045	E	E	WFAN	TO	
58046	ML	E	WFAN	TO	Asfordby Mine
58047	E	E	WFAN	TO	
58048	E	E	WFAN	TO	
58049	E	E	WFAN	TO	Littleton Colliery
58050	E	E	WFAN	TO	Toton Traction Depot

Silver Jubilee
Year 1998

PATHFINDER
TOURS

HAVE WE GOT TOURS FOR <u>YOU</u>?

Want to get some numbers underlined in this book? Then best travel with Pathfinder Tours to here, there and everywhere. Our excursions in the first half of 2000 alone will take us past the depots and stabling points at Bescot, Canton, Carlisle (DRS), Crewe, Didcot, Hither Green, Leicester, Longsight, Newport, Polmadie, Selhurst, Toton and many other places where locos and units gather. Plenty of brand new traction to be seen there.

And why just 'cop' a loco for sight? Why not go one further and record the haulage on your train?. Pathfinder trains have featured traction by more examples of classes 08, 56, 57, 58, 60 and 92 than all other tour promoters put together. Not to mention recent and future main line runs behind *Choppers, Goyles, Cromptons, Tractors, Peaks, Brush 4's, Hoovers, Deltics, Sheds, Shoe Boxes* and much, much more!! And that does not include the locos, steam and diesel, on private railways we have visited, or the many different steam locomotives that have featured on the main line.

Do you like Open days? Pathfinder Tours can take you to Crewe Works in May and Old Oak Common in August, to the Millennium Cavalcade of Steam at Darlington, to Newton Abbot Transport Festival, and everywhere else there are trains to see.

All seats are reserved and there is a buffet service on all trains. Junior fares usually available. Full Dining 'Premier Class' on many trains. All routes and motive power subject to confirmation and availability. Tickets issued subject to our standard conditions.

To get the full 'gen' and to join our **FREE** mailing list, phone

01453 835414

Pathfinder Tours, Stag House, Gydynap Lane, Inchbrook, Woodchester, Glos., GL5 5EZ

www.toursatpathfinder.freeserve.co.uk

ROAMING THE RAILS INTO THE 21ST CENTURY

CLASS 59   GENERAL MOTORS   Co-Co

Built: 1985 (59001/002/004) or 1989 (59005) by General Motors, La Grange, Illinois, USA or 1990 (59101-4), 1994 (59201) and 1995 (59202-6) by General Motors, London, Ontario, Canada.
Engine: General Motors 645E3C two stroke of 2460 kW (3300 hp) at 900 rpm.
Main Alternator: General Motors AR11 MLD-D14A.
Traction Motors: General Motors D77B.
Maximum Tractive Effort: 506 kN (113 550 lbf).
Continuous Tractive Effort: 291 kN (65 300 lbf) at 14.3 mph.
Power At Rail: 1889 kW (2533 hp).   **Train Brakes:** Air.
Brake Force: 69 t.   **Dimensions:** 21.35 x 2.65 x 3.9 m.
Weight: 121 t.   **Wheel Diameter:** 1067 mm.
Design Speed: 60 (* 75) mph.   **Maximum Speed:** 60 (* 75) mph.
Fuel Capacity: 4546 litres.   **RA:** 7.
Train Supply: Not equipped.   **Multiple Working:** AAR System.
Note: b – equipped with drophead buckeye couplers for use on use in conjunction with 'National Power' limestone hopper wagons.

Class 59/0. Owned by Foster-Yeoman Ltd.

59001	**FY**	FY	XYPO	MD	YEOMAN ENDEAVOUR
59002	**YO**	FY	XYPO	MD	ALAN J DAY
59004	**YO**	FY	XYPO	MD	PAUL A HAMMOND
59005	**FY**	FY	XYPO	MD	KENNETH J PAINTER

Class 59/1. Owned by Hanson Quarry Products.

59101	**HA**	HA	XYPA	MD	Village of Whatley
59102	**HA**	HA	XYPA	MD	Village of Chantry
59103	**HA**	HA	XYPA	MD	Village of Mells
59104	**HA**	HA	XYPA	MD	Village of Great Elm

Class 59/2. Owned by English Welsh & Scottish Railway.

59201	*	**E**	E	WDAN	FB	Vale of York
59202	*	**E**	E	WDAN	FB	Vale of White Horse
59203	*	**E**	E	WDAN	FB	Vale of Pickering
59204	*	**E**	E	WDAN	FB	Vale of Glamorgan
59205	b*	**E**	E	WDAN	FB	L. Keith McNair
59206	b*	**E**	E	WDAN	FB	Pride of Ferrybridge

CLASS 60   BRUSH/MIRRLEES   Co-Co

Built: 1989–1993 by Brush Traction at Loughborough.
Engine: Mirrlees 8MB275T of 2310 kW (3100 hp) at 1000 rpm.
Main Alternator: Brush BA1000.   **Traction Motors:** Brush TM216.
Maximum Tractive Effort: 500 kN (106500 lbf).
Continuous Tractive Effort: 336 kN (71570 lbf) at 17.4 mph.
Power At Rail: 1800 kW (2415 hp).   **Train Brakes:** Air.
Brake Force: 74 (+ 62) t.   **Dimensions:** 21.34 x 2.64 x 3.95 m.
Weight: 129 (+ 131) t.   **Wheel Diameter:** 1118 mm.
Design Speed: 100 km/h.   **Maximum Speed:** 60 mph.

Fuel Capacity: 4546 (+ 5225) litres.   **RA:** 7.
Train Supply: Not equipped.   **Multiple Working:** Within class.
Note: All equipped with Slow Speed Control.
Non-standard livery/numbering:
* 60006/033 are in British Steel livery of blue with white logos.
* 60064/070 are as **F**, with Loadhaul logos.

60001		E	E	WCAN	TO
60002	+	E	E	WCAN	TO
60003	+	E	E	WCAN	TO
60004	+	E	E	WCAN	TO
60005	+	E	E	WCAN	TO
60006		O	E	WCAN	TO
60007	+	LH	E	WCAN	TO
60008		LH	E	WCAN	TO
60009	+	MG	E	WCAN	TO
60010	+	E	E	WCAN	TO
60011		ML	E	WCAN	TO
60012	+	E	E	WCAN	TO
60013		F	E	WCAN	TO
60014		FP	E	WCAN	TO
60015	+	T	E	WCAN	TO
60016		E	E	WCAN	TO
60017	+	E	E	WCAN	TO
60018		E	E	WCAN	TO
60019		E	E	WCAN	TO
60020	+	E	E	WCAN	TO
60021	+	F	E	WCAN	TO
60022	+	E	E	WCAN	TO
60023	+	E	E	WCAN	TO
60024	+	E	E	WCAN	TO
60025	+	E	E	WCAN	TO
60026	+	E	E	WCAN	TO
60027	+	E	E	WCAN	TO
60028	+	F	E	WCAN	TO
60029		E	E	WCAN	TO
60030	+	E	E	WCAN	TO
60031		FM	E	WCAN	TO
60032		T	E	WCAN	TO
60033	+	O	E	WCAN	TO
60034		T	E	WCAN	TO
60035		T	E	WCAN	TO
60036		E	E	WCAN	TO
60037	+	E	E	WCAN	TO
60038	+	LH	E	WCAN	TO
60039		E	E	WCAN	TO
60040		E	E	WCAN	TO
60041	+	E	E	WCAN	TO
60042	+	E	E	WCAN	TO
60043		E	E	WCAN	TO
60044		ML	E	WCAN	TO

Names (right column):

60002	High Peak
60003	FREIGHT TRANSPORT ASSOCIATION
60006	Scunthorpe Ironmaster
60008	GYPSUM QUEEN II
60009	Carnedd Dafydd
60013	Robert Boyle
60014	Alexander Fleming
60015	Bow Fell
60017	Shotton Works Centenary Year 1996
60021	Pen-y-Ghent
60025	Caledonian Paper
60028	John Flamsteed
60029	Clitheroe Castle
60032	William Booth
60033	Tees Steel Express
60034	Carnedd Llewelyn[1]
60035	Florence Nightingale
60036	GEFCO
60037	Aberthaw/Aberddawan
60042	The Hundred of Hoo

60045		E	E	WCAN	TO	The Permanent Way Institution
60046	+	F	E	WCAN	TO	William Wilberforce[1]
60047	+	E	E	WCAN	TO	
60048		E	E	WCAN	TO	EASTERN
60049	+	E	E	WCAN	TO	
60050	+	E	E	WCAN	TO	
60051	+	E	E	WCAN	TO	
60052	+	E	E	WCAN	TO	Glofa Twr - The last deep mine in Wales - Tower Colliery
60053	+	E	E	WCAN	TO	NORDIC TERMINAL
60054	+	FP	E	WCAN	TO	Charles Babbage
60055	+	T	E	WCAN	TO	Thomas Barnardo
60056	+	T	E	WCAN	TO	William Beveridge
60057		FC	E	WCAN	TO	Adam Smith
60058		T	E	WCAN	TO	John Howard
60059	+	LH	E	WCAN	TO	Swinden Dalesman
60060		FC	E	WCAN	TO	James Watt
60061		T	E	WCAN	TO	Alexander Graham Bell
60062		T	E	WCAN	TO	Samuel Johnson
60063		T	E	WCAN	TO	James Murray
60064	+	O	E	WCAN	TO	Back Tor[1]
60065		T	E	WCAN	TO	Kinder Low[1]
60066		FC	E	WCAN	TO	John Logie Baird
60067	+	F	E	WCAN	TO	James Clerk-Maxwell
60068		F	E	WCAN	TO	Charles Darwin
60069		F	E	WCAN	TO	Humphry Davy
60070	+	O	E	WCAN	TO	John Loudon McAdam
60071	+	MG	E	WCAN	TO	Dorothy Garrod
60072		MG	E	WCAN	TO	Cairn Toul[1]
60073		MG	E	WCAN	TO	Cairn Gorm[1]
60074		MG	E	WCAN	TO	
60075		MG	E	WCAN	TO	
60076		MG	E	WCAN	TO	
60077	+	MG	E	WCAN	TO	Canisp[1]
60078		ML	E	WCAN	TO	
60079		MG	E	WCAN	TO	Foinaven
60080	+	T	E	WCAN	TO	Kinder Scout
60081	+	T	E	WCAN	TO	Bleaklow Hill[1]
60082		T	E	WCAN	TO	Mam Tor
60083		E	E	WCAN	TO	Mountsorrel
60084		T	E	WCAN	TO	Cross Fell
60085		T	E	WCAN	TO	
60086		MG	E	WCAN	TO	Schiehallion
60087		MG	E	WCAN	TO	Slioch
60088		MG	E	WCAN	TO	Buachaille Etive Mor[1]
60089	+	T	E	WCAN	TO	Arcuil
60090	+	FC	E	WCAN	TO	Quinag
60091	+	FC	E	WCAN	TO	An Teallach
60092		F	E	WCAN	TO	Reginald Munns
60093		T	E	WCAN	TO	Jack Stirk
60094		MG	E	WCAN	TO	Tryfan

60095	F	E	WCAN	TO	
60096	+ T	E	WCAN	TO	Ben Macdui
60097	+ T	E	WCAN	TO	
60098	+ E	E	WCAN	TO	Charles Francis Brush
60099	MG	E	WCAN	TO	Ben More Assynt
60100	MG	E	WCAN	TO	Boar of Badenoch

CLASS 66   GENERAL MOTORS   Co-Co

Built: 1998–2000 by General Motors, London, Ontario, Canada (Model JT42CWR).
Engine: General Motors 12N-710G3B-EC two stroke of 2385 kW (3200 hp) at 900 rpm.
Main Alternator: General Motors AR8/C86.
Traction Motors: General Motors D43TR.   **Max. Tractive Effort:** 409 kN (92000 lbf).
Continuous Tractive Effort: 260 kN (58390 lbf) at 15.9 mph.
Power At Rail: 1850 kW (2480 hp).   **Train Brakes:** Air.
Brake Force: 68 t.   **Dimensions:** 21.35 x 2.64 x 3.90 m.
Weight: 126 t.   **Wheel Diameter:** 1120 mm.
Design Speed: 75 mph.   **Maximum Speed:** 75 mph.
Fuel Capacity: 6550 litres.   **RA:** 7.
Train Supply: Not equipped.   **Multiple Working:** AAR System.
Note: All equipped with Slow Speed Control.

Class 66/0. EWS operated locomotives.

66001		E	A	WBAN	TO	66028		E		WBAN	TO
66002		E	A	WBAN	TO	66029	k	E	E	WBAN	TO
66003		E	A	WBAN	TO	66030		E		WBAN	TO
66004		E	A	WBAN	TO	66031		E	A	WBAN	TO
66005		E	A	WBAN	TO	66032	k	E	E	WBAN	TO
66006		E	A	WBAN	TO	66033		E	A	WBAN	TO
66007		E	A	WBAN	TO	66034		E	A	WBAN	TO
66008		E	A	WBAN	TO	66035		E	A	WBAN	TO
66009		E	A	WBAN	TO	66036	k	E		WBAN	TO
66010		E	A	WBAN	TO	66037	k	E		WBAN	TO
66011	k	E	A	WBAN	TO	66038		E		WBAN	TO
66012		E	A	WBAN	TO	66039	k	E		WBAN	TO
66013		E	A	WBAN	TO	66040		E	A	WBAN	TO
66014	k	E	A	WBAN	TO	66041		E	A	WBAN	TO
66015		E	A	WBAN	TO	66042		E	A	WBAN	TO
66016	k	E	A	WBAN	TO	66043		E	A	WBAN	TO
66017		E	A	WBAN	TO	66044		E	A	WBAN	TO
66018		E	A	WBAN	TO	66045	k	E		WBAN	TO
66019	k	E	A	WBAN	TO	66046		E		WBAN	TO
66020	k	E	A	WBAN	TO	66047	k	E		WBAN	TO
66021		E	A	WBAN	TO	66048		E		WBAN	TO
66022		E	A	WBAN	TO	66049		E		WBAN	TO
66023		E	A	WBAN	TO	66050		E		WBAN	TO
66024		E	A	WBAN	TO	66051		E		WBAN	TO
66025		E	A	WBAN	TO	66052		E		WBAN	TO
66026	k	E	A	WBAN	TO	66053		E	A	WBAN	TO
66027		E	A	WBAN	TO	66054		E	A	WBAN	TO

66055		E	A	WBAN	TO	66106		E	A	WBAN	TO
66056		E	A	WBAN	TO	66107		E	A	WBAN	TO
66057		E	A	WBAN	TO	66108		E	A	WBAN	TO
66058		E	A	WBAN	TO	66109	k	E	A	WBAN	TO
66059		E	A	WBAN	TO	66110		E	A	WBAN	TO
66060		E	A	WBAN	TO	66111		E	A	WBAN	TO
66061		E	A	WBAN	TO	66112		E	A	WBAN	TO
66062		E	A	WBAN	TO	66113		E	A	WBAN	TO
66063		E	A	WBAN	TO	66114	k	E	A	WBAN	TO
66064		E	A	WBAN	TO	66115		E	A	WBAN	TO
66065		E	A	WBAN	TO	66116		E	A	WBAN	TO
66066		E	A	WBAN	TO	66117		E	A	WBAN	TO
66067		E	A	WBAN	TO	66118		E	A	WBAN	TO
66068		E	A	WBAN	TO	66119		E	A	WBAN	TO
66069		E	A	WBAN	TO	66120		E	A	WBAN	TO
66070		E	A	WBAN	TO	66121		E	A	WBAN	TO
66071		E	A	WBAN	TO	66122		E	A	WBAN	TO
66072		E	A	WBAN	TO	66123		E	A	WBAN	TO
66073		E	A	WBAN	TO	66124		E	A	WBAN	TO
66074		E	A	WBAN	TO	66125	k	E	A	WBAN	TO
66075		E	A	WBAN	TO	66126		E	A	WBAN	TO
66076		E	A	WBAN	TO	66127		E	A	WBAN	TO
66077		E	A	WBAN	TO	66128		E	A	WBAN	TO
66078		E	A	WBAN	TO	66129		E	A	WBAN	TO
66079		E	A	WBAN	TO	66130		E	A	WBAN	TO
66080		E	A	WBAN	TO	66131		E	A	WBAN	TO
66081		E	A	WBAN	TO	66132		E	A	WBAN	TO
66082		E	A	WBAN	TO	66133		E	A	WBAN	TO
66083		E	A	WBAN	TO	66134		E	A	WBAN	TO
66084	k	E	A	WBAN	TO	66135		E	A	WBAN	TO
66085		E	A	WBAN	TO	66136		E	A	WBAN	TO
66086		E	A	WBAN	TO	66137		E	A	WBAN	TO
66087		E	A	WBAN	TO	66138		E	A	WBAN	TO
66088		E	A	WBAN	TO	66139		E	A	WBAN	TO
66089		E	A	WBAN	TO	66140		E	A	WBAN	TO
66090		E	A	WBAN	TO	66141		E	A	WBAN	TO
66091		E	A	WBAN	TO	66142		E	A	WBAN	TO
66092		E	A	WBAN	TO	66143		E	A	WBAN	TO
66093		E	A	WBAN	TO	66144		E	A	WBAN	TO
66094	k	E	A	WBAN	TO	66145		E	A	WBAN	TO
66095	k	E	A	WBAN	TO	66146		E	A	WBAN	TO
66096		E	A	WBAN	TO	66147		E	A	WBAN	TO
66097		E	A	WBAN	TO	66148		E	A	WBAN	TO
66098		E	A	WBAN	TO	66149		E	A	WBAN	TO
66099		E	A	WBAN	TO	66150		E	A	WBAN	TO
66100		E	A	WBAN	TO	66151		E	A	WBAN	TO
66101		E	A	WBAN	TO	66152		E	A	WBAN	TO
66102	k	E	A	WBAN	TO	66153		E	A	WBAN	TO
66103		E	A	WBAN	TO	66154		E	A		
66104		E	A	WBAN	TO	66155		E	A		
66105		E	A	WBAN	TO	66156		E	A	WBAN	TO

66157		E	A	WBAN	TO
66158	k	E	A	WBAN	TO
66159		E	A	WBAN	TO
66160		E	A	WBAN	TO
66161		E	A	WBAN	TO
66162		E	A	WBAN	TO
66163		E	A	WBAN	TO
66164		E	A	WBAN	TO
66165		E	A	WBAN	TO
66166		E	A	WBAN	TO
66167		E	A	WBAN	TO
66168		E	A	WBAN	TO
66169		E	A	WBAN	TO
66170		E	A	WBAN	TO
66171		E	A	WBAN	TO
66172		E	A	WBAN	TO
66173		E	A	WBAN	TO
66174		E	A	WBAN	TO
66175		E	A	WBAN	TO
66176		E	A	WBAN	TO
66177		E	A	WBAN	TO
66178		E	A	WBAN	TO
66179		E	A	WHPT	
66180		E	A	WHPT	
66181		E	A	WHPT	
66182		E	A	WHPT	
66183		E	A	WHPT	
66184		E	A	WHPT	
66185		E	A	WHPT	
66186		E	A	WHPT	
66187		E	A	WHPT	
66188		E	A	WHPT	
66189		E	A	WHPT	
66190		E	A		
66191		E	A		
66192		E	A		
66193		E	A		
66194		E	A		
66195		E	A		
66196			A		
66197			A		
66198			A		
66199			A		
66200			A		
66201	k		A		
66202	k		A		
66203	k		A		

66204	k	A
66205	k	A
66206	k	A
66207	k	A
66208	k	A
66209	k	A
66210	k	A
66211	k	A
66212	k	A
66213	k	A
66214	k	A
66215	k	A
66216	k	A
66217	k	A
66218	k	A
66219	k	A
66220	k	A
66221	k	A
66222	k	A
66223	k	A
66224	k	A
66225	k	A
66226	k	A
66227	k	A
66228	k	A
66229	k	A
66230	k	A
66231	k	A
66232	k	A
66233	k	A
66234	k	A
66235	k	A
66236	k	A
66237	k	A
66238	k	A
66239	k	A
66240	k	A
66241	k	A
66242	k	A
66243	k	A
66244	k	A
66245	k	A
66246	k	A
66247	k	A
66248	k	A
66249	k	A
66250	k	A

Class 66/5. Freightliner operated locomotives.

66501	FL	P	DFGM	FD
66502	FL	P	DFGM	FD

66503	**FL**	P	DFGM	FD
66504	**FL**	P	DFGM	FD
66505	**FL**	P	DFGM	FD
66506		H		
66507		H		
66508		H		
66509		H		
66510		H		
66511		H		
66512		H		
66513		H		
66514		H		
66515		H		
66516		H		
66517		H		
66518		H		
66519		H		
66520		H		
66521		P		
66522		P		
66523		P		
66524		P		
66525		P		
66526		P		

CLASS 67   GENERAL MOTORS   Bo-Bo

Built: 1999–2000 by Alstom at Valencia, Spain, as sub-contractors for General Motors (General Motors model JT42 HW-HS).
Engine: General Motors 12N-710G3B-EC two stroke of 2385 kW (3200 hp) at 900 rpm.
Main Alternator: General Motors AR9/HE3/CA6B.
Traction Motors: General Motors D43FM.
Maximum Tractive Effort: 141 kN (31750 lbf).
Continuous Tractive Effort: 90 kN (20200 lbf) at ?? mph.
Power At Rail: 1860 kW.   **Train Brakes:** Air.
Brake Force: 78 t.   **Dimensions:** 19.74 x 2.72 x 3.95 m.
Weight: 90 t.   **Wheel Diameter:** 965 mm.
Design Speed: 125 mph.   **Max. Speed:** 125 mph.
Fuel Capacity: 4927 litres.   **RA:** 8.
Train Supply: Electric, index 66.   **Multiple Working:** AAR System.
Note: All equipped with Slow Speed Control and swinghead knuckle automatic couplers.

67001		A		
67002		A		
67003	E	A	WAAN	TO
67004		A		
67005		A		
67006		A		
67007		A		
67008		A		
67009		A		
67010		A		
67011		A		
67012		A		
67013		A		
67014		A		
67015		A		
67016		A		
67017		A		
67018		A		
67019		A		
67020		A		
67021		A		
67022		A		
67023		A		
67024		A		
67025		A		
67026		A		
67027		A		
67028		A		
67029		A		
67030		A		

1.2. ELECTRIC & ELECTRO-DIESEL LOCOMOTIVES

Note: All electric & electro-diesel locomotives authorised to operate under their own power on the Railtrack network are listed in this section. Electric locomotives authorised to operate solely on the Eurotunnel network are listed in section 1.5.

CLASS 71   BR/ENGLISH ELECTRIC   Bo-Bo

Built: 1959 by BR at Doncaster Works.
Electric Supply System: 750 V dc from third rail.
Traction Motors: English Electric 532.
Maximum Tractive Effort: 195 kN (43800 lbf).
Continuous Rating: 1716 kW (2300 hp) giving a tractive effort of 55 kN (12400 lbf) at 69.6 mph.
Maximum Rail Power: 2239 kW (3000 hp).
Train Brakes: Air, vacuum & electro-pneumatic.
Brake Force: 41 t.   **Dimensions:** 15.42 x 2.82 x 3.99 m.
Weight: 76.2 t.   **Wheel Diameter:** 1219 mm.
Design Speed: 90 mph   **Maximum Speed:** 90 mph.
Train Supply: Electric (300 kW maximum).
Multiple Working: SR System.   **RA:** 6.
Non-standard livery/numbering:
• 71001 carries number E5001. Official RSL number is 89403.

71001   **G**   NR   MBEL   SE

UNCLASSIFIED   METROPOLITAN VICKERS   Bo-Bo

Built: 1922 by Metropolitan Vickers at Gorton.
Electric Supply System: 750 V dc from third rail or four rail system.
Traction Motors:
Maximum Tractive Effort: 100 kN (22600 lbf).
Continuous Rating: 895 kW (1200 hp) giving a tractive effort of 65 kN (14700 lbf) at ? mph.   **RA:**
Maximum Rail Power: **Train Brakes:** Air.
Brake Force: **Dimensions:**
Weight: 76.2 t.   **Wheel Diameter:** 1105 mm.
Design Speed: 65 mph   **Maximum Speed:** 65 mph.
Train Supply: Not equipped.   **Multiple Working:** Not equipped.
Non-standard livery/numbering:
• L12 is London Transport livery of red. Official RSL number is 89212.

L12   **0**   LU   MBEL   WR   SARAH SIDDONS

CLASS 73   BR/ENGLISH ELECTRIC   Bo-Bo

Built: 1962 by BR at Eastleigh Works.
Engine: English Electric 4SRKT of 447 kW (600 hp) at 850 rpm.
Main Generator: English Electric 824/3D.
Electric Supply System: 750 V dc from third rail.
Traction Motors: English Electric 542A.
Maximum Tractive Effort: Electric 187 kN (42000 lbf). Diesel 152 kN (34100 lbf).
Continuous Rating: Electric 1060 kW (1420 hp) giving a tractive effort of 43 kN (9600 lbf) at 55.5 mph.
Continuous Tractive Effort: Diesel 72 kN (16100 lbf) at 10 mph.
Maximum Rail Power: Electric 1830 kW (2450 hp) at 37 mph.
Train Brakes: Air, vacuum & electro-pneumatic († Air & electro-pneumatic).
Brake Force: 31 t.   **Dimensions:** 16.36 x 2.64 x 3.8 m.
Weight: 76.3 t.   **Wheel Diameter:** 1016 mm.
Design Speed: 80 mph   **Maximum Speed:** 60 mph.
Fuel Capacity: 1545 litres.   **RA:** 6.
Train Supply: Electric, index 66 (on electric power only). May also deliver a reduced electric train supply when on diesel power whilst stationary.
Multiple Working: SR System.
Non-standard livery/numbering:
• 73005 is in non-standard blue livery with white roof.

Class 73/0. First build. Details as above.

73002	**BL**	ME	HEBD	KK(S)
73005	**0**	ME	HEBD	BD

Class 73/1. Later build. Details as Class 73/0 except:

Built: 1965–67 by English Electric Co. at Vulcan Foundry, Newton le Willows.
Main Generator: English Electric 824/5D.
Traction Motors: English Electric 546/1B.
Maximum Tractive Effort: Electric 179 kN (40000 lbf). Diesel 160 kN (36000 lbf).
Continuous Rating: Electric 1060 kW (1420 hp) giving a tractive effort of 35 kN (7800 lbf) at 68 mph.
Continuous Tractive Effort: Diesel 60 kN (13600 lbf) at 11.5 mph.
Maximum Rail Power: Electric 2350 kW (3150 hp) at 42 mph.
Weight: 77 t.   **Dimensions:** 16.36 x 2.64 x 3.81 m.
Design Speed: 90 mph   **Maximum Speed:** 60 (90*) mph.
Fuel Capacity: 1409 litres.
Train Supply: Electric, index 66 (on electric power only).
Note: ‡ Modified cabs for use on route learning duties.

73101	*	**PC**	E	WPAN	HG	The Royal Alex'
73103		**I**	E	WNXX	EH(S)	
73104	*	**I**	E	WNXX	EH(S)	
73105	*	**CE**	E	WPAN	HG	
73106		**DG**	E	WPAN	HG	
73107	*	**CE**	E	WNXX	OC(S)	Redhill 1844-1994
73108	*	**CE**	E	WPAN	HG	
73109	*	**ST**	SW	HYSB	BM	Battle of Britain 50th Anniversary

73110		CE	E	WPAN	HG	
73114	*	ML	E	WNXX	OC(S)	
73117		I	E	WNXX	EH(S)	University of Surrey
73118	tc	EP	EU	GPSN	OC	
73119	*	CE	E	WNXX	OC(S)	Kentish Mercury
73126		N	E	WNYX	OC(S)	
73128	*	E	E	WPAN	HG	
73129	*	N	E	WPAN	HG	City of Winchester
73130	tc	EP	EU	GPSN	OC	
73131	*	E	E	WPAN	HG	
73132		I	E	WNXX	OC(S)	
73133	‡	ML	E	WPAN	HG	The Bluebell Railway
73134		I	E	WNXX	EH(S)	Woking Homes 1885-1985
73136	*	ML	E	WPAN	HG	Kent Youth Music
73138		CE	E	WNXX	OC(S)	
73139		I	E	WNXX	EH(S)	
73140		I	E	WNXX	OC(S)	
73141		I	E	WNXX	OC(S)	

Class 73/2. Gatwick Express-operated locomotives. Details as Class 73/1 except:

Maximum Speed: 90 mph.   **Train Brakes:** Air & electro-pneumatic.

73201	GX	P	IVGA	SL
73202	GX	P	IVGA	SL
73203	GX	P	IVGA	SL
73204	GX	P	IVGA	SL
73205	GX	P	IVGA	SL
73206	GX	P	IVGA	SL
73207	GX	P	IVGA	SL
73208	GX	P	IVGA	SL
73209	GX	P	IVGA	SL
73210	GX	P	IVGA	SL
73211	GX	P	IVGA	SL
73212	GX	P	IVGA	SL
73213	GX	P	IVGA	SL
73235	GX	P	IVGA	SL

Class 73/9. Merseyrail Electrics operated locomotives. Details as Class 73/0.

73901	MD	ME	HEBD	BD
73906	MD	ME	HEBD	BD

NOTES FOR CLASSES 86–91

The following common features apply to all locos of Classes 86–91 unless otherwise stated.

Supply System: 25 kV a.c. 50 Hz overhead.
Multiple Working: Time division multiplex system.

CLASS 86   BR/ENGLISH ELECTRIC   Bo-Bo

Built: 1965–66 by English Electric Co. at Vulcan Foundry, Newton le Willows or by BR at Doncaster Works.
Traction Motors: AEI 282BZ frame mounted.
Maximum Tractive Effort: 207 kN (46500 lbf).
Continuous Rating: 3010 kW (4040 hp) giving a tractive effort of 85 kN (19200 lbf) at 77.5 mph.
Maximum Rail Power: 4550 kW (6100 hp) at 49.5 mph.
Train Brakes: Air.

Brake Force: 40 t.	**Dimensions:** 17.83 x 2.65 x 3.98 m.
Weight: 83–86.8 t.	**Wheel Diameter:** 1156 mm.
Design Speed: 100 mph	**Maximum Speed:** 100 mph
Train Supply: Electric, index 74.	**RA:** 6.

Class 86/1. Revised bogies and motors. Details as above except:

Maximum Tractive Effort: 258 kN (58000 lbf).
Traction Motors: GEC 412AZ.
Continuous Rating: 3730 kW (5000 hp) giving a TE of 95 kN (21300 lbf) at 87 mph.
Maximum Rail Power: 5860 kW (7860 hp) at 50.8 mph.

Weight: 86.8 t.	**Wheel Diameter:** 1150 mm.
Design Speed: 110 mph	**Max. Speed:** 110 mph.

86101		**IS**	H	SAXL	CP(S)	Sir William A Stanier FRS
86102		**IS**	H	SAXL	CP(S)	Robert A Riddles
86103	x	**IS**	H	SAXL	ZH(S)	André Chapelon

Class 86/2. Standard Design. Details as in main class heading except:

Weight: 85–86.2 t.

86204		**IS**	H	SAXL	ZH(S)	City of Carlisle
86205		**IS**	H	IANA	NC	City of Lancaster
86206		**V**	H	ICCA	LG	City of Stoke on Trent
86207		**IS**	H	ICCA	LG	City of Lichfield
86208		**IS**	E	WNXX	CP(S)	City of Chester
86209		**V**	H	IWPA	WN	City of Coventry
86210	x	**RX**	E	WEMP	CE	C.I.T. 75th Anniversary
86212		**IS**	H	ICCA	LG	Preston Guild 1328-1992
86213		**IS**	H	SAXL	ZH(S)	Lancashire Witch
86214		**IS**	H	ICCA	LG	Sans Pareil
86215		**AR**	H	IANA	NC	
86216		**IS**	H	SAXL	ZH(S)	Meteor

86217		AR	H	IANA	NC	City University
86218		AR	H	IANA	NC	NHS 50
86219		IS	H	SAXL	ZH(S)	Phoenix
86220		AR	H	IANA	NC	The Round Tabler
86221		AR	H	IANA	NC	B.B.C. Look East
86222		V	H	ICCA	LG	Clothes Show Live
86223		AR	H	IANA	NC	Norwich Union
86224		V	H	ICCA	LG	
86225		V	H	ICCA	LG	Hardwicke
86226		V	H	ICCA	LG	CHARLES RENNIE MACKINTOSH
86227		IS	H	SAXL	ZH(S)	Sir Henry Johnson
86228		IS	H	SAXL	ZH(S)	Vulcan Heritage
86229		V	H	IWPA	WN	Lions Clubs International
86230		AR	H	IANA	NC	
86231		IS	H	ICCA	LG	Starlight Express
86232		AR	H	IANA	NC	
86233		V	H	IWPA	WN	Laurence Olivier
86234		IS	H	ICCA	LG	J B Priestley OM
86235		AR	H	IANA	NC	Crown Point
86236		V	H	ICCA	LG	Josiah Wedgwood
86237		AR	H	IANA	NC	University of East Anglia
86238		AR	H	IANA	NC	European Community
86240		V	H	ICCA	LG	Bishop Eric Treacy
86241		RX	E	WEMP	CE	Glenfiddich
86242		V	H	ICCA	LG	James Kennedy GC
86243	x	RX	E	WEMP	CE	
86244		V	H	ICCA	LG	The Royal British Legion
86245		V	H	IWPA	WN	Caledonian
86246		AR	H	IANA	NC	
86247		IS	H	IWPA	WN	Abraham Darby
86248		IS	H	ICCA	LG	Sir Clwyd/County of Clwyd
86249		IS	H	SAXL	ZH(S)	County of Merseyside
86250		AR	H	IANA	NC	
86251		V	H	ICCA	LG	The Birmingham Post
86252		IS	H	SAXL	ZH(S)	The Liverpool Daily Post
86253		IS	H	ICCA	LG	The Manchester Guardian
86254	x	RX	E	WNXX	CE(S)	
86255		IS	H	SAXL	ZH(S)	Penrith Beacon
86256		V	H	ICCA	LG	Pebble Mill
86257		AR	H	IANA	NC	
86258		IS	H	ICCA	LG	Talyllyn-The First Preserved Railway
86259		V	H	IWPA	WN	Greater MANCHESTER THE LIFE & SOUL OF BRITAIN
86260		IS	H	IWPA	WN	Driver Wallace Oakes G.C.
86261	x	E	E	WEMP	CE	THE RAIL CHARTER PARTNERSHIP

Class 86/4. EWS owned locomotives. Details as Class 86/2 except:

Maximum Tractive Effort: 258 kN (58000 lbf).
Traction Motors: AEI 412AZ.   **Weight:** 83–83.9 t.
Continuous Rating: 2680 kW (3600 hp) giving a tractive effort of 89 kN (20000 lbf) at 67 mph.
Maximum Rail Power: 4400 kW (5900 hp) at 38 mph.

86401		E	E	WEMP	CE	Hertfordshire Rail Tours
86416	x	RX	E	WEMP	CE	
86417	x	RX	E	WEMP	CE	
86419	x	RX	E	WNXX	CE(S)	
86424	x	RX	E	WNXX	CE(S)	
86425	x	RX	E	WEMP	CE	Saint Mungo
86426	x	E	E	WEMP	CE	Pride of the Nation
86430	x	RX	E	WEMP	CE	Saint Edmund

Class 86/6. Freightliner operated locomotives. Details as Class 86/4 except:

Maximum Speed: 75 mph.   **Train Supply:** Electric, isolated.

86602	FL	FL	DFNC	FE	
86603	FE	FL	DHLT	CE(S)	
86604	FF	FL	DFNC	FE	
86605	FF	FL	DFNC	FE	
86606	FF	FL	DFNC	FE	
86607	FL	FL	DFNC	FE	
86608	FL	FL	DFNC	FE	
86609	FL	FL	DFNC	FE	
86610	F	FL	DFNC	FE	
86611	FF	FL	DFNC	FE	Airey Neave
86612	FF	P	DFNC	FE	Elizabeth Garrett Anderson
86613	FL	P	DFNC	FE	
86614	FF	P	DFNC	FE	Frank Hornby
86615	F	P	DFNC	FE	Rotary International
86618	FF	P	DFNC	FE	
86620	FL	P	DFNC	FE	Philip G Walton
86621	FF	P	DFNC	FE	London School of Economics
86622	FF	P	DFNC	FE	
86623	FF	P	DFNC	FE	
86627	FL	P	DFNC	FE	
86628	FF	P	DFNC	FE	Aldaniti
86631	FL	P	DFNC	FE	
86632	FL	P	DFNC	FE	
86633	FF	P	DFNC	FE	Wulfruna
86634	FL	P	DFNC	FE	
86635	FL	P	DFNC	FE	
86636	FL	P	DFNC	FE	
86637	FF	P	DFNC	FE	
86638	FF	P	DFNC	FE	
86639	FF	P	DFNC	FE	

CLASS 87   BREL/GEC   Bo-Bo

Built: 1973–75 by BREL at Crewe Works.
Traction Motors: GEC G412AZ frame mounted.
Maximum Tractive Effort: 258 kN (58000 lbf).
Continuous Rating: 3730 kW (5000 hp) giving a TE of 95 kN (21300 lbf) at 87 mph.
Maximum Rail Power: 5860 kW (7860 hp) at 50.8 mph.
Train Brakes: Air.
Brake Force: 40 t.   **Dimensions:** 17.83 x 2.65 x 3.96 m.
Weight: 83.3 t.   **Wheel Diameter:** 1150 mm.
Design Speed: 110 mph   **Maximum Speed:** 110 mph
Train Supply: Electric, index 95 (* 66).   **RA:** 6.

Class 87/0. Standard Design.

87001		V	P	IWCA	WN	Royal Scot
87002		V	P	IWCA	WN	Royal Sovereign
87003		V	P	IWCA	WN	Patriot
87004		V	P	IWCA	WN	Britannia
87005		IS	P	IWCA	WN	City of London
87006		V	P	IWCA	WN	George Reynolds
87007		V	P	IWCA	WN	City of Manchester
87008		V	P	IWCA	WN	
87009	*	V	P	IWCA	WN	City of Birmingham
87010		V	P	IWCA	WN	King Arthur
87011		IS	P	IWCA	WN	
87012		V	P	IWCA	WN	
87013		V	P	IWCA	WN	
87014		V	P	IWCA	WN	Knight of the Thistle
87015		V	P	IWCA	WN	Howard of Effingham
87016		V	P	IWCA	WN	Willesden Intercity Depot
87017		IS	P	IWCA	WN	Iron Duke
87018		IS	P	IWCA	WN	Lord Nelson
87019		IS	P	IWCA	WN	Sir Winston Churchill
87020		IS	P	IWCA	WN	North Briton
87021		V	P	IWCA	WN	Robert The Bruce
87022		V	P	IWCA	WN	Lew Adams The Black Prince
87023		IS	P	IWCA	WN	Velocity
87024		IS	P	IWCA	WN	Lord of the Isles
87025		V	P	IWCA	WN	County of Cheshire
87026		IS	P	IWCA	WN	Sir Richard Arkwright
87027		V	P	IWCA	WN	Wolf of Badenoch
87028		IS	P	IWCA	WN	Lord President
87029	*	IS	P	IWCA	WN	Earl Marischal
87030		IS	P	IWCA	WN	Black Douglas
87031		IS	P	IWCA	WN	Hal o' the Wynd
87032		V	P	IWCA	WN	Kenilworth
87033		V	P	IWCA	WN	Thane of Fife
87034		IS	P	IWCA	WN	William Shakespeare
87035		V	P	IWCA	WN	Robert Burns

Class 87/1. Thyristor Control. Details as Class 87/0 except:

Traction Motors: GEC G412BZ frame mounted.
Continuous Rating: 3620 kW (4850 hp) giving a TE of 96 kN (21600 lbf) at 84 mph.
Maximum Speed: 75 mph.   **Weight:** 79.1 t.

87101	**B**	EF	WNXX	CE(S)	STEPHENSON

CLASS 89   BRUSH   Co-Co

Built: 1986 by BREL at Crewe Works (as sub-contractors for Brush).
Traction Motors: Brush. Frame mounted.
Maximum Tractive Effort: 205 kN (46000 lbf).
Continuous Rating: 4350 kW (5850 hp) giving a TE of 105 kN (23600 lbf) at 92 mph.
Maximum Rail Power: **Train Brakes:** Air.
Brake Force: 50 t.   **Dimensions:** 19.80 x 2.74 x 3.98 m.
Weight: 104 t.   **Wheel Diameter:** 1150 mm.
Design Speed: 125 mph   **Maximum Speed:** 125 mph.
Train Supply: Electric, index 95.   **RA:** 6.

89001	**GN**	SS	IECB	BN

CLASS 90   GEC   Bo-Bo

Built: 1987–90 by BREL at Crewe Works (as sub contractors for GEC).
Traction Motors: GEC G412CY frame mounted.
Maximum Tractive Effort: 258 kN (58000 lbf).
Continuous Rating: 3730 kW (5000 hp) giving a TE of 95 kN (21300 lbf) at 87 mph.
Maximum Rail Power: 5860 kW (7860 hp) at 68.3 mph.
Train Brakes: Air.
Brake Force: 40 t.   **Dimensions:** 18.80 x 2.74 x 3.97 m.
Weight: 84.5 t.   **Wheel Diameter:** 1156 mm.
Design Speed: 110 mph   **Maximum Speed:** 110 mph.
Train Supply: Electric, index 95.   **RA:** 7.

Non-standard liveries/numbering:
- 90028 is in Belgian National Railways style blue and yellow.
- 90029 is in German Federal Railways style red and white.
- 90130 is in French National Railways style two-tone grey.
- 90136 is as **FE**, but has a yellow roof.

Class 90/0. Standard Design. Details as above.

90001	**IS**	P	IWCA	WN	BBC Midlands Today
90002	**V**	P	IWCA	WN	Mission: Impossible
90003	**IS**	P	IWCA	WN	THE HERALD
90004	**V**	P	IWCA	WN	City of Glasgow
90005	**IS**	P	IWCA	WN	Financial Times
90006	**IS**	P	IWCA	WN	High Sheriff
90007	**IS**	P	IWCA	WN	Lord Stamp
90008	**IS**	P	IWCA	WN	The Birmingham Royal Ballet
90009	**IS**	P	IWCA	WN	The Economist
90010	**IS**	P	IWCA	WN	275 Railway Squadron (Volunteers)

90011	**IS**	P	IWCA	WN	The Chartered Institute of Transport
90012	**V**	P	IWCA	WN	British Transport Police
90013	**V**	P	IWCA	WN	The Law Society
90014	**V**	P	IWCA	WN	
90015	**V**	P	IWCA	WN	The International Brigades SPAIN 1936-1939
90016	**RX**	E	WEMP	CE	
90017	**RX**	E	WEMF	CE	Rail Express Systems Quality Assured
90018	**RX**	E	WEMF	CE	
90019	**RX**	E	WEMF	CE	Penny Black
90020	**E**	E	WEMF	CE	Sir Michael Heron
90021	**FE**	EF	WEMF	CE	
90022	**FE**	EF	WEMP	CE	Freightconnection
90023	**FE**	EF	WEMP	CE	
90024	**GN**	EF	WEMF	CE	
90025	**FD**	EF	WEMP	CE	
90026	**FE**	EF	WEMF	CE	Crewe International Electric Maintenance Depot
90027	**FD**	EF	WEMP	CE	Allerton T & RS Depot Quality Approved
90028	**0**	EF	WEMP	CE	Vrachtverbinding
90029	**0**	EF	WEMF	CE	Frachtverbindungen

No.	Former No.				
90030	(90130)	**0**	EF	WEMF	CE	Fretconnection
90031	(90131)	**FE**	EF	WEMF	CE	Intercontainer
90032	(90132)	**FE**	EF	WEMF	CE	Cerestar
90033	(90133)	**FE**	EF	WEMP	CE	
90034	(90134)	**FE**	EF	WEMP	CE	
90035	(90135)	**FE**	EF	WEMP	CE	Crewe Basford Hall
90036	(90136)	**0**	EF	WEMF	CE	
90037	(90137)	**FD**	EF	WEMF	CE	
90038	(90138)	**FE**	EF	WEMP	CE	
90039	(90139)	**FD**	EF	WEMP	CE	
90040	(90140)	**FD**	EF	WEMF	CE	

Class 90/1. Freightliner leased locomotives. Details as Class 90/0 except:

Max. Speed: 75 mph.   **Train Supply**: Electric, isolated.
Note: 90142 and 90146 are on loan to West Coast Train Care for operation by Virgin West Coast and have been temporarily reconfigured as Class 90/0.

90141	**FF**	P	DFLC	FE	
90142	**FF**	P	IWCA	WN	
90143	**FF**	P	DFLC	FE	Freightliner Coatbridge
90144	**FF**	P	DFLC	FE	
90145	**FF**	P	DFLC	FE	
90146	**FF**	P	IWCA	WN	
90147	**FF**	P	DFLC	FE	
90148	**FF**	P	DFLC	FE	
90149	**FF**	P	DFLC	FE	
90150	**FF**	P	DFLC	FE	

CLASS 91   GEC   Bo-Bo

Built: 1988–91 by BREL at Crewe Works (as sub contractors for GEC).
Traction Motors: GEC G426AZ.   **Cont. Rating:** 4540 kW (6090 hp).
Max. Rail Power: 4700 kW (6300 hp). **Train Brakes:** Air.
Brake Force: 45 t.   **Dimensions:** 19.41 x 2.74 x 3.76 m.
Weight: 84 t.   **Wheel Diameter:** 1000 mm.
Design Speed: 140 mph   **Maximum Speed:** 125 mph.
Train Supply: Electric, index 95.   **RA:** 7.

91001	**GN**	H	IECA	BN
91002	**GN**	H	IECA	BN
91003	**GN**	H	IECA	BN
91004	**GN**	H	IECA	BN	Grantham
91005	**GN**	H	IECA	BN
91006	**GN**	H	IECA	BN
91007	**GN**	H	IECA	BN
91008	**GN**	H	IECA	BN
91009	**GN**	H	IECA	BN	The Samaritans
91010	**GN**	H	IECA	BN
91011	**GN**	H	IECA	BN
91012	**GN**	H	IECA	BN
91013	**GN**	H	IECA	BN
91014	**GN**	H	IECA	BN
91015	**GN**	H	IECA	BN	Holyrood
91016	**GN**	H	IECA	BN
91017	**GN**	H	IECA	BN	City of Leeds
91018	**GN**	H	IECA	BN
91019	**GN**	H	IECA	BN
91020	**GN**	H	IECA	BN
91021	**GN**	H	IECA	BN
91022	**GN**	H	IECA	BN	Double Trigger
91023	**GN**	H	IECA	BN
91024	**GN**	H	IECA	BN
91025	**GN**	H	IECA	BN
91026	**GN**	H	IECA	BN	York Minster
91027	**GN**	H	IECA	BN
91028	**GN**	H	IECA	BN	Peterborough Cathedral
91029	**GN**	H	IECA	BN	Queen Elizabeth II
91030	**GN**	H	IECA	BN
91031	**GN**	H	IECA	BN

CLASS 92   BRUSH   Co-Co

Built: 1993–96 by Brush Traction at Loughborough.
Supply System: 25 kV a.c. 50 HZ overhead or 750 V d.c. third rail.
Traction Motors: Brush.   **Max. Tractive Effort:** 400 kN (90 000 lbf).
Continuous Rating: 5040 kW (6760 hp) on a.c., 4000 kW (5360 hp) on d.c.
Maximum Rail Power: **Train Brakes:** Air.
Brake Force: 63 t.   **Dimensions:** 21.34 x 2.67 x 3.96 m.

Weight: 126 t.   **Wheel Diameter:** 1160 mm.
Design Speed: 140 km/h (87½ mph). **Max. Speed:** 140 km/h (87½ mph).
Train Supply: Electric, index 108 (ac), 70 (dc).   **RA:** 7.
Note: Locos from pools WTAN & WTWN may also operate on the Eurotunnel network.

92001	E	E	WTWN	CE	Victor Hugo
92002	EP	E	WTWN	CE	H.G. Wells
92003	EP	E	WTWN	CE	Beethoven
92004	EP	E	WTEN	CE	Jane Austen
92005	EP	E	WTEN	CE	Mozart
92006	EP	SF	WTWN	CE	Louis Armand
92007	EP	E	WTEN	CE	Schubert
92008	EP	E	WTEN	CE	Jules Verne
92009	EP	E	WTAN	CE	Elgar
92010	EP	SF	WTWN	CE	Molière
92011	EP	E	WTEN	CE	Handel
92012	EP	E	WTWN	CE	Thomas Hardy
92013	EP	E	WTEN	CE	Puccini
92014	EP	SF	WTEN	CE	Emile Zola
92015	EP	E	WTEN	CE	D.H. Lawrence
92016	EP	E	WTEN	CE	Brahms
92017	EP	E	WTEN	CE	Shakespeare
92018	EP	SF	WTEN	CE	Stendhal
92019	EP	E	WTEN	CE	Wagner
92020	EP	EU	WTEN	CE	Milton
92021	EP	EU	WTEN	CE	Purcell
92022	EP	E	WTEN	CE	Charles Dickens
92023	EP	SF	WTEN	CE	Ravel
92024	EP	E	WTEN	CE	J.S. Bach
92025	EP	E	WTEN	CE	Oscar Wilde
92026	EP	E	WTEN	CE	Britten
92027	EP	E	WTWN	CE	George Eliot
92028	EP	SF	WTWN	CE	Saint Saëns
92029	EP	E	WTWN	CE	Dante
92030	EP	E	WTEN	CE	Ashford
92031	EP	E	WTWN	CE	
92032	EP	EU	WTEN	CE	César Franck
92033	EP	SF	WTEN	CE	Berlioz
92034	EP	E	WTEN	CE	Kipling
92035	EP	E	WTWN	CE	Mendelssohn
92036	EP	E	WTEN	CE	Bertolt Brecht
92037	EP	E	WTWN	CE	Sullivan
92038	EP	SF	WTWN	CE	Voltaire
92039	EP	E	WTWN	CE	Johann Strauss
92040	EP	EU	WTAN	CE	Goethe
92041	EP	E	WTEN	CE	Vaughan Williams
92042	EP	E	WTAN	CE	Honegger
92043	EP	SF	WTWN	CE	Debussy
92044	EP	EU	WTEN	CE	Couperin
92045	EP	EU	WTWN	CE	Chaucer
92046	EP	EU	WTEN	CE	Sweelinck

1.3. MISCELLANEOUS VEHICLES

CLASS 37 POWER UNIT TRANSPORTER/ MAINTENANCE VEHICLE

Built: 1962-63 by English Electric Company at Vulcan Foundry, Newton le Willows (025031) or by Robert Stephenson & Hawthorn at Darlington (025032). Converted to power unit transporter/maintenance vehicle in 1996 at Toton TMD. Also carry local numbers 1 & 2 respectively. Stored out of use since cessation of Class 37 overhauls by EWS.

No.	Former No.			
025031	(37070)	**DG**	E	TO(S)
025032	(37138)	**DG**	E	TO(S)

1.4. LOCO AWAITING DISPOSAL

Class 45

45015	**B**	E	WNZX	TT(S)

THE WESTERN COLLECTION

If you're a fan of the Western Class 52 diesel-hydraulics then this is the collection for you. This stunning series of booklets from A&C Services is already building up into the most comprehensive work about the fleet so far.

Already the collection has won universal acclaim from enthusiasts for providing a wealth of previously unpublished material.

Below is our current catalogue with more publications due out.

TITLE	PRICE
● Westerns On Works (Edition No. I)	£6.50
● Western Experiments Part One (D1000-29)	£6.50
● Western Revelations No. I	£6.50
● COMING SOON: Riviera Westerns	£6.50
Western Revelations No. 2	£6.50
D1014 Western Leviathan	£6.50
D1025 Western Guardsman	£6.50
Last Weeks of the Westerns	£6.50
Western Experiments Pt Two (D1030-73)	£6.50
Westerns on the Golden Hind	£6.50

PLUS HOW TO JOIN A NEW DIESEL-HYDRAULIC CLUB!

Other Publications available now from A&C Services:

Best of Classic Diesels & Electrics	£6.50
D1003 Western Pioneer	£6.50
D1006 Western Stalwart	£6.50
D1008 Western Harrier	£6.50
D1011 Western Thunderer	£6.50
D1019 Western Challenger	£6.50
D1023 Western Fusilier	£6.50
D1032 Western Marksman	£6.50
D1055 Western Advocate	£6.50
D1064 Western Regent	£6.50
D1069 Western Vanguard	£6.50

● Send your orders (all prices include p&p) to: A&C Services, The Western Collection, 3 Peddars Way, Longthorpe, Peterborough, Cambs. PE3 9NQ. Make cheques or postal orders payable to A&C Services.● Please allow 28 days for delivery ● TRADE ENQUIRIES WELCOME ● e-mail Birty003@aol.com

1.5 EUROTUNNEL LTD. LOCOMOTIVES

Depot: Coquelles (France).

Note: All locomotives authorised to operate under their own power on the Eurotunnel network are listed in this section. Locomotives authorised to operate on the Railtrack network are listed in sections 1.1–1.4.

0001–0005   MaK   Bo-Bo DIESEL

Built: 1992–93 by MaK at Kiel, Germany (Model DE1004).
Engine: MTU 12V 396 Tc of 1180 kW (1580 hp) at 1800 rpm.
Main Alternator: BBC.   **Traction Motors:** BBC.
Maximum Tractive Effort: 305 kN (68600 lbf).
Continuous Tractive Effort: 140 kN (31500 lbf) at 20 mph.
Power At Rail: 750 kW (1012 hp).

Brake Force: 120 kN.	**Dimensions:** 16.50 x ?? x ?? m.
Weight: 84 t.	**Wheel Diameter:** 1000 mm.
Design Speed: 120 km/h.	**Maximum Speed:** 120 km/h.
Fuel Capacity:	**Train Brakes:** Air.
Train Supply: Not equipped.	**Multiple Working:** Within class.
Livery: Grey and yellow.	

0001	0002	0003	0004	0005

0032–0042   HUNSLET/SCHÖMA   0-4-0 DIESEL

Built: 1989–90 by Hunslet Engine Company at Leeds as 900 mm. gauge.
Rebuilt: 1993-94 by Schöma in Germany as 1435 mm. gauge.
Engine: Deutz of 270 kW (200 hp) at ???? rpm.

Transmission: Mechanical.	**Maximum Tractive Effort:**
Continuous Tractive Effort:	**Power At Rail:**
Brake Force:	**Dimensions:**
Weight:	**Wheel Diameter:**
Design Speed: 50 km/h.	**Maximum Speed:** 50 km/h.
Fuel Capacity:	**Train Brakes:** Air.
Train Supply: Not equipped.	**Multiple Working:** Not equipped.
Livery: Yellow.	

0031	FRANCES	0037	LYDIE
0032	ELISABETH	0038	JENNY
0033	SILKE	0039	PACITA
0034	AMANDA	0040	JILL
0035	MARY	0041	KIM
0036	LAWRENCE	0042	NICOLE

9001–9105   BRUSH/ABB   Bo-Bo-Bo ELECTRIC

Built: 1993–2000 by Brush Traction at Loughborough.
Supply System: 25 kV a.c. 50 Hz overhead.
Traction Motors: ABB 6PH.
Maximum Tractive Effort: 400 kN (90 000 lbf).
Continuous Rating: 5760 kW (7725 hp) giving a TE of 310 kN at 65 km/h.
Maximum Rail Power: **Multiple Working:** TDM system.
Brake Force: 50 t.   **Dimensions:** 22.01 x 2.97 x 4.20 m.
Weight: 132 t.   **Wheel Diameter:** 1090 mm.
Design Speed: 175 km/h.   **Maximum Speed:** 160 km/h.
Train Supply: Electric.   **Train Brakes:** Air.
Livery: Two-tone grey and white with green and blue bands.

CLASS 9/0. Mixed traffic locomotives.

9001	LESLEY GARRETT	9021	TERESA BERGANZA
9002	STUART BURROWS	9022	DAME JANET BAKER
9003	BENJAMIN LUXON	9023	DAME ELISABETH LEGGE-
9004	VICTORIA DE LOS ANGELES		SCHWARZKOPF
9005	JESSYE NORMAN	9024	GOTTHARD 1882
9006	REGINE CRESPIN	9025	JUNGFRAUJOCH 1912
9007	DAME JOAN SUTHERLAND	9026	FURKATUNNEL 1982
9008	ELISABETH SODERSTROM	9027	BARBARA HENDRICKS
9009	FRANÇOIS POLLET	9028	DAME KIRI TE KANAWA
9010	JEAN-PHILLIPE COURTIS	9029	THOMAS ALLEN
9011	JOSÉ VAN DAM	9031	PLACIDO DOMINGO
9012	LUCIANO PAVAROTTI	9032	RENATA TEBALDI
9013	MARIA CALLAS	9033	MONTSERRAT CABALLE
9014	LUCIA POPP	9034	MIRELLA FRENI
9015	LÖTSCHBERG 1913	9035	Nicolai Gedda
9016	WILLARD WHITE	9036	ALAIN FONDARY
9017	JOSÉ CARRERAS	9037	GABRIEL BACQUIER
9018	WILHELMENA FERNANDEZ	9038	HILDEGARD BEHRENS
9019	MARIA EWING	9040	
9020	Nicolai Ghiaurov		

CLASS 9/1. Freight Shuttle dedicated locomotives.

9101
9102
9103
9104
9105

2. LOCO–HAULED PASSENGER COACHING STOCK

INTRODUCTION

USING THIS SECTION

Coaches are listed in batches, according to their class,

Detailed Information and Codes

After the heading, the following details are shown:

- Diagram code. This consists of the first three characters of the TOPS code followed by two numbers which relate to the particular design of vehicle.
- 'Mark' of coach (see below).
- Number of first class seats , standard class seats and lavatory compartments shown as F/S nT respectively.
- Bogie type (see below).
- Additional features.
- ETH Index.

TOPS Codes

TOPS (Total operations processing system) codes are allocated to all coaching stock. For passenger stock the code consists of:

(1) Two letters denoting the layout of the vehicle as follows:

AA Gangwayed Corridor
AB Gangwayed Corridor Brake
AC Gangwayed Open (2+2 seating)
AD Gangwayed Open (2+1 seating)
AE Gangwayed Open Brake
AF Gangwayed Driving Open Brake
AG Micro-Buffet
AH Brake Micro-Buffet
AI As 'AC' but fitted with drop-head buckeye and no gangway at one end
AJ Restaurant Buffet with Kitchen
AK Kitchen Car
AL As 'AC' but with disabled person's toilet (Mark 4 only)
AN Miniature Buffet
AP Pullman First with Kitchen
AQ Pullman Parlour First
AR Pullman Brake First
AS Sleeping Car
AT Royal Train Coach
AU Sleeping Car with Pantry
AX Generator Van
AZ Special saloon

GF DMU/EMU/Mark 4 Barrier Vehicle
NM Sandite Coach

(2) A digit for the class of passenger accommodation:

1	First	4	Unclassified
2	Standard (formerly second)	5	None
3	Composite (first & standard)		

(3) A suffix relating to the build of coach.

1	Mark 1	A	Mark 2A	C	Mark 2C	E	Mark 2E	G	Mark 3 or
Z	Mark 2	B	Mark 2B	D	Mark 2D	F	Mark 2F		Mark 3A

H	Mark 3B
J	Mark 4

Operator Codes

The normal operator codes are given in brackets after the TOPS codes. These are as follows:

B	Brake	C	Composite
F	First	O	Open
S	Standard (formerly second)	K	Side corridor with lavatory

Various other letters are in use and the meaning of these can be ascertained by referring to the titles at the head of each class.

Bogie Types

BR Mk 1 (BR1). Standard double bolster leaf spring bogie. Generally 90 m.p.h. but certain vehicles were allowed to run at 100 m.p.h. with special maintenance. Weight: 6.1 t.

BR Mk 2 (BR2). Single bolster leaf-spring bogie used on certain types of non-passenger stock and suburban stock (all now withdrawn). Weight: 5.3 t.

COMMONWEALTH (C). Heavy, cast steel coil spring bogie. 100 m.p.h. Weight: 6.75 t.

B4. Coil spring fabricated bogie for 100 m.p.h. Weight: 5.2 t.

Note: B4 bogies are allowed to run at 110 m.p.h. provided that they have a special maintenance regime. This applies to certain BGs (NBA, NHA and NIA).

B5. Heavy duty version of B4. 100 m.p.h. Weight: 5.3 t.

B5 (SR). A bogie originally used on ex Southern Region EMUs, similar in design to the B5 above. Now also used on locomotive hauled coaches. 100 m.p.h.

BT10. A fabricated bogie designed for 125 m.p.h. Air suspension.

T4. A 125 m.p.h. bogie from BREL (now Adtranz).

BT41. Fitted to Mark 4 vehicles. Manufactured by the Swiss firm of SIG. At present limited to 125 m.p.h. but designed for 140 m.p.h.

Brake Types

The standard form of braking on British main line trains is now air braking. Exceptions are shown as follows:

v	Vacuum braked.
x	Dual braked (air and vacuum).

Heating

All heating on British main-line trains is now electric. Certain coaches for use on charter trains may, however have steam heating facilities also, or steam heat only.

Public Address

It is assumed that all coaches are now fitted with public address, although certain stored coaches may not have the feature. In addition, it is assumed that all vehicles with a guard's compartment have public address transmission facilities, as have catering vehicles. BR Mark 1 catering vehicles have gas cooking, whilst Mark 2,3 and 4 vehicles have electric cooking.

Additional Feature Codes

d	Secondary door locking provided.
f	Facelifted or fluorescent lighting provided.
k	Composition brake blocks (instead of cast iron).
n	Day/night lighting.
p	Fitted with public telephone.
pg	Public address transmission and driver-guard communication.
pt	Public address transmission facility.
q	Fitted with catering staff to shore telephone.
w	Fitted with wheelchair space.
z	Fitted with disabled persons' toilet.

Note: Standard class coaches with wheelchair space also have one tip-up seat per space.

Notes on ETH Indeces

The sum of ETH indices in a train must not be more than that of the locomotive. The normal voltage on BR is 1000. Suffix 'X' denotes 600 amp wiring instead of 400 amp. Trains whose ETH index is higher than 66 must be formed completely with 600 amp wired stock. Class 55 locomotives can not provide a consistent ETH supply for Mark 2E or 2D FO 3192/3202, FK 13585–13607 & BFK 17163–17172. Class 33 locomotives can not provide an ETH supply for Mark 2D, Mark 2E, Mark 2F, Mark 3, Mark 3A, Mark 3B or Mark 4 stock.

BUILD DETAILS

Lot Numbers

Vehicles ordered under the auspices of BR were allocated a Lot (batch) number when ordered and these are quoted in class headings and sub-headings.

Vehicle Numbers

Where a coach has been renumbered, the former number is shown in parentheses. If the coach has been renumbered more than once, both the original number and last number are shown in parentheses. Where the old number of a coach due to be converted or renumbered is known and the conversion or renumbering has not yet taken place, the coach is listed both under its old number with its depot allocation, and under its new number without an allocation. This book now includes 'preserved' coaches in the main section, as there is now no official distinction between these and other coaches registered to operate on Railtrack metals, all coaches in use now being privately-owned.

Numbering Systems

Six different numbering systems were in use on BR. These were the BR series, the four pre-nationalisation companies' series' and the Pullman Car Company's series. BR number series coaches and former Pullman Car Company series coaches are listed separately. There is also a separate listing of 'Saloon' type vehicles which are registered to run on Railtrack metals. Please note that the Mark 2 Manchester Pullman vehicles were ordered after the Pullman Car Company had been nationalised and are therefore numbered in the BR series.

Layout

The layout in this section consists of number, original and last numbers in parentheses if applicable, notes (if any), livery, owner code, operation code and depot. For off-lease vehicles, the last storage location is given where known. Thus the layout is as follows:

No.	Notes	Livery	Owner	Operation	Depot
3131	x	**CC**	RS	ON	BN

THE DEVELOPMENT OF BR STANDARD COACHES

The standard BR coach built from 1951 to 1963 is the mark 1. This has a separate underframe and body. The underframe is normally 64'6" long, but certain vehicles were built on short (57') frames. Tungsten lighting is standard and until 1961, BR Mark 1 bogies were generally provided. In 1959 TSOs to Lot No. 30525 appeared with fluorescent lighting and melamine interior panels and from 1961 onwards Commonwealth bogies were fitted in an attempt to improve the quality of ride which became very poor when the tyre profiles on the wheels of the Mark 1 bogies became worn. The further batches of TSOs and BSOs retained the features of Lot 30525, but the BSKs, SKs, BCKs and CKs, whilst utilising melamine panelling in standard class, still retained tungsten lighting. Wooden interior finish was retained in first class compartments. The FOs had fluorescent lighting with wooden panelling except for lot No. 30648 which had tungsten lighting. In later years many Mark 1s had their mark 1 bogies replaced by B4s.

In 1964, a new train was introduced. Known as "XP64", it featured new seat designs, pressure heating & ventilation, aluminium compartment doors and corridor partitions, foot pedal operated toilets, and B4 bogies. The vehicles were on standard mark 1 underframes. Folding doors were fitted but these proved troublesome and were later replaced with hinged doors. All XP64 coaches have now been withdrawn, but some have been preserved.

The prototype mark 2 vehicle (W 13252) was produced in 1963. This was an FK of semi-integral construction and had pressure heating and ventilation. Tungsten lighting was provided and B4 bogies. This vehicle has been preserved by the National Railway Museum. The production build was similar, but wider windows were used. The standard class open vehicles used the new seat design similar to that in the XP64 and fluorescent lighting was provided. Interior finish reverted to wood. Mark 2s were built from 1964–66.

The Mark 2As, built 1967–68, incorporated the rest of the novel features first used in the XP64 set, i.e. foot pedal operated toilets (except BSOs), new first class seat design, aluminium compartment doors and partitions together with fluorescent lighting in first class compartments. Folding gangway doors (lime green coloured) were used instead of the traditional variety. The following list summarises the changes made in the later Mark 2 variants:

Mk 2B: Wide wrap round doors, no centre doors, slightly longer body. In standard class, one toilet at each end instead of two at one end as previously. Red gangway doors.

Mk 2C: Lowered ceiling with twin strips of fluorescent lighting, ducting for air conditioning, but no air conditioning.

Mk 2D: Air conditioning. No opening lights in windows.

Mk 2E: Smaller toilets with luggage racks opposite. Fawn gangway doors.

Mk 2F: Plastic interior panels. Inter-City 70 seats. Modified air conditioning system.

The Mark 3 coach has BT10 bogies, is 75' (23 m) long and is of fully integral construction with Inter-City 70 seats. Gangway doors were yellow (red in RFB) when new, although these are being altered on refurbishment. Loco-hauled coaches are classified Mark 3A, Mark 3 being reserved for HST trailers. A new batch of FOs and BFOs classified Mark 3B was built in 1985 with Advanced Passenger Train-style seating and revised lighting. The last vehicles in the Mark 3 series were the driving brake vehicles (officially called driving van trailers) which have been built for West Coast Main Line services.

The Mark 4 coach was built by Metro-Cammell for the East Coast Main Line electrification scheme and features a body profile suitable for tilting trains, although tilt is not fitted, and is not intended to be. They are suitable for 140 m.p.h. running, although are restricted to 125 m.p.h. pending the installation of a more advanced signalling system on the East Coast Main Line. The bogies for these coaches were built by SIG in Switzerland and are designated BT41. Driving van trailers are also a feature of this build of vehicles.

2.1. BR NUMBER SERIES STOCK

AJ11 (RF)   RESTAURANT FIRST

Dia. AJ106. Mark 1. 325 spent most of its life as a Royal Train vehicle and was numbered 2907 for a time. Built with Commonwealth bogies, but B5 bogies substituted on 325. 24/–. ETH 2.

Lot No. 30633 Swindon 1961. 42.5 t C, 41 t B5.

324	x	**CH**	NY	*ON*	NY
325		**PC**	VS	*ON*	SL

AP1Z (PK)   PULLMAN FIRST WITH KITCHEN

Dia. AP101. Mark 2. Pressure Ventilated. 18/– 2T. B5 bogies. ETH 6.

Lot No. 30755 Derby 1966. 40 t.

Non-Standard Livery: Maroon & beige.

504	**0**	WC	*ON*	CS	THE WHITE ROSE
506	**M**	WC	*ON*	CS

AQ1Z (PC)   PULLMAN PARLOUR FIRST

Dia. AQ101. Mark 2. Pressure Ventilated. 36/– 2T. B4 bogies. ETH 5.

Lot No. 30754 Derby 1966. 35 t.

Non-Standard Livery: Maroon & beige.

546	**0**	WC	*ON*	CS	CITY OF MANCHESTER
548	**0**	WC	*ON*	CS	ELIZABETHAN
549	**0**	WC	*ON*	CS	PRINCE RUPERT
550	**PC**	WC	*ON*	CS	
551	**0**	WC	*ON*	CS	CALEDONIAN
552	**PC**	WC	*ON*	CS	
553	**0**	WC	*ON*	CS	KING ARTHUR

AR1Z (PB)   PULLMAN BRAKE FIRST

Dia. AR101. Mark 2. Pressure Ventilated. 30/– 2T. B4 bogies. ETH 4.

Lot No. 30753 Derby 1966. 35 t.

Non-Standard Livery: Maroon & beige.

586	**0**	WC	*ON*	CS	TALISMAN

AJ21 (RG)   GRIDDLE CAR

Dia. AJ210. Mark 1. Rebuilt from RF. –/30. B5 bogies. ETH 2.

This vehicle was numbered DB975878 for a time when in departmental service.

Lot No. 30013 Doncaster 1952. Rebuilt Wolverton 1965. 40 t.

1105   (302)   v   **G**   MH   *ON*   RL

AJ1F (RFB)   **BUFFET OPEN FIRST**

Dia. AJ104. Mark 2F. Air conditioned. Converted 1988–9/91 at BREL, Derby
from Mark 2F FOs. 1200/1/3/6/11/14–17/20/21/50/2/5/6/9 have Stones equipment, others have Temperature Ltd. 25/– 1T 1W (except 1217 and 1253 which
are 26/– 1T). B4 bogies. p. q. d. ETH 6X.

1200/3/6/11/14/16/20/52/5/6. Lot No. 30845 Derby 1973. 33 t.
1201/4/5/7/8/10/12/13/15/17–9/21/50/1/4/7/9. Lot No. 30859 Derby 1973–
74.
33 t.
1202/9/53/8. Lot No. 30873 Derby 1974–75. 33 t.

† Fitted with new m.a. sets.

1200	(3287, 6459)	†	**V**	H	*VX*	MA
1201	(3361, 6445)	†	**V**	H	*VX*	MA
1202	(3436, 6456)	†	**V**	H	*VX*	MA
1203	(3291)	†		H	*VX*	MA
1204	(3401)	†	**V**	H	*VX*	MA
1205	(3329, 6438)	†	**V**	H	*VX*	MA
1206	(3319)	†	**V**	H	*VX*	MA
1207	(3328, 6422)	†	**V**	H	*VX*	MA
1208	(3393)		**V**	H	*VX*	MA
1209	(3437, 6457)	†	**V**	H	*VX*	MA
1210	(3405, 6462)	†	**V**	H	*VX*	MA
1211	(3305)			H	*VX*	MA
1212	(3427, 6453)	†	**V**	H	*VX*	MA
1213	(3419)	†	**V**	H	*VX*	MA
1214	(3317, 6433)			H	*VX*	MA
1215	(3377)			H	*VX*	MA
1216	(3302)	†	**V**	H	*VX*	MA
1217	(3357, 6444)			H	*SR*	IS
1218	(3332)			H	*AR*	NC
1219	(3418)			H	*AR*	NC
1220	(3315, 6432)	†	**V**	H	*VX*	MA
1221	(3371)			H	*VX*	MA
1250	(3372)	†	**V**	H	*VX*	MA
1251	(3383)	†	**V**	H	*VX*	MA
1252	(3280)	†	**V**	H	*VX*	MA
1253	(3432)	†	**V**	H	*VX*	MA
1254	(3391)	†	**V**	H	*VX*	MA
1255	(3284)	†	**V**	H	*VX*	MA
1256	(3296)	†		H	*VX*	MA
1258	(3322)	†	**V**	H	*VX*	MA
1259	(3439)	†	**V**	H	*VX*	MA
1260	(3378)	†	**V**	H	*VX*	MA

AK51 (RKB) KITCHEN BUFFET

Dia. AK502. Mark 1. No seats. B5 bogies. ETH 1.

Lot No. 30624 Cravens 1960–61. 41 t.

1566	**RB**	VS	*ON*	CP

AJ41 (RBR) RESTAURANT BUFFET

Dia. AJ403. Mark 1. Built with 23 loose chairs (Dia. AJ402). All remaining vehicles refurbished with 23 fixed polypropylene chairs and fluorescent lighting. ETH 2 (2X*).

r Further refurbished with 21 chairs, payphone, wheelchair space and carpets (Dia. AJ416).

1653–1699. Lot No. 30628 Pressed Steel 1960–61. Commonwealth bogies. 39 t.
1730. Lot No. 30512 BRCW 1960–61. B5 bogies. 37 t.

1653			CN		FK	1686	r		H		KN
1658		**BG**	RS	*ON*	BN	1689	r		H		KN
1659	x	**PC**	WT	*ON*	RL	1691	r	**G**	H		CP
1667	x		RS	*ON*	BN	1692	xr	**CH**	RV	*ON*	CP
1671	x*	**CC**	RS	*ON*	BN	1696		**G**	RS	*ON*	BN
1674			CN		BN	1697	r				CP
1679		**G**	RS	*ON*	BN	1698		**WV**	RS	*ON*	BN
1680	x*	**WV**	RS	*ON*	BN	1699	r		H		CP
1683	r	**FT**	H	*CA*	CF	1730	x	**M**	SP	*ON*	BT

AN21 (RMB) MINIATURE BUFFET CAR

Dia. AN203. Mark 1. –/44 2T. These vehicles are basically an open standard with two full window spaces removed to accommodate a buffet counter, and four seats removed to allow for a stock cupboard. All remaining vehicles now have fluorescent lighting. All vehicles have Commonwealth bogies except 1850 (B5). ETH 3.

1813–1832. Lot No. 30520 Wolverton 1960. 38 t.
1840–1850. Lot No. 30507 Wolverton 1960. 37 t (1850 is 36 t).
1859–1863. Lot No. 30670 Wolverton 1961–62. 38 t.
1871–1882. Lot No. 30702 Wolverton 1962. 38 t.

1842/50/71 have been refurbished and are fitted with a microwave oven and payphone. Dia. AN208.

1813	x	**CC**	RS	*ON*	BN	1860	x	**M**	WC	*ON*	CS
1832	x	**BG**	RS	*ON*	BN	1861	x	**M**	WC	*ON*	TM
1840	v	**G**	MH	*ON*	RL	1863	x	**CH**	RV	*ON*	CP
1842	v		H	*AR*	NC	1871	x		H		OO
1850			H		CP	1882	x	**M**	WC	*ON*	CS
1859	x	**M**	SP	*ON*	BT						

AJ41 (RBR)   RESTAURANT BUFFET

Dia. AJ414. Mark 1. This vehicle was built as an unclassified restaurant (RU). It was rebuilt with buffet counter and 23 fixed polypropylene chairs (RBS), then further refurbished by fitting fluorescent lighting and reclassified RBR. B4/B5 bogies. ETH 2X.

Lot No. 30575 Swindon 1960. 36.5 t.

1953   **RB** VS   *ON*   CP

AS41   FIRST CLASS SLEEPING CAR

Dia. AS101. Mark 1. Pressure Ventilated. 11 single-berth compartments plus an attendant's compartment. ETH 3 (3X*).

2013. Lot No. 30159 Wolverton 1958. B5 bogies. 39 t.
2127. Lot No. 30687 Wolverton 1961. Commonwealth bogies. 41 t.

2013 was numbered 2908 for a time when in use with the Royal Train.

2013   **M** FS   SZ | 2127 *   **M** GS   CS

AU51   CHARTER TRAIN STAFF COACHES

Dia. AU501. Mark 1. Converted from BCKs in 1988. Commonwealth bogies. ETH 2.

Lot No. 30732 Derby 1964. 37 t.

2833 (21270)   RS *ON*   BN | 2834 (21267)   **WV** RS *ON* BN

AT5G   HM THE QUEEN'S SALOON

Dia. AT525. Mark 3. Converted from a FO built 1972. Consists of a lounge, bedroom and bathroom for HM The Queen, and a combined bedroom and bathroom for the Queen's dresser. One entrance vestibule has double doors. Air conditioned. BT10 bogies. ETH 9X.

Lot No. 30886 Wolverton 1977. 36 t.

2903 (11001)   **RP** RK *RP*   ZN

AT5G   HRH THE DUKE OF EDINBURGH'S SALOON

Dia. AT526. Mark 3. Converted from a TSO built 1972. Consists of a combined lounge/dining room, a bedroom and a shower room for the Duke, a kitchen and a valet's bedroom and bathroom. Air conditioned. BT10 bogies. ETH 15X.

Lot No. 30887 Wolverton 1977. 36 t.

2904 (12001)   **RP** RK *RP*   ZN

AT5B   ROYAL HOUSEHOLD COUCHETTES

Dia. AT527. Mark 2B. Converted from a BFK built 1969. Consists of luggage accommodation, guard's compartment, 350 kW diesel generator and staff sleeping accommodation. Pressure ventilated. B5 bogies. ETH 5X.

Lot No. 30888 Wolverton 1977. 46 t.

2905 (14105)   **RP** RK *RP*   ZN

Dia. AT528. Mark 2B. Converted from a BFK built 1969. Consists of luggage accommodation, guards compartment and staff accommodation. Pressure ventilated. B5 bogies. ETH 4X.

Lot No. 30889 Wolverton 1977. 35.5 t.

2906 (14112)   **RP** RK *RP*   ZN

AT5G   ROYAL HOUSEHOLD SLEEPING CARS

Dia. AT531. Mark 3A. Built to similar specification as SLE 10646–732. 12 sleeping compartments for use of Royal Household with a fixed lower berth and a hinged upper berth. 2T plus shower room. Air conditioned. BT10 bogies. ETH 11X.

Lot No. 31002 Derby/Wolverton 1985. 42.5 t (44 t*).

2914   **RP** RK *RP*   ZN
2915 *   **RP** RK *RP*   ZN

AT5G   ROYAL KITCHEN/DINING CAR

Dia AT537. Mark 3. Converted from HST TRUK built 1976. Large kitchen retained, but dining area modified for Royal use seating up to 14 at central table(s). Air conditioned. BT10 bogies. ETH 13X.

Lot No. 31059 Wolverton 1988. 43 t.

2916 (40512)   **RP** RK *RP*   ZN

AT5G   ROYAL HOUSEHOLD KITCHEN/DINING CAR

Dia. AT539. Mark 3. Converted from HST TRUK built 1977. Large kitchen retained and dining area slightly modified with seating for 22 Royal Household members. Air conditioned. BT10 bogies. ETH 13X.

Lot No. 31084 Wolverton 1990. 43 t.

2917 (40514)   **RP** RK *RP*   ZN

AT5G   ROYAL HOUSEHOLD CARS

Dia. AT538 (AT540*). Mark 3. Converted from HST TRUKs built 1976/7. Air conditioned. BT10 bogies. ETH 10X.

Lot Nos. 31083 (31085*) Wolverton 1989. 41.05 t.

| 2918 | (40515) | | **RP** | RK | *RP* | ZN |
| 2919 | (40518) | * | **RP** | RK | *RP* | ZN |

AT5B   ROYAL HOUSEHOLD COUCHETTES

Dia. AT536. Mark 2B. Converted from BFK built 1969. Consists of luggage accommodation, guard's compartment, workshop area, 350 kW diesel generator and staff sleeping accommodation. B5 bogies. ETH2X.

Lot No. 31044 Wolverton 1986. 48 t.

| 2920 | (14109, 17109) | **RP** | RK | *RP* | ZN |

Dia. AT541. Mark 2B. Converted from BFK built 1969. Consists of luggage accommodation, kitchen, brake control equipment and staff accommodation. B5 bogies. ETH7X.

Lot No. 31086 Wolverton 1990. 41.5 t.

| 2921 | (14107, 17107) | **RP** | RK | *RP* | ZN |

AT5G HRH THE PRINCE OF WALES'S SLEEPING CAR

Dia. AT534. Mark 3B. BT10 bogies. Air conditioned.ETH 7X.

Lot No. 31035 Derby/Wolverton 1987.

| 2922 | **RP** | RK | *RP* | ZN |

AT5G   HRH THE PRINCE OF WALES'S SALOON

Dia. AT535. Mark 3B. BT10 bogies. Air conditioned. ETH 6X.

Lot No. 31036 Derby/Wolverton 1987.

| 2923 | **RP** | RK | *RP* | ZN |

AD11 (FO)   OPEN FIRST

Dia. AD103. Mark 1. 42/– 2T. ETH 3. Many now fitted with table lamps.

3063–3069. Lot No. 30169 Doncaster 1955. B4 bogies. 33 t.
3096–3100. Lot No. 30576 BRCW 1959. B4 bogies. 33 t.

3064 and 3068 were numbered DB 975607 and DB 975606 for a time when in departmental service for British Rail. 3065 has BR Mark 1 bogies and weighs 34 t.

3063	**BG**	VS		SL	3069	**RB**	VS	*ON*	CP
3064	**BG**	VS		SL	3096	x **M**	SP	*ON*	BT
3065	v **PC**	WT		CS	3097	**WV**	RS	*ON*	BN
3066	**RB**	VS	*ON*	CP	3098	x **CH**	RV	*ON*	CP
3068	**RB**	VS	*ON*	CP	3100	x **CC**	RS	*ON*	BN

Later design with fluorescent lighting, aluminium window frames and Commonwealth bogies.

3105–3128. Lot No. 30697 Swindon 1962–63. 36 t.

3130–3150. Lot No. 30717 Swindon 1963. 36 t.

3128/36/41/3/4/6/7/8 were renumbered 1058/60/3/5/6/8/9/70 when reclassified RUO, then 3600/5/8/9/2/6/4/10 when declassified, but have since regained their original numbers.

3105	x **M**	WC *ON*	CS	3128	x **M**	WC *ON*	CS
3107	x **BG**	RS *ON*	BN	3130	v **M**	WC *ON*	CS
3110	x **CC**	RS *ON*	BN	3131	x **CC**	RS *ON*	BN
3112	x **CH**	RV *ON*	CP	3132	x **CC**	RS *ON*	BN
3113	x **M**	WC *ON*	CS	3133	x **CC**	RS *ON*	BN
3114	**G**	RS *ON*	BN	3136		RS *ON*	BN
3115	x **BG**	RS *ON*	BN	3140	x **CH**	RV *ON*	CP
3117	x **M**	WC *ON*	CS	3141	**WV**	RS *ON*	BN
3119	x **CC**	RS *ON*	BN	3143		FS	SZ
3120	**WV**	RS *ON*	BN	3144	x **CC**	RS *ON*	BN
3121	**WV**	RS *ON*	BN	3146	**WV**	RS *ON*	BN
3122	x **CH**	RV *ON*	CP	3147	**WV**	RS *ON*	BN
3123	**G**	RS *ON*	BN	3148	**BG**	RS *ON*	BN
3124	**G**	RS *ON*	BN	3149		RS *ON*	BN
3125	**RB**	VS *ON*	CP	3150	**G**	RS *ON*	BN
3127	**G**	RS *ON*	BN				

AD1D (FO)   OPEN FIRST

Dia. AD105. Mark 2D. Air conditioned. 3172–88 have Stones equipment. 3192/ 3202 have Temperature Ltd and require at least 800 V train supply. 42/– 2T. B4 bogies. ETH 5.

Lot No. 30821 Derby 1971–72. 32.5 t.

3172		SO *SO*	ZA	3186		CN	DY
3174	**VN**	VS *ON*	CP	3187		E	KM
3178		VS	CP	3188	**RB**	RV *ON*	CP
3181	**RB**	RV *ON*	CP	3192		SO *SO*	ZA
3182		VS	CP	3202		E	KM

AD1E (FO)   OPEN FIRST

Dia. AD106. Mark 2E. Air conditioned. Stones equipment. Require at least 800 V train supply. 42/– 2T (41/– 2T 1W w). B4 bogies. ETH 5.

* Seats removed to accommodate catering module. 40F 1T.
r Refurbished with new seats.
u Fitted with power supply for Mk. 1 RBR.

3255 was numbered 3525 for a time when fitted with a pantry.

Lot No. 30843 Derby 1972–73. 32.5 t.

3221	w	H	ZC	3226		E	KN
3223		RV	OM	3228	du	H *GW*	OO
3225		E	KN	3229	d	H *GW*	OO

3230		SO	*SO*	ZA	3251 *		CN		FK
3231		RA		CP	3252 w		H		PY
3232 dr	**GW**	H	*GW*	OO	3255 dr	**GW**	H	*GW*	OO
3234 w		VS		CP	3256 w		H		PY
3235 u		H		PY	3257 w		VS		CP
3237		CN		FK	3258 n		E		KN
3239		VS		CP	3261 dw		H		OO
3240	**CH**	RV	*ON*	CP	3267	**CH**	VS	*ON*	CP
3241 dr	**GW**	H	*GW*	OO	3268		RV		KN
3242 wu		H		PY	3269 dr	**GW**	H	*GW*	OO
3244 d		H		ZC	3270		VS		CP
3246 w		RA		CP	3272		VS		CP
3247		VS		CP	3273	**CH**	VS	*ON*	CP
3248		SO	*SO*	ZA	3275		VS		CP

AD1F (FO)   OPEN FIRST

Dia. AD107. Mark 2F. Air conditioned. 3277–3318/58–81 have Stones equipment, others have Temperature Ltd. 42/– 2T. All now refurbished with power-operated vestibule doors, new panels and new seat trim. B4 bogies. d. ETH 5X.

3277–3318. Lot No. 30845 Derby 1973. 33 t.
3325–3428. Lot No. 30859 Derby 1973–74. 33 t.
3429–3438. Lot No. 30873 Derby 1974–75. 33 t.

r Further refurbished with table lamps, modified seats with burgundy seat trim and new m.a. sets.
s Further refurbished with table lamps and modified seats with burgundy seat trim.
u Fitted with power supply for Mk. 1 RBR.

3403 was numbered 6450 for a time when declassified.

3277	**AR**	H	*AR*	NC	3333 r	**V**	H	*VW*	OY
3278 r	**V**	H	*VW*	OY	3334		H	*AR*	NC
3279 u	**AR**	H	*AR*	NC	3336 u	**AR**	H	*AR*	NC
3285 s	**V**	H	*VW*	OY	3337 r	**V**	H	*VW*	OY
3290	**AR**	H	*AR*	NC	3338 u	**AR**	H	*AR*	NC
3292		H	*AR*	NC	3340 r	**V**	H	*VW*	OY
3293		H		NC	3344 r	**V**	H	*VW*	OY
3295	**AR**	H	*AR*	NC	3345 r	**V**	H	*VW*	OY
3299 r	**V**	H	*VW*	OY	3348 r	**V**	H	*VW*	OY
3300 s	**V**	H	*VW*	OY	3350 r	**V**	H	*VW*	OY
3303	**AR**	H	*AR*	NC	3351	**AR**	H	*AR*	NC
3304 r	**V**	H	*VW*	OY	3352 r	**V**	H	*VW*	OY
3309		H	*AR*	NC	3353 s	**V**	H	*VW*	OY
3312		H		OO	3354 s	**V**	H	*VW*	OY
3313 r	**V**	H	*VW*	OY	3356 r	**V**	H	*VW*	OY
3314 r	**V**	H	*VW*	OY	3358	**AR**	H	*AR*	NC
3318		H	*AR*	NC	3359 s	**V**	H	*VW*	OY
3325 r	**V**	H	*VW*	OY	3360 s	**V**	H	*VW*	OY
3326 r	**V**	H	*VW*	OY	3362 s	**V**	H	*VW*	OY
3330 r	**V**	H	*VW*	OY	3363 s	**V**	H	*VW*	OY
3331		H	*AR*	NC	3364 r	**V**	H	*VW*	OY

No.						No.				
3366	s	V	H	VW	OY	3399	u	AR	H	AR	NC
3368		AR	H	AR	NC	3400		AR	H	AR	NC
3369	s	V	H	VW	OY	3402	s	V	H	VW	OY
3373			H	AR	NC	3403	s	V	H	VW	OY
3374			H		NC	3408	s	V	H	VW	OY
3375			H	AR	NC	3411	s	V	H	VW	OY
3379	u		H	AR	NC	3414		AR	H	AR	NC
3381			H	AR	NC	3416			H	AR	NC
3384	r	V	H	VW	OY	3417			H	AR	NC
3385	r	V	H	VW	OY	3424		AR	H	AR	NC
3386	r	V	H	VW	OY	3425	s	V	H	VW	OY
3387	s	V	H	VW	OY	3426	r	V	H	VW	OY
3388		AR	H	AR	NC	3428	s	V	H	VW	OY
3389	s	V	H	VW	OY	3429	r	V	H	VW	OY
3390	r	V	H	VW	OY	3431	r	V	H	VW	OY
3392	r	V	H	VW	OY	3433	r	V	H	VW	OY
3395	r	V	H	VW	OY	3434	s	V	H	VW	OY
3397	r	V	H	VW	OY	3438	s	V	H	VW	OY

AG1E (FO (T))   OPEN FIRST (PANTRY)

Dia. AG101. Mark 2E. Air conditioned. Converted from FO. Fitted with pantry, microwave oven and payphone for use on overnight services. 36/– 1T. B4 bogies. d. ETH 5X.

Lot No. 30843 Derby 1972–73. 32.5 t.

3520	(3253)	H		OO	3523	(3238)	H	SR	IS
3521	(3271)	H		OO	3524	(3254)	H	SR	IS
3522	(3236)	H		OO			

AC21 (TSO)   OPEN STANDARD

Dia. AC204. Mark 1. These vehicles have 2+2 seating and are classified TSO ('Tourist second open'–a former LNER designation). –/64 2T. ETH 4.

3766. Lot No. 30079 York 1953. Commonwealth bogies (originally built with BR Mark 1 bogies). This coach has narrower seats than later vehicles. 36 t.
4198. Lot No. 30172 York 1956. BR Mark 1 bogies. 33 t.

3766	x	M	WC	ON	CS		4198	v	CH	NY	ON	NY

AD21 (SO)   OPEN STANDARD

Dia. AD201. Mark 1. These vehicles have 2+1 seating and were often used as second class dining cars when new. –/48 2T. BR Mark 1 bogies. ETH 4.

4786. Lot No. 30376 York 1957. 33 t.
4817. Lot No. 30473 BRCW 1957–59. 33 t.

4786	v	CH	NY	ON	NY		4817	v	CH	NY	ON	NY

AC21 (TSO)   OPEN STANDARD

Dia. AC201. Mark 1. These vehicles are a development of Dia. AC204 with fluorescent lighting and modified design of seat headrest. Built with BR Mark 1 bogies. –/64 2T. ETH 4.

4831–4836. Lot No. 30506 Wolverton 1959. Commonwealth bogies. 33 t.
4849–4880. Lot No. 30525 Wolverton 1959–60. B4 bogies. 33 t.

4831	x	**M**	SP	*ON*	BT	4866		**RR**	H	*NW*	CP
4832	x	**M**	SP	*ON*	BT	4869	x		CN		FK
4836	x	**M**	SP	*ON*	BT	4873		**RR**	H	*NW*	CP
4849		**RR**	H	*NW*	CP	4875		**RR**	H	*NW*	CP
4854		**RR**	H	*NW*	CP	4876		**RR**	H	*NW*	CP
4856	x	**M**	SP	*ON*	BT	4880		**RR**	H	*NW*	CP

Lot No. 30646 Wolverton 1961. Built with Commonwealth bogies, but BR Mark 1 bogies substituted by the SR on 4902/5/9/12/15/16. All now re-rebogied. 34 t B4, 36 t C.

4902	x B4	**CH**	RV	*ON*	CP	4915	x B4	**CC**	RS	*ON*	BN
4905	x C	**M**	WC	*ON*	CS	4916	x B4	**CC**	RS	*ON*	BN
4909	x B4		CN		FK	4917	x C	**RR**	H		CP
4912	x C	**M**	WC	*ON*	CS						

Lot No. 30690 Wolverton 1961–62. Commonwealth bogies and aluminium window frames. 37 t.

4925		**G**	RS	*ON*	BN	4998			RS	*ON*	BN
4927	x	**CH**	RV	*ON*	CP	4999		**BG**	RS	*ON*	BN
4931	v	**M**	WC	*ON*	CS	5002		**WR**	RS	*ON*	BN
4938		**BG**	RS	*ON*	BN	5005		**BG**	RS	*ON*	BN
4939			RS	*ON*	BN	5007		**G**	RS	*ON*	BN
4940	x	**M**	WC	*ON*	CS	5008	x	**CC**	RS	*ON*	BN
4946	x	**CC**	RS	*ON*	BN	5009	x	**CH**	RV	*ON*	CP
4949		**BG**	RS	*ON*	BN	5010			RV		CP
4951	x	**M**	WC	*ON*	CS	5023		**G**	RS	*ON*	BN
4954	v	**M**	WC	*ON*	CS	5025	x	**CH**	RV	*ON*	CP
4956		**BG**	RS	*ON*	BN	5027		**G**	RS	*ON*	BN
4958	v	**M**	WC	*ON*	CS	5028	x	**M**	SP	*ON*	BT
4959		**BG**	RS	*ON*	BN	5029	x	**CH**	RV	*ON*	CP
4960	x	**M**	WC	*ON*	CS	5030	x	**CH**	RV	*ON*	CP
4963	x	**CH**	RV	*ON*	CP	5032	x	**M**	WC	*ON*	CS
4973	x	**M**	WC	*ON*	CS	5033	x	**M**	WC	*ON*	CS
4977			RS	*ON*	BN	5035	x	**M**	WC	*ON*	CS
4984	v	**M**	WC	*ON*	CS	5037		**G**	RS	*ON*	BN
4986		**G**	RS	*ON*	BN	5040	x	**CH**	RV	*ON*	CP
4991		**BG**	RS	*ON*	BN	5042	x		CN		FK
4994	x	**M**	WC	*ON*	CS	5044	x	**M**	WC	*ON*	CS
4996	x	**CC**	RS	*ON*	BN						

▲ **Mark 1 Stock.** Southern green liveried restaurant buffet No. 1696 is seen at Worcester Shrub Hill with a charter train from London King's Cross on 17th April 1999. This vehicle has Commonwealth bogies. **Stephen Widdowson**

▼ Open first No. 3105 'JULIA' in BR maroon livery stabled at Carlisle on 18th September 1999. This coach is owned by the West Coast Railway Company. **Kevin Conkey**

Generator van No. 6313 now owned by VSOE is seen stabled at Worcester Shrub Hill on 25th October 1998. The vehicle is painted in Pullman umber and cream livery.

Stephen Widdowson

▲ Carmine & cream liveried corridor brake composite No. 21245 is seen stabled at Worcester Shrub Hill on 26th June 1999. The vehicle is owned by Rail Charter Services.   **Stephen Widdowson**

▼ **Mark 2A Stock.** Open standard (TSO) No. 5389 waits departure from Crewe as part of the stock of the 10.18 to Bangor on 14th August 1999.   **Peter Fox**

▲ **Mark 2D Stock.** Open first No. 3181 'MONARCH' in Regency Railtours blue and cream livery at Reading on 17th June 1997. This coach is now owned by Venice Simplon-Orient Express. **Darren Ford**

▼ **Mark 2E Stock.** Virgin Trains liveried open standard No. 5899 at Carlisle on 21st June 1998 as part of the 17.00 Edinburgh–Birmingham New Street. **Kevin Conkey**

Mark 2F Stock. Buffet first No. 1204 in Virgin Trains livery approaching Brighton on 6th March 1999 in the formation of the 06.20 ex-Preston.   **Chris Wilson**

Driving brake open standard No. 9709 pulls out of Colchester leading the 11.30 London Liverpool Street–Norwich service on 4th September 1999.

David Brown

Mark 3 Stock. First Great Western (formerly Great Western Trains) has recently modified its livery with the addition of thin green stripes on the lower bodyside together with a broad gold band. Open standard No. 42029 was photographed at Dawlish on 4th July 1999.

Colin J. Marsden

▲ **Mark 3A Stock.** Restaurant buffet first No. 10223 in Anglia Railways livery at Colchester in the formation of the 11.30 London Liverpool Street–Norwich on 4th September 1999. Anglia has eight of these vehicles which operate in sets of Mark 2F stock. **David Brown**

▼ **Mark 3B Stock.** Virgin West Coast operate three BFO vehicles which were originally built for first class only Manchester Pullman workings. One of these, No. 17173 is seen at Carlisle on 25th July 1999. **Kevin Conkey**

Mark 4 Stock. Great North Eastern Railway liveried open standard (end) No. 12212 at Doncaster on 24th July 1999 as part of the 09.30 London King's Cross–Edinburgh.

Peter Fox

▲ **Non-Passenger Carrying Coaching Stock.** Post office sorting van No. 80339 'Brian Quinn' stabled at Carlisle station on 8th June 1999. The vehicle carries Royal Mail livery.   **Peter Fox**

▼ Post office stowage van No. 80427 stabled at Carlisle on 31st July 1999.
                                                                                    Kevin Conkey

▲ Virgin Trains liveried Mark 3B driving van trailer No. 82145 at Watford at the head of the 10.30 Manchester Piccadilly–London Euston on 1st May 1999.
Kevin Conkey

▼ Mark 4 driving van trailer No. 82206 arrives at London King's Cross on 25th May 1999 at the head of the 12.00 from Edinburgh.　**Dave McAlone**

▲ Propelling control van No. 94312 stabled at Carlisle on 8th June 1999.

Peter Fox

▼ High security brake van No. 94403 at Old Oak Common, London on 21st August 1999.

Kevin Conkey

Motorail van No. 96607 on show at London Paddington. This is one of a batch built by Marcroft Engineering for First Great Western services.

Colin J. Marsden

Nightstar Stock. Nightstar coaches stored at the Alstom Birmingham works (formerly Metro-Cammell) on 15th July 1997. Pictured are seating coach No. 61 19 20-90 029-1 and sleeping car No. 61 19 70-90 028-0. These vehicles are now without work following the decision not to operate Nightstar services.

Peter Fox

Saloons. Great Western Railway first class saloon No. 9004 is also owned by Railfilms-owned and is seen at Reading on 17th June 1999 in the same train as the photograph on the previous page. **Darren Ford**

Railfilms-owned imitation LMS Club Car No. 99993 (rebuilt from Mark 1 TSO No. 5067) at Reading on 17th June 1999.
Darren Ford

AC2Z (TSO)   OPEN STANDARD

Dia. AC205. Mark 2. Pressure ventilated. –/64 2T. B4 bogies. ETH 4.

Lot No. 30751 Derby 1965–67. 32 t.

5125	v	**G**	MH	*ON*	RL	5183	v	**RR**	BM	TM
5132	v	**LN**	H		LT	5186	v	**RR**	BM	TM
5135	v	**RR**	H		LT	5191	v	**LN**	BM	TM
5148	v	**RR**	BM		TM	5193	v	**LN**	BM	TM
5154	v	**LN**	H		LT	5194	v	**RR**	BM	TM
5156	v	**RR**	H		LT	5198	v	**CH**	BM	*ON*	TM
5157	v	**RR**	BM		TM	5200	v	**G**	MH	*ON*	RL
5158	v	**RR**	H		LT	5207	v	**RR**	H		LT
5161	v	**RR**	H		LT	5209	v	**RR**	H		LT
5163	v	**RR**	H		LT	5212	v	**LN**	BM		TM
5166	v	**LN**	H		LT	5213	v	**RR**	H		LT
5167	v	**RR**	H		LT	5216	v	**G**	MH	*ON*	RL
5171	v	**G**	MH	*ON*	RL	5221	v	**RR**	BM		TM
5174	v	**RR**	H		LT	5222	v	**G**	MH	*ON*	RL
5177	v	**RR**	BM		TM	5225	v	**RR**	H		LT
5179	v	**RR**	BM		TM	5226	v	**RR**	H		LT
5180	v	**RR**	H		LT					

AD2Z (SO)   OPEN STANDARD

Dia. AD203. Mark 2. Pressure ventilated. –/48 2T. B4 bogies. ETH 4.

Lot No. 30752 Derby 1966. 32 t.

5237	v	**G**	MH	*ON*	RL	5254	**BG**	H	DY
5249	v	**G**	MH	*ON*	RL				

AC2A (TSO)   OPEN STANDARD

Dia. AC206. Mark 2A. Pressure ventilated. –/64 2T (–/62 2T w). B4 bogies. ETH 4.

5265–5345. Lot No. 30776 Derby 1967–68. 32 t.
5350–5433. Lot No. 30787 Derby 1968. 32 t.

5265	**RR**	H		KN	5299	**M**	WC	*ON*	CS
5266	**RR**	H		CW	5304	**RR**	H		CW
5267	**RR**	H		KN	5307	**FT**	H	*CA*	CF
5271	**RR**	H		KN	5309	**RR**	H	*NW*	CP
5272	**RR**	H		CP	5322	**RR**	H		CP
5275	**FT**	H	*CA*	CF	5331	**RR**	H	*NW*	CP
5276	**RR**	H		CP	5335	**RR**	H	*NW*	CP
5277	**BG**	H		KN	5341	**RR**	H		CP
5278	**RR**	H	*NW*	CP	5345	**RR**	H		CP
5282	**RR**	H		KN	5350	**FT**	H	*CA*	CF
5290	**NB**	H		KN	5353	**RR**	H		KN
5292	**RR**	H		CP	5354	**RR**	H		PY
5293	**NB**	H		KN	5364	**FT**	H	*CA*	CF

No.						No.					
5365		**FT**	H	*CA*	CF	5386	w	**RR**	H	*NW*	CP
5366		**RR**	H		KN	5389	w	**RR**	H	*NW*	CP
5373		**FT**	H	*CA*	CF	5396		**RR**	H		KN
5376		**FT**	H	*CA*	CF	5410		**N**	H		KN
5378		**FT**	H	*CA*	CF	5412	w	**RR**	H	*NW*	CP
5379		**RR**	H		KN	5419	w	**RR**	H	*NW*	CP
5381	w	**RR**	H	*NW*	CP	5420	w	**RR**	H	*NW*	CP
5384		**N**	H		CW	5433	w	**RR**	H		CP

AC2B (TSO)   OPEN STANDARD

Dia. AC207. Mark 2B. Pressure ventilated. –/62 2T. B4 bogies. ETH 4.

Lot No. 30791 Derby 1969. 32 t.

Non-Standard Livery: 5453, 5478 and 5491 are royal blue with white lining.

No.						No.					
5439		**N**	H		KN	5464		**N**	RV		CP
5443		**N**	H		KN	5471		**N**	H		KN
5446		**N**	H		KN	5472		**N**	H		KN
5447		**N**	H		PY	5475		**N**	H		KN
5449		**N**	RV		CP	5478	d	**0**	WC	*ON*	CS
5450		**N**	H		KN	5480		**N**	H		KN
5453	d	**0**	WC	*ON*	CS	5487	d	**M**	WC	*ON*	CS
5454		**N**	H		KN	5491	d	**0**	WC	*ON*	CS
5462		**N**	RV		CP	5494		**N**	RV		CP
5463	d	**M**	WC	*ON*	CS						

AC2C (TSO)   OPEN STANDARD

Dia. AC208. Mark 2C. Pressure ventilated. –/62 2T. B4 bogies. ETH 4.

Lot No. 30795 Derby 1969–70. 32 t.

No.						No.					
5554		**RR**	H		CW	5600		**M**	WC	*ON*	CS
5569	d	**M**	WC	*ON*	CS	5614		**RR**	H		CW

AC2D (TSO)   OPEN STANDARD

Dia. AC209. Mark 2D. Air conditioned. Stones equipment. –/62 2T. B4 bogies. ETH 5.

Non-Standard Livery: 5630, 5647, 5732 & 5739 are **WV** without lining.

r Refurbished with new seats and end luggage stack. –/58 2T.

Lot No. 30822 Derby 1971. 33 t.

No.						No.					
5616			CN		FK	5631	dr	**GW**	H	*GW*	OO
5618			H		PY	5632	dr	**GW**	H	*GW*	OO
5620			H		LT	5634			H		ZC
5623			H		LT	5636	dr	**GW**	H	*GW*	OO
5628			H		ZC	5640			H		LT
5629			H		LT	5645			WC		CS
5630		**0**	RV		CP	5647		**0**	RV	*ON*	CP

5650			H		LT	5710	dr	**GW**	H	*GW*	OO
5657	dr	**GW**	H	*GW*	OO	5711			H		LT
5661			H		KN	5712			WC		CS
5662			H		ZN	5714		**M**	WC *ON*		CS
5663			H		KN	5715			H		LT
5665			H		ZC	5716			H		KN
5669	dr	**GW**	H	*GW*	OO	5718			H		KN
5674			H		KN	5722			E		KM
5676			H		ZC	5724			H		LT
5679	dr	**GW**	H	*GW*	OO	5726			H		PY
5686			H		ZC	5727		**M**	WC *ON*		CS
5687			H		KN	5728			H		PY
5690			H		LT	5731			H		KN
5692			H		ZC	5732		**0**	RV		CP
5694			H		KN	5735			H	*ON*	ZC
5699			H		KN	5737	dr	**GW**	H	*GW*	OO
5700	dr	**GW**	H	*GW*	OO	5738			H		KN
5701			H		KN	5739		**0**	RV		CP
5704		**M**	WC *ON*		CS	5740	dr	**GW**	H	*GW*	OO
5709		**BG**	WC		CS						

AC2E (TSO)   OPEN STANDARD

Dia. AC210. Mark 2E. Air conditioned. Stones equipment. Require at least 800 V train supply. –/64 2T (w –/62 2T 1W). B4 bogies. d (except 5756 and 5879). ETH 5.

5744–5801. Lot No. 30837 Derby 1972. 33.5 t.
5810–5906. Lot No. 30844 Derby 1972–73. 33.5 t.

r Refurbished with new interior panelling.
s Refurbished with new interior panelling, modified design of seat headrest and centre luggage stack. –/60 2T (w –/58 2T 1W).
t Refurbished with new interior panelling and new seats.

5744			H		ZN	5789	r pt			H	*VX*	MA
5745	s	**V**	H	*VX*	MA	5791	wr			H	*VX*	MA
5746	r	**V**	H	*VX*	MA	5792	r			H	*VX*	MA
5748	r pt		H	*VX*	MA	5793	wspt	**V**	H	*VX*	MA
5750	s	**V**	H	*VX*	MA	5794	wr			H	*VX*	MA
5752	wrpt		H	*VX*	MA	5796	wr			H	*VX*	MA
5754	ws	**V**	H	*VX*	MA	5797	r			H	*VX*	MA
5756		**M**	WC *ON*		CS	5800				H	*GW*	OO
5769	r		H	*VX*	MA	5801	r		**V**	H	*VX*	MA
5773	s pt	**V**	H	*VX*	MA	5810	s		**V**	H	*VX*	MA
5775	s	**V**	H	*VX*	MA	5812	wr			H	*VX*	MA
5776	r		H	*VX*	MA	5814	r			H	*VX*	MA
5778	w		H		ZN	5815	ws		**V**	H	*VX*	MA
5779	r		H	*VX*	MA	5816	r pt			H	*VX*	MA
5780	w		H		ZN	5821	r pt		**V**	H	*VX*	MA
5781	d		H	*GW*	OO	5822	wspt	**V**	H	*VX*	MA
5784	r	**V**	H	*VX*	MA	5824	rw			H	*VX*	MA
5787	s	**V**	H	*VX*	MA	5827	r			H	*VX*	MA
5788	r		H	*VX*	MA	5828	ws		**V**	H	*VX*	MA

5831		H		ZN
5836		H	GW	OO
5843 rw		H	VX	MA
5845 s	V	H	VX	MA
5847 rw	V	H	VX	MA
5852		H	GW	OO
5853 t		H	AR	NC
5854 r		H	VX	MA
5859 s	V	H	VX	MA
5863		H	GW	OO
5866 r pt		H	VX	MA
5868 s pt	V	H	VX	MA
5869 t		H	AR	NC
5874 t		H	AR	NC
5876 s pt	V	H	VX	MA

5879			RV	OM
5881 ws	V	H	VX	MA
5886 s	V	H	VX	MA
5887 wr		H	VX	MA
5888 wr		H	VX	MA
5889 s	V	H	VX	MA
5893 s	V	H	VX	MA
5897 r		H	VX	MA
5899 s	V	H	VX	MA
5900 wspt	V	H	VX	MA
5901 s	V	H	VX	MA
5902 s	V	H	VX	MA
5903 s	V	H	VX	MA
5905 s	V	H	VX	MA
5906 wspt		H	VX	MA

AC2F (TSO)   OPEN STANDARD

Dia. AC211. Mark 2F. Air conditioned. Temperature Ltd. equipment. Inter-City 70 seats. All were refurbished in the 1980s with power-operated vestibule doors, new panels and new seat trim. –/64 2T. (w –/62 2T 1W) B4 bogies. d. ETH 5X.

5908–5958. Lot No. 30846 Derby 1973. 33 t.
5959–6170. Lot No. 30860 Derby 1973–74. 33 t.
6171–6184. Lot No. 30874 Derby 1974–75. 33 t.

* Early Mark 2 style seats.

These vehicles are now undergoing a second refurbishment with carpets and new seat trim .

Cross-Country vehicles:

r Standard refurbished vehicles with new m.a. sets.
s Also fitted with centre luggage stack. –/60 2T.
t Also fitted with centre luggage stack and wheelchair space. –/58 2T 1W.

West Coast vehicles:

r Standard refurbished vehicles with new seat trim and new m.a. sets.
u As 'r' but with two wheelchair spaces. –/60 2T 2W.
† Standard refurbished vehicles with new seat trim.

5908 r	V	H	VW	OY
5910 u	V	H	VW	OY
5911 s	V	H	VX	MA
5912 s	V	H	VX	MA
5913 s		H	VX	MA
5914 u	V	H	VW	OY
5915 r	V	H	VW	OY
5916 t		H	VX	MA
5917 s	V	H	VX	MA
5918 t	V	H	VX	MA

5919 s pt	V	H	VX	MA
5920 †	V	H	VW	OY
5921		H	AR	NC
5922	AR	H	AR	NC
5924	AR	H	AR	NC
5925 s pt		H	VX	MA
5926		H	AR	NC
5927	AR	H	AR	NC
5928	AR	H	AR	NC
5929	AR	H	AR	NC

5930	t	**V**	H	*VX*	MA		5988	r	**V**	H	*VW*	OY
5931	tw	**V**	H	*VW*	OY		5989	t	**V**	H	*VX*	MA
5932	r	**V**	H	*VW*	OY		5991	s	**V**	H	*VX*	MA
5933	r	**V**	H	*VW*	OY		5993	*	**AR**	H	*AR*	NC
5934	r	**V**	H	*VW*	OY		5994	r	**V**	H	*VX*	MA
5935		**AR**	H	*AR*	NC		5995	s		H	*VX*	MA
5936		**AR**	H	*AR*	NC		5996	s pt	**V**	H	*VX*	MA
5937	r	**V**	H	*VW*	OY		5997	r	**V**	H	*VW*	OY
5939	r	**V**	H	*VW*	OY		5998			H	*AR*	NC
5940	u	**V**	H	*VW*	OY		5999	s	**V**	H	*VX*	MA
5941	r	**V**	H	*VW*	OY		6000	t	**V**	H	*VX*	MA
5943	rw	**V**	H	*VW*	OY		6001	u	**V**	H	*VW*	OY
5944		**AR**	H	*AR*	NC		6002	†	**V**	H	*VW*	OY
5945	r	**V**	H	*VW*	OY		6005	r	**V**	H	*VX*	MA
5946	r	**V**	H	*VW*	OY		6006		**AR**	H	*AR*	NC
5947	s pt	**V**	H	*VX*	MA		6008	s	**V**	H	*VX*	MA
5948	u	**V**	H	*VW*	OY		6009	r	**V**	H	*VW*	OY
5949	u	**V**	H	*VW*	OY		6010	s	**V**	H	*VX*	MA
5950			H	*AR*	NC		6011	s	**V**	H	*VX*	MA
5951	r	**V**	H	*VX*	MA		6012	r	**V**	H	*VW*	OY
5952	r	**V**	H	*VW*	OY		6013	s		H	*VX*	MA
5953	†	**V**	H	*VW*	OY		6014	s pt		H	*VX*	MA
5954		**AR**	H	*AR*	NC		6015	t	**V**	H	*VX*	MA
5955	r	**V**	H	*VW*	OY		6016	r	**V**	H	*VW*	OY
5956			H	*AR*	NC		6018	t	**V**	H	*VX*	MA
5957	r	**V**	H	*VW*	OY		6021	r	**V**	H	*VW*	OY
5958	s		H	*VX*	MA		6022	s	**V**	H	*VX*	MA
5959	n	**AR**	H	*AR*	NC		6024	s	**V**	H	*VX*	MA
5960	s	**V**	H	*VX*	MA		6025	t	**V**	H	*VX*	MA
5961	s pt	**V**	H	*VX*	MA		6026	s	**V**	H	*VX*	MA
5962	s pt	**V**	H	*VX*	MA		6027	u	**V**	H	*VW*	OY
5963	r	**V**	H	*VW*	OY		6028		**AR**	H	*AR*	NC
5964			H	*AR*	NC		6029	r	**V**	H	*VW*	OY
5965	t		H	*VX*	MA		6030	t	**V**	H	*VX*	MA
5966		**AR**	H	*AR*	NC		6031	r	**V**	H	*VW*	OY
5967	t	**V**	H	*VX*	MA		6034		**AR**	H	*AR*	NC
5968		**AR**	H	*AR*	NC		6035	t		H	*VX*	MA
5969	u	**V**	H	*VW*	OY		6036	*	**AR**	H	*AR*	NC
5971	s		H	*VX*	MA		6037		**AR**	H	*AR*	NC
5973		**AR**	H	*AR*	NC		6038	s	**V**	H	*VX*	MA
5975	s	**V**	H	*VX*	MA		6041	s	**V**	H	*VX*	MA
5976	t	**V**	H	*VX*	MA		6042			H	*AR*	NC
5977	r	**V**	H	*VW*	OY		6043	†	**V**	H	*VW*	OY
5978	r	**V**	H	*VW*	OY		6045	tw	**V**	H	*VW*	OY
5980	r	**V**	H	*VW*	OY		6046	s	**V**	H	*VX*	MA
5981	s		H	*VX*	MA		6047	tn*	**V**	H	*VW*	OY
5983	s	**V**	H	*VX*	MA		6049	r	**V**	H	*VW*	OY
5984	r	**V**	H	*VW*	OY		6050	s		H	*VX*	MA
5985		**AR**	H	*AR*	NC		6051	r	**V**	H	*VW*	OY
5986	r	**V**	H	*VW*	OY		6052	tw		H	*VX*	MA
5987	r	**V**	H	*VW*	OY		6053	*		H	*AR*	NC

6054	r	**V**	H	*VW*	OY		6141	u	**V**	H	*VW*	OY
6055	†	**V**	H	*VW*	OY		6142	†*	**V**	H	*VW*	OY
6056	†	**V**	H	*VW*	OY		6144	†*	**V**	H	*VW*	OY
6057	r	**V**	H	*VW*	OY		6145	s pt	**V**	H	*VX*	MA
6059	s	**V**	H	*VX*	MA		6146	*	**AR**	H	*AR*	NC
6060	u	**V**	H	*VW*	OY		6147	r	**V**	H	*VW*	OY
6061	s pt	**V**	H	*VX*	MA		6148	s		H	*VX*	MA
6062	†	**V**	H	*VW*	OY		6149	u	**V**	H	*VW*	OY
6063	†w	**V**	H	*VW*	OY		6150	s		H	*VX*	MA
6064	s	**V**	H	*VX*	MA		6151	†*	**V**	H	*VW*	OY
6065	r	**V**	H	*VW*	OY		6152	*	**AR**	H	*AR*	NC
6066	s		H	*VX*	MA		6153	†	**V**	H	*VW*	OY
6067	s pt	**V**	H	*VX*	MA		6154	r pt		H	*VX*	MA
6073	s	**V**	H	*VX*	MA		6155	*	**AR**	H	*AR*	NC
6100	†*	**V**	H	*VW*	OY		6157	s	**V**	H	*VX*	MA
6101	r	**V**	H	*VW*	OY		6158	r	**V**	H	*VW*	OY
6102	r	**V**	H	*VW*	OY		6159	s pt	**V**	H	*VX*	MA
6103			H	*AR*	NC		6160	*	**AR**	H	*AR*	NC
6104	r	**V**	H	*VW*	OY		6161	†*	**V**	H	*VW*	OY
6105	tpt	**V**	H	*VX*	MA		6162	s pt	**V**	H	*VX*	MA
6106	r	**V**	H	*VW*	OY		6163	r	**V**	H	*VW*	OY
6107	r	**V**	H	*VW*	OY		6164	†	**V**	H	*VW*	OY
6110			H	*AR*	NC		6165	r	**V**	H	*VW*	OY
6111	†	**V**	H	*VW*	OY		6166			H	*AR*	NC
6112	s pt	**V**	H	*VX*	MA		6167		**AR**	H	*AR*	NC
6113	†	**V**	H	*VW*	OY		6168	s		H	*VX*	MA
6115	s		H	*VX*	MA		6170	s	**V**	H	*VX*	MA
6116	†	**V**	H	*VW*	OY		6171	†	**V**	H	*VW*	OY
6117	t	**V**	H	*VX*	MA		6172	s	**V**	H	*VX*	MA
6119	s	**V**	H	*VX*	MA		6173	s	**V**	H	*VX*	MA
6120	s	**V**	H	*VX*	MA		6174			H	*AR*	NC
6121	†	**V**	H	*VW*	OY		6175	r	**V**	H	*VW*	OY
6122	s	**V**	H	*VX*	MA		6176	t	**V**	H	*VX*	MA
6123			H	*AR*	NC		6177	s	**V**	H	*VX*	MA
6124	s pt		H	*VX*	MA		6178	s		H	*VX*	MA
6134	†	**V**	H	*VW*	OY		6179	r	**V**	H	*VW*	OY
6135	s		H	*VX*	MA		6180	†w	**V**	H	*VW*	OY
6136	r		H	*VW*	OY		6181	†wn	**V**	H	*VW*	OY
6137	s pt	**V**	H	*VX*	MA		6182	s	**V**	H	*VX*	MA
6138	†	**V**	H	*VW*	OY		6183	s	**V**	H	*VX*	MA
6139	n*		H	*AR*	NC		6184	s	**V**	H	*VX*	MA

AC2D (TSO)   OPEN STANDARD

Dia. AC217. Mark 2D. Air conditioned (Stones). Rebuilt from FO with new style 2+2 seats. –/58 2T. (–/58 1T*). B4 bogies. d. ETH 5X.

Lot No. 30821 Derby 1971–72. 33.5 t.

* One toilet converted to store room for use of attendant on sleeping car services.

6200	(3198)		H	GW	OO	6212	(3176)		H	GW	OO
6202	(3191)	*	H		CP	6213	(3208)		H	GW	LA
6203	(3180)		H	GW	OO	6219	(3213)		H	GW	OO
6206	(3183)		H	GW	LA	6221	(3173)		H		CP
6207	(3204)		H		ZN	6226	(3203)		H	GW	LA

GX51   BRAKE GENERATOR VAN

Dia. GX501. Mark 1. Renumbered 1989 from BR departmental series. Converted from NDA in 1973 to three-phase supply generator van for use with HST trailers. Modified 1999 for use with loco-hauled stock. B5 bogies.

Lot No. 30400 Pressed Steel 1958.

6310	(81448, 975325)	P	RV	ON	CP

AX51   GENERATOR VAN

Dia. AX501. Mark 1. Converted from NDA in 1992 to generator vans for use on Anglo-Scottish sleeping car services. Now normally used on trains hauled by steam locomotives. B4 bogies. ETH75.

6311. Lot No. 30162 Pressed Steel 1958. 37.25 t.
6312. Lot No. 30224 Cravens 1956. 37.25 t.
6313. Lot No. 30484 Pressed Steel 1958. 37.25 t.

Non-Standard Livery: 6311 is purple.

6313 is leased to the Venice Simplon Orient Express.

6311	(80903, 92911)	B	RS	ON	BN
6312	(81023, 92925)		FS		SZ
6313	(81553, 92167)	PC	P	ON	SL

GS5 (HSBV)   HST BARRIER VEHICLE

Various diagrams. Renumbered from departmental stock, or converted from various types. B4 bogies (Commonwealth bogies *).

6330. Mark 2A. Lot No. 30786 Derby 1968. 32 t.
6334. Mark 1. Lot No. 30400 Pressed Steel 1957–8. 31.5 t.
6336/8/44. Mark 1. Lot No. 30715 Gloucester 1962. 31 t.
6340. Mark 1. Lot No. 30669 Swindon 1962. 36 t.
6346. Mark 2A. Lot No. 30777 Derby 1967. 31.5 t.
6347. Mark 2A. Lot No. 30787 Derby 1968. 31.5 t.
6348. Mark 1. Lot No. 30163 Pressed Steel 1957. 31.5 t.

6330	(14084, 975629)		G	A	A	LA
6334	(81478, 92128)		P	P	P	NL
6336	(81591, 92185)			A	A	LA
6338	(81581, 92180)		G	A	A	LA
6340	(21251, 975678)	*	G	A	A	LA
6344	(81263, 92080)		B	A	A	EC
6346	(9422)		B	A	A	EC
6347	(5395)			A	A	LA

6348   (81233, 92963)   **G**   A   *A*   LA

GF5 (MFBV)   MARK 4 BARRIER VEHICLE

Various diagrams. Renumbered from departmental stock, or converted from
FK, BSO or BG. B4 bogies.

6351. Mark 1. Lot No. 30091 Doncaster 1954. 33 t.
6352/3. Mark 2A. Lot No. 30774 Derby 1968. 33 t.
6354–6. Mark 2C. Lot No. 30820 Derby 1970. 32 t.
6357. Mark 2C. Lot No. 30798 Derby 1970. 32 t.
6358–9. Mark 2A. Lot No. 30788 Derby 1968. 31.5 t.
6390. Mark 1. Lot No. 30136 Metro-Cammell 1955. 31.5 t.

6351	(3050, 975435)	**BG**	H	*GN*	EC
6352	(13465, 19465)	**BG**	H	*GN*	BN
6353	(13478, 19478)	**BG**	H	*GN*	EC
6354	(9459)		H	*GN*	BN
6355	(9477)	**BG**	H	*GN*	BN
6356	(9455)	**BG**	H	*GN*	BN
6357	(9443)	**BG**	H	*GN*	BN
6358	(9432)	**GN**	H	*GN*	BN
6359	(9429)	**BG**	H	*GN*	BN
6390	(80723, 92900)		H	*GN*	BN

GF5 (BV)   DMU/EMU* BARRIER VEHICLE

Various diagrams. Converted 1992 from BSO or BG*.

6360. Mark 2A. Lot No. 30777 Derby 1967. B4 bogies. 31.5 t.
6361. Mark 2C. Lot No. 30820 Derby 1970. B4 bogies. 32 t.
6364. Mark 1. Lot No. 30039 Derby 1954. BR Mark 1 bogies. 32 t.
6365. Mark 1. Lot No. 30323 Pressed Steel 1957. BR Mark 1 bogies. 32 t.

6360	(9420)		**RR**	P	*P*	NL
6361	(9460)		**RR**	P	*P*	NL
6364	(80565)	*	**RR**	P	*P*	TS
6365	(81296, 84296)	*	**RR**	P	*P*	TS

GS5 (HSBV)   HST BARRIER VEHICLE

Dia. GS507. Mark 1. Converted from BG in 1994–5. B4 bogies.

6392. Lot No. 30715 Gloucester 1962. 29.5 t.
6393/6/7. Lot No. 30716 Gloucester 1962. 29.5 t.
6394. Lot No. 30162 Pressed Steel 1956–57. 30.5 t.
6395. Lot No. 30484 Pressed Steel 1958. 30.5 t.
6398/9. Lot No. 30400 Pressed Steel 1957–58. 30.5 t.

6392	(81588, 92183)	**P**	P	*P*	LA
6393	(81609, 92196)	**P**	P	*P*	LA
6394	(80878, 92906)	**P**	P	*P*	NL
6395	(81506, 92148)	**P**	P	*P*	NL
6396	(81606, 92195)	**P**	P	*P*	LA

6397	(81600, 92190)	**P**	P	*P*	NL
6398	(81471, 92126)	**P**	P	*P*	NL
6399	(81367, 92994)	**P**	P	*P*	NL

AG2C (TSOT)   OPEN STANDARD (TROLLEY)

Dia. AG201. Mark 2C. Converted from TSO by removal of one seating bay and replacing this by a counter with a space for a trolley. Adjacent toilet removed and converted to steward's washing area/store. Pressure ventilated. –/54 1T. B4 bogies. ETH 4.

Lot No. 30795 Derby 1969–70. 32.5 t.

| 6523 | (5569) | **BG** WC | CS | | 6528 | (5592) | **M** WC *ON* | CS |

AG2D (TSOT)   OPEN STANDARD (TROLLEY)

Dia. AG202. Mark 2D. Converted from TSO by removal of one seating bay and replacing this by a counter with a space for a trolley. Adjacent toilet removed and converted to steward's washing area/store. Air conditioned. Stones equipment. –/54 1T. B4 bogies. ETH 5.

Lot No. 30822 Derby 1971. 33 t.

| 6609 | (5698) | H | KN | | 6619 | (5655) | H | KN |

AN1F (RLO)   SLEEPER RECEPTION CAR

Dia. AN101 (AN102*). Mark 2F. Converted from FO, these vehicles consist of pantry, microwave cooking facilities, seating area for passengers, telephone booth and staff toilet. 6703–8 also have a bar. Converted at RTC, Derby (6700), Ilford (6701–5) and Derby (6706–8). Air conditioned. 6700/1/3/5/–8 have Stones equipment and 6702/4 have Temperature Ltd. equipment.26/– 1T. B4 bogies. p. q. d. ETH 5X.

6700–2/4/8. Lot No. 30859 Derby 1973–74. 33.5 t.
6703/5–7. Lot No. 30845 Derby 1973. 33.5 t.

6700	(3347)		**SS**	H	*SR*	IS
6701	(3346)	*		H	*SR*	IS
6702	(3421)	*		H	*SR*	IS
6703	(3308)		**SS**	H	*SR*	IS
6704	(3341)			H	*SR*	IS
6705	(3310, 6430)			H	*SR*	IS
6706	(3283, 6421)		**SS**	H	*SR*	IS
6707	(3276, 6418)			H	*SR*	IS
6708	(3370)			H	*SR*	IS

AN1D (RMBF)   MINIATURE BUFFET CAR

Dia. AN103. Mark 2D. Converted from TSOT by the removal of another seating bay and fitting a proper buffet counter with boiler and microwave oven. Now converted to first class with new seating. Air conditioned. Stones equipment. 30/– 1T. B4 bogies. p. q. d. ETH 5.

Lot No. 30822 Derby 1971. 33 t.

6720	(5622, 6652)	**GW** H	*GW*	OO
6721	(5627, 6660)	**GW** H	*GW*	OO
6722	(5736, 6661)	**GW** H	*GW*	OO
6723	(5641, 6662)	**GW** H	*GW*	OO
6724	(5721, 6665)	**GW** H	*GW*	OO

AC2F (TSO)   OPEN STANDARD

Dia. AC224. Mark 2F. Renumbered from FO and declassified in 1985–6. Converted 1990 to TSO with mainly unidirectional seating and power-operated sliding doors. Air conditioned. 6800–14 were converted by BREL Derby and have Temperature Ltd. air conditioning. 6815–29 were converted by RFS Industries Doncaster and have Stones air conditioning. –/74 2T. B4 bogies. d. ETH 5X.

6800–07. 6810–12. 6813–14. 6819/22/28. Lot No. 30859 Derby 1973–74. 33 t.
6808–6809. Lot No. 30873 Derby 1974–75. 33.5 t.
6815–18. 6820–21. 6823–27. 6829. Lot No. 30845 Derby 1973. 33 t.

6800	(3323, 6435)	**AR** H	*AR*	NC
6801	(3349, 6442)	**AR** H	*AR*	NC
6802	(3339, 6439)	H	*AR*	NC
6803	(3355, 6443)	**AR** H	*AR*	NC
6804	(3396, 6449)	H	*AR*	NC
6805	(3324, 6436)	**AR** H	*AR*	NC
6806	(3342, 6440)	**AR** H	*AR*	NC
6807	(3423, 6452)	H	*AR*	NC
6808	(3430, 6454)	**AR** H	*AR*	NC
6809	(3435, 6455)	**AR** H	*AR*	NC
6810	(3404, 6451)	**AR** H	*AR*	NC
6811	(3327, 6437)	H	*AR*	NC
6812	(3394, 6448)	**AR** H	*AR*	NC
6813	(3410, 6463)	H	*AR*	NC
6814	(3422, 6465)	**AR** H	*AR*	NC
6815	(3282, 6420)	**AR** H	*AR*	NC
6816	(3316, 6461)	**AR** H	*AR*	NC
6817	(3311, 6431)	H	*AR*	NC
6818	(3298, 6427)	**AR** H	*AR*	NC
6819	(3365, 6446)	H	*AR*	NC
6820	(3320, 6434)	**AR** H	*AR*	NC
6821	(3281, 6458)	**AR** H	*AR*	NC
6822	(3376, 6447)	H	*AR*	NC
6823	(3289, 6424)	**AR** H	*AR*	NC
6824	(3307, 6429)	**AR** H	*AR*	NC
6825	(3301, 6460)	**AR** H	*AR*	NC
6826	(3294, 6425)	H	*AR*	NC
6827	(3306, 6428)	**AR** H	*AR*	NC
6828	(3380, 6464)	H	*AR*	NC
6829	(3288, 6423)	**AR** H	*AR*	NC

NM51   MERSEYRAIL SANDITE COACH

Dia. NM504. Mark 1. Former Class 501 750 V d.c. third rail EMU driving trailers converted for use as Sandite/de-icing coaches. BR Mark 1 Bogies.

Lot No. 30328 Eastleigh 1958.   . t.

6910	(75178, 977346)	**MD** RK	*RK*	BD	
6911	(75180, 977348)	**MD** RK	*RK*	BD	

AH2Z (BSOT)   OPEN BRAKE STANDARD (MICRO-BUFFET)

Dia. AH203. Mark 2. Converted from BSO by removal of one seating bay and replacing this by a counter with a space for a trolley. Adjacent toilet removed and converted to a steward's washing area/store. –/23 0T. B4 bogies. ETH 4.

Lot No. 30757 Derby 1966. 31 t.

9100	(9405)	v	**RR**	H		LT
9101	(9398)	v	**RR**	BM		TM
9104	(9401)	v	**G**	MH	*ON*	RL
9105	(9404)	v	**RR**	H		LT

AE21 (BSO)   OPEN BRAKE STANDARD

Dia. AE201. Mark 1. –/39 1T. BR Mark 1 bogies. ETH 3.

Lot No. 30170 Doncaster 1955–56. 34 t.

9227	xk	**M**	SP	*ON*	BT		9274	v		**CH** NY	*ON*	NY

AE2Z (BSO)   OPEN BRAKE STANDARD

Dia. AE203. Mark 2. These vehicles use the same body shell as the Mark 2 BFK and have first class seat spacing and wider tables. Pressure ventilated. –/31 1T. B4 bogies. ETH 4.

Lot No. 30757 Derby 1966. 31.5 t.

9385	v	**LN** H		LT		9388	v	**LN** H	LT

AE2A (BSO)   OPEN BRAKE STANDARD

Dia. AE204. Mark 2A. These vehicles use the same body shell as the Mark 2A BFK and have first class seat spacing and wider tables. Pressure ventilated. –/31 1T. B4 bogies. ETH 4.

9417–24. Lot No. 30777 Derby 1970. 31.5 t.
9428–35. Lot No. 30820 Derby 1970. 31.5 t.

9417	**FT** H	*CA*	CF		9428	**DR** DR	*DR*	KD
9418	**RR** H		PY		9431	**RR** H		PY
9421	**RR** H		CP		9434	**RR** H		ZN
9424	**RR** H		CP		9435	**RR** H		KN

AE2C (BSO)   OPEN BRAKE STANDARD

Dia. AE205. Mark 2C. Pressure ventilated. –/31 1T. B4 bogies. ETH 4.

 Lot No. 30798 Derby 1970. 32 t.

Non-Standard Livery: 9440 is in Royal blue with white lining.

| 9440 | d | **0** | WC | *ON* | CS | | 9448 | d | **M** | WC | *ON* | CS |

AE2D (BSO)   OPEN BRAKE STANDARD

Dia. AE206. Mark 2D. Air conditioned (Stones). –/31 1T. B4 bogies. pg. ETH 5.

r Refurbished with new interior panelling.
s Refurbished with new seating –/22 1TD.

Lot No. 30824 Derby 1971. 33 t.

9479	dr		H	*VX*	MA		9488	ds	**GW**	H	*GW*	OO
9480	d		H		OO		9489	dr	**V**	H	*VX*	MA
9481	ds	**GW**	H	*GW*	OO		9490	ds	**GW**	H	*GW*	OO
9483			H		PY		9492	d		H		OO
9484	d		H		LT		9493	ds	**GW**	H	*GW*	OO
9485			H		LT		9494	ds	**GW**	H	*GW*	OO
9486			H		PY							

AE2E (BSO)   OPEN BRAKE STANDARD

Dia. AE207. Mark 2E. Air conditioned (Stones). –/32 1T. B4 bogies. d. pg. ETH 5.

Lot No. 30838 Derby 1972. 33 t.

r Refurbished with new interior panelling.
s Refurbished with modified design of seat headrest and new interior panelling.

9496	r		H	*VX*	MA		9504	s	**V**	H	*VX*	MA
9497	r		H	*VX*	MA		9505	s		H	*VX*	MA
9498	r	**V**	H	*VX*	MA		9506	s	**V**	H	*VX*	MA
9500	r		H	*VX*	MA		9507	s	**V**	H	*VX*	MA
9501			H		ZN		9508	s	**V**	H	*VX*	MA
9502	s	**V**	H	*VX*	MA		9509	s	**V**	H	*VX*	MA
9503	s	**V**	H	*VX*	MA							

AE2F (BSO)   OPEN BRAKE STANDARD

Dia. AE208. Mark 2F. Air conditioned (Temperature Ltd.). All now refurbished with power-operated vestibule doors, new panels and seat trim. All now further refurbished with carpets and new m.a. sets. –/32 1T. B4 bogies. d. pg. ETH5X.

Lot No. 30861 Derby 1974. 34 t.

| 9513 | **V** | H | *VX* | MA | | 9520 | **V** | H | *VX* | MA |
| 9516 | **V** | H | *VX* | MA | | 9521 | **V** | H | *VX* | MA |

9522		**V**	H	*VX*	MA		9529		**V**	H	*VX*	MA
9523		**V**	H	*VX*	MA		9531		**V**	H	*VX*	MA
9524	n	**V**	H	*VX*	MA		9537	n	**V**	H	*VX*	MA
9525		**V**	H	*VX*	MA		9538		**V**	H	*VX*	MA
9526			H	*VX*	MA		9539		**V**	H	*VX*	MA
9527		**V**	H	*VX*	MA							

AF2F (DBSO) DRIVING OPEN BRAKE STANDARD

Dia. AF201. Mark 2F. Air conditioned (Temperature Ltd.). Push & pull (t.d.m. system). Converted from BSO, these vehicles originally had half cabs at the brake end. They have since been refurbished and have had their cabs widened and the cab-end gangways removed. –/30 1W 1T. B4 bogies. d. pg. Cowcatchers. ETH 5X.

9701–9710. Lot No. 30861 Derby 1974. Converted Glasgow 1979. Disc brakes. 34 t.
9711–9713. Lot No. 30861 Derby 1974. Converted Glasgow 1985. 34 t.
9714. Lot No. 30861 Derby 1974. Converted Glasgow 1986. Disc brakes. 34 t.

9701	(9528)			H	*AR*	NC		9709	(9515)	**AR**	H	*AR*	NC
9702	(9510)	**AR**	H	*AR*	NC		9710	(9518)		H	*AR*	NC
9703	(9517)	**AR**	H	*AR*	NC		9711	(9532)	**AR**	H	*AR*	NC
9704	(9512)	**AR**	H	*AR*	NC		9712	(9534)	**AR**	H	*AR*	NC
9705	(9519)		H	*AR*	NC		9713	(9535)	**AR**	H	*AR*	NC
9707	(9511)	**AR**	H	*AR*	NC		9714	(9536)	**AR**	H	*AR*	NC
9708	(9530)	**AR**	H	*AR*	NC							

AE4E (BUO) UNCLASSIFIED OPEN BRAKE

Dia. AE401. Mark 2E. Converted from TSO with new seating for use on Anglo-Scottish overnight services by Railcare, Wolverton. Air conditioned. Stones equipment. Require at least 800 V train supply. B4 bogies. d. –/31 1T. B4 bogies. ETH 4X.

9801–9803. Lot No. 30837 Derby 1972. 33.5 t.
9804–9810. Lot No. 30844 Derby 1972–73. 33.5 t.

9800	(5751)	**SS**	H	*SR*	IS		9806	(5840)	**SS**	H	*SR*	IS
9801	(5760)	**SS**	H	*SR*	IS		9807	(5851)	**SS**	H	*SR*	IS
9802	(5772)	**SS**	H	*SR*	IS		9808	(5871)		H		ZN
9803	(5799)	**SS**	H	*SR*	IS		9809	(5890)	**SS**	H	*SR*	IS
9804	(5826)	**SS**	H	*SR*	IS		9810	(5892)		H		ZN
9805	(5833)		H		ZN							

AJ1G (RFM) RESTAURANT BUFFET FIRST (MODULAR)

Dia. AJ103 (10200/1 are Dia. AJ101). Mark 3A. Air conditioned. Converted from HST TRFKs, RFBs and FOs. 24/– (r 18/– plus two seats for staff use). BT10 bogies. p. q. d. ETH 14X.

10200–10211. Lot No. 30884 Derby 1977.
10212–10229. Lot No. 30878 Derby 1975–76. 39.8 t.

10230–10260. Lot No. 30890 Derby 1979. 39.8 t.

r Refurbished with table lamps and new burgundy seat trim.

10200	(40519)			**P**	*AR*	NC	10229	(11059)	r **V**	P	*VW*	MA
10201	(40520)	r **V**	P		*VW*	OY	10230	(10021)	r **V**	P	*VW*	PC
10202	(40504)	r **V**	P		*VW*	MA	10231	(10016)	r **V**	P	*VW*	OY
10203	(40506)			**AR**	P	*AR*	NC	10232	(10027)	r **V**	P	*VW*	OY
10204	(40502)	r **V**	P		*VW*	MA	10233	(10013)	r **V**	P	*VW*	PC
10205	(40503)	r **V**	P		*VW*	OY	10234	(10004)	r **V**	P	*VW*	OY
10206	(40507)	r **V**	P		*VW*	MA	10235	(10015)	r	P	*VW*	OY
10207	(40516)	r **V**	P		*VW*	PC	10236	(10018)	r **V**	P	*VW*	PC
10208	(40517)	r **V**	P		*VW*	MA	10237	(10022)	r **V**	P	*VW*	MA
10209	(40508)	r **V**	P		*VW*	PC	10238	(10017)	r **V**	P	*VW*	OY
10210	(40509)	r **V**	P		*VW*	PC	10240	(10003)	r **V**	P	*VW*	OY
10211	(40510)	r **V**	P		*VW*	PC	10241	(10009)		**AR**	P	*AR*	NC
10212	(11049)	r **V**	P		*VW*	MA	10242	(10002)	r	P	*VW*	OY
10213	(11050)	r **V**	P		*VW*	MA	10245	(10019)	r **V**	P	*VW*	PC
10214	(11034)			**AR**	P	*AR*	NC	10246	(10014)	r **V**	P	*VW*	OY
10215	(11032)	r **V**	P		*VW*	PC	10247	(10011)		**AR**	P	*AR*	NC
10216	(11041)			**AR**	P	*AR*	NC	10248	(10005)	r **V**	P	*VW*	OY
10217	(11051)	r **V**	P		*VW*	MA	10249	(10012)	r **V**	P	*VW*	OY
10218	(11053)	r **V**	P		*VW*	MA	10250	(10020)	r **V**	P	*VW*	OY
10219	(11047)	r **V**	P		*VW*	PC	10251	(10024)	r **V**	P	*VW*	OY
10220	(11056)	r **V**	P		*VW*	OY	10252	(10008)	r **V**	P	*VW*	OY
10221	(11012)	r **V**	P		*VW*	PC	10253	(10026)	r **V**	P	*VW*	PC
10222	(11063)	r **V**	P		*VW*	MA	10254	(10006)	r **V**	P	*VW*	PC
10223	(11043)			**AR**	P	*AR*	NC	10255	(10010)	r **V**	P	*VW*	OY
10224	(11062)	r **V**	P		*VW*	MA	10256	(10028)	r **V**	P	*VW*	MA
10225	(11014)	r	P		*VW*	OY	10257	(10007)	r **V**	P	*VW*	PC
10226	(11015)	r **V**	P		*VW*	MA	10258	(10023)	r **V**	P	*VW*	MA
10227	(11057)	r **V**	P		*VW*	PC	10259	(10025)	r **V**	P	*VW*	OY
10228	(11035)			**AR**	P	*AR*	NC	10260	(10001)	r **V**	P	*VW*	MA

AJ1J (RFM)   RESTAURANT BUFFET FIRST (MODULAR)

Dia. AJ105. Mark 4. Air conditioned. 20/– 1T. BT41 bogies. ETH 6X.

Lot No. 31045 Metro-Cammell 1989 onwards. 45.5 t.

10300	**GN**	H	*GN*	BN	10312	**GN**	H	*GN*	BN
10301	**GN**	H	*GN*	BN	10313	**GN**	H	*GN*	BN
10302	**GN**	H	*GN*	BN	10314	**GN**	H	*GN*	BN
10303	**GN**	H	*GN*	BN	10315	**GN**	H	*GN*	BN
10304	**GN**	H	*GN*	BN	10316	**GN**	H	*GN*	BN
10305	**GN**	H	*GN*	BN	10317	**GN**	H	*GN*	BN
10306	**GN**	H	*GN*	BN	10318	**GN**	H	*GN*	BN
10307	**GN**	H	*GN*	BN	10319	**GN**	H	*GN*	BN
10308	**GN**	H	*GN*	BN	10320	**GN**	H	*GN*	BN
10309	**GN**	H	*GN*	BN	10321	**GN**	H	*GN*	BN
10310	**GN**	H	*GN*	BN	10322	**GN**	H	*GN*	BN
10311	**GN**	H	*GN*	BN	10323	**GN**	H	*GN*	BN

10324	**GN**	H *GN*	BN		10329	**GN**	H *GN*	BN
10325	**GN**	H *GN*	BN		10330	**GN**	H *GN*	BN
10326	**GN**	H *GN*	BN		10331	**GN**	H *GN*	BN
10327	**GN**	H *GN*	BN		10332	**GN**	H *GN*	BN
10328	**GN**	H *GN*	BN		10333	**GN**	H *GN*	BN

AU4G (SLEP)   SLEEPING CAR WITH PANTRY

Dia. AU401. Mark 3A. Air conditioned. Retention toilets. 12 compartments with a fixed lower berth and a hinged upper berth, plus an attendants compartment. 2T BT10 bogies. ETH 7X.

Lot No. 30960 Derby 1981–83. 41 t.

10500		SS			ZC		10549	d		P		ZD
10501	d	**SS**	P	*SR*	IS		10550	d		P		ZD
10502	d	**SS**	P	*SR*	IS		10551	d	**SS**	P	*SR*	IS
10503		SS			ZC		10553	d		P	*SR*	IS
10504	d	**SS**	P	*SR*	IS		10554	d		P		ZD
10506	d	**SS**	P	*SR*	IS		10555	d		P		KN
10507	d	**SS**	P	*SR*	IS		10557	d		P		ZD
10508	d		P	*SR*	IS		10558	d		P		ZC
10510	d		P	*SR*	IS		10559	d		P		KN
10512	d		P		ZG		10560	d		P		ZD
10514		SS			ZC		10561	d	**SS**	P	*SR*	IS
10515	d		P	*SR*	IS		10562	d	**SS**	P	*SR*	IS
10516	d	**SS**	P	*SR*	IS		10563	d	**GW**	P	*GW*	PZ
10519	d		P	*SR*	IS		10565	d	**SS**	P	*SR*	IS
10520	d		P	*SR*	IS		10566	d		P		ZD
10522	d	**SS**	P	*SR*	IS		10569	d	**PC**	VS	*ON*	SL
10523	d		P	*SR*	IS		10570			P		KN
10526	d		P	*SR*	IS		10571		SS			BN
10527	d	**SS**	P	*SR*	IS		10572	d		P		ZD
10529	d		P	*SR*	IS		10574			CN		FK
10530	d		P		ZD		10575		SS			ZC
10531	d		P	*SR*	IS		10577		**BG**	P		ZD
10532	d	**GW**	P	*GW*	PZ		10578			P		KN
10533			P		ZD		10579		**BG**	P		KN
10534	d	**GW**	P	*GW*	PZ		10580	d	**SS**	P	*SR*	IS
10535	d		P		ZD		10582	d		P		ZD
10536	d		P		KN		10583	d	**GW**	P	*GW*	PZ
10537	d		P		ZD		10584	d	**GW**	P	*GW*	PZ
10538	d		P		KN		10586	d		P		KN
10539	d		P		KN		10588	d	**GW**	P	*GW*	PZ
10540	d		P		ZD		10589	d	**GW**	P	*GW*	PZ
10542	d	**SS**	P	*SR*	IS		10590	d	**GW**	P	*GW*	PZ
10543	d		P	*SR*	IS		10592			P		KN
10544	d	**SS**	P	*SR*	IS		10593	d		P		KN
10546			P		ZD		10594	d	**GW**	P	*GW*	PZ
10547	d		P	*SR*	IS		10596	d		P		KN
10548	d		P	*SR*	IS		10597	d		P	*SR*	IS

10598 d	**SS**	P	*SR*	IS	10610 d		P	*SR*	IS
10600 d	**SS**	P	*SR*	IS	10612 d	**GW**	P	*GW*	PZ
10601		P		ZD	10613 d	**SS**	P	*SR*	IS
10602		P		ZD	10614 d	**SS**	P	*SR*	IS
10604		P		ZD	10616 d	**GW**	P	*GW*	PZ
10605 d	**SS**	P	*SR*	IS	10617 d	**SS**	P	*SR*	IS
10607 d	**SS**	P	*SR*	IS					

AS4G (SLE/SLED*)   SLEEPING CAR

Dia. AS403 (AS404*). Mark 3A. Air conditioned. Retention toilets. 13 compartments with a fixed lower berth and a hinged upper berth (* 11 compartments with a fixed lower berth and a hinged upper berth + one compartment for a disabled person). 2T. BT10 bogies. ETH 6X.

Notes:

10664/7/9/76/7/81/94/5/8/721 were sold to the Danish State Railways (DSB) when they were numbered in the UIC system. They have since been purchased by Angel Train Contracts and returned to Britain.

10729 is leased to Venice Simplon-Orient Express.

Lot No. 30961 Derby 1980–84. 43.5 t.

10646 d	CN			FK	10685 d		P		IS
10647	P			KN	10686 d		P		ZD
10648 d*	P		*SR*	IS	10687 d		P		ZD
10649 d	P			KN	10688 d	**SS**	P	*SR*	IS
10650 d*	P		*SR*	IS	10689 d*		P	*SR*	IS
10651 d	P			ZD	10690 d		P	*SR*	IS
10653 d	P			ZD	10691 d		P		ZD
10654 d	P			ZD	10692 d		P		ZD
10655	SS			ZC	10693 d		P	*SR*	IS
10657	SS			ZC	10694	**DS**	A		ZC
10658 d	P			KN	10695	**DS**	A		ZC
10660 d	P			ZD	10697 d		P		KN
10662	P			ZD	10698	**DS**	A		ZC
10663 d	P		*SR*	IS	10699 d*		P	*SR*	IS
10664	**DS**	A		ZC	10701 d		P		KN
10666 d*	P		*SR*	IS	10702		SS		ZC
10667	**DS**	A		ZC	10703 d	**SS**	P	*SR*	IS
10668 d	P			ZD	10704 d		P	*AE*	ZA
10669	**DS**	A		ZC	10706 d*		P	*SR*	IS
10675 d	P		*SR*	IS	10708 d		P		ZD
10676	**DS**	A		ZC	10709 d		P		ZD
10677	**DS**	A		ZC	10710 d		P		KN
10678	**BG**	P		KN	10711 d		P		ZD
10679	**BG**	P		KN	10712 d		P		ZD
10680 d*	P		*SR*	IS	10713 d		P		ZD
10681	**DS**	A		ZC	10714 d*		P	*SR*	IS
10682 d	P			ZD	10715 d		P		ZD
10683 d	**SS**	P	*SR*	IS	10716 d		P		ZD

10717	d	P		ZD	10725		SS	ZC
10718	d*	P	SR	IS	10726		SS	ZC
10719	d*	P	SR	IS	10727		SS	ZC
10720		P		KN	10729	**RB**	SS ON	CP
10721	**DS**	A		ZC	10730	d	P	ZD
10722	d*	P	SR	IS	10731	d	P	KN
10723	d*	P	SR	IS	10732	d	P	KN
10724		SS		FK				

AD1G (FO)   OPEN FIRST

Dia. AD108. Mark 3A. Air conditioned. All now refurbished with table lamps and new seat cushions and trim. 48/– 2T (* 48/– 1T 1TD). BT10 bogies. d. ETH 6X.

11005–7 were open composites 11905–7 for a time.

Lot No. 30878 Derby 1975–76. 34.3 t.

11005	V	P	VW	PC	11031	V	P	VW	MA
11006	V	P	VW	PC	11033	V	P	VW	PC
11007	V	P	VW	PC	11036	V	P	VW	MA
11011 *	V	P	VW	MA	11037	V	P	VW	PC
11013	V	P	VW	PC	11038	V	P	VW	PC
11016	V	P	VW	PC	11039	V	P	VW	PC
11017	V	P	VW	PC	11040	V	P	VW	MA
11018	V	P	VW	MA	11042	V	P	VW	MA
11019	V	P	VW	PC	11044	V	P	VW	MA
11020	V	P	VW	MA	11045	V	P	VW	PC
11021	V	P	VW	PC	11046	V	P	VW	PC
11023	V	P	VW	PC	11048	V	P	VW	MA
11024	V	P	VW	MA	11052	V	P	VW	MA
11026	V	P	VW	MA	11054	V	P	VW	PC
11027	V	P	VW	MA	11055	V	P	VW	PC
11028	V	P	VW	MA	11058	V	P	VW	MA
11029	V	P	VW	MA	11060	V	P	VW	PC
11030	V	P	VW	MA					

AD1H (FO)   OPEN FIRST

Dia. AD109. Mark 3B. Air conditioned. Inter-City 80 seats. All now refurbished with table lamps and new seat cushions and trim. 48/– 2T. BT10 bogies. d. ETH 6X.

Lot No. 30982 Derby 1985. 36.5 t.

11064	V	P	VW	MA	11070	V	P	VW	MA
11065	V	P	VW	PC	11071	V	P	VW	PC
11066	V	P	VW	MA	11072	V	P	VW	PC
11067	V	P	VW	PC	11073	V	P	VW	MA
11068	V	P	VW	MA	11074	V	P	VW	MA
11069	V	P	VW	PC	11075	V	P	VW	MA

11076		**V**	P	*VW*	PC	11089	p	**V**	P	*VW*	PC
11077		**V**	P	*VW*	MA	11090	p	**V**	P	*VW*	MA
11078		**V**	P	*VW*	PC	11091	p	**V**	P	*VW*	MA
11079		**V**	P	*VW*	MA	11092	p	**V**	P	*VW*	MA
11080		**V**	P	*VW*	MA	11093	p	**V**	P	*VW*	PC
11081		**V**	P	*VW*	PC	11094	p	**V**	P	*VW*	MA
11082		**V**	P	*VW*	PC	11095	p	**V**	P	*VW*	MA
11083	p	**V**	P	*VW*	MA	11096	p	**V**	P	*VW*	PC
11084	p	**V**	P	*VW*	MA	11097	p	**V**	P	*VW*	MA
11085	p	**V**	P	*VW*	MA	11098	p	**V**	P	*VW*	PC
11086	p	**V**	P	*VW*	PC	11099	p	**V**	P	*VW*	PC
11087	p	**V**	P	*VW*	MA	11100	p	**V**	P	*VW*	PC
11088	p	**V**	P	*VW*	PC	11101	p	**V**	P	*VW*	MA

AD1J (FO)   OPEN FIRST

Dia. AD111. Mark 4. Air conditioned. 46/- 1T. BT41 bogies. ETH 6X.

11264–71 were cancelled.

Lot No. 31046 Metro-Cammell 1989–92. 39.7 t.

11200		**GN**	H	*GN*	BN	11230		**GN**	H	*GN*	BN
11201	p	**GN**	H	*GN*	BN	11231	p	**GN**	H	*GN*	BN
11202		**GN**	H	*GN*	BN	11232		**GN**	H	*GN*	BN
11203	p	**GN**	H	*GN*	BN	11233	p	**GN**	H	*GN*	BN
11204	p	**GN**	H	*GN*	BN	11234		**GN**	H	*GN*	BN
11205		**GN**	H	*GN*	BN	11235	p	**GN**	H	*GN*	BN
11206		**GN**	H	*GN*	BN	11236		**GN**	H	*GN*	BN
11207	p	**GN**	H	*GN*	BN	11237	p	**GN**	H	*GN*	BN
11208		**GN**	H	*GN*	BN	11238		**GN**	H	*GN*	BN
11209		**GN**	H	*GN*	BN	11239	p	**GN**	H	*GN*	BN
11210		**GN**	H	*GN*	BN	11240		**GN**	H	*GN*	BN
11211	p	**GN**	H	*GN*	BN	11241		**GN**	H	*GN*	BN
11212		**GN**	H	*GN*	BN	11242	p	**GN**	H	*GN*	BN
11213	p	**GN**	H	*GN*	BN	11243	p	**GN**	H	*GN*	BN
11214	p	**GN**	H	*GN*	BN	11244		**GN**	H	*GN*	BN
11215		**GN**	H	*GN*	BN	11245	p	**GN**	H	*GN*	BN
11216		**GN**	H	*GN*	BN	11246	p	**GN**	H	*GN*	BN
11217	p	**GN**	H	*GN*	BN	11247	p	**GN**	H	*GN*	BN
11218		**GN**	H	*GN*	BN	11248		**GN**	H	*GN*	BN
11219	p	**GN**	H	*GN*	BN	11249	p	**GN**	H	*GN*	BN
11220		**GN**	H	*GN*	BN	11250		**GN**	H	*GN*	BN
11221	p	**GN**	H	*GN*	BN	11251	p	**GN**	H	*GN*	BN
11222	p	**GN**	H	*GN*	BN	11252		**GN**	H	*GN*	BN
11223		**GN**	H	*GN*	BN	11253	p	**GN**	H	*GN*	BN
11224		**GN**	H	*GN*	BN	11254		**GN**	H	*GN*	BN
11225	p	**GN**	H	*GN*	BN	11255	p	**GN**	H	*GN*	BN
11226		**GN**	H	*GN*	BN	11256		**GN**	H	*GN*	BN
11227	p	**GN**	H	*GN*	BN	11257	p	**GN**	H	*GN*	BN
11228	p	**GN**	H	*GN*	BN	11258		**GN**	H	*GN*	BN
11229	p	**GN**	H	*GN*	BN	11259	p	**GN**	H	*GN*	BN

11260		**GN**	H	*GN*	BN			
11261	p	**GN**	H	*GN*	BN			
11262		**GN**	H	*GN*	BN			
11263	p	**GN**	H	*GN*	BN			
11272		**GN**	H	*GN*	BN			
11273		**GN**	H	*GN*	BN
11274		**GN**	H	*GN*	BN
11275		**GN**	H	*GN*	BN
11276		**GN**	H	*GN*	BN

AC2G (TSO)   OPEN STANDARD

Dia. AC213 (AC220 z). Mark 3A. Air conditioned. All refurbished with modified seat backs and new layout and now further refurbished with new seat trim. – /76 2T (s –/70 2T 2W, z –/70 1TD 1T 2W). BT10 (* BREL T4) bogies. d. ETH 6X.

Note: 12169–72 were converted from open composites 11908–10/22, formerly FOs 11008–10/22.

Lot No. 30877 Derby 1975–77. 34.3 t.

12004		**V**	P	*VW*	MA	12042	s	**V**	P *VW* PC
12005		**V**	P	*VW*	PC	12043		**V**	P *VW* MA
12007		**V**	P	*VW*	MA	12044		**V**	P *VW* MA
12008		**V**	P	*VW*	MA	12045		**V**	P *VW* MA
12009		**V**	P	*VW*	MA	12046		**V**	P *VW* PC
12010		**V**	P	*VW*	MA	12047	z	**V**	P *VW* PC
12011		**V**	P	*VW*	PC	12048		**V**	P *VW* PC
12012		**V**	P	*VW*	PC	12049		**V**	P *VW* PC
12013		**V**	P	*VW*	MA	12050	s	**V**	P *VW* PC
12014		**V**	P	*VW*	PC	12051		**V**	P *VW* PC
12015		**V**	P	*VW*	PC	12052		**V**	P *VW* MA
12016		**V**	P	*VW*	PC	12053		**V**	P *VW* MA
12017		**V**	P	*VW*	MA	12054	s	**V**	P *VW* MA
12019		**V**	P	*VW*	PC	12055		**V**	P *VW* PC
12020		**V**	P	*VW*	PC	12056		**V**	P *VW* PC
12021		**V**	P	*VW*	PC	12057		**V**	P *VW* MA
12022		**V**	P	*VW*	MA	12058		**V**	P *VW* PC
12023		**V**	P	*VW*	PC	12059	s	**V**	P *VW* MA
12024	s	**V**	P	*VW*	PC	12060		**V**	P *VW* PC
12025		**V**	P	*VW*	MA	12061	s	**V**	P *VW* PC
12026		**V**	P	*VW*	PC	12062		**V**	P *VW* PC
12027		**V**	P	*VW*	MA	12063		**V**	P *VW* MA
12028		**V**	P	*VW*	MA	12064		**V**	P *VW* PC
12029		**V**	P	*VW*	MA	12065		**V**	P *VW* MA
12030		**V**	P	*VW*	PC	12066		**V**	P *VW* MA
12031		**V**	P	*VW*	PC	12067		**V**	P *VW* MA
12032		**V**	P	*VW*	PC	12068		**V**	P *VW* MA
12033	z	**V**	P	*VW*	PC	12069		**V**	P *VW* MA
12034		**V**	P	*VW*	MA	12070		**V**	P *VW* PC
12035		**V**	P	*VW*	PC	12071		**V**	P *VW* PC
12036	s	**V**	P	*VW*	PC	12072		**V**	P *VW* MA
12037		**V**	P	*VW*	PC	12073		**V**	P *VW* MA
12038		**V**	P	*VW*	PC	12075		**V**	P *VW* PC
12040		**V**	P	*VW*	PC	12076		**V**	P *VW* PC
12041		**V**	P	*VW*	PC	12077		**V**	P *VW* PC

12078	**V**	P	*VW*	MA	12125	**V**	P	*VW*	MA
12079	**V**	P	*VW*	PC	12126	**V**	P	*VW*	MA
12080	**V**	P	*VW*	PC	12127	**V**	P	*VW*	PC
12081	**V**	P	*VW*	PC	12128 s	**V**	P	*VW*	MA
12082	**V**	P	*VW*	PC	12129	**V**	P	*VW*	MA
12083	**V**	P	*VW*	MA	12130	**V**	P	*VW*	MA
12084	**V**	P	*VW*	MA	12131	**V**	P	*VW*	PC
12085 s	**V**	P	*VW*	MA	12132	**V**	P	*VW*	MA
12086 s	**V**	P	*VW*	MA	12133	**V**	P	*VW*	MA
12087 s	**V**	P	*VW*	PC	12134	**V**	P	*VW*	PC
12088 z	**V**	P	*VW*	PC	12135	**V**	P	*VW*	PC
12089	**V**	P	*VW*	MA	12136	**V**	P	*VW*	PC
12090	**V**	P	*VW*	MA	12137	**V**	P	*VW*	PC
12091	**V**	P	*VW*	PC	12138	**V**	P	*VW*	PC
12092	**V**	P	*VW*	MA	12139	**V**	P	*VW*	MA
12093	**V**	P	*VW*	PC	12140 z*	**V**	P	*VW*	PC
12094	**V**	P	*VW*	PC	12141	**V**	P	*VW*	PC
12095	**V**	P	*VW*	MA	12142 z	**V**	P	*VW*	PC
12096	**V**	P	*VW*	PC	12143	**V**	P	*VW*	PC
12097	**V**	P	*VW*	PC	12144 s	**V**	P	*VW*	PC
12098	**V**	P	*VW*	MA	12145	**V**	P	*VW*	MA
12099	**V**	P	*VW*	PC	12146	**V**	P	*VW*	PC
12100 z	**V**	P	*VW*	PC	12147	**V**	P	*VW*	PC
12101 s	**V**	P	*VW*	PC	12148	**V**	P	*VW*	PC
12102	**V**	P	*VW*	PC	12149	**V**	P	*VW*	PC
12103 s	**V**	P	*VW*	MA	12150	**V**	P	*VW*	PC
12104	**V**	P	*VW*	MA	12151	**V**	P	*VW*	PC
12105	**V**	P	*VW*	PC	12152	**V**	P	*VW*	PC
12106	**V**	P	*VW*	MA	12153	**V**	P	*VW*	PC
12107	**V**	P	*VW*	PC	12154	**V**	P	*VW*	MA
12108 s	**V**	P	*VW*	MA	12155 s	**V**	P	*VW*	PC
12109 s	**V**	P	*VW*	MA	12156	**V**	P	*VW*	MA
12110	**V**	P	*VW*	MA	12157	**V**	P	*VW*	MA
12111	**V**	P	*VW*	MA	12158	**V**	P	*VW*	PC
12112 sz	**V**	P	*VW*	MA	12159	**V**	P	*VW*	PC
12113	**V**	P	*VW*	MA	12160 s	**V**	P	*VW*	PC
12114	**V**	P	*VW*	PC	12161 z	**V**	P	*VW*	MA
12115	**V**	P	*VW*	MA	12163	**V**	P	*VW*	MA
12116	**V**	P	*VW*	PC	12164	**V**	P	*VW*	PC
12117	**V**	P	*VW*	MA	12165	**V**	P	*VW*	MA
12118	**V**	P	*VW*	MA	12166	**V**	P	*VW*	PC
12119	**V**	P	*VW*	MA	12167	**V**	P	*VW*	PC
12120	**V**	P	*VW*	MA	12168 s	**V**	P	*VW*	PC
12121	**V**	P	*VW*	PC	12169 s	**V**	P	*VW*	MA
12122 z	**V**	P	*VW*	MA	12170 s	**V**	P	*VW*	MA
12123	**V**	P	*VW*	PC	12171 s	**V**	P	*VW*	PC
12124	**V**	P	*VW*	MA	12172 s	**V**	P	*VW*	PC

AI2J (TSOE) OPEN STANDARD (END)

Dia. AI201. Mark 4. Air conditioned. –/74 2T. BT41 bogies. ETH 6X.

Lot No. 31047 Metro-Cammell 1989–91. 39.5 t.

12232 was converted from the original 12405.

12200	GN	H *GN*	BN		12216	GN	H *GN*	BN
12201	GN	H *GN*	BN		12217	GN	H *GN*	BN
12202	GN	H *GN*	BN		12218	GN	H *GN*	BN
12203	GN	H *GN*	BN		12219	GN	H *GN*	BN
12204	GN	H *GN*	BN		12220	GN	H *GN*	BN
12205	GN	H *GN*	BN		12222	GN	H *GN*	BN
12206	GN	H *GN*	BN		12223	GN	H *GN*	BN
12207	GN	H *GN*	BN		12224	GN	H *GN*	BN
12208	GN	H *GN*	BN		12225	GN	H *GN*	BN
12209	GN	H *GN*	BN		12226	GN	H *GN*	BN
12210	GN	H *GN*	BN		12227	GN	H *GN*	BN
12211	GN	H *GN*	BN		12228	GN	H *GN*	BN
12212	GN	H *GN*	BN		12229	GN	H *GN*	BN
12213	GN	H *GN*	BN		12230	GN	H *GN*	BN
12214	GN	H *GN*	BN		12231	GN	H *GN*	BN
12215	GN	H *GN*	BN		12232	GN	H *GN*	BN

AL2J (TSOD) OPEN STANDARD (DISABLED ACCESS)

Dia. AL201. Mark 4. Air conditioned. –/72 1TD 1W. BT41 bogies. p. ETH 6X.

Lot No. 31048 Metro-Cammell 1989–91. 39.4 t.

12300	GN	H *GN*	BN		12316	GN	H *GN*	BN
12301	GN	H *GN*	BN		12317	GN	H *GN*	BN
12302	GN	H *GN*	BN		12318	GN	H *GN*	BN
12303	GN	H *GN*	BN		12319	GN	H *GN*	BN
12304	GN	H *GN*	BN		12320	GN	H *GN*	BN
12305	GN	H *GN*	BN		12321	GN	H *GN*	BN
12306	GN	H *GN*	BN		12322	GN	H *GN*	BN
12307	GN	H *GN*	BN		12323	GN	H *GN*	BN
12308	GN	H *GN*	BN		12324	GN	H *GN*	BN
12309	GN	H *GN*	BN		12325	GN	H *GN*	BN
12310	GN	H *GN*	BN		12326	GN	H *GN*	BN
12311	GN	H *GN*	BN		12327	GN	H *GN*	BN
12312	GN	H *GN*	BN		12328	GN	H *GN*	BN
12313	GN	H *GN*	BN		12329	GN	H *GN*	BN
12314	GN	H *GN*	BN		12330	GN	H *GN*	BN
12315	GN	H *GN*	BN					

AC2J (TSO) OPEN STANDARD

Dia. AC214. Mark 4. Air conditioned. –/74 2T. BT41 bogies. ETH 6X.

Lot No. 31049 Metro-Cammell 1989 onwards. 39.9 t.

12405 is the second coach to carry that number. It was built from the bodyshell originally intended for 12221. The original 12405 is now 12232. 12490–12512 were cancelled.

12400	**GN**	H *GN*	BN	12447	**GN**	H *GN*	BN
12401	**GN**	H *GN*	BN	12448	**GN**	H *GN*	BN
12402	**GN**	H *GN*	BN	12449	**GN**	H *GN*	BN
12403	**GN**	H *GN*	BN	12450	**GN**	H *GN*	BN
12404	**GN**	H *GN*	BN	12451	**GN**	H *GN*	BN
12405	**GN**	H *GN*	BN	12452	**GN**	H *GN*	BN
12406	**GN**	H *GN*	BN	12453	**GN**	H *GN*	BN
12407	**GN**	H *GN*	BN	12454	**GN**	H *GN*	BN
12408	**GN**	H *GN*	BN	12455	**GN**	H *GN*	BN
12409	**GN**	H *GN*	BN	12456	**GN**	H *GN*	BN
12410	**GN**	H *GN*	BN	12457	**GN**	H *GN*	BN
12411	**GN**	H *GN*	BN	12458	**GN**	H *GN*	BN
12412	**GN**	H *GN*	BN	12459	**GN**	H *GN*	BN
12413	**GN**	H *GN*	BN	12460	**GN**	H *GN*	BN
12414	**GN**	H *GN*	BN	12461	**GN**	H *GN*	BN
12415	**GN**	H *GN*	BN	12462	**GN**	H *GN*	BN
12416	**GN**	H *GN*	BN	12463	**GN**	H *GN*	BN
12417	**GN**	H *GN*	BN	12464	**GN**	H *GN*	BN
12418	**GN**	H *GN*	BN	12465	**GN**	H *GN*	BN
12419	**GN**	H *GN*	BN	12466	**GN**	H *GN*	BN
12420	**GN**	H *GN*	BN	12467	**GN**	H *GN*	BN
12421	**GN**	H *GN*	BN	12468	**GN**	H *GN*	BN
12422	**GN**	H *GN*	BN	12469	**GN**	H *GN*	BN
12423	**GN**	H *GN*	BN	12470	**GN**	H *GN*	BN
12424	**GN**	H *GN*	BN	12471	**GN**	H *GN*	BN
12425	**GN**	H *GN*	BN	12472	**GN**	H *GN*	BN
12426	**GN**	H *GN*	BN	12473	**GN**	H *GN*	BN
12427	**GN**	H *GN*	BN	12474	**GN**	H *GN*	BN
12428	**GN**	H *GN*	BN	12475	**GN**	H *GN*	BN
12429	**GN**	H *GN*	BN	12476	**GN**	H *GN*	BN
12430	**GN**	H *GN*	BN	12477	**GN**	H *GN*	BN
12431	**GN**	H *GN*	BN	12478	**GN**	H *GN*	BN
12432	**GN**	H *GN*	BN	12479	**GN**	H *GN*	BN
12433	**GN**	H *GN*	BN	12480	**GN**	H *GN*	BN
12434	**GN**	H *GN*	BN	12481	**GN**	H *GN*	BN
12435	**GN**	H *GN*	BN	12482	**GN**	H *GN*	BN
12436	**GN**	H *GN*	BN	12483	**GN**	H *GN*	BN
12437	**GN**	H *GN*	BN	12484	**GN**	H *GN*	BN
12438	**GN**	H *GN*	BN	12485	**GN**	H *GN*	BN
12439	**GN**	H *GN*	BN	12486	**GN**	H *GN*	BN
12440	**GN**	H *GN*	BN	12487	**GN**	H *GN*	BN
12441	**GN**	H *GN*	BN	12488	**GN**	H *GN*	BN
12442	**GN**	H *GN*	BN	12489	**GN**	H *GN*	BN
12443	**GN**	H *GN*	BN	12513	**GN**	H *GN*	BN
12444	**GN**	H *GN*	BN	12514	**GN**	H *GN*	BN
12445	**GN**	H *GN*	BN	12515	**GN**	H *GN*	BN
12446	**GN**	H *GN*	BN	12516	**GN**	H *GN*	BN

12517	**GN**	H	*GN*	BN	12528	**GN**	H *GN*	BN
12518	**GN**	H	*GN*	BN	12529	**GN**	H *GN*	BN
12519	**GN**	H	*GN*	BN	12530	**GN**	H *GN*	BN
12520	**GN**	H	*GN*	BN	12531	**GN**	H *GN*	BN
12521	**GN**	H	*GN*	BN	12532	**GN**	H *GN*	BN
12522	**GN**	H	*GN*	BN	12533	**GN**	H *GN*	BN
12523	**GN**	H	*GN*	BN	12534	**GN**	H *GN*	BN
12524	**GN**	H	*GN*	BN	12535	**GN**	H *GN*	BN
12525	**GN**	H	*GN*	BN	12536	**GN**	H *GN*	BN
12526	**GN**	H	*GN*	BN	12537	**GN**	H *GN*	BN
12527	**GN**	H	*GN*	BN	12538	**GN**	H *GN*	BN

AA11 (FK)   CORRIDOR FIRST

Dia. AA101. Mark 1. 42/– 2T. ETH 3.

13225–13230. Lot No. 30381 Swindon 1959. B4 bogies. 33 t.
13318–13341. Lot No. 30667 Swindon 1962. Commonwealth bogies. 36 t.

f Fitted with fluorescent lighting.

13225	k	**RR**	H		EC	13318		RS *ON*	BN
13227	xk	**CH**	RV	*ON*	CP	13321	x	**M** WC *ON*	CS
13228	xk	**M**	SP		BT	13323	xf	**M** WC	CS
13229	xk	**M**	SP	*ON*	BT	13331	vf	**N** LW	CP
13230	xk	**M**	SP	*ON*	BT	13341	f	**WR** RS *ON*	BN

AA1D (FK)   CORRIDOR FIRST

Dia. AA109. Mark 2D. Air conditioned (Stones). 13585–13607 require at least 800 V train supply. 42/– 2T. B4 bogies. ETH 5.

Lot No. 30825 Derby 1971–72. 34.5 t.

13582		E	KN		13604	CN	BN
13585		RV	KN		13607	CN	FK

AB11 (BFK)   CORRIDOR BRAKE FIRST

Dia. AB101. Mark 1. 24/– 1T. Commonwealth bogies. ETH 2.

17007. Lot No. 30382 Swindon 1959. 35 t.
17013–17019. Lot No. 30668 Swindon 1961. 36 t.
17023. Lot No. 30718 Swindon 1963. Metal window frames. 36 t.

Originally numbered 14007/13/15/18/19/23.

17007	x	**PC**	MN *OS*	SL	17018	v	**CH** BM *ON*	TM
17013		**M**	FS *OS*	SZ	17019	x	**M** NE *OS*	BQ
17015	x	**BG**	RS *ON*	BN	17023	x	**G** RS *ON*	BN

AB1Z (BFK)   CORRIDOR BRAKE FIRST

Dia. AB102. Mark 2. Pressure ventilated. 24/– 1T. B4 bogies. ETH 4.

Lot No. 30756 Derby 1966. 31.5 t.

Originally numbered 14039.

17039 v   **RX** H   *E*   CD

AB1A (BFK)   CORRIDOR BRAKE FIRST

Dia. AB103. Mark 2A. Pressure ventilated. 24/– 1T. B4 bogies. ETH 4.

17056–17077. Lot No. 30775 Derby 1967–8. 32 t.
17086–17102. Lot No. 30786 Derby 1968. 32 t.

Originally numbered 14056–102. 17090 was numbered 35503 for a time when declassified.

17056	**CH**	RV	*ON*	CP		17090	v	**RR**	BM	TM
17058	**N**	H		KN		17091	v	**RR**	H	LT
17064	v **RR**	H		LT		17096		**G**	MN	SL
17077	**H**	H	*CA*	CF		17099	v	**RR**	H	LT
17086	**H**	H	*CA*	CF		17102		**M**	WC	*ON*	CS

AB1D (BFK)   CORRIDOR BRAKE FIRST

Dia. AB106. Mark 2D. Air conditioned (Stones equipment). 17163–17172 require at least 800 V train supply. 24/– 1T. B4 Bogies. ETH 5.

Lot No. 30823 Derby 1971–72. 33.5 t.

Non-Standard Livery: 17141 & 17164 are as **WV** without lining.

Originally numbered 14141–72.

17141	**O**	CN		FK		17163		H		KN
17144		SO	*SO*	ZA		17164	**O**	RV	*ON*	CP
17146		SO	*SO*	ZA		17165		CN		FK
17148		H		KN		17166		H		LT
17151		VS		CP		17167	**VN**	VS	*ON*	CP
17153	**WR**	CN		CS		17168	**M**	WC	*ON*	CS
17155		H		KN		17169		CN		CS
17156		CN		DY		17170		CN		DY
17159	**CH**	RV	*ON*	CP		17171		E		KM
17161		E		OM		17172		CN		FK

AE1G (BFO)   OPEN BRAKE FIRST

Dia. AE101. Mark 3B. Air conditioned. Fitted with hydraulic handbrake. Refurbished with table lamps and burgundy seat trim. 36/– 1T (w 35/– 1T) BT10 bogies. pg. d. ETH 5X.

Lot No. 30990 Derby 1986. 35.81 t.

17173	**V**	P	*VW*	PC		17175	w **V**	P	*VW*	PC
17174	**V**	P	*VW*	PC						

AB31 (BCK)   CORRIDOR BRAKE COMPOSITE

Dia. AB301 (AB302*). Mark 1. There are two variants depending upon whether the standard class compartments have armrests. Each vehicle has two first class and three standard class compartments. 12/18 2T (12/24 2T *). ETH 2.

21224. Lot No. 30245. Metro-Cammell 1958. B4 bogies. 33 t.
21236–21246. Lot No. 30669 Swindon 1961–62. Commonwealth bogies. 36 t.
21252–21256. Lot No. 30731 Derby 1963. Commonwealth bogies. 37 t.
21266–21272. Lot No. 30732 Derby 1964. Commonwealth bogies. 37 t.

21224	**RB**	VS	*ON*	CP	21256	x **M**	WC	*ON*	CS
21236	v **M**	ER	*OS*	ZG	21266	*	FS		SZ
21241	x **M**	SP	*ON*	BT	21268	*	FS		SZ
21245	x **CC**	RS	*ON*	BN	21269	* **WV**	RS	*ON*	BN
21246	**BG**	RS	*ON*	BN	21272	x* **CH**	RV	*ON*	CP
21252	v **G**	MH	*ON*	RL					

AA21 (SK)   CORRIDOR STANDARD

Dia. AA201 (AA202*). Mark 1. There are two variants depending upon whether the standard class compartments have armrests. Each vehicle has eight compartments. All remaining vehicles have metal window frames and melamine interior panelling. Commonwealth bogies. –/48 2T (–/64 2T *). ETH 4.

25729–25893. Lot No. 30685 Derby 1961–62. 36 t.
25955. Lot No. 30686 Derby 1962. 36 t.
26013. Lot No. 30719 Derby 1962. 37 t.

Non-Standard Livery: 25837 and 26013 are Pilkington's K (green with white red chevron and light blue block).

f Facelifted with fluorescent lighting.
t Rebuilt internally as TSO using components from 4936. -/64 2T.

These coaches were renumbered 18729–19013 for a time.

25729	x*f **M**	WC	*ON*	TM	25837	x **0**	WC	*ON*	CS
25756	x **M**	WC	*ON*	TM	25862	x **M**	WC	*ON*	TM
25767	x **CH**	WC	*ON*	TM	25893	x **CH**	WC	*ON*	TM
25806	xt **M**	WC	*ON*	CS	25955	x*f **M**	WC	*ON*	CS
25808	x **M**	WC	*ON*	TM	26013	x **0**	WC	*ON*	CS

AB21 (BSK)   CORRIDOR BRAKE STANDARD

Dia. AB201 (AB202*). Mark 1. There are two variants depending upon whether the standard class compartments have armrests. Each vehicle has four compartments. Lots 30699, 30721 and 30728 have metal window frames and melamine interior panelling. –/24 1T (–/32 1T*). ETH2.

g Fitted with an e.t.s. generator.

34525. Lot No. 30095 Wolverton 1955. Commonwealth bogies. 36 t.
34991. Lot No. 30229 Metro-Cammell 1956–57. Commonwealth bogies. 36 t.

35185–35207. Lot No. 30427 Wolverton 1959. B4 bogies. 33 t.
35317–35333. Lot No. 30699 Wolverton 1962–63. Commonwealth bogies. 37 t.
35407, 35452–35486. Lot No. 30721 Wolverton 1963. Commonwealth Bogies. 37 t.
35449. Lot No. 30728 Wolverton 1963. Commonwealth bogies. 37 t.

Non-Standard Livery: 35407 is in London & North Western Railway livery.

34525	g	**M**	GS		CS		35457	v	**M**	IE *OS*	NY
34991	*	**PC**	VS	*ON*	SL		35459	x	**M**	WC *ON*	CS
35185	x	**M**	SP		BT		35461	x	**CH**	RV *OS*	CP
35207	x*	**CC**	VS	*OS*	SL		35463	v	**M**	WC *OS*	CS
35317	x	**M**	WT	*ON*	CS		35465	x	**WV**	LW *OS*	CP
35322	x	**M**	SH	*ON*	CJ		35467	v	**M**	SV *OS*	KR
35329	v	**G**	MH	*ON*	RL		35468	v	**M**	NR *OS*	YM
35333	x	**CH**	24	*OS*	DI		35469	xg	**CC**	RS *ON*	BN
35407	xg	**O**	SH	*ON*	CJ		35470	v	**CH**	BM *OS*	TM
35449	x	**CH**	14	*OS*	BQ		35476	v	**CC**	62 *OS*	SK
35452	x	**RR**	H	*NW*	CP		35479	v	**M**	SV *OS*	KR
35453	x	**CH**	RV	*ON*	CP		35486	v	**M**	SV *OS*	KR

AB2A/AB2C (BSK)   CORRIDOR BRAKE STANDARD

Dia. AB204. Mark 2A (c 2C). Pressure ventilated. Renumbered from BFK. –/24 1T. B4 bogies. ETH 4.

35507/8/11. Lot No. 30796 Derby 1969–70. 32.5 t.
35510/12–14. Lot No. 30775 Derby 1967–68. 32 t.
35515–18. Lot No. 30786 Derby 1968. 32 t.

* Cage removed from brake compartment.

35507	(14123, 17123)	c	**RR**	H		KN
35508	(14128, 17128)	c	**RR**	RV		CP
35510	(14075, 17075)		**RR**	H		KN
35511	(14130, 17130)	c	**RR**	H		KN
35512	(14057, 17057)	*	**RR**	H		CP
35513	(14063, 17063)	*	**RR**	H	*NW*	CP
35514	(14069, 17069)	*	**RR**	H		CP
35515	(14079, 17079)	*	**RR**	H	*NW*	CP
35516	(14080, 17080)	*	**RR**	H	*NW*	CP
35517	(14088, 17088)	*	**RR**	H	*NW*	CP
35518	(14097, 17097)	*	**RR**	H	*NW*	CP

NAMED COACHES

The following miscellaneous coaches carry names:

1566	CAR 1566		5193	CLAN MACLEOD
1659	CAMELOT		5212	CAPERKAILZIE
1683	Carol		5275	Wendy
1953	LANCASTRIAN		5307	Beverley
3065	ORCHID		5350	Dawn
3066	CHATSWORTH		5364	Andrea
3068	BEAULIEU		5365	Deborah
3069	ALNWICK		5373	Felicity
3105	JULIA		5376	Michaela
3125	LOCH SHIEL		5378	Sarah
3130	PAMELA		9385	BALMACARA
3174	GLAMIS		9388	BAILECHAUL
3181	MONARCH		9417	Ellen
3188	SOVEREIGN		10569	LEVIATHAN
3240	PENDENNIS		10729	OLYMPIC
3267	TREGENNA		17007	MERCATOR
3273	RESTORMEL		17077	Catherine
5132	CLAN MUNRO		17086	Georgina
5154	CLAN FRASER		17167	ASPINALL
5166	CLAN MACKENZIE		21224	DIRECTORS CAR
5191	CLAN DONALD		35449	ELIZABETH

2.2. HIGH SPEED TRAIN TRAILER CARS

HSTs normally run in formations of 7 or 8 trailer cars with a Class 43 power car at each end. All trailer cars are classified Mark 3 and have BT10 bogies with disc brakes and central door locking. Heating is by a 415 V three-phase supply and vehicles have air conditioning. Max. Speed is 125 m.p.h.

All vehicles underwent a mid-life refurbishment in the 1980s, and they are at present undergoing a further refurbishment, each train operating company having a different scheme as follows:

First Great Western. Green seat covers and extra partitions between seat bays.
Great North Eastern Railway. New ceiling lighting panels and brown seat covers. First class vehicles have table lamps and imitation walnut plastic end panels.
Virgin Cross-Country. Green seat covers. Standard class vehicles have four seats in the centre of each carriage replaced with a luggage stack.
Virgin West Coast. Red seat covers in first class and light blue seat covers in standard class.
Midland Mainline. Grey seat covers, redesigned seat squabs, side carpeting and two seats in the centre of each carriage replaced with a luggage stack.

All Midland Mainline, First Great Western, Virgin West Coast , GNER and most Virgin Cross-Country vehicles have now been refurbished.

Tops Type Codes

TOPS type codes for HST trailer cars are made up as follows:

(1) Two letters denoting the layout of the vehicle as follows:

GH	Open
GJ	Open with Guard's compartment.
GK	Buffet
GL	Kitchen
GN	Buffet

(2) A digit for the class of passenger accommodation

1	First
2	Standard (formerly second)
4	Unclassified

(3) A suffix relating to the build of coach.

G	Mark 3

Operator Codes

The normal operator codes are given in brackets after the TOPS codes. These are as follows:

TF	Trailer First		TRFK	Trailer Kitchen First
TGS	Trailer Guard's Standard		TRFM	Trailer Modular Buffet First
TRB	Trailer Buffet First		TRSB	Trailer Buffet Standard
TRFB	Trailer Buffet First		TS	Trailer Standard

GN4G (TRB)   TRAILER BUFFET FIRST

Dia. GN401. Converted from TRSB by fitting first class seats. Renumbered from 404xx series by subtracting 200. 23/–. p. q.

40204–40228. Lot No. 30883 Derby 1976–77. 36.12 t.
40231. Lot No. 30899 Derby 1978–79. 36.12 t.

40204	**GW**	A	*GW*	PM	40210	**GW**	A	*GW*	PM
40205	**GW**	A	*GW*	PM	40213	**GW**	A		ZC
40206	**GW**	A	*GW*	PM	40221	**GW**	A	*GW*	PM
40207	**GW**	A	*GW*	PM	40228	**GW**	A	*GW*	PM
40208	**GW**	A	*GW*	PM	40231	**GW**	A	*GW*	PM
40209	**GW**	A	*GW*	PM					

GK2G (TRSB)   TRAILER BUFFET STANDARD

Dia. GK202. Renumbered from 400xx series by adding 400. –/33 1W. p. q.

40401–40427. Lot No. 30883 Derby 1976–77. 36.12 t.
40429–40437. Lot No. 30899 Derby 1978–79. 36.12 t.

40411/2/32–4 were numbered 40211/2/32–4 for a time when fitted with first class seats.

40401	**V**	P	*VX*	LA	40423	**V**	P	*VX*	LA
40402	**V**	P	*VX*	LA	40424		P	*VX*	LA
40403		P	*VX*	LA	40425	**V**	P	*VX*	LA
40411	**V**	P	*VX*	LA	40426		P	*VX*	LA
40412	**V**	P	*VX*	LA	40427	**V**	P	*VX*	LA
40414	**V**	P	*VX*	LA	40429	**V**	P	*VX*	LA
40415	**V**	P	*VX*	LA	40430	**V**	P	*VX*	LA
40416		P	*VX*	LA	40432	**V**	P	*VX*	LA
40417		P	*VX*	LA	40433	**V**	P	*VX*	LA
40418	**V**	P	*VX*	LA	40434	**V**	P	*VX*	LA
40419	**V**	P	*VX*	LA	40435	**V**	P	*VX*	LA
40420	**V**	P	*VX*	LA	40436	**V**	P	*VX*	LA
40422	**V**	P	*VX*	LA	40437	**V**	P	*VX*	LA

GL1G (TRFK)   TRAILER KITCHEN FIRST

Dia. GL101. Reclassified from TRUK. p. q. 24/–.

Lot No. 30884 Derby 1976–77. 37 t.

40501		P		ZD	40513		P		ZD

GK1G (TRFM)   TRAILER MODULAR BUFFET FIRST

Dia. GK102. Converted to modular catering from TRFB 40719. 17/– 1T. p. q.

Lot No. 30921 Derby 1978–79. 38.16 t.

40619	P	*VX*	LA

GK1G (TRFB)   TRAILER BUFFET FIRST

Dia. GK101. These vehicles have larger kitchens than the 402xx and 404xx series vehicles, and are used in trains where full meal service is required. They were renumbered from the 403xx series (in which the seats were unclassified) by adding 400 to previous number. 17/–. p. q.

40700–40721. Lot No. 30921 Derby 1978–79. 38.16 t.
40722–40735. Lot No. 30940 Derby 1979–80. 38.16 t.
40736–40753. Lot No. 30948 Derby 1980–81. 38.16 t.
40754–40757. Lot No. 30966 Derby 1982. 38.16 t.

40700	**MM**	P	*MM*	NL	40730	**MM**	P	*MM*	NL
40701	**MM**	P	*MM*	NL	40731	**GW**	A	*GW*	LA
40702	**MM**	P	*MM*	NL	40732	**V**	A	*VW*	LA
40703	**GW**	A	*GW*	LA	40733	**GW**	A	*GW*	LA
40704	**GN**	A	*GN*	EC	40734	**GW**	A	*GW*	PM
40705	**GN**	A	*GN*	EC	40735	**GN**	A	*GN*	EC
40706	**GN**	A	*GN*	EC	40736	**GW**	A	*GW*	LA
40707	**GW**	A	*GW*	LA	40737	**GN**	A	*GN*	EC
40708	**MM**	P	*MM*	NL	40738	**GW**	A	*GW*	LA
40709	**GW**	A	*GW*	LA	40739	**GW**	A	*GW*	PM
40710	**GW**	A	*GW*	LA	40740	**GN**	A	*GN*	EC
40711	**GN**	A	*GN*	EC	40741	**MM**	P	*MM*	NL
40712	**GW**	A	*GW*	LA	40742	**V**	A	*VW*	LA
40713	**GW**	A	*GW*	LA	40743	**GW**	A	*GW*	LA
40714	**GW**	A	*GW*	PM	40744	**GW**	A	*GW*	PM
40715	**GW**	A	*GW*	PM	40745	**GW**	A	*GW*	LA
40716	**GW**	A	*GW*	PM	40746	**MM**	P	*MM*	NL
40717	**GW**	A	*GW*	PM	40747	**GW**	A	*GW*	PM
40718	**GW**	A	*GW*	LA	40748	**GN**	A	*GN*	EC
40720	**GN**	A	*GN*	EC	40749	**MM**	P	*MM*	NL
40721	**GW**	A	*GW*	LA	40750	**GN**	A	*GN*	EC
40722	**GW**	A	*GW*	LA	40751	**MM**	P	*MM*	NL
40723	**V**	A	*VW*	LA	40752	**GW**	A	*GW*	LA
40724	**GW**	A	*GW*	PM	40753	**MM**	P	*MM*	NL
40725	**GW**	A	*GW*	LA	40754	**MM**	P	*MM*	NL
40726	**GW**	A	*GW*	LA	40755	**GW**	A	*GW*	LA
40727	**GW**	A	*GW*	LA	40756	**MM**	P	*MM*	NL
40728	**MM**	P	*MM*	NL	40757	**GW**	A	*GW*	LA
40729	**MM**	P	*MM*	NL					

GH1G (TF)   TRAILER FIRST

Dia. GH102. 48/– 2T (w 47/– 2T 1W).

41003–41056. Lot No. 30881 Derby 1976–77. 33.66 t.
41057–41120. Lot No. 30896 Derby 1977–78. 33.66 t.
41121–41148. Lot No. 30938 Derby 1979–80. 33.66 t.
41149–41166. Lot No. 30947 Derby 1980. 33.66 t.
41167–41169. Lot No. 30963 Derby 1982. 33.66 t.

41170. Lot No. 30967 Derby 1982. Former prototype vehicle. 33.66 t.
41179/80. Lot No. 30884 Derby 1976–77. 33.60 t.

s Fitted with centre luggage stack. 46/– 2T 1TD 1W.

41170 was converted from 41001. 41179/80 have been converted from 40505
and 40511 respectively.

41003 p	**GW**	A	*GW*	LA		41051	**GW**	A	*GW*	LA
41004	**GW**	A	*GW*	PM		41052	**GW**	A	*GW*	LA
41005 p	**GW**	A	*GW*	PM		41055	**GW**	A	*GW*	LA
41006	**GW**	A	*GW*	PM		41056	**GW**	A	*GW*	LA
41007 p	**GW**	A	*GW*	PM		41057	**MM**	P	*MM*	NL
41008	**GW**	A	*GW*	PM		41058 s	**MM**	P	*MM*	NL
41009 p	**GW**	A	*GW*	PM		41059 w	**V**	P	*VX*	LA
41010	**GW**	A	*GW*	PM		41060	**GW**	A		ZC
41011 p	**GW**	A	*GW*	PM		41061	**MM**	P	*MM*	NL
41012	**GW**	A	*GW*	PM		41062 w	**MM**	P	*MM*	NL
41013 p	**GW**	A	*GW*	PM		41063	**MM**	P	*MM*	NL
41014	**GW**	A	*GW*	PM		41064 s	**MM**	P	*MM*	NL
41015 p	**GW**	A	*GW*	PM		41065	**GW**	A	*GW*	LA
41016	**GW**	A	*GW*	PM		41066 p	**V**	A	*VW*	LA
41017 p	**GW**	A	*GW*	PM		41067 s	**MM**	P	*MM*	NL
41018	**GW**	A	*GW*	PM		41068 s	**MM**	P	*MM*	NL
41019 p	**GW**	A	*GW*	PM		41069 s	**MM**	P	*MM*	NL
41020	**GW**	A	*GW*	PM		41070 s	**MM**	P	*MM*	NL
41021 p	**GW**	A	*GW*	PM		41071	**MM**	P	*MM*	NL
41022	**GW**	A	*GW*	PM		41072 s	**MM**	P	*MM*	NL
41023 p	**GW**	A	*GW*	LA		41075	**MM**	P	*MM*	NL
41024	**GW**	A	*GW*	LA		41076 s	**MM**	P	*MM*	NL
41025 p	**V**	A	*VW*	LA		41077	**MM**	P	*MM*	NL
41026	**V**	A	*VW*	LA		41078	**MM**	P	*MM*	NL
41027 p	**GW**	A	*GW*	LA		41079	**MM**	P	*MM*	NL
41028	**GW**	A	*GW*	LA		41080 s	**MM**	P	*MM*	NL
41029 p	**GW**	A	*GW*	LA		41081 w	**V**	P	*VX*	LA
41030	**GW**	A	*GW*	LA		41082 w		P	*VX*	LA
41031 p	**GW**	A	*GW*	LA		41083	**MM**	P	*MM*	NL
41032	**GW**	A	*GW*	LA		41084 s	**MM**	P	*MM*	NL
41033 p	**GW**	A	*GW*	LA		41085 w	**V**	P	*VX*	LA
41034	**GW**	A	*GW*	LA		41086 w	**V**	P	*VX*	LA
41035 p	**V**	A	*VW*	LA		41087	**GN**	A	*GN*	EC
41036 w	**V**	A	*VW*	LA		41088 w	**GN**	A	*GN*	EC
41037 p	**GW**	A	*GW*	LA		41089	**GW**	A	*GW*	LA
41038	**GW**	A	*GW*	LA		41090 w	**GN**	A	*GN*	EC
41039	**GN**	A	*GN*	EC		41091	**GN**	A	*GN*	EC
41040	**GN**	A	*GN*	EC		41092 w	**GN**	A	*GN*	EC
41041 ps	**MM**	P	*MM*	NL		41093	**GW**	A	*GW*	LA
41042	**MM**	A		ZC		41094	**GW**	A	*GW*	LA
41043 w	**GN**	A	*GN*	EC		41095 w	**V**	P	*VX*	LA
41044	**GN**	A	*GN*	EC		41096 w	**V**	P	*VX*	LA
41045 w	**V**	P	*VX*	LA		41097 w	**GN**	A	*GN*	EC
41046 s	**MM**	P	*MM*	NL		41098 w	**GN**	A	*GN*	EC

No.						No.					
41099		GN	A	GN	EC	41136		GW	A	GW	LA
41100	w	GN	A	GN	EC	41137	p	GW	A	GW	PM
41101		GW	A	GW	LA	41138		GW	A	GW	PM
41102		GW	A	GW	LA	41139	p	GW	A	GW	LA
41103		GW	A	GW	LA	41140		GW	A	GW	LA
41104		GW	A	GW	LA	41141	p	GW	A	GW	PM
41105		GW	A	GW	PM	41142		GW	A	GW	PM
41106		GW	A	GW	PM	41143	p	GW	A	GW	LA
41107	w	V	P	VX	LA	41144		GW	A	GW	LA
41108	w	V	P	VX	LA	41145	p	GW	A	GW	PM
41109	w	V	P	VX	LA	41146		GW	A	GW	PM
41110		GW	A	GW	PM	41147	w	V	P	VX	LA
41111		MM	P	MM	NL	41148	w	V	P	VX	LA
41112		MM	P	MM	NL	41149	w	V	P	VX	LA
41113	s	MM	P	MM	NL	41150	w	GN	A	GN	EC
41114	w		P	VX	LA	41151		GN	A	GN	EC
41115			P	VX	LA	41152		GN	A	GN	EC
41116		GW	A	GW	LA	41153		MM	P	MM	NL
41117		MM	P	MM	NL	41154	s	MM	P	MM	NL
41118	w	GN	A	GN	EC	41155		MM	P	MM	NL
41119	w	V	P	VX	LA	41156		MM	P	MM	NL
41120		GN	A	GN	EC	41157		GW	A	GW	LA
41121	p	GW	A	GW	LA	41158		GW	A	GW	LA
41122		GW	A	GW	LA	41159	w	V	P	VX	LA
41123	p	GW	A	GW	PM	41160	w	V	P	VX	LA
41124		GW	A	GW	PM	41161	w	V	P	VX	LA
41125		GW	A	GW	PM	41162	w	V	P	VX	LA
41126	p	GW	A	GW	PM	41163	w		P	VX	LA
41127	p	GW	A	GW	PM	41164	p	V	A	VW	LA
41128		GW	A	GW	PM	41165	w		P	VX	LA
41129	p	GW	A	GW	PM	41166	w		P	VX	LA
41130		GW	A	GW	PM	41167	w	V	P	VX	LA
41131	p	GW	A	GW	LA	41168	w	V	P	VX	LA
41132		GW	A	GW	LA	41169	w	V	P	VX	LA
41133	p	GW	A	GW	LA	41170		GN	A	GN	EC
41134		GW	A	GW	LA	41179		GW	A	GW	PM
41135	p	GW	A	GW	LA	41180		GW	A	GW	PM

GH2G (TS)   TRAILER STANDARD

Dia. GH203. –/76 2T. (§ –/70 2T 2W).

42003–42090/42362. Lot No. 30882 Derby 1976–77. 33.60 t.
42091–42250. Lot No. 30897 Derby 1977–79. 33.60 t.
42251–42305. Lot No. 30939 Derby 1979–80. 33.60 t.
42306–42322. Lot No. 30969 Derby 1982. 33.60 t.
42323–42341. Lot No. 30983 Derby 1984–85. 33.60 t.
42342/60. Lot No. 30949 Derby 1982. 33.47 t. Converted from TGS.
42343/5. Lot No. 30970 Derby 1982. 33.47 t. Converted from TGS.
42344/61. Lot No. 30964 Derby 1982. 33.47 t. Converted from TGS.
42346/7/50/1. Lot No. 30881 Derby 1976–77. 33.66 t. Converted from TF.

42348/9. Lot No. 30896 Derby 1977–78. 33.66 t. Converted from TF.
42353/5–7. Lot No. 30967 Derby 1982. Ex prototype vehicles. 33.66 t.
42352/4. Lot No. 30897 Derby 1977. Were TF from 1983 to 1992. 33.66 t.
s Centre luggage stack –/72 2T.
t Centre luggage stack –/72 2T. Fitted with pt.
u Centre luggage stack –/74 2T (w –72 2T 1W).
* disabled persons toilet and 5 tip-up seats. –/65 1T 1TD.

42158 was also numbered 41177 for a time when fitted with first class seats.

42003		**GW**	A	*GW*	PM	42046	**GW**	A	*GW*	LA
42004	*	**GW**	A	*GW*	LA	42047	**GW**	A	*GW*	LA
42005		**GW**	A	*GW*	PM	42048	**GW**	A	*GW*	LA
42006		**GW**	A	*GW*	PM	42049	**GW**	A	*GW*	LA
42007	*	**GW**	A	*GW*	LA	42050	**GW**	A	*GW*	LA
42008	*	**GW**	A	*GW*	PM	42051	§	**V**	A	*VW*	LA
42009		**GW**	A	*GW*	PM	42052		**V**	A	*VW*	LA
42010		**GW**	A	*GW*	PM	42053		**V**	A	*VW*	LA
42012	*	**GW**	A	*GW*	PM	42054	**GW**	A	*GW*	PM
42013		**GW**	A	*GW*	PM	42055	**GW**	A	*GW*	LA
42014		**GW**	A	*GW*	PM	42056	**GW**	A	*GW*	LA
42015	*	**GW**	A	*GW*	PM	42057	**GN**	A	*GN*	EC
42016		**GW**	A	*GW*	PM	42058	**GN**	A	*GN*	EC
42017		**GW**	A	*GW*	PM	42059	**GN**	A	*GN*	EC
42018	*	**GW**	A	*GW*	PM	42060	**GW**	A	*GW*	PM
42019		**GW**	A	*GW*	PM	42061	**GW**	A	*GW*	PM
42020		**GW**	A	*GW*	PM	42062	*	**GW**	A	*GW*	LA
42021	*	**GW**	A	*GW*	PM	42063	**GN**	A	*GN*	EC
42022		**GW**	A	*GW*	PM	42064	**GN**	A	*GN*	EC
42023		**GW**	A	*GW*	PM	42065	**GN**	A	*GN*	EC
42024	*	**GW**	A	*GW*	PM	42066	*	**GW**	A	*GW*	LA
42025		**GW**	A	*GW*	PM	42067	**GW**	A	*GW*	LA
42026		**GW**	A	*GW*	PM	42068	**GW**	A	*GW*	LA
42027		**GW**	A	*GW*	PM	42069	*	**GW**	A	*GW*	PM
42028		**GW**	A	*GW*	PM	42070	**GW**	A	*GW*	PM
42029		**GW**	A	*GW*	PM	42071	**GW**	A	*GW*	PM
42030	*	**GW**	A	*GW*	PM	42072	**GW**	A	*GW*	PM
42031		**GW**	A	*GW*	PM	42073	**GW**	A	*GW*	PM
42032		**GW**	A	*GW*	PM	42074	**GW**	A	*GW*	PM
42033		**GW**	A	*GW*	LA	42075	**GW**	A	*GW*	PM
42034		**GW**	A	*GW*	LA	42076	**GW**	A	*GW*	LA
42035		**GW**	A	*GW*	LA	42077	**GW**	A	*GW*	LA
42036		**V**	A	*VW*	LA	42078	**GW**	A	*GW*	LA
42037		**V**	A	*VW*	LA	42079	**GW**	A	*GW*	PM
42038		**V**	A	*VW*	LA	42080	**GW**	A	*GW*	PM
42039		**GW**	A	*GW*	LA	42081	*	**GW**	A	*GW*	LA
42040		**GW**	A	*GW*	LA	42082	*	**GW**	A		ZC
42041		**GW**	A	*GW*	LA	42083	**GW**	A	*GW*	LA
42042		**GW**	A	*GW*	LA	42084	s	**V**	P	*VX*	LA
42043		**GW**	A	*GW*	LA	42085	t	**V**	P	*VX*	LA
42044		**GW**	A	*GW*	LA	42086	s	**V**	P	*VX*	LA
42045		**GW**	A	*GW*	LA	42087	s	**V**	P	*VX*	LA

42088	s	**V**	P	*VX*	LA	42140	u	**MM**	P	*MM*	NL
42089		**GW**	A	*GW*	PM	42141	u	**MM**	P	*MM*	NL
42090	s	**V**	P	*VX*	LA	42143		**GW**	A	*GW*	LA
42091	s	**V**	P	*VX*	LA	42144		**GW**	A	*GW*	LA
42092			P	*VX*	LA	42145		**GW**	A	*GW*	LA
42093			P	*VX*	LA	42146		**GN**	A	*GN*	EC
42094			P	*VX*	LA	42147	u	**MM**	P	*MM*	NL
42095			P	*VX*	LA	42148	u	**MM**	P	*MM*	NL
42096		**GW**	A	*GW*	LA	42149	u	**MM**	P	*MM*	NL
42097	§	**V**	A	*VW*	LA	42150		**GN**	A	*GN*	EC
42098		**GW**	A	*GW*	PM	42151	uw	**MM**	P	*MM*	NL
42099		**GW**	A	*GW*	LA	42152	u	**MM**	P	*MM*	NL
42100	u	**MM**	P	*MM*	NL	42153	u	**MM**	P	*MM*	NL
42101	uw	**MM**	P	*MM*	NL	42154			A	*GN*	EC
42102	u	**MM**	P	*MM*	NL	42155	uw	**MM**	P	*MM*	NL
42103	s	**V**	P	*VX*	LA	42156	u	**MM**	P	*MM*	NL
42104		**GN**	A	*GN*	EC	42157	u	**MM**	P	*MM*	NL
42105	s	**V**	P	*VX*	LA	42158		**GN**	A	*GN*	EC
42106		**GN**	A	*GN*	EC	42159			P	*VX*	LA
42107		**GW**	A	*GW*	LA	42160			P	*VX*	LA
42108			P	*VX*	LA	42161			P	*VX*	LA
42109			P	*VX*	LA	42162	s	**V**	P	*VX*	LA
42110			P	*VX*	LA	42163	uw	**MM**	P	*MM*	NL
42111	u	**MM**	P	*MM*	NL	42164	u	**MM**	P	*MM*	NL
42112	u	**MM**	P	*MM*	NL	42165	u	**MM**	P	*MM*	NL
42113	u	**MM**	P	*MM*	NL	42166	t	**V**	P	*VX*	LA
42115	t	**V**	P	*VX*	LA	42167	s	**V**	P	*VX*	LA
42116	s	**V**	P	*VX*	LA	42168	t	**V**	P	*VX*	LA
42117	s	**V**	P	*VX*	LA	42169	s	**V**	P	*VX*	LA
42118		**GW**	A	*GW*	PM	42170	s	**V**	P	*VX*	LA
42119	u	**MM**	P	*MM*	NL	42171		**GN**	A	*GN*	EC
42120	u	**MM**	P	*MM*	NL	42172		**GN**	A	*GN*	EC
42121	u	**MM**	P	*MM*	NL	42173	s	**V**	P	*VX*	LA
42122		**V**	A	*VW*	LA	42174	s	**V**	P	*VX*	LA
42123	u	**MM**	P	*MM*	NL	42175	s	**V**	P	*VX*	LA
42124	u	**MM**	P	*MM*	NL	42176	t	**V**	P	*VX*	LA
42125	u	**MM**	P	*MM*	NL	42177	s	**V**	P	*VX*	LA
42126		**GW**	A	*GW*	LA	42178	s	**V**	P	*VX*	LA
42127	s	**V**	P	*VX*	LA	42179		**GN**	A	*GN*	EC
42128	s	**V**	P	*VX*	LA	42180		**GN**	A	*GN*	EC
42129		**GW**	A	*GW*	LA	42181		**GN**	A	*GN*	EC
42130	s	**V**	P	*VX*	LA	42182		**GN**	A	*GN*	EC
42131	u	**MM**	P	*MM*	NL	42183	*	**GW**	A	*GW*	LA
42132	u	**MM**	P	*MM*	NL	42184		**GW**	A	*GW*	LA
42133	u	**MM**	P	*MM*	NL	42185		**GW**	A	*GW*	LA
42134		**V**	A	*VW*	LA	42186		**GN**	A	*GN*	EC
42135	u	**MM**	P	*MM*	NL	42187	t	**V**	P	*VX*	LA
42136	u	**MM**	P	*MM*	NL	42188	s	**V**	P	*VX*	LA
42137	u	**MM**	P	*MM*	NL	42189	s	**V**	P	*VX*	LA
42138	*	**GW**	A	*GW*	PM	42190		**GN**	A	*GN*	EC
42139	u	**MM**	P	*MM*	NL	42191		**GN**	A	*GN*	EC

No.					
42192		**GN**	A	*GN*	EC
42193		**GN**	A	*GN*	EC
42194	uw	**MM**	P	*MM*	NL
42195	s	**V**	P	*VX*	LA
42196		**GW**	A	*GW*	LA
42197		**GW**	A	*GW*	PM
42198		**GN**	A	*GN*	EC
42199		**GN**	A	*GN*	EC
42200	*	**GW**	A	*GW*	LA
42201	*	**GW**	A	*GW*	LA
42202	*	**GW**	A	*GW*	LA
42203		**GW**	A	*GW*	LA
42204		**GW**	A	*GW*	LA
42205	u	**MM**	P	*MM*	NL
42206	*	**GW**	A	*GW*	LA
42207	*	**GW**	A	*GW*	LA
42208		**GW**	A	*GW*	LA
42209		**GW**	A	*GW*	LA
42210	u	**MM**	P	*MM*	NL
42211	*	**GW**	A	*GW*	PM
42212		**GW**	A	*GW*	PM
42213		**GW**	A	*GW*	PM
42214		**GW**	A	*GW*	PM
42215		**GN**	A	*GN*	EC
42216		**GW**	A	*GW*	LA
42217	t	**V**	P	*VX*	LA
42218	t	**V**	P	*VX*	LA
42219		**GN**	A	*GN*	EC
42220	uw	**MM**	P	*MM*	NL
42221		**GW**	A	*GW*	LA
42222	t	**V**	P	*VX*	LA
42223	s	**V**	P	*VX*	LA
42224	s	**V**	P	*VX*	LA
42225	u	**MM**	P	*MM*	NL
42226		**GN**	A	*GN*	EC
42227	u	**MM**	P	*MM*	NL
42228	u	**MM**	P	*MM*	NL
42229	u	**MM**	P	*MM*	NL
42230	u	**MM**	P	*MM*	NL
42231			P	*VX*	LA
42232			P	*VX*	LA
42233			P	*VX*	LA
42234			P	*VX*	LA
42235		**GN**	A	*GN*	EC
42236		**GW**	A	*GW*	PM
42237		**V**	P	*VX*	LA
42238		**V**	P	*VX*	LA
42239		**V**	P	*VX*	LA
42240		**GN**	A	*GN*	EC
42241		**GN**	A	*GN*	EC
42242		**GN**	A	*GN*	EC
42243		**GN**	A	*GN*	EC
42244		**GN**	A	*GN*	EC
42245		**GW**	A	*GW*	LA
42246	s	**V**	P	*VX*	LA
42247	t	**V**	P	*VX*	LA
42248	s	**V**	P	*VX*	LA
42249	s	**V**	P	*VX*	LA
42250		**GW**	A	*GW*	LA
42251	*	**GW**	A	*GW*	PM
42252		**GW**	A	*GW*	LA
42253		**GW**	A	*GW*	LA
42254	s	**V**	P	*VX*	LA
42255	*	**GW**	A	*GW*	PM
42256		**GW**	A	*GW*	PM
42257		**GW**	A	*GW*	PM
42258	t	**V**	P	*VX*	LA
42259	*	**GW**	A	*GW*	PM
42260		**GW**	A	*GW*	PM
42261		**GW**	A	*GW*	PM
42262	s	**V**	P	*VX*	LA
42263		**GW**	A	*GW*	PM
42264	*	**GW**	A	*GW*	PM
42265		**GW**	A	*GW*	LA
42266	s	**V**	P	*VX*	LA
42267	*	**GW**	A	*GW*	PM
42268	*	**GW**	A	*GW*	LA
42269		**GW**	A	*GW*	PM
42270	s	**V**	P	*VX*	LA
42271	*	**GW**	A	*GW*	LA
42272		**GW**	A	*GW*	LA
42273		**GW**	A	*GW*	LA
42274	t	**V**	P	*VX*	LA
42275	*	**GW**	A	*GW*	LA
42276		**GW**	A	*GW*	LA
42277		**GW**	A	*GW*	LA
42278	s	**V**	P	*VX*	LA
42279	*	**GW**	A	*GW*	LA
42280		**GW**	A	*GW*	LA
42281		**GW**	A	*GW*	LA
42282	s	**V**	P	*VX*	LA
42283		**GW**	A	*GW*	LA
42284		**GW**	A	*GW*	PM
42285		**GW**	A	*GW*	PM
42286	s	**V**	P	*VX*	LA
42287	*	**GW**	A	*GW*	LA
42288		**GW**	A	*GW*	LA
42289		**GW**	A	*GW*	LA
42290	t	**V**	P	*VX*	LA
42291	*	**GW**	A	*GW*	PM
42292	*	**GW**	A	*GW*	LA
42293		**GW**	A	*GW*	PM

42294	s	**V**	P	*VX*	LA	42318	s	**V**	P	*VX*	LA
42295	*	**GW**	A	*GW*	LA	42319	t	**V**	P	*VX*	LA
42296		**GW**	A	*GW*	LA	42320	s	**V**	P	*VX*	LA
42297		**GW**	A	*GW*	LA	42321	s	**V**	P	*VX*	LA
42298	s	**V**	P	*VX*	LA	42322			P	*VX*	LA
42299	*	**GW**	A	*GW*	PM	42323		**GN**	A	*GN*	EC
42300		**GW**	A	*GW*	PM	42324	uw	**MM**	P	*MM*	NL
42301		**GW**	A	*GW*	PM	42325		**GW**	A	*GW*	PM
42302	s	**V**	P	*VX*	LA	42326	s	**V**	P	*VX*	LA
42303	t	**V**	P	*VX*	LA	42327	uw	**MM**	P	*MM*	NL
42304	s	**V**	P	*VX*	LA	42328	uw	**MM**	P	*MM*	NL
42305	s	**V**	P	*VX*	LA	42329	uw	**MM**	P	*MM*	NL
42306			P	*VX*	LA	42330		**V**	P	*VX*	LA
42307			P	*VX*	LA	42331	uw	**MM**	P	*MM*	NL
42308			P	*VX*	LA	42332		**GW**	A	*GW*	PM
42309			P	*VX*	LA	42333		**GW**	A	*GW*	LA
42310	s	**V**	P	*VX*	LA	42334	s	**V**	P	*VX*	LA
42311	t	**V**	P	*VX*	LA	42335	uw	**MM**	P	*MM*	NL
42312	s	**V**	P	*VX*	LA	42336	s	**V**	P	*VX*	LA
42313	s	**V**	P	*VX*	LA	42337	uw	**MM**	P	*MM*	NL
42314	s	**V**	P	*VX*	LA	42338	s	**V**	P	*VX*	LA
42315	t	**V**	P	*VX*	LA	42339	uw	**MM**	P	*MM*	NL
42316	s	**V**	P	*VX*	LA	42340		**GN**	A	*GN*	EC
42317	s	**V**	P	*VX*	LA	42341	uw	**MM**	P	*MM*	NL

42342	(44082)		**V**	A	*VW*	LA
42343	(44095)		**GW**	A	*GW*	LA
42344	(44092)	*	**GW**	A	*GW*	PM
42345	(44096)	*	**GW**	A	*GW*	LA
42346	(41053)		**GW**	A	*GW*	PM
42347	(41054)	*	**GW**	A	*GW*	PM
42348	(41073)	*	**GW**	A	*GW*	LA
42349	(41074)		**GW**	A	*GW*	PM
42350	(41047)		**GW**	A	*GW*	LA
42351	(41048)		**GW**	A	*GW*	PM
42352	(42142, 41176)	u	**MM**	P	*MM*	NL
42353	(42001, 41171)	s	**V**	P	*VX*	LA
42354	(42114, 41175)		**GN**	A	*GN*	EC
42355	(42000, 41172)	§	**V**	A	*VW*	LA
42356	(42002, 41173)		**GW**	A	*GW*	PM
42357	(41002, 41174)		**V**	A	*VW*	LA
42360	(44084, 45084)		**GW**	A	*VW*	PM
42361	(44099)		**GW**	A	*GW*	PM
42362	(42011, 41178)		**GW**	A	*GW*	PM

GJ2G (TGS)   TRAILER GUARD'S STANDARD

Dia. GJ205. –/65 1T (w –/63 1T 1W). pg.

44000. Lot No. 30953 Derby 1980. 33.47 t.
44001–44090. Lot No. 30949 Derby 1980–82. 33.47 t.
44091–44094. Lot No. 30964 Derby 1982. 33.47 t.

44097–44101. Lot No. 30970 Derby 1982. 33.47 t.

s t Fitted with centre luggage stack s –/63 1T, t –/61 1T.

44000	t	**V**	P	*VX*	LA	44048	s	**MM**	P	*MM*	NL
44001	w	**GW**	A	*GW*	LA	44049	w	**GW**	A	*GW*	LA
44002	w	**GW**	A	*GW*	PM	44050	s	**MM**	P	*MM*	NL
44003	w	**GW**	A	*GW*	PM	44051	s	**MM**	P	*MM*	NL
44004	w	**GW**	A	*GW*	PM	44052	s	**MM**	P	*MM*	NL
44005	w	**GW**	A	*GW*	PM	44053	w		P	*VX*	LA
44006	w	**GW**	A	*GW*	PM	44054		**MM**	P	*MM*	NL
44007	w	**GW**	A	*GW*	PM	44055	t	**V**	P	*VX*	LA
44008	w	**GW**	A	*GW*	PM	44056	w	**GN**	A	*GN*	EC
44009	w	**GW**	A	*GW*	PM	44057	t	**V**	P	*VX*	LA
44010	w	**GW**	A	*GW*	PM	44058	w	**GN**	A	*GN*	EC
44011	w	**GW**	A	*GW*	LA	44059	w	**GW**	A	*GW*	LA
44012		**V**	A	*VW*	LA	44060		**V**	P	*VX*	LA
44013	w	**GW**	A	*GW*	LA	44061	w	**GN**	A	*GN*	EC
44014	w	**GW**	A	*GW*	LA	44062	t	**V**	P	*VX*	LA
44015	w	**GW**	A	*GW*	LA	44063	w	**GN**	A	*GN*	EC
44016	w	**GW**	A	*GW*	LA	44064	w	**GW**	A	*GW*	LA
44017		**V**	A	*VW*	LA	44065	t	**V**	P	*VX*	LA
44018	w	**GW**	A	*GW*	LA	44066	w	**GW**	A	*GW*	LA
44019	w	**GN**	A	*GN*	EC	44067	w	**GW**	A	*GW*	PM
44020	w	**GW**	A	*GW*	PM	44068	t	**V**	P	*VX*	LA
44021	t	**V**	P	*VX*	LA	44069	t	**V**	P	*VX*	LA
44022	w	**GW**	A	*GW*	LA	44070	s	**MM**	P	*MM*	NL
44023	w	**GW**	A	*GW*	PM	44071	s	**MM**	P	*MM*	NL
44024	w	**GW**	A	*GW*	PM	44072	t	**V**	P	*VX*	LA
44025	w	**GW**	A	*GW*	LA	44073	s	**MM**	P	*MM*	NL
44026	w	**GW**	A	*GW*	PM	44074			P	*VX*	LA
44027	s	**MM**	P	*MM*	NL	44075	t	**V**	P	*VX*	LA
44028	w	**GW**	A	*GW*	LA	44076			P	*VX*	LA
44029	w	**GW**	A	*GW*	PM	44077	w	**GN**	A	*GN*	EC
44030	w	**GW**	A	*GW*	PM	44078	t	**V**	P	*VX*	LA
44031		**V**	A	*VW*	LA	44079	t	**V**	P	*VX*	LA
44032	w	**GW**	A	*GW*	PM	44080	w	**GN**	A	*GN*	EC
44033	w	**GW**	A	*GW*	LA	44081	t	**V**	P	*VX*	LA
44034	w	**GW**	A	*GW*	LA	44083	s	**MM**	P	*MM*	NL
44035	w	**GW**	A	*GW*	LA	44085	s	**MM**	P	*MM*	NL
44036	w	**GW**	A	*GW*	PM	44086	w	**GW**	A	*GW*	LA
44037	w	**GW**	A	*GW*	LA	44087			P	*VX*	LA
44038	w	**GW**	A	*GW*	PM	44088			P	*VX*	LA
44039	w	**GW**	A	*GW*	LA	44089	t	**V**	P	*VX*	LA
44040	w	**GW**	A	*GW*	PM	44090	t	**V**	P	*VX*	LA
44041	s	**MM**	P	*MM*	NL	44091	t	**V**	P	*VX*	LA
44042	t	**V**	P	*VX*	LA	44093	w	**GW**	A	*GW*	LA
44043	w	**GW**	A	*GW*	LA	44094	w	**GN**	A	*GN*	EC
44044	s	**MM**	P	*MM*	NL	44097	t	**V**	P	*VX*	LA
44045	w	**GN**	A	*GN*	EC	44098	w	**GN**	A	*GN*	EC
44046	s	**MM**	P	*MM*	NL	44100	t	**V**	P	*VX*	LA
44047	s	**MM**	P	*MM*	NL	44101	t	**V**	P	*VX*	LA

2.3. NIGHTSTAR STOCK

These coaches were designed for use on new 'Nightstar' services between Britain and Continental Europe via the Channel Tunnel. This new generation of overnight trains was to offer high quality accommodation to both business and leisure customers.

The venture was being developed by European Night Services Limited (ENS), a joint company of Eurostar (UK) Ltd., SNCF, DB and NS. It was originally intended that the trains would operate on the following routes:

London Waterloo–Amsterdam CS.
London Waterloo–Dortmund Hbf./Frankfurt Hbf.
Glasgow Central/Manchester Piccadilly–Paris Nord.
Plymouth/Swansea–Paris Nord.

Unfortunately the project has now been completely cancelled because of both technical and commercial problems, e.g. there is no locomotive in Belgium which has enough power for the train heating and air conditioning for the length of train envisaged!

Both sleeping cars and reclining seat coaches have been built. Each train was due to be formed of two half-sets, London services having two reclining seat coaches, a service vehicle and five sleeping cars in each half-set to form a sixteen coach train, whilst services from the Provinces to Paris were to be fourteen coaches long with each portion consisting of three sleeping cars, a service vehicle and three reclining seat coaches. The "regional" half-sets were to be numbered 1–9, whilst the "London" half-sets were to be numbered 10–18.

In the following lists, the UIC number for each vehicle is followed by the set number to which it was to belong. All stock is the property of Alstom, the manufacturer. Stock is stored at MoD Kineton, MoD Bicester or the Alstom works at Washwood Heath, Birmingham. Current locations are shown where known.

RECLINING SEAT CARS   SO End

Each car has 50 seats which are fully reclining, with generous leg space. A table and footrests are provided at each seat. The seats are mounted on plinths and main luggage is stored beneath the seat, while hand baggage is stored in overhead lockers. Individually controlled reading lights are provided, with different levels of ambient lighting for sleeping and non-sleeping hours. Each car has three toilet compartments with shaver sockets.

61 19 20-90 001-0	1	KN	61 19 20-90 010-1	10	
61 19 20-90 002-8	2	KN	61 19 20-90 011-9	11	
61 19 20-90 003-6	3	KN	61 19 20-90 012-7	12	
61 19 20-90 004-4	4	KN	61 19 20-90 013-5	13	
61 19 20-90 005-1	5	ZE	61 19 20-90 014-3	14	
61 19 20-90 006-9	6	KN	61 19 20-90 015-0	15	
61 19 20-90 007-7	7		61 19 20-90 016-8	16	
61 19 20-90 008-5	8		61 19 20-90 017-6	17	
61 19 20-90 009-3	9		61 19 20-90 018-4	18	

RECLINING SEAT CAR   SO

Details as above, but no coupling for locomotive.

61 19 20-90 019-2	1	KN	61 19 20-90 034-1	8	
61 19 20-90 020-0	1	KN	61 19 20-90 035-8	9	
61 19 20-90 021-8	2	KN	61 19 20-90 036-6	9	
61 19 20-90 022-6	2	KN	61 19 20-90 037-4	10	
61 19 20-90 023-4	3	KN	61 19 20-90 038-2	11	
61 19 20-90 024-2	3	KN	61 19 20-90 039-0	12	
61 19 20-90 025-9	4	KN	61 19 20-90 040-8	13	
61 19 20-90 026-7	4	KN	61 19 20-90 041-6	14	
61 19 20-90 027-5	5	KN	61 19 20-90 042-4	15	
61 19 20-90 028-3	5	KN	61 19 20-90 043-2	16	
61 19 20-90 029-1	6	ZE	61 19 20-90 044-0	17	
61 19 20-90 030-9	6	KN	61 19 20-90 045-7	18	
61 19 20-90 031-7	7		61 19 20-90 046-5	S	KN
61 19 20-90 032-5	7		61 19 20-90 047-3	S	KN
61 19 20-90 033-3	8				

SLEEPING CARS   SLF End

Each sleeping car has 10 cabins. Six of these have a compact en-suite shower room, with a washbasin, toilet and hairdryers. The remaining four cabins include en-suite toilet and washing facilities, but without the shower.

All cabins are convertible so that when the bunks are folded away by the attendant after passengers have got up, two comfortable armchairs with fold-out tables are revealed. The bunks themselves are generously sized one above the other and will already be made up with duvets, sheets and pillows when passengers arrive. Each cabin has a fitted wardrobe and cupboard, together with facilities for making hot drinks. Cabin telephones are provided for room service.

61 19 70-90 001-9	1	KN	61 19 70-90 010-0	10	
61 19 70-90 002-7	2	KN	61 19 70-90 011-8	11	
61 19 70-90 003-5	3	KN	61 19 70-90 012-6	12	
61 19 70-90 004-3	4	KN	61 19 70-90 013-4	13	
61 19 70-90 005-0	5	KN	61 19 70-90 014-2	14	
61 19 70-90 006-8	6	ZE	61 19 70-90 015-9	15	
61 19 70-90 007-6	7		61 19 70-90 016-7	16	
61 19 70-90 008-4	8		61 19 70-90 017-5	17	
61 19 70-90 009-2	9		61 19 70-90 018-3	18	

SLEEPING CARS   SLF

Details as above, but no coupling for locomotive.

61 19 70-90 019-1	1	KN	61 19 70-90 046-4	12	
61 19 70-90 020-9	1	KN	61 19 70-90 047-2	12	
61 19 70-90 021-7	2	KN	61 19 70-90 048-0	12	
61 19 70-90 022-5	2	KN	61 19 70-90 049-8	13	
61 19 70-90 023-3	3	KN	61 19 70-90 050-6	13	
61 19 70-90 024-1	3	KN	61 19 70-90 051-4	13	
61 19 70-90 025-8	4	KN	61 19 70-90 052-2	13	
61 19 70-90 026-6	4	KN	61 19 70-90 053-0	14	
61 19 70-90 027-4	5	KN	61 19 70-90 054-8	14	
61 19 70-90 028-2	5	KN	61 19 70-90 055-5	14	
61 19 70-90 029-0	6	ZE	61 19 70-90 056-3	14	
61 19 70-90 030-8	6	KN	61 19 70-90 057-1	15	
61 19 70-90 031-6	7		61 19 70-90 058-9	15	
61 19 70-90 032-4	7		61 19 70-90 059-7	15	
61 19 70-90 033-2	8		61 19 70-90 060-5	15	
61 19 70-90 034-0	8		61 19 70-90 061-3	16	
61 19 70-90 035-7	9		61 19 70-90 062-1	16	
61 19 70-90 036-5	9		61 19 70-90 063-9	16	
61 19 70-90 037-3	10	KN	61 19 70-90 064-7	16	
61 19 70-90 038-1	10		61 19 70-90 065-4	17	
61 19 70-90 039-9	10		61 19 70-90 066-2	17	
61 19 70-90 040-7	10		61 19 70-90 067-0	17	
61 19 70-90 041-5	11		61 19 70-90 068-8	17	
61 19 70-90 042-3	11		61 19 70-90 069-6	18	
61 19 70-90 043-1	11		61 19 70-90 070-4	18	
61 19 70-90 044-9	11		61 19 70-90 071-2	18	
61 19 70-90 045-6	11		61 19 70-90 072-0	18	

SERVICE VEHICLE/LOUNGE CAR   SV

Lounge cars are positioned in each half of the train, between the sleeping cars and the seated accommodation. These vehicles consist of of a sleeping cabin for a disabled passenger and companion with en-suite washroom, a parcels room, offices for train manager and control authority, a lounge with bar for sleeping car passengers and public telephone and a bar for seated passengers.

The vehicle also acts as a base for the sleeping car attendants and for the trolley service which is provided for the seated passengers in the evening. There is also a seated passengers' counter so that snacks and drinks can be obtained during sleeping hours.

61 19 89-90 001-8	1	KN	61 19 89-90 011-7	11	
61 19 89-90 002-6	2	KN	61 19 89-90 012-5	12	
61 19 89-90 003-4	3	KN	61 19 89-90 013-3	13	
61 19 89-90 004-2	4	KN	61 19 89-90 014-1	14	
61 19 89-90 005-9	5	KN	61 19 89-90 015-8	15	
61 19 89-90 006-7	6	KN	61 19 89-90 016-6	16	
61 19 89-90 007-5	7		61 19 89-90 017-4	17	
61 19 89-90 008-3	8		61 19 89-90 018-2	18	
61 19 89-90 009-1	9		61 19 89-90 019-0	S	
61 19 89-90 010-9	10		61 19 89-90 020-8	S	

2.4. SALOONS

Several specialist passenger carrying vehicles, normally referred to as saloons are permitted to run on the Railtrack system. Many of these are to pre-nation-alisation designs.

LNER GENERAL MANAGERS SALOON

Dia. AO133. Built 1945 by LNER, York. Gangwayed at one end with a veran-dah at the other. The interior has a dining saloon seating twelve, kitchen, toi-let, office and nine seat lounge. 21/– 1T. B4 bogies. ETH3. 35.7 t.

1999   (902260)   **M**   GS   *ON*   EN

GNR FIRST CLASS SALOON

Dia. AO132. Built 1912 by GNR, Doncaster. Contains entrance vestibule, lava-tory, two seperate saloons and luggage space. Gresley bogies. 19/– 1T. 75 m.p.h. 29.4 t.

Non-Standard Livery: Teak.

4807   (807)   x   **0**   SH   *ON*   CJ

LNWR DINING SALOON

Dia. AO131. Built 1890 by LNWR, Wolverton. Mounted on the underframe of LMS GUV 37908 in the 1980s. Contains kitchen and dining area seating 10 at two tables. Gresley bogies. 10/–. 75 m.p.h. 25.4 t.

Non-Standard Livery: London & North Western Railway.

5159   (159)   x   **0**   SH   *ON*   CJ

GENERAL MANAGER'S SALOON

Dia. AZ501. Renumbered 1989 from London Midland Region departmental series. Formerly the LMR General Manager's saloon. Rebuilt from LMS period 1 BFK M 5033 M to dia. 1654 and mounted on the underframe of BR suburban BS M 43232. Screw couplings have been removed. B4 bogies. 100 m.p.h. ETH2X.

LMS Lot No. 326 Derby 1927. 27.5 t.

Non-Standard Livery: Aircraft blue with gold lining.

6320   (5033, DM 395707) x   **0**   RV   *ON*   CP

GWR FIRST CLASS SALOON

Dia. AO103. Built 1930 by GWR, Swindon. Contains saloons at either end with body end observation windows, staff compartment, central kitchen and pantry/bar. Numbered DE321011 when in departmental service with British Railways. 20/– 1T. GWR bogies. 75 m.p.h. 34 t.

GWR Lot No. 1431 1930.

9004   x   **CH**   RA   *ON*   CP

WCJS OBSERVATION SALOON

Dia. AO102. Built 1892 by LNWR, Wolverton. Originally dining saloon mounted on six-wheel bogies. Rebuilt with new underframe with four-wheel bogies in 1927. Rebuilt 1960 as observation saloon with DMU end. Gangwayed at other end. The interior has a saloon, kitchen, guards vestibule and observation lounge. Gresley bogies. 19/– 1T. 28.5 t. 75 m.p.h.

Non-Standard Livery: London & North Western Railway.

45018 (484, 15555)   x   **0**   SH   *ON*   CJ

LMS INSPECTION SALOONS

Dia. QX035 (*QX504). Built as engineers inspection saloons. Non-gangwayed. Observation windows at each end. The interior layout consists of two saloons interspersed by a central lavatory/kitchen/guards section. BR Mark 1 bogies. 80 m.p.h. 31.5 t.

45020–45026. Lot No. LMS 1356 Wolverton 1944.
45029. Lot No. LMS 1327 Wolverton 1942.
999503–999504. Lot No. BR Wagon Lot. 3093 Wolverton 1957.

45026 & 999503 are currently hired to Racal-BRT who have contracted maintenance to the Severn Valley Railway.

45020		**RR**	E	*ON*	ML	999503	v*	**M**	E	*ON*	KR
45026	v	**M**	E	*ON*	KR	999504	v*	**E**	E	*ON*	TO
45029	v	**E**	E	*ON*	ML						

ROYAL SCOTSMAN SALOONS

Dia. AO427. Mark 3A. Converted from SLEP at Carnforth Railway Restoration and Engineering Services in 1997. BT10 bogies. Attendant's and adjacent two sleeping compartments converted to generator room containing a 160 kW Volvo unit. In 99968 four sleeping compartments remain for staff use with another converted for use as a staff shower and toilet. The remaining five sleeping compartments have been replaced by two passenger cabins. In 99969 seven sleeping compartments remain for staff use. A further sleeping compartment, along with one toilet, have been converted to store rooms. The other two sleeping compartments have been combined to form a crew mess. ETH7X. 41.5 t.

Lot. No. 30960 Derby 1981–3.

99968 (10541)	M	GS	*ON*	EN	STATE CAR 5
99969 (10556)	M	GS	*ON*	EN	SERVICE CAR

RAILFILMS 'LMS CLUB CAR'

Dia. AO239. Converted from BR Mark 1 TSO at Carnforth Railway Restoration and Engineering Services in 1994. Contains kitchenette, pantry, coupé, lounge/reception area with two setees and two dining saloons. 24/– 1T. Commonwealth bogies. ETH 4.

Lot. No. 30724 York 1963. 37 t.

99993 (5067)	M	RA	*ON*	CP	LMS CLUB CAR

BR INSPECTION SALOON

Dia. QX505. Mark 1. Short frames. Non-gangwayed. Observation windows at each end. The interior layout consists of two saloons interspersed by a central lavatory/kitchen/guards/luggage section. BR Mark 1 bogies.

Lot No. BR Wagon Lot. 3379 Swindon 1960.

999509	E	E	*ON*	ML

2.5. PULLMAN CAR COMPANY SERIES

Pullman cars have never generally been numbered as such, although many
have carried numbers, instead they have carried titles. However, a scheme of
schedule numbers exists which generally lists cars in chronological order. In
this section those numbers are shown followed by the cars title. Cars described as 'kitchen' contain a kitchen in addition to passenger accomodation
and have gas cooking unless otherwise stated. Cars described as 'parlour'
consist entirely of passenger accomodation. cars described as 'brake' contain a compartment for the use of the guard and a luggage compartment in
addition to passenger accommodation.

PULLMAN PARLOUR FIRST

Dia. AO418. Built 1927 by Midland Carriage and Wagon Company. Gresley
bogies. 26/–. ETH 2. 41 t.

213 MINERVA   **PC** VS *ON* SL

PULLMAN BRAKE THIRD

Dia. AO412. Built 1928 by Metropolitan Carriage and Wagon Company.
Gresley bogies. –/30. 37.5 t.

232 CAR No. 79   v   **PC** NY *ON* NY

PULLMAN PARLOUR FIRST

Dia. AO419. Built 1928 by Metropolitan Carriage and Wagon Company. Gresley
bogies. 24/–. ETH 4. 40 t.

239 AGATHA   **PC** VS   SL
243 LUCILLE   **PC** VS *ON* SL

PULLMAN KITCHEN FIRST

Dia. AO417. Built 1925 by BRCW. Rebuilt by Midland Carriage & Wagon Company in 1928. Gresley bogies. 20/–. ETH 4. 41 t.

245 IBIS   **PC** VS *ON* SL

PULLMAN PARLOUR FIRST

Built 1928 by Metropolitan Carriage and Wagon Company. Gresley bogies.
24/–. ETH 4.

254 ZENA   **PC** VS *ON* SL

PULLMAN KITCHEN FIRST

Dia. AO416. Built 1928 by Metropolitan Carriage and Wagon Company. Gresley bogies. 20/–. ETH 4. 42 t.

255 IONE   **PC** VS *ON* SL

PULLMAN PARLOUR THIRD

Built 1931 by Birmingham Railway Carriage and Wagon Company. Gresley bogies. –/42.

261 CAR No. 83   **PC** VS   SL

PULLMAN KITCHEN COMPOSITE

Built 1932 by Metropolitan Carriage and Wagon Company. Originally included in 6-Pul EMU. Electric cooking. EMU bogies. 12/16.

264 RUTH   **PC** VS   SL

PULLMAN KITCHEN FIRST

Dia. AO420. Built 1932 by Metopolitan Carriage and Wagon Company. Originally included in 'Brighton Belle' EMUs but now used as hauled stock. Electric cooking. B5 (SR) bogies (§ EMU bogies). 20/–. ETH 2. 44 t.

280	AUDREY		**PC**	VS	*ON*	SL
281	GWEN		**PC**	VS	*ON*	SL
283	MONA	§	**PC**	VS		SL
284	VERA		**PC**	VS	*ON*	SL

PULLMAN PARLOUR THIRD

Built 1932 by Metropolitan Carriage and Wagon Company. Originally included in 'Brighton Belle' EMUs. EMU bogies. –/56.

285 CAR No. 85   **PC** VS   SL
286 CAR No. 86   **PC** VS   SL

PULLMAN BRAKE THIRD

Built 1932 by Metropolitan Carriage and Wagon Company. Originally driving motor cars in 'Brighton Belle' EMUs. Traction and control equipment removed for use as hauled stock. EMU bogies. –/48.

288 CAR No. 88   **PC** VS   SL
292 CAR No. 92   **PC** VS   SL
293 CAR No. 93   **PC** VS   SL

PULLMAN PARLOUR FIRST

Dia. AO414. Built 1951 by Birmingham Railway Carriage and Wagon Company. Gresley bogies. 32/–. ETH 3. 39 t.

301 PERSEUS   **PC**   VS   *ON*   SL

Dia. AO415. Built 1952 by Pullman Car Company, Preston Park using underframe and bogies from 176 RAINBOW, the body of which had been destroyed by fire. Gresley bogies. 26/–. ETH 4. 38 t.

302 PHOENIX   **PC**   VS   *ON*   SL

PULLMAN KITCHEN FIRST

Built 1951 by Birmingham Railway Carriage & Wagon Company. Gresley bogies. 22/–.

307 CARINA   **PC**   VS   SL

PULLMAN PARLOUR FIRST

Dia. AO414. Built 1951 by Birmingham Railway Carriage & Wagon Company. Gresley bogies. 32/–. ETH 3. 39 t.

308 CYGNUS   **PC**   VS   *ON*   SL

PULLMAN FIRST BAR

Built 1951 by Birmingham Railway Carriage & Wagon Company. Rebuilt 1999 by Blake Fabrications, Edinburgh with original timber-framed body replaced by a new fabricated steel body. Contains kitchen, bar, dining saloon and coupé. Electric cooking. Gresley bogies. 14/– 1T. ETH 3.

310 PEGASUS   **PC**   RA   CP

Also carries "THE TRIANON BAR" branding.

PULLMAN KITCHEN FIRST

Built by Metro-Cammell 1960/1 for East Coast Main-line services. Commonwealth bogies. 20/– 2T. ETH4. 40 t. Those vehicles used in the 'Royal Scotsman' charter train set have been modified and do not carry their names. Their current title and use is shown.

311	EAGLE	x	**PC**	NR	*ON*	NY	On loan to North Yorkshire Moors Rly.
313	FINCH	x	**M**	GS	*ON*	EN	STATE CAR 4 Sleeping Car
317	RAVEN	x	**M**	GS	*ON*	EN	DINING CAR 1 Kitchen & Dining Car
318	ROBIN	x	**PC**	NY	*ON*	NY	
319	SNIPE	x	**M**	GS	*ON*	EN	OBSERVATION CAR Observation Car

PULLMAN PARLOUR FIRST

Built by Metro-Cammell 1960/1 for East Coast Main-line services. Common-wealth bogies. 29/– 2T. 38.5 t. Those vehicles used in the 'Royal Scotsman' charter train set have been modified and do not carry their names. Their current title and use is shown.

324	AMBER	x	M	GS	ON	EN	STATE CAR 1	Sleeping Car
325	AMETHYST	x	PC	FS		SZ		
328	OPAL	x	PC	NY	ON	NY		
329	PEARL	x	M	GS	ON	EN	STATE CAR 2	Sleeping Car
331	TOPAZ	x	M	GS	ON	EN	STATE CAR 3	Sleeping Car

PULLMAN KITCHEN SECOND

Built by Metro-Cammell 1960/1 for East Coast Main-line services. Common-wealth bogies. –/30 1T. 40 t.

335	AMETHYST	x	PC	FS	SZ

PULLMAN PARLOUR SECOND

Built by Metro-Cammell 1960/1 for East Coast Main-line services. Common-wealth bogies. –/42 2T. 38.5 t.

347	CAR No. 347	x	PC	FS	SZ
348	CAR No. 348	x	PC	FS	SZ
349	CAR No. 349	x	PC	FS	On loan to Kent & East Sussex Railway
350	CAR No. 350	x	PC	FS	SZ
351	CAR No. 351	x	PC	FS	SZ
352	CAR No. 352	x	PC	FS	SZ
353	CAR No. 353	x	PC	FS	SZ

PULLMAN FIRST BAR

Built by Metro-Cammell 1961 for East Coast Main-line services. Common-wealth bogies. 24/– + bar seating 1T. 38.5 t.

354	THE HADRIAN BAR	x	PC	FS	SZ

2.6. COACHING STOCK AWAITING DISPOSAL

This list contains the last known locations of coaching stock awaiting disposal. The definition of which vehicles are "awaiting disposal" is somewhat vague, but generally speaking these are vehicles of types not now in normal service or vehicles which have been damaged by fire, vandalism or collision.

1644	CS		6345	EC
1650	CS		6362	LL
1652	CS		6363	LL
1655	KM		6500	Healey Mills Yard
1663	CS		6501	Healey Mills Yard
1670	CS		6521	Healey Mills Yard
1684	KM		6527	Healey Mills Yard
1688	CS		6900	Cambridge Station Yard
4858	KM		6901	Cambridge Station Yard
4860	CS		7183	Crewe Brook Sidings
4932	CS		9458	ZB
4997	CS		9482	NL
5038	OM		13306	KM
5476	Neville Hill Up Sidings		13320	CS
5505	CS		17054	Crewe Brook Sidings
5533	Neville Hill Up Sidings		18416	Crewe Brook Sidings
5574	Neville Hill Up Sidings		18750	Crewe Brook Sidings
5585	Neville Hill Up Sidings		19500	Crewe Brook Sidings
5595	Neville Hill Up Sidings		21265	KM
6335	LA		34952	SL
6339	EC		35509	ZH
6343	HT			

2.7. 99xxx RANGE NUMBER CONVERSION TABLE

The following table is presented to help readers identify vehicles which may carry numbers in the 99xxx range, the former private owner number series which is no longer in general use.

99xxx	BR No.	99xxx	BR No.	99xxx	BR No.	99xxx	BR No.
99035	35322	99327	5044	99672	549	99824	4831
99041	35476	99328	5033	99673	550	99826	13229
99052	45018	99329	4931	99674	551	99827	3096
99053	9004	99371	3128	99675	552	99828	13230
99121	3105	99405	35486	99676	553	99829	4856
99125	3113	99530	301	99677	586	99830	5028
99127	3117	99531	302	99678	504	99880	5159
99128	3130	99532	308	99679	506	99881	4807
99131	1999	99534	245	99680	17102	99886	35407
99241	35449	99535	213	99710	25767	99887	2127
99304	21256	99536	254	99712	25893	99953	35468
99311	1882	99537	280	99713	26013	99961	324
99312	35463	99538	34991	99716	25808	99962	329
99314	25729	99539	255	99717	25837	99963	331
99315	25955	99540	3069	99718	25862	99964	313
99316	13321	99541	243	99721	25756	99965	319
99317	3766	99542	889202	99722	25806	99966	34525
99318	4912	99543	284	99723	35459	99967	317
99319	14168	99545	80207	99782	17007	99970	232
99321	5299	99546	281	99783	84025	99971	311
99322	5600	99566	3066	99792	17019	99972	318
99323	5704	99568	3068	99821	9227	99973	324
99324	5714	99670	546	99822	1859	99974	328
99325	5727	99671	548	99823	4832	99995	35457
99326	4954						

The following table lists support coaches and the BR numbers of the locomotives which they normally support at present. These coaches can spend considerable periods of time off the Railtrack network when the locomotives they support are not being used on that network.

17007	35028	35333	6024	35465	46035 §	35476	80098
17013	60103 *	35449	34027	35467	KR locos	35479	KR locos
17019	45407	35457	60532	35468	YM locos	35486	KR locos
21236	30828	35461	5029	35470	TM locos	80217	75014
35207	VS locos	35463	CS locos				

* Carries former LNER number 4472.
§ Carries original number D 172.

3. DIESEL MULTIPLE UNITS

USING THIS SECTION – LAYOUT OF INFORMATION

DMUs are listed in numerical order of class, then in numerical order of set – using current numbers as allocated by the RSL. Individual 'loose' vehicles are listed in numerical order after vehicles formed into fixed formations. Where numbers carried are differ from those officially allocated these are noted in class headings where appropriate. Where sets or vehicles have been renumbered since the previous edition of this book, former numbering detail is shown in parentheses. Each entry is laid out as in the following example:

Set No.	Detail	Livery	Owner	Operation	Depot	Formation		Name
150 257	r*	**PS**	P	*AR*	NC	52257	57257	QUEEN BOADICEA

CLASS HEADINGS

Principal details and dimensions are quoted for each class in metric and/or imperial units as considered appropriate bearing in mind common usage in the UK.

All dimensions and weights are quoted for vehicles in an 'as new' condition with all necessary supplies (e.g. oil and water) on board. Dimensions are quoted in the order Length – Width. All lengths quoted are over buffers or couplings as appropriate. All width dimensions quoted are maxima.

DETAIL DIFFERENCES

Only detail differences which currently affect the areas and types of train which vehicles may work are shown. All other detail differences are specifically excluded. Where such differences occur within a class, these are shown either in the heading information or alongside the individual set or vehicle number. The following standard abbreviation is used:

r   Radio Electronic Token Block (RETB) equipment.

In all cases use of the above abbreviation indicates the equipment indicated is normally operable. Meaning of non-standard abbreviations is detailed in individual class headings.

LIVERY CODES

Livery codes are used to denote the various liveries carried. Readers should note it is impossible in a publication of this size to list every livery variation which currently exists. In particular items ignored for the purposes of this book include minor colour variations, all numbering, lettering and branding and omission of logos.

The descriptions are thus a general guide only and may be subject to slight variation between individual vehicles. Logos as appropriate for each livery are normally deemed to be carried. A complete list of livery codes used appears in section 6.1.

OWNER CODES

Owner codes are used in this to denote the owners of vehicles listed. Most vehicles are leased by the TOCs from specialist leasing companies. A complete list of owner codes used appears in section 6.2.

OPERATION CODES

Operation codes are used to denote the normal usage of the vehicles listed – i.e. A guide to the services of which train operating company any vehicle will normally be used upon. Where vehicles are used for non revenue earning purposes, an indication to the normal type of usage is given in the class heading. Where no operation code is shown, vehicles are currently not in use. A complete list of operation codes used appears in section 6.4.

DEPOT & LOCATION CODES

Depot codes are used to denote the normal maintenance base of each operational vehicle. However, maintenance may be carried out at other locations and may also be carried out by mobile maintenance teams.

Location codes are used to denote common storage locations. A complete list of depot and location codes used appears in section 6.5.

SET FORMATIONS

Regular set formations are shown where these are normally maintained. Readers should note set formations might be temporarily varied from time to time to suit maintenance and/or operational requirements. Vehicles shown as 'Spare' are not formed in any regular set formation.

NAMES

Only names carried with official sanction are listed. As far as possible names are shown in UPPER/lower case characters as actually shown on the name carried on the vehicle(s). Unless otherwise shown, complete units are regarded as named rather than just the individual car(s) which carry the name. Inscriptions carried on crests and/or plates additional to the main name are not shown.

GENERAL INFORMATION

CLASSIFICATION AND NUMBERING

First generation ('Heritage') DMUs are classified in the series 100–139.

Second generation DMUs are classified in the series 140–199.
Diesel-electric multiple units are classified in the series 200–249.
Service units are classified in the series 930–999.
Individual cars are numbered in the series 50000–59999 and 79000–79999.

DEMU individual cars are numbered in the series 60000–60999, except for a few former EMU vehicles which retain their EMU numbers.

Individual cars renumbered into service stock are numbered in the series 975000–975999 and 977000–977999, although these series are not exclusively used for DMU vehicles. Purpose built service stock is numbered in the series 999600–999602.

OPERATING CODES

These codes are used by train operating company staff to describe the various different types of vehicles and normally appear on data panels on the inner (i.e. non driving) ends of vehicles.

DM	Driving Motor.	DTCso	Driving Trailer Composite (semi-open).
DMB	Driving Motor Brake.		
DMBS	Driving Motor Brake Standard	MF	Motor First.
DMC	Driving Motor Composite.	MS	Motor Standard.
DMS	Driving Motor Standard.	MSLRB	Motor Standard with buffet.
DMF	Driving Motor First.	T	Trailer
DT	Driving Trailer.	TC	Trailer Composite.
DTC	Driving Trailer Composite.	TCso	Trailer Composite (semi-open).
DTS	Driving Trailer Standard.	TS	Trailer Standard.

All vehicles are of open configuration except where shown. A semi-open vehicle features both open and compartment accommodation, with first class accommodation usually in compartments in composite vehicles. Where two vehicles of the same type are formed within the same unit, the above codes may be suffixed by (A) and (B) to differentiate between the vehicles. The suffix 'L' denotes vehicles with a lavatory compartment.

A composite is a vehicle containing both first and standard class accommodation, although first class accommodation on first generation DMU vehicles has now all been permanently declassified. The distinction is maintained in this publication in respect of these vehicles to indicate the differing style of seating still fitted.

A brake vehicle is a vehicle containing separate specific accommodation for the conductor.

DESIGN CODES AND DIAGRAM CODES

For each type of vehicle the RSL issues a seven character 'Design Code' consisting of two letters plus four numbers and a suffix letter. (e.g. DP2010A). The first five characters of the Design Code are known as the 'Diagram Code' and these are quoted in this publication in sub-headings. The meaning of the various characters of the Design Code is as follows:

First Character

D   Diesel Multiple Unit vehicle.

Second Character

B   DEMU Driving motor passenger vehicle with brake compartment.
C   DEMU Driving motor passenger vehicle.
D   DEMU Non-driving motor passenger vehicle.
E   DEMU Driving trailer passenger vehicle.
F   DEMU Driving motor passenger vehicle (tilting).
G   DEMU Non-driving motor passenger vehicle (tilting).
H   DEMU Trailer passenger vehicle.
P   DMU (excl. DEMU) Driving motor passenger vehicle.
Q   DMU (excl. DEMU) Driving motor passenger vehicle with brake com-
           partment.
R   DMU (excl. DEMU) Non-driving motor passenger vehicle.
S   DMU (excl. DEMU) Driving trailer passenger vehicle.
T   DMU (excl. DEMU) Trailer passenger vehicle.
X   DMU (excl. DEMU) Single unit railcar.
Z   All types of service vehicle.

Third Character

2   Standard class accommodation.
3   Composite accommodation.
5   No passenger accommodation.

Fourth & Fifth Characters

These distinguish between different designs of vehicle, each design being
allocated a unique two digit number.

Special Note

Where vehicles have been declassified, the correct design code for a declassified vehicle is quoted in this publication, even though this may be at variance with RSL records, which do not always show the reality of the current
position.

ACCOMMODATION

The information given in class headings and sub-headings is in the form F/S nT
(or TD) nW. For example 12/54 1T 1W denotes 12 first class and 54 standard
class seats, 1 toilet and 1 wheelchair space. In declassified vehicles the capacity is still shown in terms of first and standard class seats whilst different types
of seat remain fitted. TD denotes a toilet suitable for a disabled person.

BUILD DETAILS

Lot Numbers

Vehicles ordered under the auspices of BR were allocated a Lot (batch) number
when ordered and these are quoted in class headings and sub-headings. Details
of the meaning of abbreviations used to denote builders are shown in Section 6.8.

Branch Line Society

Now you know about the traction, you should find out about the branches they work in a UK and global scale.

When did they open or close?
Who owned and worked the lines?
Have you been there on a Railtour?
Are you going there on a Railtour?

Too many questions? Need to know more, then **join us now** and make the difference.

Make contact with the Membership Secretary, By email: bls.membership@tesco.net
By post: JJJ Holmes, Rose Grove, 23 Church View, Gillingham, Dorset SP8 4XE

NEW GUIDES published every year
PSUL - Passenger Services over Unusual Lines for those hard to identify lines in the British Isles.

Minor Railways Every year a new edition of this guide gives a complete list of all Standard gauge, Narrow gauge, Miniature, Cliff railways and Tramways in the British Isles.

For your copies contact the Sales Officer, 37 Osberton Place, Hunters Bar, Sheffield S11 8XL

3.1. FIRST GENERATION DMUS

Very few first generation diesel multiple units remain. These are now referred to as 'heritage' units. Standard features are as follows:

Transmission: Mechanical. Cardan shaft and freewheel to a four-speed epicyclic gearbox with a further cardan shaft to the final drive, each engine driving the inner axle of one bogie.
Brakes: All units are vacuum braked.
Lighting: All cars are now fitted with fluorescent lighting.
Doors: Slam.
Couplings: Screw couplings are used on all vehicles.
Gangways: British Standard gangways are fitted.
Multiple Working: 'Blue Square' coupling code. All remaining first generation vehicles may be coupled together to work in multiple up to a maximum of 6 motor cars or 12 cars in total in a formation. First generation vehicles may not be coupled in multiple with second generation vehicles.

Maximum Speed: 70 m.p.h.

CLASS 101   METRO-CAMMELL 2-CAR UNITS

DMBS–DTSL (Refurbished) or DMBS–DMSL (Refurbished) or DMBS–DMCL (Facelifted).
Construction: Steel underframe and aluminium alloy bodies.
Engines: Two Leyland 680/1 of 112 kW (150 h.p.) at 1800 r.p.m. per power car.
Gangways: Midland scissors type. Within unit only.
Bogies: DD15 (motor) and DT11 (trailer).
Dimensions: 18.49 x 2.82 m.
Seating Layout: 3+2 unidirectional (2+2 facing in first class).

51175–51253. DMBS. Dia. DQ202. Lot No. 30467 1958–59. –/52. 32.5 t.
51426–51463. DMBS. Dia. DQ202. Lot No. 30500 1959. –/52. (–/49 51432 – Dia. DQ232) 32.5 t.
53164. DMBS. Dia. DQ202. Lot No. 30254 1956. –/52. 32.5 t.
53204. DMBS. Dia. DQ202. Lot No. 30259 1957. –/52. 32.5 t.
53211–53228. DMBS. Dia. DQ202. Lot No. 30261 1957. –/52. 32.5 t.
53253–53256. DMBS. Dia. DQ202. Lot No. 30266 1957. –/52. 32.5 t.
53311–53314. DMBS. Dia. DQ232. Lot No. 30275 1958. –/49 . 32.5 t.
51800. DMBS. Dia. DQ202. Lot No. 30587 1956. –/52. 32.5 t.
51496–51533. DMCL or DMSL. Dia. DP317 or DP210. Lot No. 30501 1959. 12/46 1T. 32.5t.
51803. DMSL. Dia. DP210. Lot No. 30588 1959. –/72 1T. 32.5 t.
53160–53163. DMSL. Dia. DP214. Lot No. 30253 1956. –/72 1T. 32.5 t.
53170–53171. DMSL. Dia. DP214. Lot No. 30255 1957. –/72 1T. 32.5 t.
53177. DMSL. Dia. DP214. Lot No. 30256 1957. –/72 1T. 32.5 t.
53266–53269. DMSL. Dia. DP210. Lot No. 30267 1957. –/72 1T. 32.5 t.
53322–53327. DMCL. Dia. DP317. Lot No. 30276 1958. 12/46 1T. 32.5 t.
53746. DMSL. Dia. DP210. Lot No. 30271 1957. –/72 1T. 32.5 t.
54055–54061. DTSL. DS206. Lot No. 30260 1957. –/72 1T. 25.5 t.
54062–54091. DTSL. Dia. DS206. Lot No. 30262 1957. –/71 1T. 25.5 t.

54343–54408. DTSL. Dia. DS206. Lot No. 30468 1958. –/72 1T. 25.5 t.
59303. TSL. Dia DT202. Lot No. 30273 1957. –/71 1T. 25.5 t.
59539. TSL. Dia DT202. Lot No. 30502 1959. –/71 1T. 25.5 t.

Refurbished 2-car Sets. DMBS–DTSL.

101 653	**RR**	A	*NW*	LO	51426	54358
101 654	**RR**	A	*NW*	LO	51800	54408
101 655	**RR**	A	*NW*	LO	51428	54062
101 656	**RR**	A	*NW*	LO	51230	54056
101 657	**RR**	A	*NW*	LO	53211	54085
101 658	**RR**	A	*NW*	LO	51175	54091
101 659	**RR**	A	*NW*	LO	51213	54352
101 660	**RR**	A	*NW*	LO	51189	54343
101 661	**RR**	A	*NW*	LO	51463	54365
101 662	**RR**	A	*NW*	LO	53228	54055
101 663	**RR**	A	*NW*	LO	51201	54347
101 664	**RR**	A	*NW*	LO	51442	54061
101 665	**RR**	A	*NW*	LO	51429	54393

Refurbished Twin Power Car Sets. DMBS–DMSL.

Non-Standard livery: Caledonian Blue with yellow/orange stripes..

101 676	**RR**	A	*NW*	LO	51205	51803
101 677	**RR**	A	*NW*	LO	51179	51496
101 678	**RR**	A	*NW*	LO	51210	53746
101 679	**RR**	A	*NW*	LO	51224	51533
101 680	**RR**	A	*NW*	LO	53204	53163
101 681	**RR**	A	*NW*	LO	51228	51506
101 682	**RR**	A	*NW*	LO	53256	51505
101 683	**RR**	A	*NW*	LO	51177	53269
101 684	**S**	A	*SR*	CK	51187	51509
101 685	**G**	A	*NW*	LO	53164	53160
101 686	**S**	A	*NW*	CK(S)	51231	51500
101 687	**S**	A	*SR*	CK	51247	51512
101 689	**S**	A	*SR*	CK	51185	51511
101 690	**S**	A	*SR*	CK	51435	53177
101 691	**S**	A	*SR*	CK	51253	53171
101 692	**0**	A	*SR*	CK	53253	53170
101 693	**S**	A	*SR*	CK	51192	53266
101 694	**S**	A	*SR*	CK	51188	53268
101 695	**S**	A	*SR*	CK	51226	51499
Spare TSL	**RR**	A	*NW*	BP(S)	59303	
Spare TSL	**G**	A	*NW*	BP(S)	59539	

Facelifted Twin Power Car Sets. DMBS–DMCL. These sets have seats removed and additional luggage racks. These modifications were carried out when they were used on Reading–Gatwick Airport services.

Note: These units show L835, L840 and L842 instead of the official set number.

101 835	**RR**	A	*NW*	LO	51432	51498
101 840	**N**	A	*NW*	LO	53311	53322
101 842	**N**	A		ZA (S)	53314	53327

CLASS 117   PRESSED STEEL SUBURBAN

DMBS–DMS or DMBS–TSL–DMS.
Construction: Steel.
Engines: Two Leyland 680/1 of 112 kW (150 h.p.) at 1800 r.p.m. per power car.
Gangways: GWR suspension type. Within unit only.
Bogies: DD10 (motor) and Dt9 (trailer).
Dimensions: 20.45 x 2.82 m.
Seating Layout: 3+2 facing.

DMBS. Dia. DQ220. Lot No. 30546 1959–60. –/65. 36.5 t.
TSL. Dia. DP230. Lot No. 30547 1959–60. –/89. 30.5 t.
DMS. Dia. DP221. Lot No. 30548 1959–60. –/89. 36.5 t.

Refurbished Sets.

117 301	**RR**	A	PH (S)	51353		51395		
117 306	**RR**	A	PH (S)	51369		51411		
117 308	**RR**	A	PH (S)	51371		51413		
117 310	**RR**	A	HA (S)	51353	59486	51381		
117 311	**RR**	A	HA (S)	51352		51376		
117 313	**RR**	A	PH (S)	51339		51382		
Spare TSL	**RR**	A	PH (S)	59492	59500	59505	59509	59521

Facelifted Sets.

Note: 117 704–721 carry L 704–721 instead of their official set number.

117 701	**N**	A		PY (S)	51350	51392
117 702	**N**	A	SL	BY	51356	51398
117 704	**N**	A		PY (S)	51341	51383
117 705	**N**	A		PY (S)	51358	51400
117 706	**N**	A		PY (S)	51366	51408
117 707	**N**	A		PY (S)	51335	51377
117 720	**N**	A		PY (S)	51354	51396
117 721	**N**	A		PY (S)	51363	51405

CLASS 121   PRESSED STEEL SUBURBAN

DMBS.
Construction: Steel.
Engines: Two Leyland 1595 of 112 kW (150 h.p.) at 1800 r.p.m.
Gangways: Non gangwayed single cars with cabs at each end.
Bogies: DD10.
Dimensions: 20.45 x 2.82 m.
Seating Layout: 3+2 facing.

Dia. DX201. Lot No. 30518 1960. –/65. 38.0 t.

121 027	**SL**	A	SL	BY	55027	Bletchley TMD
121 029	**N**	A	SL	BY	55029	MARSTON VALE
121 031	**N**	A	SL	BY	55031	LESLIE CRABBE

3.2. SECOND GENERATION DMUS

All second generation DMUs have air brakes. They are equipped with public address, with transmission equipment on driving vehicles. All vehicles have flexible diaphragm gangways. Except where otherwise stated, transmission is Voith T211r hydraulic with a cardan shaft to a Gmeinder GM190 final drive.

CLASS 142   BREL/LEYLAND PACER

DMS–DMSL.

Construction: Steel. Leyland National bus parts on four-wheeled underframes.
Engines: One Cummins LTA10-R of 172 kW (230 h.p.) at 2100 r.p.m. (* One Perkins 2006-TWH of 172 kW (230 h.p.) at 2100 r.p.m.) per car.
Dimensions: 15.66 x 2.80 m.
Couplers: BSI at outer ends, bar couplers within unit.
Seating Layout: 3+2 mainly unidirectional bus style.
Gangways: Within unit only.   **Wheel Arrangement:** 1-A A-1.
Doors: Folding.   **Maximum Speed:** 75 m.p.h.
Non-Standard Livery: O 55709 is in original Provincial 'Pacer' two-tone blue.

55542–55591. DMS. Dia. DP234 (s DP271). Lot No. 31003 BREL Derby 1985–86. –/62. (s –/56) 23.26 t.
55592–55641. DMSL. Dia. DP235 (s DP272). Lot No. 31004 BREL Derby 1985–86. –/59 1T. (s –/50) 24.97 t.
55701–55746. DMS. Dia. DP234 (s DP271). Lot No. 31013 BREL Derby 1986–87. –/62. (s –/56) 23.26 t.
55747–55792. DMSL. Dia. DP235 (s DP272). Lot No. 31014 BREL Derby 1986–87. –/59 1T. (s –/50) 24.97 t.

s Fitted with 2+2 individual high-backed seating.
t DMS fitted with luggage rack. Accommodation –/55.

142 001	t	GM	A	NW	NH	55542	55592
142 002		GM	A	NW	NH	55543	55593
142 003		GM	A	NW	NH	55544	55594
142 004	t	GM	A	NW	NH	55545	55595
142 005	t	GM	A	NW	NH	55546	55596
142 006		GM	A	NW	NH	55547	55597
142 007	t	GM	A	NW	NH	55548	55598
142 008	t	GM	A	NW	ZC (S)	55549	55599
142 009	t	GM	A	NW	NH	55550	55600
142 010		GM	A	NW	NH	55551	55601
142 011	t	GM	A	NW	NH	55552	55602
142 012	t	GM	A	NW	NH	55553	55603
142 013		GM	A	NW	NH	55554	55604
142 014	t	GM	A	NW	NH	55555	55605
142 015	s	RR	A	NS	HT	55556	55606
142 016	s	RR	A	NS	HT	55557	55607
142 017	s	TW	A	NS	HT	55558	55608
142 018	s	TW	A	NS	HT	55559	55609
142 019	s	TW	A	NS	HT	55560	55610

142 020	s	TW	A	NS	HT	55561	55611
142 021	s	TW	A	NS	HT	55562	55612
142 022	s	TW	A	NS	HT	55563	55613
142 023	t	RR	A	NW	NH	55564	55614
142 024	s	RR	A	NS	HT	55565	55615
142 025	s	NS	A	NS	HT	55566	55616
142 026	s	NS	A	NS	HT	55567	55617
142 027	t	GM	A	NW	NH	55568	55618
142 028	t	GM	A	NW	NH	55569	55619
142 029		GM	A	NW	NH	55570	55620
142 030		GM	A	NW	NH	55571	55621
142 031	t	GM	A	NW	NH	55572	55622
142 032	t	GM	A	NW	NH	55573	55623
142 033	t	RR	A	NW	NH	55574	55624
142 034	t	GM	A	NW	NH	55575	55625
142 035	t	GM	A	NW	NH	55576	55626
142 036	t	RR	A	NW	NH	55577	55627
142 037	t	GM	A	NW	NH	55578	55628
142 038		GM	A	NW	NH	55579	55629
142 039	t	GM	A	NW	NH	55580	55630
142 040		GM	A	NW	NH	55581	55631
142 041		GM	A	NW	NH	55582	55632
142 042		GM	A	NW	NH	55583	55633
142 043		GM	A	NW	NH	55584	55634
142 044		RR	A	NW	NH	55585	55635
142 045		GM	A	NW	NH	55586	55636
142 046		GM	A	NW	NH	55587	55637
142 047		RR	A	NW	NH	55588	55638
142 048		RR	A	NW	NH	55589	55639
142 049		GM	A	NW	NH	55590	55640
142 050	s	NS	A	NS	HT	55591	55641
142 051		MT	A	NW	NH	55701	55747
142 052		MT	A	NW	NH	55702	55748
142 053		MT	A	NW	NH	55703	55749
142 054		MT	A	NW	NH	55704	55750
142 055		MT	A	NW	NH	55705	55751
142 056		MT	A	NW	NH	55706	55752
142 057		MT	A	NW	NH	55707	55753
142 058		MT	A	NW	NH	55708	55754
142 060	t	GM	A	NW	NH	55710	55756
142 061		GM	A	NW	NH	55711	55757
142 062		GM	A	NW	NH	55712	55758
142 063		GM	A	NW	NH	55713	55759
142 064	t	GM	A	NW	NH	55714	55760
142 065	s	NS	A	NS	HT	55715	55761
142 066	s	NS	A	NS	NL	55716	55762
142 067		GM	A	NW	NH	55717	55763
142 068		GM	A	NW	NH	55718	55764
142 069		GM	A	NW	NH	55719	55765
142 070		GM	A	NW	NH	55720	55766
142 071	s	RR	A	NS	HT	55721	55767

142 072		**RR**	A	*NS*	NL	55722	55768
142 073		**RR**	A	*NS*	NL	55723	55769
142 074		**RR**	A	*NS*	NL	55724	55770
142 075		**RR**	A	*NS*	NL	55725	55771
142 076		**RR**	A	*NS*	NL	55726	55772
142 077		**RR**	A	*NS*	NL	55727	55773
142 078	s	**RR**	A	*NS*	NL	55728	55774
142 079		**RR**	A	*NS*	NL	55729	55775
142 080		**RR**	A	*NS*	NL	55730	55776
142 081		**RR**	A	*NS*	NL	55731	55777
142 082		**RR**	A	*NS*	NL	55732	55778
142 083		**RR**	A	*NS*	NL	55733	55779
142 084	s*	**RR**	A	*NS*	NL	55734	55780
142 085	s	**RR**	A	*CA*	CF	55735	55781
142 086	s	**RR**	A	*CA*	CF	55736	55782
142 087	s	**RR**	A	*CA*	CF	55737	55783
142 088	s	**RR**	A	*CA*	CF	55738	55784
142 089	s	**RR**	A	*CA*	CF	55739	55785
142 090	s	**RR**	A	*CA*	CF	55740	55786
142 091	s	**RR**	A	*CA*	CF	55741	55787
142 092	s	**RR**	A	*CA*	CF	55742	55788
142 093	s	**RR**	A	*CA*	CF	55743	55789
142 094	s	**RR**	A	*CA*	CF	55744	55790
142 095	s	**RR**	A	*NS*	NL	55745	55791
142 096	s	**RR**	A	*CA*	CF	55746	55792
Spare		**0**	A		NH(S)	55709	

CLASS 143   ALEXANDER/BARCLAY PACER

DMS–DMSL. Similar design to Class 142, but bodies built by W. Alexander with Barclay underframes.

Construction: Steel. Alexander bus bodywork on four-wheeled underframes.
Engines: One Cummins LTA10-R of 172 kW (230 h.p.) at 2100 r.p.m. per car.
Dimensions: 15.55 x 2.70 m.
Couplers: BSI at outer ends of unit, bar couplers within unit.
Seating Layout: 3+2 mainly unidirectional bus style.
Gangways: Within unit only.   **Wheel Arrangement:** 1-A A-1.
Doors: Folding.   **Maximum Speed:** 75 m.p.h.

DMS. Dia. DP236 Lot No. 31005 Barclay 1985–86. –/62. 24.5 t.
DMSL. Dia. DP237 Lot No. 31006 Barclay 1985–86. –/60 1T. 25.0 t.

Note: 143 601/10/4 are owned by Mid-Glamorgan County Council, 143 609 is owned by South Glamorgan County Council. These units and 143 617-9 are managed by Porterbrook Leasing Company.

143 601	**RR**	P	*WW*	CF	55642	55667
143 602	**RR**	P	*CA*	CF	55651	55668
143 603	**RR**	P	*CA*	CF	55658	55669
143 604	**RR**	P	*CA*	CF	55645	55670
143 605	**RR**	P	*CA*	CF	55646	55671
143 606	**RR**	P	*CA*	CF	55647	55672

143 607	**RR**	P	*CA*	CF	55648	55673	
143 608	**RR**	P	*CA*	CF	55649	55674	
143 609	**RR**	P	*CA*	CF	55650	55675	TOM JONES
143 610	**RR**	P	*WW*	CF	55643	55676	
143 611	**AL**	P	*CA*	CF	55652	55677	
143 612	**RR**	P	*WW*	CF	55653	55678	
143 613	**AL**	P	*CA*	CF	55654	55679	
143 614	**RR**	P	*WW*	CF	55655	55680	
143 615	**RR**	P	*CA*	CF	55656	55681	
143 616	**RR**	P	*CA*	CF	55657	55682	
143 617	**RR**	RI	*CA*	CF	55644	55683	BEWICK'S SWAN
143 618	**RR**	RI	*CA*	CF	55659	55684	MUTE SWAN
143 619	**RR**	RI	*WW*	CF	55660	55685	WHOOPER SWAN
143 620	**RR**	P	*WW*	CF	55661	55686	
143 621	**RR**	P	*WW*	CF	55662	55687	
143 622	**RR**	P	*WW*	CF	55663	55688	
143 623	**RR**	P	*WW*	CF	55664	55689	
143 624	**RR**	P	*WW*	CF	55665	55690	
143 625	**RR**	P	*WW*	CF	55666	55691	

CLASS 144 ALEXANDER/BREL PACER

DMS–DMSL or DMS–MS–DMSL. As Class 143, but underframes built by BREL.

Construction: Steel. Alexander bus bodywork on four-wheeled underframes.
Engines: One Cummins LTA10-R of 172 kW (230 h.p.) at 2100 r.p.m. per car.
Dimensions: 15.11 x 2.73 m.
Couplers: BSI at outer ends of unit, bar couplers within unit.
Seating Layout: 3+2 mainly unidirectional bus style.
Gangways: Within unit only. **Wheel Arrangement:** 1-A A-1.
Doors: Folding. **Maximum Speed:** 75 m.p.h.

DMS. Dia. DP240 Lot No. 31015 BREL Derby 1986–87. –/62 1W. 24.2 t.
MS. Dia. DR205 Lot No. 31037 BREL Derby 1987. –/73. 22.6 t.
DMSL. Dia. DP241 Lot No. 31016 BREL Derby 1986–87. –/60 1T. 25.0 t.

Note: The centre cars of the three-car units are owned by West Yorkshire PTE, although managed by Porterbrook Leasing Company.

144 001	**WY**	P	*NS*	NL	55801		55824
144 002	**WY**	P	*NS*	NL	55802		55825
144 003	**WY**	P	*NS*	NL	55803		55826
144 004	**WY**	P	*NS*	NL	55804		55827
144 005	**WY**	P	*NS*	NL	55805		55828
144 006	**WY**	P	*NS*	NL	55806		55829
144 007	**WY**	P	*NS*	NL	55807		55830
144 008	**WY**	P	*NS*	NL	55808		55831
144 009	**WY**	P	*NS*	NL	55809		55832
144 010	**WY**	P	*NS*	NL	55810		55833
144 011	**RR**	P	*NS*	NL	55811		55834
144 012	**RR**	P	*NS*	NL	55812		55835
144 013	**RR**	P	*NS*	NL	55813		55836
144 014	**WY**	P	*NS*	NL	55814	55850	55837

144 015	**WY**	P	*NS*	NL	55815	55851	55838
144 016	**WY**	P	*NS*	NL	55816	55852	55839
144 017	**WY**	P	*NS*	NL	55817	55853	55840
144 018	**WY**	P	*NS*	NL	55818	55854	55841
144 019	**WY**	P	*NS*	NL	55819	55855	55842
144 020	**WY**	P	*NS*	NL	55820	55856	55843
144 021	**WY**	P	*NS*	NL	55821	55857	55844
144 022	**WY**	P	*NS*	NL	55822	55858	55845
144 023	**WY**	P	*NS*	NL	55823	55859	55846

CLASS 150/0   BREL PROTOTYPE SPRINTER

DMSL–MS–DMS. Prototype Sprinter.

Construction: Steel.
Engines: One Cummins NT-855-R4 of 213 kW (285 h.p.) at 2100 r.p.m. per car.
Bogies: BX8P (powered), BX8T (non-powered).
Couplings: BSI at outer end of driving vehicles, bar non-driving ends.
Dimensions: 20.06 x 2.82 m (outer cars), 20.18 x 2.82 m (inner car).
Seating Layout: 3+2 (mainly unidirectional).
Gangways: Within unit only.   **Wheel Arrangement:** 2-B – 2-B – B-2.
Doors: Sliding.   **Maximum Speed:** 75 m.p.h.

DMSL. Dia. DP230. Lot No. 30984 BREL York 1984. –/72 1T. 35.8 t.
MS. Dia. DR202. Lot No. 30986 BREL York 1984. –/92. 34.4 t.
DMS. Dia. DP231. Lot No. 30985 BREL York 1984. –/76. 35.6 t.

Note: 150 001 was converted to 154 002 at RTC Derby in 1986, but was later converted back to a Class 150.

| 150 001 | **CO** | A | *CT* | TS | 55200 | 55400 | 55300 |
| 150 002 | **CO** | A | *CT* | TS | 55201 | 55401 | 55301 |

CLASS 150/1   BREL SPRINTER

DMSL–DMS or DMSL–DMSL–DMS or DMSL–DMS–DMS.

Construction: Steel.
Engines: One Cummins NT855R5 of 213 kW (285 h.p.) at 2100 r.p.m. per car.
Bogies: BP38 (powered), BT38 (non-powered).
Couplers: BSI.
Dimensions: 20.06 x 2.82 m.
Seating Layout: 3+2 facing as built but 150 010–150 132 were reseated with mainly unidirectional seating.
Gangways: Within unit only.   **Wheel Arrangement:** 2-B (– 2–B) – B-2.
Doors: Sliding.   **Maximum Speed:** 75 m.p.h.

DMSL. Dia. DP238. Lot No. 31011 York 1985–86. –/72 1T (s –/58 1T, t –/64 1T, u –/68 1T). 36.5 t.
DMS. Dia. DP239. Lot No. 31012 York 1985–86. –/76 (s –/64, t –/70, u –/66). 38.45 t.
Notes: The centre cars of three-car units are Class 150/2 vehicles. For details see Class 150/2.
Units reliveried in **NW** livery have been fitted with new seating.

150 010	r	**CO**	A	*CT*	TS	52110	57226	57110
150 011	r	**CO**	A	*CT*	TS	52111	57206	57111
150 012	r	**CO**	A	*CT*	TS	52112	52204	57112
150 013	r	**CO**	A	*CT*	TS	52113	52226	57113
150 014	r	**CO**	A	*CT*	TS	52114	57204	57114
150 015	r	**CO**	A	*CT*	TS	52115	52206	57115
150 016	r	**CO**	A	*CT*	TS	52116	57212	57116
150 017	r	**CO**	A	*CT*	TS	52117	57209	57117
150 018	r	**CO**	A	*CT*	TS	52118	52220	57118
150 019	r	**CO**	A	*CT*	TS	52119	57220	57119
150 101	r	**CO**	A	*CT*	TS	52101		57101
150 102	r	**CO**	A	*CT*	TS	52102		57102
150 103	r	**CO**	A	*CT*	TS	52103		57103
150 104	r	**CO**	A	*CT*	TS	52104		57104
150 105	r	**CO**	A	*CT*	TS	52105		57105
150 106	r	**CO**	A	*CT*	TS	52106		57106
150 107	r	**CO**	A	*CT*	TS	52107		57107
150 108	r	**CO**	A	*CT*	TS	52108		57108
150 109	r	**CO**	A	*CT*	TS	52109		57109
150 120		**CO**	A	*SL*	BY	52120		57120
150 121	r	**CO**	A	*CT*	TS	52121		57121
150 122	r	**CO**	A	*CT*	TS	52122		57122
150 123		**CO**	A	*SL*	BY	52123		57123
150 124	r	**CO**	A	*CT*	TS	52124		57124
150 125	r	**CO**	A	*CT*	TS	52125		57125
150 126	r	**CO**	A	*CT*	TS	52126		57126
150 127		**CO**	A	*SL*	BY	52127		57127
150 128		**CO**	A	*SL*	BY	52128		57128
150 129		**CO**	A	*SL*	BY	52129		57129
150 130		**CO**	A	*SL*	BY	52130		57130
150 131		**CO**	A	*SL*	BY	52131		57131
150 132	r	**CO**	A	*CT*	TS	52132		57132
150 133	s	**NW**	A	*NW*	NH	52133		57133
150 134	s	**NW**	A	*NW*	NH	52134		57134
150 135	s	**NW**	A	*NW*	NH	52135		57135
150 136	s	**NW**	A	*NW*	NH	52136		57136
150 137	s	**NW**	A	*NW*	NH	52137		57137
150 138	s	**NW**	A	*NW*	NH	52138		57138
150 139	s	**NW**	A	*NW*	NH	52139		57139
150 140	t	**GM**	A	*NW*	NH	52140		57140
150 141	t	**GM**	A	*NW*	NH	52141		57141
150 142	s	**NW**	A	*NW*	NH	52142		57142
150 143	s	**NW**	A	*NW*	NH	52143		57143
150 144	u	**PS**	A	*NW*	NH	52144		57144
150 145	s	**NW**	A	*NW*	NH	52145		57145
150 146	s	**NW**	A	*NW*	NH	52146		57146
150 147	s	**NW**	A	*NW*	NH	52147		57147
150 148	u	**PS**	A	*NW*	NH	52148		57148
150 149	u	**PS**	A	*NW*	NH	52149		57149
150 150	u	**PS**	A	*NW*	NH	52150		57150

▲ 101 655 in Regional Railways livery leaves Bamford on the Hope Valley line with the 12.46 Manchester Piccadilly–Sheffield service on 14th August 1998. **Les Nixon**

▼ 121 027 in Silverlink livery and 121 029 in Network SouthEast livery approach Ridgmont with the 11.50 Bletchley–Bedford on 29th May 1999. **Kevin Conkey**

142 029 in Greater Manchester PTE livery approaches Porton on 22nd July 1999 with the 11.04 Carlisle–Barrow-in-Furness. **Dave McAlone**

▲ 143 601 arrives at Pylle on the 09.40 Swansea–Weston-super-Mare on 30th April 1998.   **Hugh Ballantyne**

▼ 144 020 in West Yorkshire PTE livery seen east of Hatfield & Stainforth forming a Doncaster–Scunthorpe working on 27th March 1999.   **Hugh Ballantyne**

▲ Refurbished Class 150/1 No. 150 133, in North Western Trains livery, stands at Leyland whilst working the 09.34 Manchester Airport–Blackpool North on 21st August 1999.   **Martyn Hilbert**

▼ Merseytravel-liveried Class 150/2 No. 150 205 at Heysham Port having arrived on the 13.47 from Morecambe on 28th August 1999.   **Martyn Hilbert**

▲ 153 304 forms the 13.12 Chesterfield–York via Pontefract stopping service at Meadowhall Interchange on 26th June 1999. **Peter Fox**

▼ 155 344 in West Yorkshire PTE livery west of Selby with the 14.53 Selby–Manchester Victoria on 15th October 1998. **John G. Teasdale**

▲ 156 460 in North West Regional Railways livery arrives at Carnforth on 13th September 1999 on the 13.03 Carlisle–Lancaster via Barrow-in-Furness service.
Martyn Hilbert

▼ A pair of Class 158s in Scotrail livery, Nos 158 730 and 158 727 at Aberdeen on 25th July 1999 with the Sundays-only15.25 Inverness–Glasgow Queen Street via Aberdeen.
Bob Sweet

▲ 158 797 in Central Trains livery passes the site of Heeley Carriage Sidings with the 13.50 Norwich–Liverpool Lime Street on 13th July 1999.   **Wolfram Stein**

▼ 158 869, recently repainted in Wales & West Passenger Trains livery, at Cwmbran on the 14.33 Manchester Piccadilly–Cardiff Central on 29th June 1999.
Bob Sweet

159 008 in South West Trains livery at Shell Cove, Dawlish, on 1st August 1999 with the Sunday 11.05 London Waterloo–Paignton on 1st August 1999.

Hugh Ballantyne

▲ A pair of Class 165/0 units Nos. 165 018 and 165 033 passing Hatton on the 11.30 Chiltern Railways service from Birmingham Snow Hill to London Marylebone on 4th September 1999.   **Hugh Ballantyne**

▼ On 21st August 1999, Thames Trains Class 166s Nos. 166 216 and 166 209 pass Hinksey Yard, south of Oxford, with the 14.10 Stratford-upon-Avon–London Paddington.   **David Brown**

▲ "Chiltern Clubman" No. 168 001 arrives at Leamington Spa with the 13.30 Birmingham Snow Hill–London Marylebone on 4th September 1999.
Hugh Ballantyne

▼ "Coradia 1000" No. 175 101 at Highley, on the Severn Valley Railway, following a test run from Kidderminster. **Bob Sweet**

Midland Mainline Class 170 "Turbostar" No. 170 104 passes through Cricklewood on 21st August 1999 with the 12.23 Derby–London St. Pancras   **Kevin Conkey**

▲ Anglia Railways' variant of the Turbostar is the Class 170/4 which has better seating than the Midland Mainline and Central Trains' variants. 170 204, 170 202 and 170 203 leave Colchester on 4th September 1999 with the 11.00 London Liverpool Street–Norwich service. **David Brown**

▼ Central Trains Class 170/5 No. 170 510 arrives at Stoke-on-Trent on 4th October 1999 with the 12.31 Manchester Airport–Skegness. **Hugh Ballantyne**

▲ Hastings Diesels' preserved Class 201 unit 1001 (officially 201 001) at Harwich International on 25th September 1999 with the "Farewell to Thumper" tour.
Michael J. Collins

▼ Class 205/0 DEMU No. 205 028 is the leading unit on the 06.57 Uckfield–London Bridge as it is seen near Norwood Junction on 14th September 1998.
Brian Denton

▲ The 17.22 Ashford–Hastings service on 2nd April 1999 formed of Class 207/2 DEMU 207 201 'Ashford Fayre'. Note the wider bodied ex-Class 411 EMU trailer in the middle.   **David Brown**

▼ BREL-built track recording unit 999600/1 approaches Birkett Common north of Kirkby Stephen on 23rd June 1999.   **Kevin Conkey**

▲ **Midland Metro.** Car No. 05 at Soho Benson Road on a Wolverhampton–Birmingham Snow Hill service on the 31st May 1999, the first day of normal service.
Peter Fox

▼ **Stagecoach Supertram.** Car No. 119 approaches Moss Way in the Owlthorpe district of Sheffield with a Halfway–Malin Bridge working on 19th April 1999.
Peter Fox

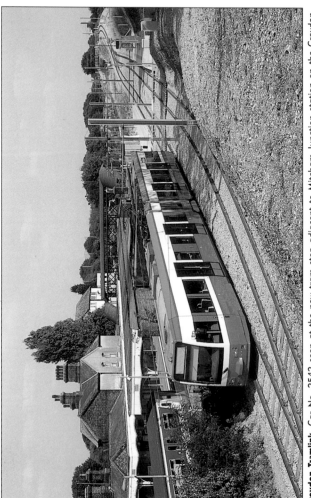

Croydon Tramlink. Car No. 2542 seen at the new tram stop adjacent to Mitcham Junction station on the Croydon–Wimbledon line with a Wimbledon–Wandle Park driver training run. **Chris Wilson**

CLASS 150/2   BREL SPRINTER

DMSL–DMS.

Construction: Steel.
Engines: One Cummins NT855R5 of 213 kW (285 h.p.) at 2100 r.p.m. per car.
Bogies: BP38 (powered), BT38 (non-powered).
Couplers: BSI.
Dimensions: 20.06 x 2.82 m.
Seating Layout: 3+2 mainly unidirectional seating.
Gangways: Throughout.   **Wheel Arrangement:** 2-B – B-2.
Doors: Sliding.   **Maximum Speed:** 75 m.p.h.

DMSL. Dia. DP242. Lot No. 31017 BREL York 1986–87. –/73 1T (t –70 1T). 35.8 t.
DMS. Dia. DP243. Lot No. 31018 BREL York 1986–87. –/76 (* –/68, u –/73). 34.90 t.

150 201	t	**MT**	A	*NW*	NH	52201	57201
150 202		**CO**	A	*CT*	TS	52202	57202
150 203	t	**MT**	A	*NW*	NH	52203	57203
150 205	t	**MT**	A	*NW*	NH	52205	57205
150 207	u	**MT**	A	*NW*	NH	52207	57207
150 208		**RR**	P	*SR*	HA	52208	57208
150 210		**CO**	A	*CT*	TS	52210	57210
150 211	u	**MT**	A	*NW*	NH	52211	57211
150 213	r*	**PS**	P	*AR*	NC	52213	57213	LORD NELSON
150 214		**CO**	A	*CT*	TS	52214	57214
150 215		**GM**	A	*NW*	NH	52215	57215
150 216		**CO**	A	*CT*	TS	52216	57216
150 217	r*	**PS**	P	*AR*	NC	52217	57217	OLIVER CROMWELL
150 218	tu	**GM**	A	*NW*	NH	52218	57218
150 219	r	**RR**	P	*WW*	CF	52219	57219
150 221	r	**RR**	P	*WW*	CF	52221	57221
150 222	tu	**GM**	A	*NW*	NH	52222	57222
150 223	t	**GM**	A	*NW*	NH	52223	57223
150 224	t	**GM**	A	*NW*	NH	52224	57224
150 225	u	**GM**	A	*NW*	NH	52225	57225
150 227	r*	**PS**	P	*AR*	NC	52227	57227	SIR ALF RAMSEY
150 228		**RR**	P	*SR*	HA	52228	57228
150 229	r*	**PS**	P	*AR*	NC	52229	57229	GEORGE BORROW
150 230	r	**RR**	P	*WW*	CF	52230	57230
150 231	r*	**PS**	P	*AR*	NC	52231	57231	KING EDMUND
150 232	r	**RR**	P	*WW*	CF	52232	57232
150 233	r	**RR**	P	*WW*	CF	52233	57233
150 234	r	**RR**	P	*WW*	CF	52234	57234
150 235	r*	**PS**	P	*AR*	NC	52235	57235	CARDINAL WOLSEY
150 236	r	**RR**	P	*WW*	CF	52236	57236
150 237	r*	**PS**	P	*AR*	NC	52237	57237	HEREWARD THE WAKE
150 238	r	**RR**	P	*WW*	CF	52238	57238
150 239	r	**RR**	P	*WW*	CF	52239	57239
150 240	r	**RR**	P	*WW*	CF	52240	57240
150 241	r	**RR**	P	*WW*	CF	52241	57241

150 242		**RR**	P	*CT*	TS	52242	57242
150 243	r	**RR**	P	*WW*	CF	52243	57243
150 244	r	**RR**	P	*WW*	CF	52244	57244
150 245		**RR**	P	*SR*	HA	52245	57245
150 246	r	**RR**	P	*WW*	CF	52246	57246
150 247	r	**RR**	P	*WW*	CF	52247	57247
150 248	r	**RR**	P	*WW*	CF	52248	57248
150 249	r	**RR**	P	*WW*	CF	52249	57249
150 250		**RR**	P	*SR*	HA	52250	57250
150 251	r	**RR**	P	*WW*	CF	52251	57251
150 252		**RR**	P	*SR*	HA	52252	57252
150 253	r	**RR**	P	*WW*	CF	52253	57253
150 254	r	**RR**	P	*WW*	CF	52254	57254
150 255	r*	**PS**	P	*AR*	NC	52255	57255	HENRY BLOGG
150 256		**RR**	P	*SR*	HA	52256	57256
150 257	r*	**PS**	P	*AR*	NC	52257	57257	QUEEN BOADICEA
150 258		**RR**	P	*SR*	HA	52258	57258
150 259		**RR**	P	*SR*	HA	52259	57259
150 260		**RR**	P	*SR*	HA	52260	57260
150 261	r	**RR**	P	*WW*	CF	52261	57261
150 262		**RR**	P	*SR*	HA	52262	57262
150 263	r	**RR**	P	*WW*	CF	52263	57263
150 264		**RR**	P	*SR*	HA	52264	57264
150 265	r	**RR**	P	*WW*	CF	52265	57265
150 266	r	**RR**	P	*WW*	CF	52266	57266
150 267	r	**RR**	P	*WW*	CF	52267	57267
150 268		**RR**	P	*NS*	NL	52268	57268
150 269		**RR**	P	*NS*	NL	52269	57269
150 270		**RR**	P	*NS*	NL	52270	57270
150 271		**RR**	P	*NS*	NL	52271	57271
150 272		**RR**	P	*NS*	NL	52272	57272
150 273		**RR**	P	*NS*	NL	52273	57273
150 274		**RR**	P	*NS*	NL	52274	57274
150 275		**RR**	P	*NS*	NL	52275	57275
150 276		**RR**	P	*NS*	NL	52276	57276
150 277		**RR**	P	*NS*	NL	52277	57277
150 278	r	**RR**	P	*WW*	CF	52278	57278
150 279		**RR**	P	*CA*	CF	52279	57279
150 280		**RR**	P	*CA*	CF	52280	57280
150 281		**RR**	P	*CA*	CF	52281	57281
150 282		**RR**	P	*CA*	CF	52282	57282
150 283		**RR**	P	*SR*	HA	52283	57283
150 284		**RR**	P	*SR*	HA	52284	57284
150 285		**RR**	P	*SR*	HA	52285	57285	EDINBURGH–BATHGATE 1986–1996

CLASS 153   LEYLAND BUS SUPER SPRINTER

DMSL. Converted by Hunslet-Barclay, Kilmarnock from Class 155 two-car units.

Construction: Steel. Built from Leyland National bus parts on conventional

bogied underframes.
Engine: One Cummins NT855R5 of 213 kW (285 h.p.) at 2100 r.p.m.
Bogies: One P3-10 (powered) and one BT38 (non-powered).
Couplers: BSI.
Seating Layout: 2+2 facing/unidirectional.
Dimensions: 23.29 x 2.70 m.

Gangways: Throughout.	**Wheel Arrangement:** 2-B.
Doors: Sliding plug.	**Maximum Speed:** 75 m.p.h.

52301–52335. DMSL. Dia. DX203. Lot No. 31026 1987–88. Converted under
Lot No. 31115 1991–2. –/72 1TD 1W (* –/66 1TD 1W). 41.2 t.
57301–57335. DMSL. Dia. DX203. Lot No. 31027 1987–88. Converted under
Lot No. 31115 1991–2. –/72 1TD (* –/66 1TD). 41.2 t.

Notes:

Cars numbered in the 573XX series have been renumbered by adding 50 to
the number so that the last two digits correspond with the set number.
Certain Central Trains units have been fitted with new-style seating.

153 301		**RR**	A	*NS*	HT	52301
153 302	r	**RR**	A	*WW*	CF	52302
153 303	r	**RR**	A	*WW*	CF	52303
153 304		**RR**	A	*NS*	HT	52304
153 305	r	**RR**	A	*WW*	CF	52305
153 306	r*	**PS**	P	*AR*	NC	52306	EDITH CAVELL
153 307		**RR**	A	*NS*	HT	52307
153 308	r	**RR**	A	*WW*	CF	52308
153 309	r*	**PS**	P	*AR*	NC	52309	GERARD FIENNES
153 310		**RR**	P	*NW*	NH	52310
153 311	r*	**PS**	P	*AR*	NC	52311	JOHN CONSTABLE
153 312	r	**RR**	A	*WW*	CF	52312
153 313		**RR**	P	*NW*	NH	52313
153 314	r*	**PS**	P	*AR*	NC	52314	DELIA SMITH
153 315		**RR**	A	*NS*	HT	52315
153 316		**RR**	P	*NW*	NH	52316
153 317		**RR**	A	*NS*	HT	52317
153 318	r	**RR**	A	*WW*	CF	52318
153 319		**RR**	A	*NS*	HT	52319
153 320	r	**RR**	P	*CT*	TS	52320
153 321	r	**RR**	P	*CT*	TS	52321
153 322	r*	**PS**	P	*AR*	NC	52322	BENJAMIN BRITTEN
153 323	r	**RR**	P	*CT*	TS	52323
153 324		**RR**	P	*NW*	NH	52324
153 325	r	**RR**	P	*CT*	TS	52325
153 326	r*	**PS**	P	*AR*	NC	52326	TED ELLIS
153 327	r	**RR**	A	*WW*	CF	52327
153 328		**RR**	A	*NS*	HT	52328
153 329	r	**RR**	P	*CT*	TS	52329
153 330		**RR**	P	*NW*	NH	52330
153 331		**RR**	A	*NS*	HT	52331
153 332		**RR**	P	*NW*	NH	52332
153 333	r	**RR**	P	*CT*	TS	52333

153 334	r	RR	P	CT	TS	52334
153 335	r*	PS	P	AR	NC	52335
153 351		RR	A	NS	HT	57351
153 352		RR	A	NS	HT	57352
153 353	r	RR	A	WW	CF	57353
153 354	r	RR	P	CT	TS	57354
153 355	r	RR	A	WW	CF	57355
153 356	r	RR	P	CT	TS	57356
153 357		RR	A	NS	HT	57357
153 358		RR	P	NW	NH	57358
153 359		RR	P	NW	NH	57359
153 360		RR	P	NW	NH	57360
153 361		RR	P	NW	NH	57361
153 362	r	RR	A	WW	CF	57362
153 363		RR	P	NW	NH	57363
153 364	r	RR	P	CT	TS	57364
153 365	r	RR	P	CT	TS	57365
153 366	r	RR	P	CT	TS	57366
153 367		RR	P	NW	NH	57367
153 368	r	RR	A	WW	CF	57368
153 369	r	RR	P	CT	TS	57369
153 370	r	RR	A	WW	CF	57370
153 371	r	RR	P	CT	TS	57371
153 372	r	RR	A	WW	CF	57372
153 373	r	RR	A	WW	CF	57373
153 374	r	RR	A	WW	CF	57374
153 375	r	RR	P	CT	TS	57375
153 376	r	RR	P	CT	TS	57376
153 377	r	RR	A	WW	CF	57377
153 378		RR	A	NS	HT	57378
153 379	r	RR	P	CT	TS	57379
153 380	r	RR	A	WW	CF	57380
153 381	r	RR	P	CT	TS	57381
153 382	r	RR	A	WW	CF	57382
153 383	r	RR	P	CT	TS	57383
153 384	r	RR	P	CT	TS	57384
153 385	r	RR	P	CT	TS	57385

MICHAEL PALIN

CLASS 155   LEYLAND BUS SUPER SPRINTER

DMSL–DMS.

Construction: Steel. Built from Leyland National bus parts on conventional bogied underframes.
Engines: One Cummins NT855R5 of 213 kW (285 h.p.) at 2100 r.p.m. per car
Bogies: One P3-10 (powered) and one BT38 (non-powered).
Couplers: BSI.
Seating Layout: 2+2 facing/unidirectional.
Dimensions: 23.21 x 2.70 m.
Gangways: Throughout.   **Wheel Arrangement:** 2-B – B-2.
Doors: Sliding plug.   **Maximum Speed:** 75 m.p.h.

DMSL. Dia. DP248. Lot No. 31057 1988. –/80 1TD 1W. 39.0 t.
DMS. Dia. DP249. Lot No. 31058 1988. –/80. 38.7 t.

Note: These units are owned by West Yorkshire PTE, although managed by Porterbrook Leasing Company.

155 341	**Y**	P	*NS*	NL	52341	57341
155 342	**Y**	P	*NS*	NL	52342	57342
155 343	**Y**	P	*NS*	NL	52343	57343
155 344	**Y**	P	*NS*	NL	52344	57344
155 345	**Y**	P	*NS*	NL	52345	57345
155 346	**Y**	P	*NS*	NL	52346	57346
155 347	**Y**	P	*NS*	NL	52347	57347

CLASS 156   METRO-CAMMELL SUPER SPRINTER

DMSL–DMS.

Construction: Steel.
Engines: One Cummins NT855R5 of 213 kW (285 h.p.) at 2100 r.p.m. per car
Bogies: One P3-10 (powered) and one BT38 (non-powered).
Couplers: BSI.
Seating Layout: 2+2 facing/unidirectional.
Dimensions: 23.03 x 2.73 m.
Gangways: Throughout.   **Wheel Arrangement:** 2-B – B-2.
Doors: Sliding.   **Maximum Speed:** 75 m.p.h.

DMSL. Dia. DP244 (q Dia DP261). Lot No. 31028 1988–89. –/74 (†* –/72, st$ –/70, u –/68) 1TD 1W. 36.1 t.
DMS. Dia. DP245. (q Dia. DP262) Lot No. 31029 1987–89. –/76 (q –/78, † –/74, tu$§ –/72) 35.5 t.

Notes: 156 500–514 are owned by Strathclyde PTE, although managed by Angel Trains Contracts.
Units reliveried in **RE**, **RN** or **NS** livery have been fitted with new seating.

156 401	r*	**RE**	P	*CT*	TS	52401	57401
156 402	r*	**RE**	P	*CT*	TS	52402	57402
156 403	r*	**RE**	P	*CT*	TS	52403	57403
156 404	r*	**RE**	P	*CT*	TS	52404	57404
156 405	r*	**RE**	P	*CT*	TS	52405	57405
156 406	r*	**RE**	P	*CT*	TS	52406	57406
156 407	r*	**CT**	P	*CT*	TS	52407	57407
156 408	r*	**RE**	P	*CT*	TS	52408	57408
156 409	r*	**RE**	P	*CT*	TS	52409	57409
156 410	r*	**RE**	P	*CT*	TS	52410	57410
156 411	r*	**RE**	P	*CT*	TS	52411	57411
156 412	r*	**RE**	P	*CT*	TS	52412	57412
156 413	r*	**RE**	P	*CT*	TS	52413	57413
156 414	r*	**RE**	P	*CT*	TS	52414	57414
156 415	r*	**RE**	P	*CT*	TS	52415	57415
156 416	r*	**RE**	P	*CT*	TS	52416	57416
156 417	r*	**RE**	P	*CT*	TS	52417	57417
156 418	r*	**RE**	P	*CT*	TS	52418	57418

156 419	r*	**RE**	P	*CT*	TS	52419	57419	
156 420	s	**RN**	P	*NW*	NH	52420	57420	
156 421	s	**RN**	P	*NW*	NH	52421	57421	
156 422	r*	**RE**	P	*CT*	TS	52422	57422	
156 423	s	**RN**	P	*NW*	NH	52423	57423	
156 424	s	**RN**	P	*NW*	NH	52424	57424	
156 425	s	**RN**	P	*NW*	NH	52425	57425	
156 426	s	**RN**	P	*NW*	NH	52426	57426	
156 427	s	**RN**	P	*NW*	NH	52427	57427	
156 428	s	**RN**	P	*NW*	NH	52428	57428	
156 429	s	**RN**	P	*NW*	NH	52429	57429	
156 430	rt	**CC**	A	*SR*	CK	52430	57430	
156 431	t	**PS**	A	*SR*	CK	52431	57431	
156 432	t	**PS**	A	*SR*	CK	52432	57432	
156 433	t	**CC**	A	*SR*	CK	52433	57433	The Kilmarnock Edition
156 434	rt	**PS**	A	*SR*	CK	52434	57434	
156 435	t	**PS**	A	*SR*	CK	52435	57435	
156 436	t	**PS**	A	*SR*	CK	52436	57436	
156 437	rt	**PS**	A	*SR*	CK	52437	57437	
156 438		**PS**	A	*NS*	NL	52438	57438	
156 439	rt	**CC**	A	*SR*	CK	52439	57439	
156 440	s	**RN**	P	*NW*	NH	52440	57440	
156 441	s	**RN**	P	*NW*	NH	52441	57441	
156 442	rt	**PS**	A	*SR*	CK	52442	57442	
156 443		**PS**	A	*NS*	HT	52443	57443	
156 444		**PS**	A	*NS*	HT	52444	57444	
156 445	ru	**PS**	A	*SR*	CK	52445	57445	
156 446	rt	**PS**	A	*SR*	IS	52446	57446	
156 447	ru	**PS**	A	*SR*	CK	52447	57447	
156 448		**PS**	A	*NS*	HT	52448	57448	
156 449	ru	**PS**	A	*SR*	CK	52449	57449	saint columba
156 450	t	**PS**	A	*SR*	CK	52450	57450	
156 451		**PS**	A	*NS*	HT	52451	57451	
156 452	s	**RN**	P	*NW*	NH	52452	57452	
156 453	ru	**PS**	A	*SR*	CK	52453	57453	
156 454	q	**NS**	A	*NS*	HT	52454	57454	
156 455	s	**RN**	P	*NW*	NH	52455	57455	
156 456	rt	**PS**	A	*SR*	CK	52456	57456	
156 457	rt	**PS**	A	*SR*	IS	52457	57457	
156 458	rt	**PS**	A	*SR*	IS	52458	57458	
156 459	s	**RN**	P	*NW*	NH	52459	57459	
156 460	s	**RN**	P	*NW*	NH	52460	57460	
156 461	s	**RN**	P	*NW*	NH	52461	57461	
156 462	r	**PS**	A	*SR*	CK	52462	57462	
156 463		**PS**	A	*NS*	HT	52463	57463	
156 464	s	**RN**	P	*NW*	NH	52464	57464	
156 465	u	**PS**	A	*SR*	CK	52465	57465	Bonnie Prince Charlie
156 466	s	**RN**	P	*NW*	NH	52466	57466	
156 467	rt	**PS**	A	*SR*	CK	52467	57467	
156 468		**PS**	A	*NS*	NL	52468	57468	
156 469		**PS**	A	*NS*	HT	52469	57469	

156 470		**PS**	A	*NS*	NL	52470	57470
156 471	q	**NS**	A	*NS*	NL	52471	57471
156 472		**PS**	A	*NS*	NL	52472	57472
156 473		**PS**	A	*NS*	NL	52473	57473
156 474	r†	**PS**	A	*SR*	IS	52474	57474
156 475	q	**NS**	A	*NS*	NL	52475	57475
156 476	t	**PS**	A	*SR*	CK	52476	57476
156 477	r†	**PS**	A	*SR*	IS	52477	57477	HIGHLAND FESTIVAL
156 478	r†	**PS**	A	*SR*	IS	52478	57478
156 479		**PS**	A	*NS*	NL	52479	57479
156 480	q	**NS**	A	*NS*	NL	52480	57480
156 481		**PS**	A	*NS*	NL	52481	57481
156 482	q	**NS**	A	*NS*	NL	52482	57482
156 483		**PS**	A	*NS*	NL	52483	57483
156 484	q	**NS**	A	*NS*	NL	52484	57484
156 485	ru	**PS**	A	*SR*	CK	52485	57485
156 486		**PS**	A	*NS*	NL	52486	57486
156 487		**PS**	A	*NS*	NL	52487	57487
156 488		**PS**	A	*NS*	NL	52488	57488
156 489		**PS**	A	*NS*	NL	52489	57489
156 490	q	**NS**	A	*NS*	NL	52490	57490
156 491		**PS**	A	*NS*	NL	52491	57491
156 492	r$	**PS**	A	*SR*	CK	52492	57492
156 493	r†	**PS**	A	*SR*	CK	52493	57493
156 494	§	**CC**	A	*SR*	CK	52494	57494
156 495	ru	**PS**	A	*SR*	CK	52495	57495
156 496	r†	**PS**	A	*SR*	CK	52496	57496
156 497		**PS**	A	*NS*	NL	52497	57497
156 498		**PS**	A	*NS*	NL	52498	57498
156 499	r†	**PS**	A	*SR*	IS	52499	57499
156 500	u	**CC**	A	*SR*	CK	52500	57500
156 501		**CC**	A	*SR*	CK	52501	57501
156 502		**CC**	A	*SR*	CK	52502	57502
156 503		**S**	A	*SR*	CK	52503	57503
156 504		**CC**	A	*SR*	CK	52504	57504
156 505		**CC**	A	*SR*	CK	52505	57505
156 506		**CC**	A	*SR*	CK	52506	57506
156 507		**CC**	A	*SR*	CK	52507	57507
156 508		**CC**	A	*SR*	CK	52508	57508
156 509		**CC**	A	*SR*	CK	52509	57509
156 510		**CC**	A	*SR*	CK	52510	57510
156 511		**CC**	A	*SR*	CK	52511	57511
156 512		**CC**	A	*SR*	CK	52512	57512
156 513		**CC**	A	*SR*	CK	52513	57513
156 514		**CC**	A	*SR*	CK	52514	57514

CLASS 158/0   BREL EXPRESS

DMSL (B)–DMSL (A) or DMCL–DMSL or DMCL–MSL–DMSL.

Construction: Welded aluminium.

Engines: 158 701–158 814: One Cummins NTA855R of 260 kW (350 h.p.) at
1900 r.p.m. per car.
158 815–158 862: One Perkins 2006-TWH of 260 kW (350 h.p.) at 1900 r.p.m.
per car.
158 863–158 872: One Cummins NTA855R of 300 kW (400 h.p.) at 2100 r.p.m.
per car.
Bogies: One BREL P4 (powered) and one BREL T4 (non-powered) per car.
Couplers: BSI.
Seating Layout: 2+2 facing/unidirectional in standard class and in Scotrail
first class. 2+2 facing in Northern Spirit first class, 2+1 facing/unidirectional
in Virgin Cross-Country first class.
Dimensions: 22.57 x 2.70 m.
Gangways: Throughout.   **Wheel Arrangement:** 2-B – B-2.
Doors: Sliding plug.   **Maximum Speed:** 90 m.p.h.
Non-Standard Livery: 0 Grey, orange, light blue and dark blue with orange
doors.

DMSL (B).. Dia. DP252. Lot No. 31051 BREL Derby 1989–92. –/68 1TD 1W. (†–
/66 1TD 1W). Public telephone and trolley space. 38.5 t.
MSL. Dia. DR207. Lot No. 31050 BREL Derby 1991. 37.1 t. –/70 2T. 37.1 t.
DMSL (A). Dia. DP251 Lot No. 31052 BREL Derby 1989–92. –/70 († –/68; § 32/
32) 1T. 37.8 t.

The above details refer to the "as built" condition. The following DMSL(B)
have now been converted to DMCL as follows:

52701–52746 (Scotrail). Dia. DP318. 15/51 1TD 1W (*15/53 1TD 1W).
52747–52751. (Virgin Cross-Country). Dia. DP323. 9/51 1TD 1W.
52757–52759. (First North-Western). Dia. DP333. 16/51 1TD 1W.
52760–779/781. (Northern Spirit 2-car Units). Dia. DP331. 16/48 1TD 1W.
52798–810/812–814 (Northern Spirit 3-car Units). Dia. DP332. 32/32 1TD 1W.
57811 (Northern Spirit 3-car Unit). Dia. DP330. 32/32 1TD 1W.

s Refurbished with new shape seat cushions, new saloon cladding and table
lamps in first class.
† Fitted with new seating.

158 701		**SR**	P	*SR*	HA	52701	57701
158 702		**SR**	P	*SR*	HA	52702	57702	BBC Scotland 75 Years
158 703		**SR**	P	*SR*	HA	52703	57703
158 704		**SR**	P	*SR*	HA	52704	57704
158 705		**SR**	P	*SR*	HA	52705	57705
158 706		**SR**	P	*SR*	HA	52706	57706
158 707		**SR**	P	*SR*	HA	52707	57707	Far North Line 125th ANNIVERSARY
158 708		**SR**	P	*SR*	HA	52708	57708
158 709		**SR**	P	*SR*	HA	52709	57709
158 710		**SR**	P	*SR*	HA	52710	57710
158 711		**SR**	P	*SR*	HA	52711	57711
158 712	*	**SR**	P	*SR*	HA	52712	57712
158 713		**SR**	P	*SR*	HA	52713	57713
158 714		**SR**	P	*SR*	HA	52714	57714
158 715		**SR**	P	*SR*	HA	52715	57715	Haymarket

158 716	*	**SR**	P	*SR*	HA	52716	57716
158 717	*	**SR**	P	*SR*	HA	52717	57717
158 718	*	**SR**	P	*SR*	HA	52718	57718
158 719		**SR**	P	*SR*	HA	52719	57719
158 720		**SR**	P	*SR*	HA	52720	57720
158 721		**SR**	P	*SR*	HA	52721	57721
158 722	*	**SR**	P	*SR*	HA	52722	57722
158 723		**SR**	P	*SR*	HA	52723	57723
158 724		**SR**	P	*SR*	HA	52724	57724
158 725		**SR**	P	*SR*	HA	52725	57725
158 726	*	**SR**	P	*SR*	HA	52726	57726
158 727		**SR**	P	*SR*	HA	52727	57727
158 728		**RE**	P	*SR*	HA	52728	57728
158 729		**RE**	P	*SR*	HA	52729	57729
158 730		**SR**	P	*SR*	HA	52730	57730
158 731		**SR**	P	*SR*	HA	52731	57731
158 732		**RE**	P	*SR*	HA	52732	57732
158 733		**SR**	P	*SR*	HA	52733	57733
158 734		**SR**	P	*SR*	HA	52734	57734
158 735		**SR**	P	*SR*	HA	52735	57735
158 736		**RE**	P	*SR*	HA	52736	57736
158 737		**RE**	P	*SR*	HA	52737	57737
158 738		**RE**	P	*SR*	HA	52738	57738
158 739		**RE**	P	*SR*	HA	52739	57739
158 740	*	**SR**	P	*SR*	HA	52740	57740
158 741		**SR**	P	*SR*	HA	52741	57741
158 742		**RE**	P	*SR*	HA	52742	57742
158 743		**RE**	P	*SR*	HA	52743	57743
158 744		**RE**	P	*SR*	HA	52744	57744
158 745		**RE**	P	*SR*	HA	52745	57745
158 746		**RE**	P	*SR*	HA	52746	57746
158 747		**RE**	P	*VX*	NH	52747	57747
158 748		**RE**	P	*VX*	NH	52748	57748
158 749		**RE**	P	*VX*	NH	52749	57749
158 750		**RE**	P	*VX*	NH	52750	57750
158 751		**RE**	P	*VX*	NH	52751	57751
158 752		**NW**	P	*NW*	NH	52752	57752
158 753		**NW**	P	*NW*	NH	52753	57753
158 754		**NW**	P	*NW*	NH	52754	57754
158 755		**NW**	P	*NW*	NH	52755	57755
158 756		**NW**	P	*NW*	NH	52756	57756
158 757		**NW**	P	*NW*	NH	52757	57757
158 758		**NW**	P	*NW*	NH	52758	57758
158 759		**NW**	P	*NW*	NH	52759	57759
158 760	s	**TX**	P	*NS*	NL	52760	57760
158 761	s	**TX**	P	*NS*	NL	52761	57761
158 762	s	**TX**	P	*NS*	NL	52762	57762
158 763	s	**TX**	P	*NS*	NL	52763	57763
158 764	s	**TX**	P	*NS*	NL	52764	57764
158 765	s	**TX**	P	*NS*	NL	52765	57765
158 766	s	**TX**	P	*NS*	NL	52766	57766

158 767	s	TX	P	NS	NL	52767		57767
158 768	s	TX	P	NS	NL	52768		57768
158 769	s	TX	P	NS	NL	52769		57769
158 770	s	TX	P	NS	NL	52770		57770
158 771	s	TX	P	NS	HT	52771		57771
158 772	s	TX	P	NS	NL	52772		57772
158 773	s	TX	P	NS	NL	52773		57773
158 774	s	TX	P	NS	HT	52774		57774
158 775	s	TX	P	NS	HT	52775		57775
158 776	s	TX	P	NS	HT	52776		57776
158 777	s	TX	P	NS	HT	52777		57777
158 778	s	TX	P	NS	HT	52778		57778
158 779	s	TX	P	NS	HT	52779		57779
158 780	r	CT	A	CT	TS	52780		57780
158 781	s	TX	P	NS	HT	52781		57781
158 782	r	RE	A	CT	TS	52782		57782
158 783	r	CT	A	CT	TS	52783		57783
158 784	r	CT	A	CT	TS	52784		57784
158 785	r	CT	A	CT	TS	52785		57785
158 786	r	CT	A	CT	TS	52786		57786
158 787	r	CT	A	CT	TS	52787		57787
158 788	r	CT	A	CT	TS	52788		57788
158 789	r	CT	A	CT	TS	52789		57789
158 790	r	CT	A	CT	TS	52790		57790
158 791	r	CT	A	CT	TS	52791		57791
158 792	r	RE	A	CT	TS	52792		57792
158 793	r	RE	A	CT	TS	52793		57793
158 794	r	RE	A	CT	TS	52794		57794
158 795	r	RE	A	CT	TS	52795		57795
158 796	r	RE	A	CT	TS	52796		57796
158 797	r	CT	A	CT	TS	52797		57797
158 798	s	TX	P	NS	HT	52798	58715	57798
158 799	s	TX	P	NS	HT	52799	58716	57799
158 800	s	TX	P	NS	HT	52800	58717	57800
158 801	s	TX	P	NS	HT	52801	58701	57801
158 802	s	TX	P	NS	HT	52802	58702	57802
158 803	s	TX	P	NS	HT	52803	58703	57803
158 804	s	TX	P	NS	HT	52804	58704	57804
158 805	s	TX	P	NS	HT	52805	58705	57805
158 806	s	TX	P	NS	HT	52806	58706	57806
158 807	s	TX	P	NS	HT	52807	58707	57807
158 808	s	TX	P	NS	HT	52808	58708	57808
158 809	s	TX	P	NS	HT	52809	58709	57809
158 810	s	TX	P	NS	HT	52810	58710	57810
158 811	s	TX	P	NS	HT	52811	58711	57811
158 812	s	TX	P	NS	HT	52812	58712	57812
158 813	s	TX	P	NS	HT	52813	58713	57813
158 814	s	TX	P	NS	HT	52814	58714	57814
158 815	†	RE	A	WW	CF	52815		57815
158 816	†	RE	A	WW	CF	52816		57816
158 817	†	RE	A	WW	CF	52817		57817

158 818	†	RE	A	*WW*	CF	52818	57818
158 819	†	RE	A	*WW*	CF	52819	57819
158 820	†	RE	A	*WW*	CF	52820	57820
158 821	†	RE	A	*WW*	CF	52821	57821
158 822	†	RE	A	*WW*	CF	52822	57822
158 823	†	RE	A	*WW*	CF	52823	57823
158 824	†	RE	A	*WW*	CF	52824	57824
158 825	†	RE	A	*WW*	CF	52825	57825
158 826	†	RE	A	*WW*	CF	52826	57826
158 827	†	RE	A	*WW*	CF	52827	57827
158 828	†	RE	A	*WW*	CF	52828	57828
158 829	†	RE	A	*WW*	CF	52829	57829
158 830	†	RE	A	*WW*	CF	52830	57830
158 831	†	RE	A	*WW*	CF	52831	57831
158 832	†	RE	A	*WW*	CF	52832	57832
158 833	†	RE	A	*WW*	CF	52833	57833
158 834	†	RE	A	*WW*	CF	52834	57834
158 835	†	RE	A	*WW*	CF	52835	57835
158 836	†	RE	A	*WW*	CF	52836	57836
158 837	†	RE	A	*WW*	CF	52837	57837
158 838	†	RE	A	*WW*	CF	52838	57838
158 839	†	RE	A	*WW*	CF	52839	57839
158 840	†	RE	A	*WW*	CF	52840	57840
158 841	†	RE	A	*WW*	CF	52841	57841
158 842	†	RE	A	*WW*	CF	52842	57842
158 843	†	RE	A	*WW*	CF	52843	57843
158 844	r	RE	A	*CT*	TS	52844	57844
158 845	r	RE	A	*CT*	TS	52845	57845
158 846	r	RE	A	*CT*	TS	52846	57846
158 847	r	RE	A	*CT*	TS	52847	57847
158 848	r	RE	A	*CT*	TS	52848	57848
158 849	r	RE	A	*CT*	TS	52849	57849
158 850	r	RE	A	*CT*	TS	52850	57850
158 851	r	RE	A	*CT*	TS	52851	57851
158 852	r	RE	A	*CT*	TS	52852	57852
158 853	r	CT	A	*CT*	TS	52853	57853
158 854	r	RE	A	*CT*	TS	52854	57854
158 855	r	RE	A	*CT*	TS	52855	57855
158 856	r	RE	A	*CT*	TS	52856	57856
158 857	r	RE	A	*CT*	TS	52857	57857
158 858	r	RE	A	*CT*	TS	52858	57858
158 859	r	RE	A	*CT*	TS	52859	57859
158 860	r	CT	A	*CT*	TS	52860	57860
158 861	r	RE	A	*CT*	TS	52861	57861
158 862	r	RE	A	*CT*	TS	52862	57862
158 863	†	RE	A	*WW*	CF	52863	57863
158 864	†	RE	A	*WW*	CF	52864	57864
158 865	†	RE	A	*WW*	CF	52865	57865
158 866	†	RE	A	*WW*	CF	52866	57866
158 867	†	0	A	*WW*	CF	52867	57867
158 868	†	RE	A	*WW*	CF	52868	57868

158 869	†	**RE**	A	*WW*	CF	52869	57869
158 870	†	**RE**	A	*WW*	CF	52870	57870
158 871	†	**RE**	A	*WW*	CF	52871	57871
158 872	†	**RE**	A	*WW*	CF	52872	57872

CLASS 158/9   BREL EXPRESS

DMSL–DMS. Units leased by West Yorkshire PTE. Details as for Class 158/0 except for seating layout and toilets.

DMSL.. Dia. DP252. Lot No. 31051 BREL Derby 1990–92. –/70 1TD 1W. Public telephone and trolley space. 38.1 t.
DMS. Dia. DP251. Lot No. 31052 BREL Derby 1990–92. –/72 and parcels area. 37.8 t.

Note: These units are leased by West Yorkshire PTE and are managed by Porterbrook Leasing Company.

158 901	**WY**	P	*NS*	NL	52901	57901
158 902	**WY**	P	*NS*	NL	52902	57902
158 903	**WY**	P	*NS*	NL	52903	57903
158 904	**WY**	P	*NS*	NL	52904	57904
158 905	**WY**	P	*NS*	NL	52905	57905
158 906	**WY**	P	*NS*	NL	52906	57906
158 907	**WY**	P	*NS*	NL	52907	57907
158 908	**WY**	P	*NS*	NL	52908	57908
158 909	**YN**	P	*NS*	NL	52909	57909
158 910	**WY**	P	*NS*	NL	52910	57910

CLASS 159   BREL EXPRESS

DMCL–MSL–DMSL. Built as Class 158 by BREL. Converted before entering passenger service to Class 159 by Rosyth Dockyard.

Construction: Welded aluminium.
Engines: One Cummins NTA855R of 300 kW (400 h.p.) at 2100 r.p.m. per car.
Bogies: One BREL P4 (powered) and one BREL T4 (non-powered) per car.
Couplers: BSI.
Seating Layout: 2+2 facing/unidirectional (standard class), 2+1 facing (first class).
Dimensions: 23.21 x 2.82 m.
Gangways: Throughout.   **Wheel Arrangement:** 2-B – B-2 – B-2.
Doors: Sliding plug.   **Maximum Speed:** 90 m.p.h.

DMCL.. Dia. DP322. Lot No. 31051 BREL Derby 1992–93. 24/28 1TD 1W. 38.5 t.
MSL. Dia. DR209. Lot No. 31050 BREL Derby 1992–93. 38 t. –/72 2T.
DMSL. Dia. DP260. Lot No. 31052 BREL Derby 1992–93. –/72 1T and parcels area. 37.8 t.

159 001	**NT**	P	*SW*	SA	52873	58718	57873	CITY OF EXETER
159 002	**NT**	P	*SW*	SA	52874	58719	57874	CITY OF SALISBURY
159 003	**SW**	P	*SW*	SA	52875	58720	57875	TEMPLECOMBE
159 004	**NT**	P	*SW*	SA	52876	58721	57876	BASINGSTOKE AND DEANE
159 005	**SW**	P	*SW*	SA	52877	58722	57877	
159 006	**NT**	P	*SW*	SA	52878	58723	57878	

159 007	**SW**	P	*SW*	SA	52879	58724	57879
159 008	**SW**	P	*SW*	SA	52880	58725	57880
159 009	**NT**	P	*SW*	SA	52881	58726	57881
159 010	**NT**	P	*SW*	SA	52882	58727	57882
159 011	**NT**	P	*SW*	SA	52883	58728	57883
159 012	**NT**	P	*SW*	SA	52884	58729	57884
159 013	**NT**	P	*SW*	SA	52885	58730	57885
159 014	**NT**	P	*SW*	SA	52886	58731	57886
159 015	**NT**	P	*SW*	SA	52887	58732	57887
159 016	**NT**	P	*SW*	SA	52888	58733	57888
159 017	**NT**	P	*SW*	SA	52889	58734	57889
159 018	**NT**	P	*SW*	SA	52890	58735	57890
159 019	**NT**	P	*SW*	SA	52891	58736	57891
159 020	**NT**	P	*SW*	SA	52892	58737	57892
159 021	**NT**	P	*SW*	SA	52893	58738	57893
159 022	**NT**	P	*SW*	SA	52894	58739	57894

CLASS 165/0   BREL NETWORK TURBO

DMCL–DMS or DMCL–MS–DMS. Built for Chiltern Line services.

Construction: Welded aluminium.
Engines: One Perkins 2006-TWH of 260 kW (350 h.p.) at 1900 r.p.m. per car.
Bogies: BREL P3-17 (powered), BREL T3-17 (non-powered).
Couplers: BSI.
Seating Layout: 3+2 facing/unidirectional (standard class), 2+2 facing (first class).
Dimensions: 23.50 x 2.85 m.
Gangways: Within unit only.   **Wheel Arrangement:** 2-B (– B-2) – B-2.
Doors: Sliding plug.   **Maximum Speed:** 75 m.p.h.

58801–58822. 58873–58878. DMCL. Dia. DP319. Lot No. 31087 York 1990. 16/72 1T. 37.0 t.
58823–58833. DMCL. Dia. DP320. Lot No. 31089 BREL York 1991–92. 24/60 1T. 37.0 t.
MS. Dia. DR208. Lot No. 31090 BREL York 1991–92. –/106. 37.0 t.
DMS. Dia. DP253. Lot No. 31088 BREL York 1991–92. –/98. 37.0 t.

Note: All Chiltern Railways units are fitted with tripcocks for working over London Underground tracks between Harrow-on-the-Hill and Amersham.

165 001	**NT**	A	*TT*	RG	58801	58834
165 002	**NT**	A	*TT*	RG	58802	58835
165 003	**NT**	A	*TT*	RG	58803	58836
165 004	**NT**	A	*TT*	RG	58804	58837
165 005	**NT**	A	*TT*	RG	58805	58838
165 006	**NT**	A	*CR*	AL	58806	58839
165 007	**NT**	A	*CR*	AL	58807	58840
165 008	**NT**	A	*CR*	AL	58808	58841
165 009	**NT**	A	*CR*	AL	58809	58842
165 010	**NT**	A	*CR*	AL	58810	58843
165 011	**NT**	A	*CR*	AL	58811	58844
165 012	**NT**	A	*CR*	AL	58812	58845
165 013	**NT**	A	*CR*	AL	58813	58846

165 014	**NT**	A	*CR*	AL	58814		58847
165 015	**NT**	A	*CR*	AL	58815		58848
165 016	**NT**	A	*CR*	AL	58816		58849
165 017	**NT**	A	*CR*	AL	58817		58850
165 018	**NT**	A	*CR*	AL	58818		58851
165 019	**NT**	A	*CR*	AL	58819		58852
165 020	**NT**	A	*CR*	AL	58820		58853
165 021	**NT**	A	*CR*	AL	58821		58854
165 022	**NT**	A	*CR*	AL	58822		58855
165 023	**NT**	A	*CR*	AL	58873		58867
165 024	**NT**	A	*CR*	AL	58874		58868
165 025	**NT**	A	*CR*	AL	58875		58869
165 026	**NT**	A	*CR*	AL	58876		58870
165 027	**NT**	A	*CR*	AL	58877		58871
165 028	**NT**	A	*CR*	AL	58878		58872
165 029	**NT**	A	*CR*	AL	58823	55404	58856
165 030	**NT**	A	*CR*	AL	58824	55405	58857
165 031	**NT**	A	*CR*	AL	58825	55406	58858
165 032	**NT**	A	*CR*	AL	58826	55407	58859
165 033	**NT**	A	*CR*	AL	58827	55408	58860
165 034	**NT**	A	*CR*	AL	58828	55409	58861
165 035	**NT**	A	*CR*	AL	58829	55410	58862
165 036	**NT**	A	*CR*	AL	58830	55411	58863
165 037	**NT**	A	*CR*	AL	58831	55412	58864
165 038	**NT**	A	*CR*	AL	58832	55413	58865
165 039	**NT**	A	*CR*	AL	58833	55414	58866

CLASS 165/1   BREL NETWORK TURBO

DMCL–DMS or DMCL–MS–DMS. Built for Thames Trains services.

Construction: Welded aluminium.
Engines: One Perkins 2006-TWH of 260 kW (350 h.p.) at 1900 r.p.m. per car.
Bogies: BREL P3-17 (powered), BREL T3-17 (non-powered).
Couplers: BSI.
Seating layout: 3+2 facing/unidirectional (standard class), 2+2 facing (first class).
Dimensions: 23.50 x 2.85 m.
Gangways: Within unit only.   **Wheel Arrangement:** 2-B (– B-2) – B-2.
Doors: Sliding plug.   **Maximum Speed:** 90 m.p.h.

58953–58969. DMCL. Dia. DP320. Lot No. 31098 BREL/ABB York 1992. 24/60
1T. 37.0 t.
58879–58898. DMCL. Dia. DP319. Lot No. 31096 BREL/ABB York 1992. 16/72
1T. 37.0 t.
MS. Dia. DR208. Lot No. 31099 BREL/ABB York 1992. –/106. 37.0 t.
DMS. Dia. DP253. Lot No. 31097 BREL/ABB York 1992. –/98. 37.0 t.

165 101	**NT**	A	*TT*	RG	58916	55415	58953
165 102	**NT**	A	*TT*	RG	58917	55416	58954
165 103	**NT**	A	*TT*	RG	58918	55417	58955
165 104	**NT**	A	*TT*	RG	58919	55418	58956
165 105	**NT**	A	*TT*	RG	58920	55419	58957
165 106	**NT**	A	*TT*	RG	58921	55420	58958

165 107	**NT**	A	*TT*	RG	58922	55421	58959
165 108	**NT**	A	*TT*	RG	58923	55422	58960
165 109	**NT**	A	*TT*	RG	58924	55423	58961
165 110	**NT**	A	*TT*	RG	58925	55424	58962
165 111	**NT**	A	*TT*	RG	58926	55425	58963
165 112	**NT**	A	*TT*	RG	58927	55426	58964
165 113	**NT**	A	*TT*	RG	58928	55427	58965
165 114	**NT**	A	*TT*	RG	58929	55428	58966
165 116	**NT**	A	*TT*	RG	58931	55430	58968
165 117	**NT**	A	*TT*	RG	58932	55431	58969
165 118	**NT**	A	*TT*	RG	58879		58933
165 119	**NT**	A	*TT*	RG	58880		58934
165 120	**NT**	A	*TT*	RG	58881		58935
165 121	**NT**	A	*TT*	RG	58882		58936
165 122	**NT**	A	*TT*	RG	58883		58937
165 123	**NT**	A	*TT*	RG	58884		58938
165 124	**NT**	A	*TT*	RG	58885		58939
165 125	**NT**	A	*TT*	RG	58886		58940
165 126	**NT**	A	*TT*	RG	58887		58941
165 127	**NT**	A	*TT*	RG	58888		58942
165 128	**NT**	A	*TT*	RG	58889		58943
165 129	**NT**	A	*TT*	RG	58890		58944
165 130	**NT**	A	*TT*	RG	58891		58945
165 131	**NT**	A	*TT*	RG	58892		58946
165 132	**NT**	A	*TT*	RG	58893		58947
165 133	**NT**	A	*TT*	RG	58894		58948
165 134	**NT**	A	*TT*	RG	58895		58949
165 135	**NT**	A	*TT*	RG	58896		58950
165 136	**NT**	A	*TT*	RG	58897		58951
165 137	**NT**	A	*TT*	RG	58898		58952
Spare	**NT**	A		ZC (S)	58930	55429	

CLASS 166   ABB NETWORK EXPRESS TURBO

DMCL (A)–MS–DMCL (B). Built for London Paddington–Oxford/Newbury services. Air conditioned.

Construction: Welded aluminium.
Engines: One Perkins 2006-TWH of 260 kW (350 h.p.) at 1900 r.p.m. per car.
Bogies: BREL P3-17 (powered), BREL T3-17 (non-powered).
Couplers: BSI.
Seating Layout: 3+2 facing/unidirectional (standard class) with 20 standard class seats in 2+2 format in DMCL(B), 2+2 facing (first class).
Dimensions: 22.91 x 2.81 m (DMCL), 22.72 x 2.81 m (MS).
Gangways: Within unit only.   **Wheel Arrangement:** 2-B – B-2 – B-2.
Doors: Sliding plug.   **Maximum Speed:** 90 m.p.h.

DMCL (A). Dia. DP321. Lot No. 31116 ABB York 1992–3. 16/75 1T. 40.62 t.
MS. Dia. DR209. Lot No. 31117 ABB York 1992–93. –/96. 38.04 t.
DMCL (B). Dia. DP321. Lot No. 31116 ABB York 1992–93. 16/72 1T. 40.64 t.

166 201	**NT**	A	*TT*	RG	58101	58601	58122

166 202	**NT**	A	*TT*	RG	58102	58602	58123
166 203	**NT**	A	*TT*	RG	58103	58603	58124
166 204	**NT**	A	*TT*	RG	58104	58604	58125
166 205	**NT**	A	*TT*	RG	58105	58605	58126
166 206	**NT**	A	*TT*	RG	58106	58606	58127
166 207	**NT**	A	*TT*	RG	58107	58607	58128
166 208	**NT**	A	*TT*	RG	58108	58608	58129
166 209	**NT**	A	*TT*	RG	58109	58609	58130
166 210	**NT**	A	*TT*	RG	58110	58610	58131
166 211	**NT**	A	*TT*	RG	58111	58611	58132
166 212	**NT**	A	*TT*	RG	58112	58612	58133
166 213	**NT**	A	*TT*	RG	58113	58613	58134
166 214	**NT**	A	*TT*	RG	58114	58614	58135
166 215	**NT**	A	*TT*	RG	58115	58615	58136
166 216	**NT**	A	*TT*	RG	58116	58616	58137
166 217	**NT**	A	*TT*	RG	58117	58617	58138
166 218	**NT**	A	*TT*	RG	58118	58618	58139
166 219	**NT**	A	*TT*	RG	58119	58619	58140
166 220	**NT**	A	*TT*	RG	58120	58620	58141
166 221	**NT**	A	*TT*	RG	58121	58621	58142

CLASS 168   ADTRANZ CLUBMAN

DMSL (A)–MSL–MS–DMSL (B). Air conditioned.

Construction: Welded aluminium underframes, sides and roofs and steel ends bolted together.
Engines: One MTU 6R183TD13H of 315 kW (422 h.p.) at 1900 r.p.m. per car.
Bogies: One Adtranz P3–23 and one BREL T3–23 per car.
Couplers: BSI.
Transmission: Hydraulic. Voith T211rzze to ZF final drive.
Gangways: Within unit only.
Doors: Swing plug.
Seating Layout: 2+2 facing/unidirectional.
Dimensions: 22.93 x 2.69 m (DMSL), 22.80 x 2.69 m (MS).
Gangways: Within unit only.   **Wheel Arrangement:** 2-B (– B-2 – B-2) – B-2.
Doors: Swing plug.   **Maximum Speed:** 100 m.p.h.

58151–58155. DMSL(A). Dia. DP270. Adtranz Derby 1997-8. –/60 1TD 1W. 43.7 t.
58156–58159. DMSL(A). Dia. DP280. Adtranz Derby 2000. –/59 1TD 2W. 43.7 t.
MSL. Dia. DR211. Adtranz Derby 1998. –/73 1T. 41.0 t.
MS. Dia. DR211. Adtranz Derby 1998. –/77. 40.5 t.
58251–58255. DMSL(B). Dia. DP270. Adtranz Derby 1998. –/66 1T. 43.6 t.
58256–58259. DMSL(B). Dia. DP281. Adtranz Derby 2000. –/69 1T. 43.6 t.

Notes:

All Chiltern Railways units are fitted with tripcocks for working over London Underground tracks between Harrow-on-the-Hill and Amersham.
It is intended to reform these units as 10 three-car sets with 58451–6 being renumbered 58656–60.

| 168 001 | **CR** | P | *CR* | AL | 58151 | 58651 | 58451 | 58251 |
| 168 002 | **CR** | P | *CR* | AL | 58152 | 58652 | 58452 | 58252 |

168 003	**CR**	P	*CR*	AL	58153	58653	58453	58253
168 004	**CR**	P	*CR*	AL	58154	58654	58454	58254
168 005	**CR**	P	*CR*	AL	58155	58655	58455	58255
168 106	**CR**	P	*CR*		58156			58256
168 107	**CR**	P	*CR*		58157			58257
168 108	**CR**	P	*CR*		58158			58258
168 109	**CR**	P	*CR*		58159			58259
168 110	**CR**	P	*CR*		58160			58260

CLASS 170   ADTRANZ TURBOSTAR

Various formations. Air conditioned.

Construction: Welded aluminium underframes, sides and roofs and steel ends bolted together.
Engines: One MTU 6R183TD13H of 315 kW (422 h.p.) at 1900 r.p.m. per car.
Bogies: One Adtranz P3–23 and one BREL T3–23 per car.
Couplers: BSI.
Transmission: Hydraulic. Voith T211rzze to ZF final drive.
Seating Layout: facing/unidirectional (2+2 in standard class and in first class on Class 170/1, 2+1 in first class on Class 170/2 and 170/4).
Dimensions: 22.93 x 2.69 m (DMSL), 22.80 x 2.69 m (MS).
Gangways: Within unit only.   **Wheel Arrangement:** 2-B (– B-2) – B-2.
Doors: Swing plug.   **Maximum Speed:** 100 m.p.h.

Class 170/1. Midland Mainline Units. DMCL–DMCL.

DMCL (A). Dia. DP324. Adtranz Derby 1998–1999. 12/45 1TD 2W. 45.19 t.
DMCL (B). Dia. DP325. Adtranz Derby 1998–1999. 12/52 1T. Catering point. 45.22 t

170 101	**MM**	P	*MM*	DY	50101	79101
170 102	**MM**	P	*MM*	DY	50102	79102
170 103	**MM**	P	*MM*	DY	50103	79103
170 104	**MM**	P	*MM*	DY	50104	79104
170 105	**MM**	P	*MM*	DY	50105	79105
170 106	**MM**	P	*MM*	DY	50106	79106
170 107	**MM**	P	*MM*	DY	50107	79107
170 108	**MM**	P	*MM*	DY	50108	79108
170 109	**MM**	P	*MM*	DY	50109	79109
170 110	**MM**	P	*MM*	DY	50110	79110
170 111	**MM**	P	*MM*	DY	50111	79111
170 112	**MM**	P	*MM*	DY	50112	79112
170 113	**MM**	P	*MM*	DY	50113	79113
170 114	**MM**	P	*MM*	DY	50114	79114
170 115	**MM**	P	*MM*	DY	50115	79115
170 116	**MM**	P	*MM*	DY	50116	79116
170 117	**MM**	P	*MM*	DY	50117	79117

Class 170/2. Anglia Railways Units. DMCL–MSLRB–DMSL.

DMCL. Dia. DP326. Adtranz Derby 1999. 30/3 1TD 2W. 44.30 t.
MSLRB. Dia. DR212. Adtranz Derby 1999. –/58 1T. Buffet and conductor's office 42.76 t.

DMSL. Dia. DP274. Adtranz Derby 1999. –/66 1T. 44.70 t.

170 201	**AR**	P	*AR*	NC	50201	56201	79201
170 202	**AR**	P	*AR*	NC	50202	56202	79202
170 203	**AR**	P	*AR*	NC	50203	56203	79203
170 204	**AR**	P	*AR*	NC	50204	56204	79204
170 205	**AR**	P	*AR*	NC	50205	56205	79205
170 206	**AR**	P	*AR*	NC	50206	56206	79206
170 207	**AR**	P	*AR*	NC	50207	56207	79207
170 208	**AR**	P	*AR*		50208	56208	79208

Class 170/3. South West Trains Units. DMCL–DMCL. On order.

DMCL(A). Dia. DP329. Adtranz Derby 1999–2000. 9/43 1TD 2W. 45.80 t.
DMCL(B). Dia. DP330. Adtranz Derby 1999–2000. 9/53 1T. 45.80 t.

170 301		P	*SW*		50301	79301
170 302		P	*SW*		50302	79302
170 303		P	*SW*		50303	79303
170 304		P	*SW*		50304	79304
170 305		P	*SW*		50305	79305
170 306		P	*SW*		50306	79306
170 307		P	*SW*		50307	79307
170 308		P	*SW*		50308	79308

Class 170/4. Scotrail Units. DMCL–MS–DMCL. Under construction.

DMCL(A). Dia. DP329. Adtranz Derby 1999–2000. 9/43 1TD 2W. 45.80 t.
MS. Dia. DR213. Adtranz Derby 1999–2000. –/76. 43.00 t.
DMCL(B). Dia. DP330. Adtranz Derby 1999–2000. 9/53 1T. 45.80 t.

170 401	**SR**	P	*SR*	HA	50401	56401	79401
170 402	**SR**	P	*SR*	HA	50402	56402	79402
170 403	**SR**	P	*SR*	HA	50403	56403	79403
170 404	**SR**	P	*SR*	HA	50404	56404	79404
170 405	**SR**	P	*SR*	HA	50405	56405	79405
170 406	**SR**	P	*SR*	HA	50406	56406	79406
170 407	**SR**	P	*SR*	HA	50407	56407	79407
170 408	**SR**	P	*SR*	HA	50408	56408	79408
170 409	**SR**	P	*SR*	HA	50409	56409	79409
170 410	**SR**	P	*SR*	HA	50410	56410	79410
170 411	**SR**	P	*SR*	HA	50411	56411	79411
170 412	**SR**	P	*SR*	HA	50412	56412	79412
170 413	**SR**	P	*SR*	HA	50413	56413	79413
170 414	**SR**	P	*SR*	HA	50414	56414	79414
170 415	**SR**	P	*SR*	HA	50415	56415	79415
170 416	**SR**	H	*SR*		50416	56416	79416
170 417	**SR**	H	*SR*		50417	56417	79417
170 418	**SR**	H	*SR*		50418	56418	79418
170 419	**SR**	H	*SR*		50419	56419	79419
170 420	**SR**	H	*SR*		50420	56420	79420
170 421	**SR**	H	*SR*		50421	56421	79421
170 422	**SR**	H	*SR*		50422	56422	79422

Class 170/5. Central Trains Two-car Units. DMSL–DMSL. Under construction.

DMSL(A). Dia. DP275. Adtranz Derby 1999–2000. –/55 1TD 2W. 45.80 t.
DMSL(B). Dia. DP276. Adtranz Derby 1999–2000. –/73 1T. 46.80 t.

170 501	**CT**	P	*CT*	TS	50501	79501
170 502	**CT**	P	*CT*	TS	50502	79502
170 503	**CT**	P	*CT*	TS	50503	79503
170 504	**CT**	P	*CT*	TS	50504	79504
170 505	**CT**	P	*CT*	TS	50505	79505
170 506	**CT**	P	*CT*	TS	50506	79506
170 507	**CT**	P	*CT*	TS	50507	79507
170 508	**CT**	P	*CT*	TS	50508	79508
170 509	**CT**	P	*CT*	TS	50509	79509
170 510	**CT**	P	*CT*	TS	50510	79510
170 511	**CT**	P	*CT*	TS	50511	79511
170 512	**CT**	P	*CT*	TS	50512	79512
170 513	**CT**	P	*CT*	TS	50513	79513
170 514	**CT**	P	*CT*		50514	79514
170 515	**CT**	P	*CT*		50515	79515
170 516	**CT**	P	*CT*		50516	79516
170 517	**CT**	P	*CT*		50517	79517
170 518	**CT**	P	*CT*		50518	79518
170 519	**CT**	P	*CT*		50519	79519
170 520	**CT**	P	*CT*		50520	79520
170 521	**CT**	P	*CT*		50521	79521
170 522	**CT**	P	*CT*		50522	79522
170 523	**CT**	P	*CT*		50523	79523

Class 170/6. Central Trains Three-car Units. DMSL–MS–DMSL. Under construction.

DMSL(A). Dia. DP275. Adtranz Derby 2000. –/55 1TD 2W. 45.80 t.
MS. Dia. DR214. Adtranz Derby 2000. –/74. 43.00 t.
DMSL(B). Dia. DP276. Adtranz Derby 2000. –/73 1T. 46.80 t.

170 630	**CT**	P	*CT*	50630	56630	79630
170 631	**CT**	P	*CT*	50631	56631	79631
170 632	**CT**	P	*CT*	50632	56632	79632
170 633	**CT**	P	*CT*	50633	56633	79633
170 634	**CT**	P	*CT*	50634	56634	79634
170 635	**CT**	P	*CT*	50635	56635	79635
170 636	**CT**	P	*CT*	50636	56636	79636
170 637	**CT**	P	*CT*	50637	56637	79637
170 638	**CT**	P	*CT*	50638	56638	79638
170 639	**CT**	P	*CT*	50639	56639	79639

CLASS 175 ALSTOM CORADIA 1000

New units under construction for First North Western.

Construction: Steel.
Engines: One Cummins N14 of 335 kW (450 h.p.).
Transmission: Hydraulic. Voith T211rzze to ZF final drive.
Bogies:
Couplers: Scharfenberg.
Seating Layout: 2+2 facing/unidirectional.
Dimensions: 23.06 x 2.80.
Gangways: Within unit only.   **Wheel Arrangement:** 2-B (– B-2 – B-2) – B-2.
Doors: Swing plug.   **Maximum Speed:** 100 m.p.h.

Class 175/0. DMSL–DMSL. Two-car units.

DMSL(A). Dia. DP278. Alstom Birmingham 1999–2000. –/54 1TD 2W. 51.00 t.
DMSL(B). Dia. DP279. Alstom Birmingham 1999–2000. –/64 1T. 51.00 t.

175 001	**FN**	W	NW	CH	50701 79701
175 002	**FN**	W	NW	CH	50702 79702
175 003	**FN**	W			50703 79703
175 004	**FN**	W			50704 79704
175 005	**FN**	W			50705 79705
175 006	**FN**	W			50706 79706
175 007	**FN**	W			50707 79707
175 008	**FN**	W			50708 79708
175 009	**FN**	W			50709 79709
175 010	**FN**	W			50710 79710
175 011	**FN**	W			50711 79711

Class 175/1. DMSL(A)–MSL–DMSL(B). Three-car units.

DMSL(A). Dia. DP278. Alstom Birmingham 1999–2000. –/54 1TD 2W. 51.00 t.
MSL. Dia. DR216. Alstom Birmingham 1999–2000. –/68 1T. 47.50 t.
DMSL(B). Dia. DP279. Alstom Birmingham 1999–2000. –/64 1T. 51.00 t.

175 101	**FN**	W	50751	56751	79751
175 102	**FN**	W	50752	56752	79752
175 103	**FN**	W	50753	56753	79753
175 104	**FN**	W	50754	56754	79754
175 105	**FN**	W	50755	56755	79755
175 106	**FN**	W	50756	56756	79756
175 107	**FN**	W	50757	56757	79757
175 108	**FN**	W	50758	56758	79758
175 109	**FN**	W	50759	56759	79759
175 110	**FN**	W	50760	56760	79760
175 111	**FN**	W	50761	56761	79761
175 112	**FN**	W	50762	56762	79762
175 113	**FN**	W	50763	56763	79763
175 114	**FN**	W	50764	56764	79764
175 115	**FN**	W	50765	56765	79765
175 116	**FN**	W	50766	56766	79766

CLASS 180   ALSTOM CORADIA 1000

New units under construction for First Great Western.

Construction: Steel.
Engines: One Cummins QSK 19 of 560 kW (750 h.p.).
Transmission: Hydraulic. Voith T211rzze to ZF final drive.
Couplers: Scharfenberg.
Bogies:
Gangways: Within unit only.
Doors: Swing plug.
Seating Layout: facing/unidirectional (2+2 in standard class and 2+1 in first class).
Dimensions: .
Gangways: Within unit only.   **Wheel Arrangement:** 2-B – B-2 – B-2 – B-2 – B-2.
Doors: Swing plug.   **Maximum Speed:** 125 m.p.h.

DMSL(A). Dia. DP2   . Alstom Birmingham 2000. –/46 2W 1TD. 53.00 t.
MFL. Dia. DR1   . Alstom Birmingham 2000. 42/– 1T 1W + catering point. 51.50 t.
MSL. Dia. DR2   . Alstom Birmingham 2000. –/68 1T. 51.50 t.
MSLRB. Dia. DR2   . Alstom Birmingham 2000. –/56 1T. 51.50 t.
DMSL(B). Dia. DP276. Alstom Birmingham 2000. –/56 1T. 53.00 t.

180 101	**GW**	W	*GW*	50801	56801	56831	56861 79801
180 102	**GW**	W	*GW*	50802	56802	56832	56862 79802
180 103	**GW**	W	*GW*	50803	56803	56833	56863 79803
180 104	**GW**	W	*GW*	50804	56804	56834	56864 79804
180 105	**GW**	W	*GW*	50805	56805	56835	56865 79805
180 106	**GW**	W	*GW*	50806	56806	56836	56866 79806
180 107	**GW**	W	*GW*	50807	56807	56837	56867 79807
180 108	**GW**	W	*GW*	50808	56808	56838	56868 79808
180 109	**GW**	W	*GW*	50809	56809	56839	56869 79809
180 110	**GW**	W	*GW*	50810	56810	56840	56870 79810
180 111	**GW**	W	*GW*	50811	56811	56841	56871 79811
180 112	**GW**	W	*GW*	50812	56812	56842	56872 79812
180 113	**GW**	W	*GW*	50813	56813	56843	56873 79813
180 114	**GW**	W	*GW*	50814	56814	56844	56874 79814

3.3. DIESEL ELECTRIC MULTIPLE UNITS

The following features are standard to ex-BR Southern Region diesel-electric multiple unit power cars (Classes 201–207):

Construction: Steel.
Engine: One English Electric 4SRKT Mk. 2 of 450 kW (600 h.p.) at 850 r.p.m.
Main Generator: English Electric EE824.
Traction Motors: Two English Electric EE507 mounted on the inner bogie.

The following features are standard to all diesel-electric multiple unit cars (Classes 201–207):

Couplings: Drophead buckeye.
Doors: Manually operated slam.
Brakes: Electro-pneumatic and automatic air.
Bogies: SR Mk. 4. (Former EMU TSOL vehicles have Commonwealth bogies).
Maximum Speed: 75 m.p.h.
Multiple Working: Other ex BR Southern Region DEMU vehicles.

CLASS 201/202   'HASTINGS' UNIT

DMBSO–3TSOL–DMBSO.

Preserved unit made up from 2 Class 201 short-frame cars and 2 Class 202 long-frame cars. The 'Hastings' units were made with narrow body-profiles for use on the section between Tonbridge and Battle which had tunnels of restricted loading gauge. These tunnels were converted to single track operation in the 1980s thus allowing standard loading gauge stock to be used. The set also contains a Class 411 EMU trailer (not Hastings line gauge).

Gangways: Within unit only.
Seating Layout: 2+2 facing.
Dimensions: 18.36 x 2.50 m (60000/60501), 20.34 x 2.50 m. (60118/60529) 20.34 x 2.82 m (70262).

60000. DMBSO. Dia DB203. Lot No. 30329 1957. –/22. 54 t.
60118. DMBSO. Dia DB203. Lot No. 30395 1957. –/30. 55 t. Renumbered from 60018.
60501. TSOL. Dia DB204. Lot No. 30331 1957. –/52 2T. 29 t.
60529. TSOL. Dia DH203. Lot No. 30397 1957. –/60 2T. 30 t.
70262. TSOL (ex Class 411/5 EMU). Dia. EH282. Lot No. 30455 1958–99. –/64 2T. 33.78 t.

Note: This unit carries set No. 1001.

201 001	G	HD *ON*	SE	60000	60501	70262	60529	60118

Names:

60000	Hastings		60118	Tunbridge Wells

CLASS 205/0 (3H)   BR EASTLEIGH 'HAMPSHIRE'

DMBSO–TSOL–DTCsoL or DMBSO–DTCsoL.

Gangways: Non-gangwayed.
Seating Layout: 3+2 facing or compartments.
Dimensions: 20.33 x 2.82 m (DMBSO), 20.28 x 2.82 m (TSO), 20.36 x 2.82 m (DTCsoL).

60111/117/154. DMBSO. Dia DB203. Lot No. 30332 1957. –/52. 56 t.
60122–124. DMBSO. Dia DB203. Lot No. 30540 1958–59. –/52. 56 t.
60146–151. DMBSO. Dia DB204. Lot No. 30671 1960–62. –/42. 56 t.
60650–670. TSO. Dia DH203. Lot No. 30542 1958–59. –/104. 30 t.
60673–678. TSO. Dia DH203. Lot No. 30672 1960–62. –/104. 30 t.
60800. DTCsoL. Dia DE301. Lot. No. 30333 1956–57. 13/50 2T. 32 t.
60811. DTCsoL. Dia DE302. Lot No. 30333 1956–57. 19/50 2T. 32 t.
60820. DTCsoL. Dia DE301. Lot No. 30399 1957–58. 13/50 2T. 32 t.
60823/824. DTCsoL. Dia DE301. Lot No. 30541 1958–59. 13/50 2T. 32 t.
60827–832. DTCsoL. Dia DE303. Lot No. 30673 1960–62. 13/62 2T. 32 t.

Note: 60154 was renumbered from 60100.

Unit					DMBSO	TSO	DTCsoL
205 001	CX	P	SC	SU	60154		60800
205 009	CX	P	SC	SU	60108	60658	60808
205 012	CX	P	SC	SU	60111		60811
205 018	CX	P	SC	SU	60117	60674	60828
205 023	G	HD		SE	60122		60820
205 024	N	P	SC	SU (U)	60123		60823
205 025	CX	P	SC	SU	60124		60824
205 028	CX	P	SC	SU	60146	60673	60827
205 032	N	P	SC	SU	60150	60677	60831
205 033	CX	P	SC	SU	60151	60678	60832
Spare	CX	P	SC	SU (S)	60650		
Spare	N	P	SC	SU (S)	60661		
Spare	N	P	SC	SU (S)	60669		
Spare	N	P	SC	SU (S)	60670		
Spare	N	P	SC	SE (S)	60668		

CLASS 205/2 (3H)   BR EASTLEIGH 'HAMPSHIRE'

DMBSO–TSOL (ex Class 411/5 EMU)–DTSOL. Refurbished 1980. Fluorescent lighting.

Details as for Class 205/0 except:

Gangways: Within unit only.   **Seating Layout:** 3+2 facing.

DMBSO. Dia DB203. Lot No. 30332 1957. –/39. 57 t.
TSOL. Dia. EH282. Converted from loco-hauled TSO 4059 Lot No. 30149 Swindon 1955–57. –/64 2T. 33.78 t.
DTSOL. Dia DE204. Lot No. 30333 1957. –/76 2T. 32 t.
Note: This unit operates as a two-car set in winter.

205 205	N	P	SC	SU	60110	71634	60810

CLASS 207/0 (2D)   BR EASTLEIGH 'OXTED'

DMBSO–DTSO (formerly DMBSO–TCsoL–DTSO).

This class was built for the Oxted line and the units are therefore referred to as 'Oxted' units.
Gangways: Non-gangwayed.   **Seating Layout:** 3+2 facing or compartments.
Dimensions: 20.33 x 2.74 m. (DMBSO), 20.32 x 2.74 m. (DTSO), 20.33 x 2.74 m.(TCsoL).

DMBSO. Dia DB205. Lot No. 30625 1962. –/42. 56 t.
TCsoL. Dia DH301. Lot No. 30626 1962. 24/42 1T. 31 t.
DTSO. Dia DE201. Lot No. 30627 1962. –/76. 32 t.

207 017	N	P	*SC*	SU	60142	60916

CLASS 207/1 (3D)   BR EASTLEIGH 'OXTED'

DMBSO–TSOL–DTSO.
Gangwayed sets with a Class 411 EMU trailer in the centre.

Gangways: Within unit only. **Seating Layout:** 2+2 facing.
Dimensions: 20.34 x 2.74 m. (DMBSO), 20.32 x 2.74 m. (DTS).

DMBSO. Dia DB205. Lot No. 30625 1962. –/40. 56 t.
70286. TSOL. Dia. DH206. Lot No. 30455 1958–59. –/64 2T. 33.78 t.
70547/9. TSOL. Dia. DH206. Lot No. 30620 1960–61 –/64 2T. 33.78 t.
DTSO. Dia DE201. Lot No. 30627 1962. –/75. 32 t.
Note: These units operate as two-car sets in winter.

207 201	CX	P	*SC*	SU	60129	70286	60901	Ashford Fayre
207 202	N	P	*SC*	SU	60130	70549	60904	Brighton Royal Pavilion
207 203	CX	P	*SC*	SU	60127	70547	60903	

CLASS 220   BOMBARDIER VOYAGER

DMSO–MSORB–MSO–DMFO. New units under construction for Virgin Cross-Country.

Construction: Steel.
Engine: Cummins of 750 h.p. (560 kW) at 1800 r.p.m.
Transmission: Alstom three-phase traction motors on inner bogie.
Couplers: Dellner.
Seating Layout: 2+2 mainly unidirectional (standard class, 2+1 facing/unidirectional (first class).
Dimensions: 23.85 x . m. (outer cars),   . x . m. (inner cars).
Gangways: Within unit only.
Wheel Arrangement: 2-B – B-2 – B-2 – B-2.
Doors: Swing plug.   **Maximum Speed:** 125 m.p.h.

DMSO. Dia DC201. Bombardier Eurorail 2000. –/42 1TD 1W.   . t.
MSORB. Dia DD201. Bombardier Eurorail 2000. –/58.   . t.
MSO. Dia DD202. Bombardier Eurorail 2000. –/62 1TD 1W.   . t.

DMFO. Dia DC101. Bombardier Prorail 2000. 26/– 1TD 1W.   .   t.

220 001	GR	*VX*	60301	60201	60701	60401
220 002	GR	*VX*	60302	60202	60702	60402
220 003	GR	*VX*	60303	60203	60703	60403
220 004	GR	*VX*	60304	60204	60704	60404
220 005	GR	*VX*	60305	60205	60705	60405
220 006	GR	*VX*	60306	60206	60706	60406
220 007	GR	*VX*	60307	60207	60707	60407
220 008	GR	*VX*	60308	60208	60708	60408
220 009	GR	*VX*	60309	60209	60709	60409
220 010	GR	*VX*	60310	60210	60710	60410
220 011	GR	*VX*	60311	60211	60711	60411
220 012	GR	*VX*	60312	60212	60712	60412
220 013	GR	*VX*	60313	60213	60713	60413
220 014	GR	*VX*	60314	60214	60714	60414
220 015	GR	*VX*	60315	60215	60715	60415
220 016	GR	*VX*	60316	60216	60716	60416
220 017	GR	*VX*	60317	60217	60717	60417
220 018	GR	*VX*	60318	60218	60718	60418
220 019	GR	*VX*	60319	60219	60719	60419
220 020	GR	*VX*	60320	60220	60720	60420
220 021	GR	*VX*	60321	60221	60721	60421
220 022	GR	*VX*	60322	60222	60722	60422
220 023	GR	*VX*	60323	60223	60723	60423
220 024	GR	*VX*	60324	60224	60724	60424
220 025	GR	*VX*	60325	60225	60725	60425
220 026	GR	*VX*	60326	60226	60726	60426
220 027	GR	*VX*	60327	60227	60727	60427
220 028	GR	*VX*	60328	60228	60728	60428
220 029	GR	*VX*	60329	60229	60729	60429
220 030	GR	*VX*	60330	60230	60730	60430
220 031	GR	*VX*	60331	60231	60731	60431
220 032	GR	*VX*	60332	60232	60732	60432
220 033	GR	*VX*	60333	60233	60733	60433
220 034	GR	*VX*	60334	60234	60734	60434

CLASS 221   BOMBARDIER VOYAGER

DMSO–MSORB–MSO(–MSO)–DMFO. New tilting units under construction for Virgin Cross-Country (five-car units) and Virgin West Coast (four-car units).

Construction: Steel.
Engine: Cummins of 750 h.p. (560 kW) at 1800 r.p.m.
Transmission: Alstom three-phase traction motors on inner bogie.
Couplers: Dellner.
Seating Layout: 2+2 mainly unidirectional (standard class, 2+1 facing/unidirectional (first class).
Dimensions: 23.85 x   . m. (outer cars),   . x   . m. (inner cars).
Gangways: Within unit only.
Wheel Arrangement: 2-B – B-2 – B-2 (– B-2) – B-2.
Doors: Swing plug.   **Maximum Speed:** 125 m.p.h.

DMSO. Dia DF201. Bombardier Prorail 2000. –/42 1TD 1W.   .   t.
MSORB. Dia. DG201. Bombardier Prorail 2000. –/58.   .   t.
MSO. Dia. DDG02. Bombardier Prorail 2000. –/62 1TD 1W.   .   t.
DMFO. Dia DF101. Bombardier Prorail 2000. 26/– 1TD 1W.   .   t.

221 001	GR	VX	60351	60851	60951	60751	60451
221 002	GR	VX	60352	60852	60952	60752	60452
221 003	GR	VX	60353	60853	60953	60753	60453
221 004	GR	VX	60354	60854	60954	60754	60454
221 005	GR	VX	60355	60855	60955	60755	60455
221 006	GR	VX	60356	60856	60956	60756	60456
221 007	GR	VX	60357	60857	60957	60757	60457
221 008	GR	VX	60358	60858	60958	60758	60458
221 009	GR	VX	60359	60859	60959	60759	60459
221 010	GR	VX	60360	60860	60960	60760	60460
221 011	GR	VX	60361	60861	60961	60761	60461
221 012	GR	VX	60362	60862	60962	60762	60462
221 013	GR	VX	60363	60863	60963	60763	60463
221 014	GR	VX	60364	60864	60964	60764	60464
221 015	GR	VX	60365	60865	60965	60765	60465
221 016	GR	VX	60366	60866	60966	60766	60466
221 017	GR	VX	60367	60867	60967	60767	60467
221 018	GR	VX	60368	60868	60968	60768	60468
221 019	GR	VX	60356	60869	60969	60769	60456
221 020	GR	VX	60370	60870	60970	60770	60470
221 021	GR	VX	60371	60871	60971	60771	60471
221 022	GR	VX	60372	60872	60972	60772	60472
221 023	GR	VX	60373	60873	60973	60773	60473
221 024	GR	VX	60374	60874	60974	60774	60474
221 025	GR	VX	60375	60875	60975	60775	60475
221 026	GR	VX	60376	60876	60976	60776	60476
221 027	GR	VX	60377	60877	60977	60777	60477
221 028	GR	VX	60378	60878	60978	60778	60478
221 029	GR	VX	60379	60879	60979	60779	60479
221 030	GR	VX	60380	60880	60980	60780	60480
221 031	GR	VX	60381	60881	60981	60781	60481
221 032	GR	VX	60382	60882	60982	60782	60482
221 033	GR	VX	60383	60883	60983	60783	60483
221 034	GR	VX	60384	60884	60984	60784	60484
221 035	GR	VX	60385	60885	60985	60785	60485
221 036	GR	VX	60386	60886	60986	60786	60486
221 037	GR	VX	60387	60887	60987	60787	60487
221 038	GR	VX	60388	60888	60988	60788	60488
221 039	GR	VX	60389	60889	60989	60789	60489
221 040	GR	VX	60390	60890	60990	60790	60490
221 041	GR	VW	60391		60991	60791	60491
221 042	GR	VW	60392		60992	60792	60492
221 043	GR	VW	60393		60993	60793	60493
221 044	GR	VW	60394		60994	60794	60494

3.4. SERVICE DMUS

This section lists vehicles not used for revenue earning purposes. Some vehicles are numbered in the special service stock number series or in the internal user series (An internal user vehicle is a vehicle specifically for use in one location/area which is not otherwise permitted over the Railtrack network without special authority).

CLASS 101   INTERNAL USER OFFICE VEHICLE

Converted 1990 from Class 101 DTC. Gangwayed.
Maximum Speed: 70 mph.
Bogies: DT11.   **Couplings:** Screw.
Brakes: Twin pipe vacuum.   **Multiple Working:** Blue Square.
Doors: Manually operated slam.   **Dimensions:** 18.49 x 2.82 m.
Note: Allocated Internal User number 042222, but this is not carried.

54342. DT. Dia. DZ5??. Lot No. 30468 Metro-Cammell 1958. 22.5 t.

Spare	**BG**	NS	NL(S)	54342

CLASS 114/1   ROUTE LEARNING UNIT

DMB–DT. Converted 1992 from Class 114/1. Gangwayed within unit.
Engines: Two Leyland TL11/40 of 153 kW (205 hp) at 1950 rpm per car.
Transmission: Mechanical. Cardan shaft and freewheel to a four-speed epicyclic gearbox with a further cardan shaft to the final drive, each engine driving the inner axle of one bogie.
Maximum Speed: 70 mph.
Bogies: DD9 + DT9.   **Couplings:** Screw.
Brakes: Twin pipe vacuum.   **Multiple Working:** Blue Square.
Doors: Manually operated slam/roller shutter.   **Dimensions:** 20.45 x 2.82 m.
Non-Standard Livery: Grey, red and yellow.

977775. DMB. Dia. DZ518. Lot No. 30209 Derby 1957. 39.0 t.
977776. DT. Dia. DZ516. Lot No. 30210 Derby 1957. 29.2 t.

-		**0**	E *E*	TE	977775	977776

CLASS 122   ROUTE LEARNING UNIT

DM. Converted 1995 from DMBS.
Engines: Two Leyland 1595 of 112 kW (150 hp) at 1800 rpm.
Gangways: Non gangwayed single car with cab at each end.
Bogies: DD10.   **Dimensions:** 20.45 x 2.82 x m.
Note: Allocated number 977941, but this is not carried.

DM. Dia. DZ5??. Lot No. 30419 Gloucester 1958. Converted by ABB Doncaster 1995. 36.5 t.

-		**LH**	E *E*	TE	55012

CLASS 141   WEEDSPRAY UNIT

DM–DM. Built from Leyland National bus components on BREL underframe. 141 105 and 141 112 await conversion.
Engines: One Leyland TL11/65 of 157 kW (210 hp) at 1950 rpm per car.
Transmission: Mechanical. SCG R500 4-speed epicyclic gearbox with cardan shafts to SCG RF420i final drive.
Doors: Four-leaf folding.   **Dimensions:** 15.45 x 2.50 m.

55505/12/18. DM. Dia. DZ540. Lot No. 30978 BREL Derby. Converted Serco Railtest Derby 1998. . t.
55525/32/38. DM. Dia. DZ541. Lot No. 30977 BREL Derby. Converted Serco Railtest Derby 1998. . t.

141 105	WY	P	SO	ZA (S) 55505	55525	
141 112	WY	P	SO	ZA (S) 55512	55532	
–	SO	P	SO	ZA 55518	55538	FLOWER

CLASS 210   TRACK INSPECTION UNIT

DM–DMB. Prototype DEMU currently undergoing conversion.
Engines: One MTU 12V396TC12 of 914 kW (1225 hp) at 1500 rpm (* One Paxman Valenta 6RP200 of 842 kW (1129 hp) at 1500 rpm.
Main Alternator: GEC G563AZ (* Brush BA1002A).
Transmission: Electric. Four GEC (* Brush) traction motors.
Maximum Speed: 90 mph.   **Bogies:** BP20.
Brakes: Electro-pneumatic.   **Doors:** Power operated sliding.
Couplers: Tightlock (outer), bar (inner) end.
Multiple Working: Within class only.   **Dimensions:** 20.52 x 2.82 m.

999603. DM. Dia. DZ5 . Lot No. 30931 BREL Derby 1982.
999604. DMB. Dia. DZ5 . Lot No. 30930 BREL Derby 1982.

210 001	N	AY	ZG(S)	999603	999604*

CLASS 930   SANDITE/DEICING UNIT

DMB–T–DMB. Converted 1993 from Class 205. Gangwayed within unit. Sandite trailer 977870 is replaced by de-icing trailer 977364 as required.
Engine: One English Electric 4SRKT Mk. 2 of 450 kW (600 hp) at 850 rpm per power car.
Transmission: Electric. Two English Electric EE507 traction motors mounted on the inner bogie of each power car. **Multiple Working:** Classes 201–207.
Maximum Speed: 75 mph.   **Bogies:** SR Mk. 4.
Brakes: Electro-pneumatic and automatic air.
Doors: Manually operated slam.   **Couplings:** Drophead buckeye.
Dimensions: 20.33 (DMB) or 20.28 (T) x 2.82 m.

977939–977940. DMB. Dia. DZ537. Lot No. 30671 Eastleigh 1962. 56.0 t.
977870. T. Dia. DZ533. Lot No. 30542 Eastleigh 1960. 30.5 t.

930 301	RO	RK	RK	SU	977939	977870	977940

CLASS 960   ULTRASONIC TEST TRAIN

DM–DM. Converted 1986 from Class 101. Gangwayed within unit. Often operates as a tractor unit with either 975091, 999550 or 999602 as a centre car.
Engines: Two Leyland 680/1 of 112 kW (150 hp) at 1800 rpm per car.
Transmission: Mechanical. Cardan shaft and freewheel to a four-speed epicyclic gearbox with a further cardan shaft to the final drive, each engine driving the inner axle of one bogie.   **Dimensions:** 18.49 x 2.82 m.
Maximum Speed: 70 mph.   **Doors:** Manually operated slam.
Bogies: DD15.   **Couplings:** Screw.
Brakes: Twin pipe vacuum.   **Multiple Working:** Blue Square.

977391. DM. Dia. DZ503. Lot No. 30500 Metro-Cammell 1959. 32.5 t.
977392. DM. Dia. DZ503. Lot No. 30254 Metro-Cammell 1956. 32.5 t.

-	**S0**	SO	*SO*	RG	977391	977392

CLASS 960   TEST UNIT

DM–DM. Converted 1991 from Class 101. Gangwayed within unit.
Engines: Two Leyland 680/1 of 112 kW (150 hp) at 1800 rpm per car.
Transmission: Mechanical. Cardan shaft and freewheel to a four-speed epicyclic gearbox with a further cardan shaft to the final drive, each engine driving the inner axle of one bogie.   **Maximum Speed:** 70 mph.
Bogies: DD15.   **Couplings:** Screw.
Brakes: Twin pipe vacuum.   **Multiple Working:** Blue Square.
Doors: Manually operated slam.   **Dimensions:** 18.49 x 2.82 m.

977693. DM. Dia. DZ503. Lot No. 30261 Metro-Cammell 1957. 32.5 t.
977694. DM. Dia. DZ503. Lot No. 30276 Metro-Cammell 1958. 32.5 t.

-	**S0**	SO	*SO*	BY	977693	977694	Iris 2

CLASS 960   SANDITE UNITS

DMB. Converted 1991/93 from Class 121. Non gangwayed.
Engines: Two Leyland 1595 of 112 kW (150 hp) at 1800 rpm.
Transmission: Mechanical. Cardan shaft and freewheel to a four-speed epicyclic gearbox with a further cardan shaft to the final drive, each engine driving the inner axle of one bogie.
Maximum Speed: 70 mph.
Bogies: DD10.   **Couplings:** Screw.
Brakes: Twin pipe vacuum.   **Multiple Working:** Blue Square.
Doors: Manually operated slam.   **Dimensions:** 20.45 x 2.82 m.

977722-977723. DMB. Dia. DZ515. Lot No. 30518 Pressed Steel 1960. 38.0 t.
977858–60/66/73. DMB. Dia. DZ526. Lot No. 30518 Pressed Steel 1960. 38.0 t.

960 002	**N**	RK		AL(S)	977722
121 021	**R0**	RK	*RK*	BY	977723
55024	**M**	RK	*RK*	AL	977858
960 011	**N**	RK		LO(S)	977859

960 012	**N**	RK	*RK*	AL	977860
960 013	**RO**	RK	*RK*	NC	977866
960 014	**N**	RK	*RK*	RG	977873

CLASS 960   SANDITE UNIT

DMB. Converted 1991 from Class 122 vehicle. Non gangwayed.
Engines: Two Leyland 1595 of 112 kW (150 hp) at 1800 rpm.
Transmission: Mechanical. Cardan shaft and freewheel to a four-speed
epicyclic gearbox with a further cardan shaft to the final drive, each engine
driving the inner axle of one bogie.   **Maximum Speed:** 70 mph.
Bogies: DD10.   **Couplings:** Screw.
Brakes: Twin pipe vacuum.   **Multiple Working:** Blue Square.
Doors: Manually operated slam.   **Dimensions:** 20.45 x 2.82 m.

DM. Dia. DX516. Lot No. 30419 Gloucester 1958. 36.5 t.

| 122 019 | **RO** | RK | *RK* | BY | 975042 |

CLASS 960/9   SANDITE & ROUTE LEARNING UNITS

DM–DM. Converted 1993 from Class 101 vehicles. Gangwayed within unit.
Engines: Two Leyland 680/1 of 112 kW (150 hp) at 1800 rpm per car.
Transmission: Mechanical. Cardan shaft and freewheel to a four-speed
epicyclic gearbox with a further cardan shaft to the final drive, each engine
driving the inner axle of one bogie.   **Maximum Speed:** 70 mph.
Bogies: DD15.   **Couplings:** Screw.
Brakes: Twin pipe vacuum.   **Multiple Working:** Blue Square.
Doors: Manually operated slam.   **Dimensions:** 18.49 x 2.82 m.

977895. DM. Dia. DZ503. Lot No. 30275 Metro-Cammell 1958. 32.5 t.
977896/900. DM. Dia. DZ504. Lot No. 30276 Metro-Cammell 1958. 32.5 t.
977897/901/903. DM. Dia. DZ503. Lot No. 30259 Metro-Cammell 1957. 32.5 t.
977898. DM. Dia. DZ515. Lot No. 30256 Metro-Cammell 1957. 32.5 t.
977899. DM. Dia. DZ503. Lot No. 30500 Metro-Cammell 1959. 32.5 t.
977902. DM. Dia. DZ503. Lot No. 30261 Metro-Cammell 1957. 32.5 t.
977904. DM. Dia. DZ503. Lot No. 30270 Metro-Cammell 1957. 32.5 t.

960 991	**N**	RK		LO(S)	977895	977896
960 992	**BG**	RK		LO(S)	977897	977898
960 993	**BG**	RK		LO(S)	977899	977900
960 994	**BG**	RK		LO(S)	977901	977902
960 995	**BG**	RK		LO(S)	977903	977904

UNCLASSIFIED   TEST UNIT

DMB. Converted 1968 from Unclassified DMBS. Non gangwayed.
Engines: Two Leyland 680/1 of 112 kW (150 hp) at 1800 rpm.
Transmission: Mechanical. Cardan shaft and freewheel to a four-speed
epicyclic gearbox with a further cardan shaft to the final drive, each engine

driving the inner axle of one bogie. **Maximum Speed:** 70 mph.
Bogies: **Couplings:** Screw.
Brakes: Twin pipe vacuum.   **Dimensions:** 18.49 x 2.79 m.
Doors: Manually operated slam.
Multiple Working: Obsolete Yellow Diamond system/Blue Square.

Note: Also carries former number 79900.

DMB. Dia. DZ530. Lot No. 30380 Derby 1956. 27.2 t.

| - | G | SO | | ZA(S) | 975010 | | Iris |

UNCLASSIFIED   DE-ICING TRAILER

T. Converted 1960 from 4-Sub EMU vehicle. Non gangwayed. Operates with
977939/40.
Maximum Speed: 70 m.p.h.   **Couplings:** Drophead buckeye.
Bogies: Central 43 inch.   **Multiple Working:** SR system.
Brakes: Electro-pneumatic and automatic air.
Doors: Manually operated slam.   **Dimensions:**

T. Dia. EZ520. Eastleigh 1946. 29.0 t.

| - | RO | RK | *RK* | SU | 977364 |

UNCLASSIFIED   TRACK ASSESSMENT UNIT

DM–DM. Purpose built service unit. Gangwayed within unit.
Engine: One Cummins NT-855-RT5 of 213 kW (285 hp) at 2100 rpm per power car.
Transmission: Hydraulic. Voith T211r with cardan shafts to Gmeinder GM190
final drive.
Maximum Speed: 75 m.p.h.   **Couplers:** BSI automatic.
Bogies: BP38 (powered), BT38 (non-powered).
Brakes: Electro-pneumatic.   **Dimensions:** 20.06 x 2.82 m.
Doors: Manually operated slam & power operated sliding.
Multiple Working: With classes 141–158 and 170 only.
Non-Standard Livery: Grey, red and blue.

999600. DM. Dia. DZ536. Lot No. 4060 BREL York 1987. 36.5 t.
999601. DM. Dia. DZ536. Lot No. 4061 BREL York 1987. 36.5 t.

| - | 0 | SO | *SO* | NC | 999600 | 999601 |

UNCLASSIFIED   ULTRASONIC TEST CAR

T. Converted 1986 from Class 432 EMU. Gangwayed. Operates with 977391/2.
Maximum Speed: 70 m.p.h.
Bogies: SR Mk. 6.   **Couplings:** Screw.
Brakes: Twin pipe vacuum.   **Multiple Working:** Blue Square.
Doors: Manually operated slam.   **Dimensions:** 19.66 x 2.82 m.

999602. T. Dia. DZ531. Lot No. 30862 York 1974. 55.5 t.

| - | SO | SO | *SO* | ZA | 999602 |

3.5. DMUS AWAITING DISPOSAL

This section lists vehicles awaiting disposal of classes or types not otherwise represented in this publication (except as Internal User vehicles). Notes regarding common detail applicable to first and second generation units also apply to this section as appropriate.

CLASS 141   BREL/LEYLAND PACER

DMS–DMSL. Built from Leyland National bus parts on four-wheeled underframes.

Construction: Steel. Leyland National bus parts on four-wheeled underframes.
Engines: One Leyland TL11/65 of 157 kW (210 h.p.) at 1950 r.p.m. (* Cummins LTA10-R of 172 kW at 2100 r.p.m.) per car.
Transmission: Mechanical. SCG R500 4-speed epicyclic gearbox with cardan shafts to SCG RF420i final drive (* Hydraulic. Voith T211r with Gmeinder final drive).
Dimensions: 15.45 x 2.50 m.
Seating Layout: 2+2 mainly unidirectional bus style.
Gangways: Within unit only.   **Wheel Arrangement:** 1-A A-1.
Doors: Power-operated folding.   **Maximum Speed:** 75 m.p.h.

DMS. Dia. DP228 Lot No. 30977 BREL Derby 1984. Modified by Barclay 1988–89. –/50. 26.0 t.
DMSL. Dia. DP229 Lot No. 30978 BREL Derby 1984. Modified by Barclay 1988–89. –/44 1T. 26.5 t.

141 101	**WY**	P	NL (S)	55521	55541
141 102	**WY**	P	HT (S)	55502	55522
141 103	**WY**	P	ZB (S)	55503	55523
141 106	**WY**	P	ZB (S)	55506	55526
141 107	**WY**	P	ZB (S)	55507	55527
141 108	**WY**	P	ZB (S)	55508	55528
141 109	**WY**	P	HT (S)	55509	55529
141 110	**WY**	P	ZB (S)	55510	55530
141 111	**WY**	P	HT (S)	55511	55531
141 113 *	**WY**	P	NL (S)	55513	55533
141 114	**WY**	P	NL (S)	55514	55534
141 115	**WY**	P	HT (S)	55515	55535
141 116	**WY**	P	MM (S)	55516	55536
141 117	**WY**	P	HT (S)	55517	55537
141 119	**WY**	P	NL(S)	55519	55539
141 120	**WY**	P	ZB(S)	55520	55540

CLASS 151   METRO-CAMMELL SPRINTER

DMS–MS († MS)–DMS. Prototype Metro-Cammell Sprinter.

Construction: Aluminium body on steel underframe.
Engines: One Cummins NT-855-R4 of 213 kW (285 hp) at 2100 rpm per car.
Transmission: Hydraulic. Twin Disc TA-33-1316 with cardan shafts to Gmeinder GM190 final drive.

Bogies: BX9P (powered), BX9T(non-powered).
Gangways: Within unit only.
Dimensions: 19.98 x 2.81 x 3.89 m.
Non-Standard Livery: 0 Unpainted.
55202–55203. DMS. Dia. DP233. Lot No. 30987 Metro-Cammell 1985. –/72 1T. 32.4 t.
55402. MS. Dia. DR204. Lot No. 30989 Metro-Cammell 1985. –/76. 36.5 t.
55403. MS. Dia. DR2??. Lot No. 30989 Metro-Cammell 1985. –/73. 37.50 t.
55302–55303. DMS. Dia. DP232. Lot No. 30988 Met-Camm. 1985. –/76. 36.70 t.

| 151 003 | **0** | A | ZA | 55202 | 55402 | 55302 |
| 151 004 | **0** | A | ZA | 55203 | 55403 | 55303 |

MISCELLANEOUS VEHICLES

No.	Location		Type
54350	CB		101 DTCL

Former Service Vehicles:

No.	Former No.	Location	Type
977191	(56106)	CB	100 QXV (ex DTSL)
977696	(60522)	ZG(S)	951 TSOL

4. ELECTRIC MULTIPLE UNITS

USING THIS SECTION – LAYOUT OF INFORMATION

25 kV a.c. 50 Hz overhead Electric Multiple Units (EMUs) and 'Versatile' EMUs (units capable of utilising more than one type of electrical supply system) are listed in numerical order of class number, then in numerical order of set number – using official numbers as allocated by the Rolling Stock Library. Individual 'loose' vehicles are listed in numerical order after vehicles formed into fixed formations. Where numbers carried are different to those officially allocated, these are noted in class headings where appropriate.

750 V d.c. third rail EMUs are listed in numerical order of set numbers actually carried. Some of these differ from the six digit numbers allocated by the RSL.

Where sets or vehicles have been renumbered since the previous edition of this book, former numbering detail is shown alongside current detail.

Each entry is laid out as in the following example:

Set No.	Detail	Livery	Owner	OperationDepot	Formation			
1706	†	**CX**	A	*SC* BI	76094	63035	70713	76040

CLASS HEADINGS

Principal details and dimensions are quoted for each class in metric and/or imperial units as considered appropriate bearing in mind common UK usage. Abbreviations used are shown in Section 6.9.

All dimensions and weights are quoted for vehicles in an 'as new' condition with all necessary supplies on board. Dimensions are quoted in the order Length – Width – Height. All lengths are quoted are over buffers or couplings as appropriate. All dimensions quoted are maxima. Height of vehicles is quoted over body, ignoring pantographs (where fitted).

Bogie Types are quoted in the format motored/non-motored (e.g. BP20/BT13 denotes BP20 motored bogies and BT non-motored bogies).

DETAIL DIFFERENCES

Only detail differences which currently affect the areas and types of train which vehicles may work are shown. All other detail differences are specifically excluded. Where such differences occur within a class or part class, these are shown alongside the individual set or vehicle number. Meaning of abbreviations used in this context is detailed in individual class headings.

LIVERY CODES

Livery codes are used in this publication to denote the various liveries carried by vehicles. Readers should note it is impossible in a publication of this size to list every livery variation which currently exists. In particular items ignored for the purposes of this book include:

• Minor colour variations;
• Omission of logos;
• All numbering, lettering and branding.

The descriptions quoted are thus a general guide only and may be subject to slight variation between individual vehicles. Logos as appropriate for each livery are normally deemed to be carried.

A complete list of livery codes used in this publication appears in Section 6.1.

OWNER CODES

Owner codes are used in this publication to denote the owners of vehicles listed. Most vehicles are leased by the TOCs from specialist leasing companies.

A complete list of owner codes used in this publication appears in Section 6.2.

OPERATION CODES

Operation codes are used in this publication to denote the normal usage of the units/vehicles listed – i.e. A guide to the services of which train operating company any unit/vehicle will normally be used upon. Where a unit/vehicle is used for non-revenue earning purposes, an indication to the normal type of usage is given in the class heading.

Where no operation code is shown, a unit/vehicle is currently not in use. In this instance the symbol (S) – denoting stored – will appear immediately after the location code.

Where an operation code is shown, but a unit/vehicle is also shown as stored – then the unit/vehicle remains available for use (i.e. on hire), but is currently out of use.

Readers should appreciate some units/vehicles are only operational for certain periods of the year (e.g. Sandite and De-Icing units). As such units/vehicles are normally stored at other times of the year, locations during such store periods are not shown in this publication.

A complete list of operation codes used in this publication appears in Section 6.4.

DEPOT & LOCATION CODES

Depot codes are used to denote the normal maintenance base of each operational vehicle. However, maintenance may be carried out at other locations and may also be carried out by mobile maintenance teams.

Location codes are used to denote the current actual location of stored vehicles. A location code will always be followed by (S) to denote stored.

A complete list of depot and location codes used in this publication appears in Section 6.5.

SET FORMATIONS

Set formations shown are those normally maintained. Readers should note some set formations might be temporarily varied from time to time to suit maintenance and/or operational requirements. Vehicles shown as 'Spare' are not formed in any regular set formation.

NAMES

Only names carried with official sanction are listed in this publication. As far as possible names are shown in UPPER/lower case characters as actually shown on the name carried on the vehicle(s). Inscriptions carried on crests and/or plates additional to the main name are not shown. Complete units are regarded as named rather than just the individual car(s) which carry the name.

GENERAL INFORMATION

CLASSIFICATION AND NUMBERING

25 kV a.c. 50 Hz overhead and 'Versatile' EMUs are classified in the series 300–399.

750 V d.c. third rail EMUs are classified in the series 400–599.

Service units are classified in the series 900–949.

EMU individual cars are numbered in the series 61000–78999, except for vehicles used on the Isle of Wight – which are numbered in a separate series.

Prior to privatisation, Service Stock individual cars were numbered in the series 975000–975999 and 977000–977999, although this series was not used exclusively for EMU vehicles. Since privatisation, use of these series has been sporadic, vehicles often now retaining their former numbers.

Where a vehicle carries an incorrect number which duplicates another correct number, the actual number carried is shown followed by " to indicate a duplicate number. Correct number details are noted in the class heading.

Any vehicle constructed to replace another vehicle following accident damage and carring the same number as the original vehicle is denoted by the suffix [2] in this publication.

DESIGN CONSIDERATIONS

Unless otherwise stated all vehicles listed have bar couplings at non-driving ends and tread brakes. In all types of vehicle except 'Express' stock, seating is 3 + 2 (i.e. three seats on one side of the gangway plus two on the other side) in standard class open vehicles, 2 + 2 in first class open vehicles, 8 per compartment in standard class and 6 per compartment in first class. In Express stock, seating is 2 + 2 in standard class open vehicles and 2 + 1 in first class open vehicles.

OPERATING CODES

These codes are used by TOC staff to describe the various different types of vehicles and normally appear on data panels on the non-driving ends of vehicles.

ATC	Auxiliary Equipment Trailer Composite
ATS	Auxiliary Equipment Trailer Standard
BDBS	Battery Driving Trailer Brake Standard
BDMS	Battery Driving Motor Standard
BDTC	Battery Driving Trailer Composite
BDTS	Battery Driving Trailer Standard
DM	Driving Motor
DMBS	Driving Motor Brake Standard
DMC	Driving Motor Composite
DMF	Driving Motor First
DMLF	Driving Motor Lounge First
DMLV	Driving Motor Luggage Van
DMFRK	Driving Motor First with Kitchen
DMS	Driving Motor Standard
DT	Driving Trailer
DTB	Driving Trailer Brake
DTBS	Driving Trailer Brake Standard
DTC	Driving Trailer Composite
DTF	Driving Trailer First
DTV	Driving Trailer Van
DTS	Driving Trailer Standard
M	Motor
MB	Motor Brake
MBLS	Motor Brake Restaurant Buffet Lounge Standard
MBS	Motor Brake Standard
MF	Motor First
MFD	Motor First with disabled accommodation
MS	Motor Standard
MSD	Motor Standard with disabled accommodation
PMB	Pantograph Motor Buffet Standard
PMS	Pantograph Motor Standard
PMV	Pantograph Motor Van
PTF	Pantograph Trailer First
PTS	Pantograph Trailer Standard
PTSRMB	Pantograph Trailer Standard with Buffet/Shop
TAV	Trailer Auxiliary Equipment Van
TBC	Trailer Brake Composite
TBF	Trailer Brake First
TBS	Trailer Brake Standard
TC	Trailer Composite
TF	Trailer First
TFH	Trailer First with Handbrake
TRBS	Trailer Restaurant Buffet Standard
TS	Trailer Standard

TSD   Trailer Standard with Disabled Persons' toilet.
TSH   Trailer Standard with Handbrake
TSW   Trailer Standard with Wheelchair Accommodation

The letters 'O' (denoting Open), 'K' (denoting Corridor) or 'L' (denoting Lavatory) may be added to the above codes on some vehicle data panels. Where two vehicles of the same type are formed within the same unit, the above codes may be suffixed by (A) and (B) to differentiate between the vehicles.

A composite is a vehicle containing both first and standard class accommodation, although first class accommodation on some EMU vehicles has now all been permanently declassified. A brake vehicle is a vehicle containing separate specific accommodation for the conductor (as opposed to the use of rear or intermediate cabs on some units).

Single motor coach 25 kV a.c. 50 Hz overhead EMUs (except Class 306) all have the pantograph mounted on the motor coach. Units with more than one motor coach have the pantograph mounted on a trailer car denoted as shown above.

DESIGN CODES AND DIAGRAM CODES

For each type of vehicle the Rolling Stock Library issues a seven character 'Design Code' consisting of two letters plus four numbers and a suffix letter. (e.g. EF2110A). The first five characters of the Design Code are known as the 'Diagram Code' and these are quoted in this publication in sub-headings. The meaning of the various characters of the Design Code is as follows:

First Character
E   Electric Multiple Unit
L   Eurostar Unit

Second Character (EMU vehicles)
A   Driving Motor
B   Driving Motor Brake
C   Non-driving Motor
D   Non-driving Motor Brake
E   Driving Trailer
F   Battery Driving Trailer
G   Driving Trailer Brake
H   Trailer
I   Battery Driving Motor
J   Trailer Brake
N   Trailer Buffet
O   Battery Driving Trailer Brake
P   Trailer with Handbrake
X   Driving Motor Van
Z   All types of service vehicle

Second Character (Eurostar vehicles)
A   Driving Motor
B   Non-driving Motor
C   Trailer (with train manager's compartment) – position 3

D	Trailer – position 4
E	Trailer (with public telephone) – position 5
F	Trailer – position 6
G	Kitchen/Bar
H	Trailer – position 8
J	Trailer (with public telephone) – position 9
K	Trailer (with staff compartment) – position 10

Third Character

1	First class accommodation
2	Standard class accommodation
3	Composite accommodation
4	Unclassified accommodation
5	No passenger accommodation

Fourth & Fifth Characters
These distinguish between different designs of vehicle, each design being allocated a unique two-digit number.

Special Note
Where vehicles have been declassified, the correct design code for a declassified vehicle is quoted in this publication, even though this may be at variance with RSL records, which do not always show the reality of the current position.

ACCOMMODATION

The information given in class headings and sub-headings is in the form F/S nT (or TD) nW. For example 12/54 1T 1W denotes 12 first class and 54 standard class seats, 1 toilet and 1 wheelchair space.

BUILD DETAILS

Lot Numbers
Vehicles ordered under the auspices of BR were allocated a Lot (batch) number when ordered and these are quoted in class headings and sub-headings.

Builders/Heavy Maintenance Providers
Abbreviations used to denote builders are shown in Section 6.8.

The previous practice of showing dual builder details (e.g. Ashford/Eastleigh) where vehicle underframe and body were built at two separate locations has been discontinued as this is now virtually the industry norm rather than an exceptional circumstance.

4.1. 25 kV a.c. 50 Hz OVERHEAD & 'VERSATILE' EMUs

Supply System: Except where otherwise stated, all units in this section operate on 25 kV a.c. 50 Hz overhead only.

CLASS 303   PRESSED STEEL SUBURBAN

DTS–MBS–BDTS. Gangwayed within unit. 2 + 2 (* 2 + 3) seating.
Construction: Steel.
Traction Motors: Four Metropolitan Vickers MV155 of 155 kW each.
Dimensions: 20.18 x 2.82 x 3.86 m.
Maximum Speed: 75 mph.   **Doors:** Power operated sliding.
Couplings: Buckeye.   **Bogies:** Gresley ED3/ET3.
Multiple Working: Classes 303–312 only.

61481–61515. MBS. Dia. ED220. Lot No. 30580 Pressed Steel 1959–60. –/48. 56.4 t.
61812–61867. MBS. Dia. ED220. Lot No. 30630 Pressed Steel 1960–61. –/48. 56.4 t.
75566–75600. DTS. Dia. EE241. Lot No. 30579 Pressed Steel 1959–60. –/56. 34.4 t.
75601–75635. BDTS. Dia. EF217. Lot No. 30581 Pressed Steel 1959–60. –/56. 38.4 t.
75746–75801. DTS. Dia. EE241 (* EE206). Lot No. 30629 Pressed Steel 1960–61. –/56 (* –/83). 34.4 (* 34.5) t.
75802–75857. BDTS. Dia. EF217. Lot No. 30631 Pressed Steel 1960–61. –/56. 38.4 t.

303 001	S	A	SR	GW	75566	61481	75601
303 003	S	A	SR	GW	75568	61483	75603
303 004	S	A	SR	GW	75569	61484	75604
303 006	S	A	SR	GW	75571	61486	75606
303 008	S	A	SR	GW	75573	61488	75608
303 009	S	A	SR	GW	75574	61489	75609
303 010	S	A	SR	GW	75575	61490	75610
303 011	S	A	SR	GW	75576	61491	75611
303 012	S	A	SR	GW	75577	61492	75612
303 013	S	A	SR	GW	75578	61493	75613
303 014	S	A	SR	GW	75579	61494	75614
303 016	S	A	SR	GW	75750	61496	75616
303 019	CC	A	SR	GW	75584	61499	75619
303 020	S	A	SR	GW	75585	61500	75620
303 021	CC	A	SR	GW	75586	61501	75621
303 023	CC	A	SR	GW	75588	61503	75623
303 024	S	A		GW(S)	75589	61504	75624
303 025	S	A	SR	GW	75590	61505	75625
303 027	S	A	SR	GW	75592	61507	75627

303 028	S	A		GW(S)	75600	61813	75845
303 032	S	A	SR	GW	75597	61512	75632
303 033	S	A	SR	GW	75595	61860	75817
303 034	S	A	SR	GW	75599	61514	75634
303 037	S	A	SR	GW	75781	61508	75803
303 040	S	A	SR	GW	75581	61816	75806
303 043	S	A	SR	GW	75572	61819	75809
303 045	S	A	SR	GW	75755	61821	75811
303 047	S	A	SR	GW	75757	61823	75813
303 054	S	A	SR	GW	75764	61830	75820
303 055	S	A	SR	GW	75765	61831	75821
303 056	S	A	SR	GW	75766	61832	75822
303 058	S	A	SR	GW	75768	61834	75824
303 061	S	A	SR	GW(S)	75771	61837	75827
303 065	S	A	SR	GW	75775	61841	75831
303 070	S	A	SR	GW	75780	61846	75836
303 077	S	A	SR	GW	75787	61853	75843
303 079	S	A	SR	GW	75789	61855	75635
303 080	S	A	SR	GW	75790	61856	75846
303 083	S	A	SR	GW	75793	61859	75849
303 085	S	A	SR	GW	75795	61861	75851
303 087	CC	A	SR	GW	75797	61863	75853
303 088	S	A	SR	GW	75798	61864	75854
303 089	S	A	SR	GW	75799	61865	75855
303 090	S	A	SR	GW	75800	61866	75856
303 091	S	A	SR	GW	75801	61867	75857
Spare	* BG	A		LT(S)	75773		

Name (carried on MBS):

303 089   COWAL HIGHLAND GATHERING 1894–1994

CLASS 305   BR SUBURBAN

BDTC (declassified)–MBS–DTS or BDTS–MBS–TS–DTS. Gangwayed within unit.
Construction: Steel.
Traction Motors: Four GEC WT380 of 153 kW each.
Dimensions: 20.35 (BDTC, BDTS & DTS) or 20.29 (MBS & TS) x 2.8 x 3.84 m.
Maximum Speed: 75 mph.   **Doors:** Manually operated slam.
Couplings: Buckeye.   **Bogies:** Gresley ED5/ET5.
Multiple Working: Classes 303–312 only.

61410–61428. MBS. Dia. ED216. Lot No. 30567 Doncaster 1960. –/76 (*–/58; †–/72). 56.5 t.
70356–70374. TS. Dia. EH223. Lot No. 30568 Doncaster 1960. –/86 1T. 31.5 t.
75424–75442. BDTC († BDTS). Dia. EF304 († EF2??). Lot No. 30566 Doncaster 1960. 24/52 (*20/40; †–/80) 1T. 36.5 t.
75443–75461. DTS. Dia. EE220. Lot No. 30569 Doncaster 1960. –/88 (* –/70). 32.7 t.

305 501	†	**RR**	A	*SR*	GW	75424	61410	70356	75443
305 502	†	**RR**	A	*SR*	GW	75425	61421	70357	75444
305 506		**GM**	A	*NW*	LG	75429	61415		75448
305 508	†	**RR**	A	*SR*	GW	75431	61417	70363	75450
305 511	*	**GM**	A	*NW*	LG	75434	61420		75453
305 516		**GM**	A	*NW*	LG	75439	61425		75458
305 517	†	**RR**	A	*SR*	GW	75440	61426	70372	75459
305 519	†	**RR**	A	*SR*	GW	75442	61428	70374	75461

CLASS 306   METRO-CAMMELL/BRCW SUBURBAN

DMS–TBS–DTS. Non gangwayed. 2 + 2 seating. Original supply system 1500 V
d.c. overhead, converted 1960–61. Retained for special workings only, not
normally used on timetabled services.
Construction: Steel.
Traction Motors: Four Crompton Parkinson of 155 kW each.
Dimensions: 19.24 (DMS & DTS) or 17.40 (TBS) x 2.89 x 3.84 m.
Maximum Speed: 70 mph.   **Doors:** Power operated sliding.
Couplings: Screw.   **Bogies:** LNER ED6/ET6.
Multiple Working: Classes 303–312 only.

65201–65292. DMS. Dia. EA203. Lot No. 363 Metro-Cammell 1949. –/62. 51.7 t.
65401–65492. TBS. Dia. EJ201. Lot No. 365 BRCW 1949. –/46. 26.4 t.
65601–65692. DTS. Dia. EE211. Lot No. 364 Metropolitan-Cammell 1949. –/60. 27.9 t.

| 306 017 | | **G** | H | *GE* | IL(S) | 65217 | 65417 | 65617 |

CLASS 308   BR SUBURBAN

BDTC (declassified)–MBS–DTS. Gangwayed within unit. Originally 4-car units,
but surviving TS cars are all now spare.
Construction: Steel.
Traction Motors: Four English Electric 536A of 143.5 kW each.
Dimensions: 19.88 (BDTC & DTS) or 19.35 (MBS & TS) x 2.82 x 3.86 m.
Maximum Speed: 75 mph.   **Doors:** Manually operated slam.
Couplings: Buckeye.   **Bogies:** Gresley ED5/ET5.
Multiple Working: Classes 303–312 only.

61883–61891. MBS. Dia. ED216. Lot No. 30653 York 1961–62. –/76. 55.0 t.
61893–61915. MBS. Dia. ED216. Lot No. 30657 York 1961–62. –/76. 55.0 t.
70611–70619. TS. Dia. EH223. Lot No. 30654 York 1961. Converted from TC. –/86
1T. 30.0 t.
70620–70643. TS. Dia. EH223. Lot No. 30658 York 1961–62. Converted from
TC. –/86 1T. 30.0 t.
75878–75886. BDTC. Dia. EF304. Lot No. 30652 York 1961–62. 24/50 1T. 36.3 t.
75887–75895. DTS. Dia. EE220. Lot No. 30655 York 1961–62. –/88. 33.0 t.
75896–75928. BDTC. Dia. EF304. Lot No. 30656 York 1961–62. 24/52 1T. 36.3 t.
75929–75961. DTS. Dia. EE220. Lot No. 30659 York 1961–62. –/88. 33.0 t.

308 134	**WY**	A	*NS*	ZH(S)	75879	61884	75888
308 136	**WY**	A	*NS*	NL	75881	61886	75890
308 137	**WY**	A	*NS*	NL	75882	61887	75891

308 138	**WY**	A	*NS*	NL	75883	61888	75892	
308 141	**WY**	A	*NS*	NL	75886	61891	75895	
308 143	**WY**	A	*NS*	NL	75897	61893	75930	
308 144	**WY**	A	*NS*	NL	75880	61894	75931	
308 145	**WY**	A	*NS*	NL	75899	61895	75932	
308 147	**WY**	A	*NS*	NL	75901	61897	75934	
308 152	**WY**	A	*NS*	NL	75913	61902	75939	
308 153	**WY**	A	*NS*	NL	75907	61903	75940	
308 154	**WY**	A	*NS*	NL	75908	61904	75941	
308 155	**WY**	A	*NS*	NL	75909	61905	75942	
308 157	**WY**	A	*NS*	NL	75915	61907	75944	
308 158	**WY**	A	*NS*	NL	75912	61908	75945	
308 159	**WY**	A	*NS*	NL	75906	61909	75946	
308 161	**WY**	A	*NS*	NL	75911	61911	75948	
308 162	**WY**	A	*NS*	NL	75916	61912	75949	
308 163	**WY**	A	*NS*	NL	75917	61913	75950	
308 164	**WY**	A	*NS*	NL	75918	61914	75951	
308 165	**WY**	A	*NS*	NL	75919	61915	75952	

Spare TS.

| Spare | **N** | A | | CB(S) | 70612 | 70621 | 70622 | 70631 |
| Spare | **N** | A | | CB(S) | 70640 | | | |

CLASS 309   BR 'CLACTON' EXPRESS

BDTC–MBS–TS–DTS. Gangwayed throughout.
Construction: Steel.
Traction Motors: Four GEC WT401 of 210 kW each.
Dimensions: 20.18 x 2.82 x 3.90 m.
Maximum Speed: 100 mph.   **Doors:** Manually operated slam.
Couplings: Buckeye.   **Bogies:** Commonwealth.
Multiple Working: Classes 303–312 only.
Advertising Livery:
• 309 624 'Manchester Airport Air Express'.

61925–61931. MBS. Dia. ED218. Lot No. 30676 York 1962. –/52. 57.7 t.
61932–61939. MBS. Dia. ED218. Lot No. 30680 York 1962. –/52. 57.7 t.
70253–70259. TS. Dia. EH229. Lot No. 30677 York 1962. –/68. 34.8 t.
71754–71761. TS. Dia. EH228. Lot No. 31001 BREL Wolverton 1984–87. Converted from loco-hauled vehicles built to Lot No. 30724 York 1962–63. –/68. 34.8 t.
75637–75644. BDTC. Dia. EF305. Lot No. 30679 York 1962. 18/32 2T. 40.0 t.
75962–75968. BDTC. Dia. EF305. Lot No. 30675 York 1962. 18/32 2T. 40.0 t.
75969–75975. DTS. Dia. EE229. Lot No. 30678 York 1962. –/56 2T. 36.6 t.
75976–75983. DTS. Dia. EE229. Lot No. 30682 York 1962–63. –/56 2T. 36.6 t.

309 613	**RN**	A	*NW*	LG	75639	61934	71756	75978
309 616	**RN**	A	*NW*	LG	75642	61937	71759	75981
309 617	**RN**	A	*NW*	LG	75643	61938	71760	75982
309 623	**RN**	A	*NW*	LG	75641	61927	71758	75980
309 624	**AL**	A	*NW*	LG	75965	61928	70256	75972
309 627	**RN**	A	*NW*	LG(S)	75644	61931	70259	75975

CLASS 310   BR OUTER SUBURBAN

Various formations, see below. Gangwayed within unit. Disc brakes.
Construction: Steel.   **Dimensions:** 20.18 x 2.82 x 3.86 m.
Traction Motors: Four English Electric 546 of 201.5 kW each.
Maximum Speed: 75 mph.   **Doors:** Manually operated slam.
Couplings: Buckeye.   **Bogies:** B4.
Multiple Working: Classes 303–312 only.
Note: 310 081 carries car numbers 76991, 62526, 71210, 78042 in error on
one side only.

62071–62120. MBS. Dia. ED219. Lot No. 30746 Derby 1965–67. –/68. 57.2 t.
70731–70780. TS. Dia. EH232. Lot No. 30747 Derby 1965–67. –/98. 31.7 t.
76130–76179. BDTS. Dia. EF211. Lot No. 30745 Derby 1965–67. –/80 2T. 37.3 t.
**76180/181/183–186/190–195/198–205/208/209/211/213–223/225/76227/229.
DTC.** Dia. EE306. Lot No. 30748 Derby 1965–67. 25/43 2T. 34.4 t.
76182/187–189/196/197/206/207/210/212/224. DTS. Dia. EE237. Lot No.
30748 Derby 1965–67. Converted from DTC. –/75 2T. 34.4 t.
76228. BDTS. Dia. EF210. Lot No. 30748 Derby 1967. Converted from DTC. –/68
2T. 34.5 t.
76998. BDTS. Dia. EF214. Lot No. 30747 Derby 1965–67. Converted from TS.
–/75 2T. 35.0 t.

Class 310/0. 4-car units. BDTS–MBS–TS–DTC (declassified).

310 046	N	H	LS	EM	76130	62071	70731	76180
310 047	N	H	LS	EM	76131	62072	70732	76181
310 049	N	H	LS	EM	76133	62074	70734	76183
310 050	N	H	LS	EM	76134	62075	70735	76184
310 051	N	H	LS	EM	76135	62076	70736	76185
310 052	N	H	LS	EM	76136	62077	70737	76186
310 057	N	H	LS	EM	76141	62082	70742	76191
310 058	N	H	LS	EM	76142	62083	70743	76192
310 059	N	H	LS	EM	76143	62084	70744	76205
310 060	N	H	LS	EM	76144	62085	70745	76194
310 064	N	H	LS	EM	76148	62089	70749	76198
310 066	N	H	LS	EM	76228	62091	70751	76200
310 067	N	H	LS	EM	76151	62092	70752	76201
310 068	N	H	LS	EM	76152	62093	70753	76202
310 069	N	H	LS	EM	76153	62094	70754	76203
310 070	N	H	LS	EM	76154	62095	70755	76204
310 074	N	H	LS	EM	76145	62099	70759	76208
310 075	N	H	LS	EM	76159	62100	70760	76209
310 077	N	H	LS	EM	76161	62102	70762	76221
310 079	N	H	LS	EM	76163	62104	70764	76222
310 080	N	H	LS	EM	76164	62105	70765	76214
310 081	N	H	LS	EM	76165	62106	70766	76215
310 082	N	H	LS	EM	76166	62107	70767	76216
310 083	N	H	LS	EM	76167	62108	70768	76217
310 084	N	H	LS	EM	76168	62109	70769	76218
310 085	N	H	LS	EM	76169	62110	70770	76219

310 086	N	H	LS	EM	76170	62111	70771	76220
310 087	N	H	LS	EM	76171	62112	70772	76221
310 088	N	H	LS	EM	76172	62113	70773	76213
310 089	N	H	LS	EM	76173	62114	70774	76223
310 091	N	H	LS	EM	76175	62116	70776	76225
310 092	N	H	LS	EM	76176	62117	70777	76226
310 093	N	H	LS	EM	76177	62118	70778	76190
310 094	N	H	LS	EM	76998	62119	70780	76193
310 095	N	H	LS	EM	76179	62120	70779	76229

Name (carried on MBS):

310 058   Chafford Hundred.

Class 310/1. 3-car units. BDTS–MBS–DTS (*DTC (declassified)).

310 101	RR	H		EM(S)	76157	62098	76207
310 102	RR	H	LS	EM	76139	62080	76189
310 103	RR	H		EM(S)	76160	62101	76210
310 104	RR	H	LS	EM	76162	62103	76212
310 105	RR	H	CT	SI	76174	62115	76224
310 106	RR	H	LS	EM	76156	62097	76206
310 107	RR	H	CT	SI	76146	62087	76196
310 108	RR	H	CT	SI	76132	62073	76182
310 109	RR	H		EM(S)	76137	62078	76187
310 110	RR	H	LS	EM	76138	62079	76188
310 111	RR	H	CT	SI	76147	62088	76197
310 112 *	RR	H	CT	SI	76140	62086	76227
310 113 *	RR	H	CT	SI	76158	62090	76195

Spare TS.

Spare	PM	H	KN(S)	70733	70747	70748	70757
Spare	PM	H	KN(S)	70763

CLASS 312   BREL OUTER SUBURBAN

BDTS–MBS–TS–DTC. Gangwayed within unit. Disc brakes. All DTC vehicles operated by LTS Rail are declassified.
Construction: Steel.   **Dimensions:** 20.18 x 2.82 x 3.86 m.
Traction Motors: Four English Electric 546 of 201.5 kW each.
Maximum Speed: 90 mph.   **Doors:** Manually operated slam.
Couplings: Buckeye.   **Bogies:** B4.
Multiple Working: Classes 303–312 only.
Note: 76949 carries number 76946 in error on one side only.

Class 312/0. Built to operate on 25 kV 50 Hz a.c. overhead only.

62484–62509. MBS. Dia. ED212. Lot No. 30864 BREL York 1977–78. –/68. 56.0 t.
62571–62560. MBS. Dia. ED214. Lot No. 30893 BREL York 1976. –/68. 56.0 t.
71168–71193. TS. Dia. EH209. Lot No. 30865 BREL York 1977–78. –/98. 30.5 t.
71277–71280. TS. Dia. EH209. Lot No. 30893 BREL York 1976. –/98. 30.5 t.
76949–76974. BDTS. Dia. EF213. Lot No. 30863 BREL York 1977–78. –/84 1T. 34.9 t.
76994–76997. BDTS. Dia. EF213. Lot No. 30891 BREL York 1976. –/84 1T. 34.9 t.

78000–78025. DTC. Dia. EE305. Lot No. 30866 BREL York 1977–78. 25/47 2T. 33.0 t.

78045–78048. DTC. Dia. EE305. Lot No. 30894 BREL York 1976. 25/47 2T. 33.0 t.

312 701	GE	A	GE	IL	76949	62484	71168	78000
312 702	GE	A	GE	IL	76950	62485	71169	78001
312 703	GE	A	GE	IL	76951	62486	71170	78002
312 704	GE	A	LS	EM	76952	62487	71171	78003
312 705	GE	A	GE	IL	76953	62488	71172	78004
312 706	GE	A	GE	IL	76954	62489	71173	78005
312 707	GE	A	GE	IL	76955	62490	71174	78006
312 708	GE	A	LS	EM	76956	62491	71175	78007
312 709	GE	A	GE	IL	76957	62492	71176	78008
312 710	GE	A	GE	IL	76958	62493	71177	78009
312 711	GE	A	GE	IL	76959	62494	71178	78010
312 712	GE	A	GE	IL	76960	62495	71179	78011
312 713	GE	A	GE	IL	76961	62496	71180	78012
312 714	GE	A	GE	IL	76962	62497	71181	78013
312 715	GE	A	GE	IL	76963	62498	71182	78014
312 716	GE	A	GE	IL	76964	62499	71183	78015
312 717	GE	A	GE	IL	76965	62500	71184	78016
312 718	GE	A	GE	IL	76966	62501	71185	78017
312 719	GE	A	GE	IL	76967	62502	71186	78018
312 720	GE	A	GE	IL	76968	62503	71187	78019
312 721	GE	A	GE	IL	76969	62504	71188	78020
312 722	GE	A	GE	IL	76970	62505	71189	78021
312 723	GE	A	GE	IL	76971	62506	71190	78022
312 724	GE	A	GE	IL	76972	62507	71191	78023
312 725	N	A	LS	EM	76973	62509	71193	78025
312 726	N	A	LS	EM	76974	62508	71192	78024
312 727	N	A	LS	EM	76994	62657	71277	78045
312 728	N	A	LS	EM	76995	62658	71278	78046
312 729	N	A	LS	EM	76996	62659	71279	78047
312 730	N	A	LS	EM	76997	62660	71280	78048

Class 312/1. Built to operate on 25 kV 50 Hz a.c. or 6.25 kV 50 Hz a.c. overhead.

62510–62528. MBS. Dia. ED213. Lot No. 30868 BREL York 1975–76. –/68. 56.0 t.

71194–71212. TS. Dia. EH209. Lot No. 30869 BREL York 1975–76. –/98. 30.5 t.

76975–76993. BDTS. Dia. EF213. Lot No. 30867 BREL York 1975–76. –/84 2T. 34.9 t.

78026–78044. DTC. Dia. EE305. Lot No. 30870 BREL York 1975–76. 25/47 2T. 33.0 t.

312 781	N	A	LS	EM	76975	62510	71194	78026
312 782	N	A	LS	EM	76976	62511	71195	78027
312 783	N	A	LS	EM	76977	62512	71196	78028
312 784	N	A	LS	EM	76978	62513	71197	78029
312 785	N	A	LS	EM	76979	62514	71198	78030
312 786	N	A	LS	EM	76980	62515	71199	78031
312 787	N	A	LS	EM	76981	62516	71200	78032
312 788	N	A	LS	EM	76982	62517	71201	78033
312 789	N	A	LS	EM	76983	62518	71202	78034

312 790	N	A	LS	EM	76984	62519	71203	78035
312 791	N	A	LS	EM	76985	62520	71204	78036
312 792	N	A	LS	EM	76986	62521	71205	78037
312 793	N	A	LS	EM	76987	62522	71206	78038
312 794	N	A	LS	EM	76988	62523	71207	78039
312 795	N	A	LS	EM	76989	62524	71208	78040
312 796	N	A	LS	EM	76990	62525	71209	78041
312 797	N	A	LS	EM	76991	62526	71210	78042
312 798	N	A	LS	EM	76992	62527	71211	78043
312 799	N	A	LS	EM	76993	62528	71212	78044

CLASS 313   BREL SUBURBAN

DMS–PTS–BDMS. Gangwayed within unit. End doors. Disc and rheostatic brakes.
Construction: Steel underframe, aluminium alloy body and roof.
Supply System: 25 kV 50 Hz a.c. overhead or 750 V d.c. third rail.
Traction Motors: Four GEC G310AZ of 82.125 kW each per motor car.
Dimensions: 19.80 (DMS & BDMS) or 19.92 (PTS) x 2.82 x 3.58 m.
Maximum Speed: 75 mph.   **Doors:** Power operated sliding.
Couplers: Tightlock.   **Bogies:** BREL BX1.
Multiple Working: Classes 313–323.
Notes: 71217 carries number 71277 in error on one side only. 71733[§] is actually 71233.

62529–62592. DMS. Dia. EA204. Lot No. 30879 BREL York 1976–77. –/74. 36.4 t.
62593–62656. BDMS. Dia. EI201. Lot No. 30885 BREL York 1976–77. –/74. 37.6 t.
71213–71276. PTS. Dia. EH210. Lot No. 30880 BREL York 1976–77. –/84 (*–/80). 30.5 t.

Class 313/0. Operated by West Anglia Great Northern Railway.

Note: † Refurbished 1998 onwards by Adtranz Ilford with high back seats.
Advertising Liveries:
• 313 024/027/043/050/057/064 'WAGN Family Travelcard'
• 313 060 'Intalink'

313 018		N	H	WN	HE	62546	71230	62610
313 024	†	U	H	WN	HE	62552	71236	62616
313 025		N	H	WN	HE	62553	71237	62617
313 026		N	H	WN	HE	62554	71238	62618
313 027	†	U	H	WN	HE	62555	71239	62619
313 028	†	U	H	WN	HE	62556	71240	62620
313 029		N	H	WN	HE	62557	71241	62621
313 030	†	U	H	WN	HE	62558	71242	62622
313 031		N	H	WN	HE	62559	71243	62623
313 032		N	H	WN	HE	62560	71244	62643
313 033		N	H	WN	HE	62561	71245	62625
313 035		N	H	WN	HE	62563	71247	62627
313 036		N	H	WN	HE	62564	71248	62628
313 037		N	H	WN	HE	62565	71249	62629

313 038	†	**U**	H	*WN*	HE	62566	71250	62630
313 039		**N**	H	*WN*	HE	62567	71251	62631
313 040		**N**	H	*WN*	HE	62568	71252	62632
313 041		**N**	H	*WN*	HE	62569	71253	62633
313 042		**N**	H	*WN*	HE	62570	71254	62634
313 043	†	**AL**	H	*WN*	HE	62571	71255	62635
313 044		**N**	H	*WN*	HE	62572	71256	62636
313 045		**N**	H	*WN*	HE	62573	71257	62637
313 046		**N**	H	*WN*	HE	62574	71258	62638
313 047		**N**	H	*WN*	HE	62575	71259	62639
313 048		**N**	H	*WN*	HE	62576	71260	62640
313 049		**N**	H	*WN*	HE	62577	71261	62641
313 050	†	**AL**	H	*WN*	HE	62578	71262	62649
313 051		**N**	H	*WN*	HE	62579	71263	62624
313 052		**N**	H	*WN*	HE	62580	71264	62644
313 053		**N**	H	*WN*	HE	62581	71265	62645
313 054		**N**	H	*WN*	HE	62582	71266	62646
313 055		**N**	H	*WN*	HE	62583	71267	62647
313 056		**N**	H	*WN*	HE	62584	71268	62648
313 057	†	**AL**	H	*WN*	HE	62585	71269	62642
313 058		**N**	H	*WN*	HE	62586	71270	62650
313 059		**N**	H	*WN*	HE	62587	71271	62651
313 060	†	**AL**	H	*WN*	HE	62588	71272	62652
313 061		**N**	H	*WN*	HE	62589	71273	62653
313 062		**N**	H	*WN*	HE	62590	71274	62654
313 063		**N**	H	*WN*	HE	62591	71275	62655
313 064	†	**U**	H	*WN*	HE	62592	71276	62656

Class 313/1. Operated by Silverlink Train Services. Equipped with additional shoegear for working on LUL 750 V d.c. 4-rail system. Units are renumbered and reclassified from Class 313/0 upon completion of facelift by Railcare Wolverton, retaining last two digits of previous number.

Number Former No.

	313 001	**N**	H	*SL*	BY	62529	71213	62593
313 102	(313 002) *	**SL**	H	*SL*	BY	62530	71214	62594
313 103	(313 003) *	**SL**	H	*SL*	BY	62531	71215	62595
	313 004	**N**	H	*SL*	BY	62532	71216	62596
313 105	(313 005) *	**SL**	H	*SL*	BY	62533	71217	62597
313 106	(313 006) *	**N**	H	*SL*	BY	62534	71218	62598
313 107	(313 007) *	**SL**	H	*SL*	BY	62535	71219	62599
	313 008	**N**	H	*SL*	BY	62536	71220	62600
	313 009	**N**	H	*SL*	BY	62537	71221	62601
313 110	(313 010) *	**SL**	H	*SL*	BY	62538	71222	62602
	313 011	**N**	H	*SL*	BY	62539	71223	62603
313 112	(313 012) *	**SL**	H	*SL*	BY	62540	71224	62604
	313 013	**N**	H	*SL*	BY	62541	71225	62605
313 114	(313 014) *	**SL**	H	*SL*	BY	62542	71226	62606
313 115	(313 015) *	**SL**	H	*SL*	BY	62543	71227	62607
	313 016	**N**	H	*SL*	BY	62544	71228	62608
313 117	(313 017) *	**SL**	H	*SL*	BY	62545	71229	62609
	313 019	**N**	H	*SL*	BY	62547	71231	62611

313 120	(313 020) *	**SL**	H	*SL*	BY	62548	71232	62612
313 121	(313 021) *	**SL**	H	*SL*	BY	62549	71733[II]	62613
	313 022	**SL**	H	*SL*	BY	62550	71234	62614
	313 023	**N**	H	*SL*	BY	62551	71235	62615
313 134	(313 034) *	**SL**	H	*SL*	BY	62562	71246	62626

Name (carried on PTS):

313 120   PARLIAMENT HILL

CLASS 314   BREL SUBURBAN

DMS–PTS–DMS. Gangwayed within unit. End doors. Disc and rheostatic brakes.
Construction: Steel underframe, aluminium alloy body and roof.
Traction Motors: Four Brush TM61-53 or GEC G310AZ of 82.125 kW each per motor car.
Dimensions: 19.80 (DMS or 19.92 (PTS) x 2.82 x 3.58 m.
Maximum Speed: 75 mph.   **Doors:** Power operated sliding.
Couplers: Tightlock.   **Bogies:** BREL BX1.
Multiple Working: Classes 313–323.

64583–64613 (Odd numbers). DMS(A). Dia. EA206. Lot No. 30912 BREL York 1979. –/68. 34.5 t.
64584–64614 (Even numbers). DMS(B). Dia. EA206. Lot No. 30912 BREL York 1979. –/68. 34.5 t.
64588[2]. DMS(B). Dia. EA206. Lot No. 30908 BREL York 1978–80. Rebuilt Railcare Glasgow 1996 from Class 507 DMS. –/74. 35.6 t.
71450–71465. PTS. Dia. EH211. Lot No. 30913 BREL York 1979. –/76. 33.0 t.

Units 314 201–314 206. Brush traction motors.

314 201	**S**	A	*SR*	GW	64583	71450	64584
314 202	**S**	A	*SR*	GW	64585	71451	64586
314 203	**S**	A	*SR*	GW	64587	71452	64588[2]
314 204	**CC**	A	*SR*	GW	64589	71453	64590
314 205	**CC**	A	*SR*	GW	64591	71454	64592
314 206	**CC**	A	*SR*	GW	64593	71455	64594

Units 314 207–314 216. GEC traction motors.

314 207	**S**	A	*SR*	GW	64595	71456	64596
314 208	**S**	A	*SR*	GW	64597	71457	64598
314 209	**S**	A	*SR*	GW	64599	71458	64600
314 210	**CC**	A	*SR*	GW	64601	71459	64602
314 211	**CC**	A	*SR*	GW	64603	71460	64604
314 212	**S**	A	*SR*	GW	64605	71461	64606
314 213	**S**	A	*SR*	GW	64607	71462	64608
314 214	**S**	A	*SR*	GW	64609	71463	64610
314 215	**CC**	A	*SR*	GW	64611	71464	64612
314 216	**CC**	A	*SR*	GW	64613	71465	64614

Name (carried on PTS):

314 203   European Union

CLASS 315   BREL SUBURBAN

DMS–TS–PTS–DMS. Gangwayed within unit. End doors. Disc and rheostatic brakes.
Construction: Steel underframe, aluminium alloy body and roof.
Traction Motors: Four GEC G310AZ or Brush TM61-53) of 82.125 kW each per motor car.
Dimensions: 19.80 (DMS) or 19.92 (TS & PTS) x 2.82 x 3.58 m.
Maximum Speed: 75 mph.   **Doors:** Power operated sliding.
Couplers: Tightlock.   **Bogies:** BREL BX1.
Multiple Working: Classes 313–323.
Advertising Livery:
• 315 844/845 'WAGN Family Travelcard'.

64461–64581 (Odd numbers). DMS(A). Dia. EA207. Lot No. 30902 BREL York 1980–81. –/74. 35.0 t.
64462–64582 (Even numbers). DMS(B). Dia. EA207. Lot No. 30902 BREL York 1980–81. –/74. 35.0 t.
71281–71341. TS. Dia. EH216. Lot No. 30904 BREL York 1980–81. –/86. 25.5 t.
71389–71449. PTS. Dia. EH217. Lot No. 30903 BREL York 1980–81. –/84. 32.0 t.

Units 315 801–315 841. GEC traction motors.

315 801	**GE**	H	*GE*	IL	64461	71281	71389	64462
315 802	**GE**	H	*GE*	IL	64463	71282	71390	64464
315 803	**GE**	H	*GE*	IL	64465	71283	71391	64466
315 804	**GE**	H	*GE*	IL	64467	71284	71392	64468
315 805	**GE**	H	*GE*	IL	64469	71285	71393	64470
315 806	**GE**	H	*GE*	IL	64471	71286	71394	64472
315 807	**GE**	H	*GE*	IL	64473	71287	71395	64474
315 808	**GE**	H	*GE*	IL	64475	71288	71396	64476
315 809	**GE**	H	*GE*	IL	64477	71289	71397	64478
315 810	**GE**	H	*GE*	IL	64479	71290	71398	64480
315 811	**GE**	H	*GE*	IL	64481	71291	71399	64482
315 812	**GE**	H	*GE*	IL	64483	71292	71400	64484
315 813	**GE**	H	*GE*	IL	64485	71293	71401	64486
315 814	**GE**	H	*GE*	IL	64487	71294	71402	64488
315 815	**GE**	H	*GE*	IL	64489	71295	71403	64490
315 816	**GE**	H	*GE*	IL	64491	71296	71404	64492
315 817	**GE**	H	*GE*	IL	64493	71297	71405	64494
315 818	**GE**	H	*GE*	IL	64495	71298	71406	64496
315 819	**GE**	H	*GE*	IL	64497	71299	71407	64498
315 820	**GE**	H	*GE*	IL	64499	71300	71408	64500
315 821	**GE**	H	*GE*	IL	64501	71301	71409	64502
315 822	**GE**	H	*GE*	IL	64503	71302	71410	64504
315 823	**GE**	H	*GE*	IL	64505	71303	71411	64506
315 824	**GE**	H	*GE*	IL	64507	71304	71412	64508
315 825	**GE**	H	*GE*	IL	64509	71305	71413	64510
315 826	**GE**	H	*GE*	IL	64511	71306	71414	64512
315 827	**GE**	H	*GE*	IL	64513	71307	71415	64514
315 828	**GE**	H	*GE*	IL	64515	71308	71416	64516

315 829	**GE**	H	*GE*	IL	64517	71309	71417	64518
315 830	**GE**	H	*GE*	IL	64519	71310	71418	64520
315 831	**GE**	H	*GE*	IL	64521	71311	71419	64522
315 832	**GE**	H	*GE*	IL	64523	71312	71420	64524
315 833	**GE**	H	*GE*	IL	64525	71313	71421	64526
315 834	**GE**	H	*GE*	IL	64527	71314	71422	64528
315 835	**GE**	H	*GE*	IL	64529	71315	71423	64530
315 836	**GE**	H	*GE*	IL	64531	71316	71424	64532
315 837	**GE**	H	*GE*	IL	64533	71317	71425	64534
315 838	**GE**	H	*GE*	IL	64535	71318	71426	64536
315 839	**GE**	H	*GE*	IL	64537	71319	71427	64538
315 840	**GE**	H	*GE*	IL	64539	71320	71428	64540
315 841	**GE**	H	*GE*	IL	64541	71321	71429	64542

Units 315 842–315 861. Brush traction motors.

315 842	**GE**	H	*GE*	IL	64543	71322	71430	64544
315 843	**GE**	H	*GE*	IL	64545	71323	71431	64546
315 844	**AL**	H	*WN*	HE	64547	71324	71432	64548
315 845	**AL**	H	*WN*	HE	64549	71325	71433	64550
315 846	**U**	H	*WN*	HE	64551	71326	71434	64552
315 847	**U**	H	*WN*	HE	64553	71327	71435	64554
315 848	**N**	H	*WN*	HE	64555	71328	71436	64556
315 849	**U**	H	*WN*	HE	64557	71329	71437	64558
315 850	**N**	H	*WN*	HE	64559	71330	71438	64560
315 851	**N**	H	*WN*	HE	64561	71331	71439	64562
315 852	**N**	H	*WN*	HE	64563	71332	71440	64564
315 853	**N**	H	*WN*	HE	64565	71333	71441	64566
315 854	**N**	H	*WN*	HE	64567	71334	71442	64568
315 855	**N**	H	*WN*	HE	64569	71335	71443	64570
315 856	**N**	H	*WN*	HE	64571	71336	71444	64572
315 857	**N**	H	*WN*	HE	64573	71337	71445	64574
315 858	**N**	H	*WN*	HE	64579	71340	71446	64580
315 859	**N**	H	*WN*	HE	64577	71339	71447	64578
315 860	**N**	H	*WN*	HE	64575	71338	71448	64576
315 861	**N**	H	*WN*	HE	64581	71341	71449	64582

CLASS 317   BREL OUTER SUBURBAN

Various formations, see below. Gangwayed throughout. Disc brakes.
Construction: Steel.
Traction Motors: Four GEC G315BZ of 247.5 kW each.
Dimensions: 20.13 (DTS & DTC) or 20.18 (ATC, ATS & PMS) x 2.82 x 3.77 m.
Maximum Speed: 100 mph.   **Doors:** Power operated sliding.
Couplers: Tightlock.   **Bogies:** BREL BP20/BT13.
Multiple Working: Classes 313–323.

Class 317/1 († 317/3). Pressure heating & ventilation. DTS(A)–PMS–ATC († ATS)–DTS(B).

62661–62708. PMS. Dia. EC208. Lot No. 30958 BREL York 1981–82. –/79. 49.8 t.
71577–71624. ATC († ATS). Dia. EH307 († EH242). Lot No. 30957 BREL Derby 1981–82. 22/46 († –/68) 2T. 28.8 t.
77000–77047. DTS(A). Dia. EE216. Lot No. 30955 BREL York 1981–82. –/74. 29.4 t.
77048–77095. DTS(B). Dia. EE235 (*EE232). Lot No. 30956 York 1981–82. –/70. (* –/71). 29.3 t.

317 301	†	LS	A	LS	EM	77024	62661	71577	77048
317 302	†	LS	A	LS	EM	77001	62662	71578	77049
317 303	†	LS	A	LS	EM	77002	62663	71579	77050
317 304	†	LS	A	LS	EM	77003	62664	71580	77051
317 305	†	LS	A	LS	EM	77004	62665	71581	77052
317 306	†	LS	A	LS	EM	77005	62666	71582	77053
317 307	†	LS	A	LS	EM	77006	62667	71583	77054
317 309		N	A	WN	HE	77008	62669	71585	77056
317 310		N	A	WN	HE	77009	62670	71586	77057
317 311	†	LS	A	LS	EM	77010	62697	71587	77058
317 312	†	LS	A	LS	EM	77011	62672	71588	77059
317 313	†	LS	A	LS	EM	77012	62673	71589	77060
317 314		LS	A	WN	HE	77013	62674	71590	77061
317 315		N	A	WN	HE	77014	62675	71591	77062
317 316		N	A	WN	HE	77015	62676	71592	77063
317 317		N	A	TR	HE	77016	62677	71593	77064
317 318		N	A	WN	HE	77017	62678	71594	77065
317 319	†	LS	A	LS	EM	77018	62679	71595	77066
317 320		N	A	WN	HE	77019	62680	71596	77067
317 321		N	A	WN	HE	77020	62681	71597	77068
317 324		N	A	TR	HE	77023	62684	71600	77071
317 325		N	A	WN	HE	77000	62685	71601	77072
317 326		N	A	TR	HE	77025	62686	71602	77073
317 327		N	A	WN	HE	77026	62687	71603	77074
317 328		N	A	WN	HE	77027	62688	71604	77075
317 330		N	A	WN	HE	77043	62704	71606	77077
317 331		N	A	WN	HE	77030	62691	71607	77078
317 332	†	LS	A	LS	EM	77031	62692	71608	77079
317 333		N	A	WN	HE	77032	62693	71609	77080
317 334		N	A	WN	HE	77033	62694	71610	77081

317 335		N	A	*WN*	HE	77034	62695	71611	77082
317 336		N	A	*WN*	HE	77035	62696	71612	77083
317 337	*	N	A	*WN*	HE	77036	62671	71613	77084
317 338	*	N	A	*WN*	HE	77037	62698	71614	77085
317 339	*	N	A	*WN*	HE	77038	62699	71615	77086
317 340	*	N	A	*WN*	HE	77039	62700	71616	77087
317 341	*	N	A	*WN*	HE	77040	62701	71617	77088
317 342	*	N	A	*WN*	HE	77041	62702	71618	77089
317 343	*	N	A	*WN*	HE	77042	62703	71619	77090
317 344	*	N	A	*WN*	HE	77029	62690	71620	77091
317 345	*	N	A	*WN*	HE	77044	62705	71621	77092
317 346	*	N	A	*WN*	HE	77045	62706	71622	77093
317 347	*	N	A	*WN*	HE	77046	62707	71623	77094
317 348	*	N	A	*WN*	HE	77047	62708	71624	77095
317 392	†	LS	A	*LS*	EM	77021	62682	71598	77069
317 393	†	LS	A	*TR*	HE	77022	62683	71599	77070

Class 317/6. Convection heating. DTS–PMS–ATS–DTC. 2 + 2 seating.

62846–62865. PMS. Dia. EC222. Lot No. 30996 BREL York 1985–86. Refurbished Railcare Wolverton 1998–99. –/70. 50.1 t.
62886–62889. PMS. Dia. EC222. Lot No. 31009 BREL York 1987. Refurbished Railcare Wolverton 1998–99. –/70. 50.1 t.
71734–71753. ATS. Dia. EH247. Lot No. 30997 BREL York 1985–86. Refurbished Railcare Wolverton 1998–99. –/62 2T. 28.8 t.
71762–71765. ATS. Dia. EH247. Lot No. 31010 BREL York 1987. Refurbished Railcare Wolverton 1998–99. –/62 2T. 28.8 t.
77200–77219. DTS. Dia. EE247. Lot No. 30994 BREL York 1985–86. Refurbished Railcare Wolverton 1998–99. –/64. 29.3 t.
77280–77283. DTS. Dia. EE247. Lot No. 31007 BREL York 1987. Refurbished Railcare Wolverton 1998–99. –/64. 29.3 t.
77220–77239. DTC. Dia. EE375. Lot No. 30995 BREL York 1985–86. Refurbished Railcare Wolverton 1998–99. 24/48. 29.3 t.
77284–77287. DTC. Dia. EE375. Lot No. 31008 BREL York 1987. Refurbished Railcare Wolverton 1998–99. 24/48. 29.3 t.

Number	Former No.								
317 649	(317 349)	**WN**	A	*WN*	HE	77200	62846	71734	77220
317 650	(317 350)	**WN**	A	*WN*	HE	77201	62847	71735	77221
317 651	(317 351)	**WN**	A	*WN*	HE	77202	62848	71736	77222
317 652	(317 352)	**WN**	A	*WN*	HE	77203	62849	71739	77223
317 653	(317 353)	**WN**	A	*WN*	HE	77204	62850	71738	77224
317 654	(317 354)	**WN**	A	*WN*	HE	77205	62851	71737	77225
317 655	(317 355)	**WN**	A	*WN*	HE	77206	62852	71740	77226
317 656	(317 356)	**WN**	A	*WN*	HE	77207	62853	71742	77227
317 657	(317 357)	**WN**	A	*WN*	HE	77208	62854	71741	77228
317 658	(317 358)	**WN**	A	*WN*	HE	77209	62855	71743	77229
317 659	(317 359)	**WN**	A	*WN*	HE	77210	62856	71744	77230
317 660	(317 360)	**WN**	A	*WN*	HE	77211	62857	71745	77231
317 661	(317 361)	**WN**	A	*WN*	HE	77212	62858	71746	77232
317 662	(317 362)	**WN**	A	*WN*	HE	77213	62859	71747	77233
317 663	(317 363)	**WN**	A	*WN*	HE	77214	62860	71748	77234

317 664	(317 364)	**WN**	A	WN	HE	77215	62861	71749	77235
317 665	(317 365)	**WN**	A	WN	HE	77216	62862	71750	77236
317 666	(317 366)	**WN**	A	WN	HE	77217	62863	71752	77237
317 667	(317 367)	**WN**	A	WN	HE	77218	62864	71751	77238
317 668	(317 368)	**WN**	A	WN	HE	77219	62865	71753	77239
317 669	(317 369)	**WN**	A	WN	HE	77280	62886	71762	77284
317 670	(317 370)	**WN**	A	WN	HE	77281	62887	71763	77285
317 671	(317 371)	**WN**	A	WN	HE	77282	62888	71764	77286
317 672	(317 372)	**WN**	A	WN	HE	77283	62889	71765	77287

Class 317/7. Dedicated units to be converted for services to/from Stansted Airport. Pressure heating & ventilation. Final details awaited.

62661–62708. PMS. Dia. EC2??. Lot No. 30958 BREL York.1981–82. Refurbished Railcare Wolverton 1999–2000. –/64.
71577–71624. TS. Dia. EH2??. Lot No. 30957 BREL Derby 1981–82. Refurbished Railcare Wolverton 1999–2000. –/46. 1T 1TD.
77000–77047. DTS. Dia. EE2??. Lot No. 30955 BREL York 1981–82. Refurbished Railcare Wolverton 1999–2000. –/54.
77048–77095. DTC. Dia. EE3??. Lot No. 30956 York 1981–82. Refurbished Railcare Wolverton 1999–2000. 23/16.

Number	Former No.								
317 701	(317 308)		A	WN	HE	77007	62668	71584	77055
317 702	(317 329)		A	WN	HE	77028	62689	71605	77076
317 703	(317 392)								
317 704	(317 319)								
317 705	(317 314)								
317 706	(317 3								
317 707	(317 3								
317 708	(317 3								
317 709	(317 3								

CLASS 318   BREL OUTER SUBURBAN

DTS(B)–PMS–DTS(A). Gangwayed throughout. Disc brakes.
Construction: Steel.
Traction Motors: Four Brush TM 2141 of 268 kW each.
Dimensions: 20.13 (DTS) or 20.18 (PMS) x 2.82 x 3.77 m.
Maximum Speed: 90 mph.   **Doors:** Power operated sliding.
Couplers: Tightlock.   **Bogies:** BREL BP20/BT13.
Multiple Working: Classes 313–323.
Note: DTS(A) fitted with Controlled Emission Toilet to permit use on the Argyle Line.

62866–62885. PMS. Dia. EC207. Lot No. 30998 BREL York 1985–86. –/79. 50.9 t.
62890. PMS. Dia. EC207. Lot No. 31019 BREL York 1987. –/79. 50.9 t.
77240–77259. DTS(A). Dia. EE227. Lot No. 30999 BREL York 1985–86. –/66 1T 1W. 30.0 t.
77260–77279. DTS(B). Dia. EE228. Lot No. 31000 BREL York 1985–86. –/71. 26.6 t.
77288. DTS(A). Dia. EE227. Lot No. 31020 BREL York 1987. –/66 1T 1W. 30.0 t.
77289. DTS(B). Dia. EE228. Lot No. 31021 BREL York 1987. –/71. 26.6 t.

318 250	S	H	*SR*	GW	77260	62866	77240
318 251	CC	H	*SR*	GW	77261	62867	77241
318 252	CC	H	*SR*	GW	77262	62868	77242
318 253	CC	H	*SR*	GW	77263	62869	77243
318 254	CC	H	*SR*	GW	77264	62870	77244
318 255	CC	H	*SR*	GW	77265	62871	77245
318 256	CC	H	*SR*	GW	77266	62872	77246
318 257	CC	H	*SR*	GW	77267	62873	77247
318 258	CC	H	*SR*	GW	77268	62874	77248
318 259	CC	H	*SR*	GW	77269	62875	77249
318 260	S	H	*SR*	GW	77270	62876	77250
318 261	S	H	*SR*	GW	77271	62877	77251
318 262	CC	H	*SR*	GW	77272	62878	77252
318 263	CC	H	*SR*	GW	77273	62879	77253
318 264	CC	H	*SR*	GW	77274	62880	77254
318 265	S	H	*SR*	GW	77275	62881	77255
318 266	CC	H	*SR*	GW	77276	62882	77256
318 267	S	H	*SR*	GW	77277	62883	77257
318 268	S	H	*SR*	GW	77278	62884	77258
318 269	CC	H	*SR*	GW	77279	62885	77259
318 270	CC	H	*SR*	GW	77289	62890	77288

Names (carried on PMS):

| 318 259 | Citizens' Network | | 318 266 | STRATHCLYDER |

CLASS 319   BREL OUTER SUBURBAN

Various formations, see below. Gangwayed within unit. End doors. Disc brakes.
Construction: Steel.
Supply System: 25 kV 50 Hz a.c. overhead and/or 750 V d.c. third rail.
Traction Motors: Four GEC G315BZ of 247.5 kW each.
Dimensions: 20.13 (DTC & DTS) or 20.18 (ATS & PMS) x 2.82 x 3.77 m.
Maximum Speed: 100 mph.   **Doors:** Power operated sliding.
Couplers: Tightlock.   **Bogies:** BREL P7-4/T3-7.
Multiple Working: Classes 313–323.

Class 319/0. DTS(A)–PMS–ATS–DTS(B). 25 kV 50 Hz a.c. overhead or 750 V
d.c. third rail supply.

Note: Two units are loaned to Thameslink Rail on a daily basis.

62891–62903. PMS. Dia. EC209. Lot No. 31023 BREL York 1987–88. –/77 2T. 51.0 t.
71772–71784. ATS. Dia. EH234. Lot No. 31024 BREL York 1987–88. –/77 2T.
31.0 t.
77290–77314 (Even numbers). DTS(B). Dia. EE234. Lot No. 31025 BREL York
1987–88. –/78. 30.0 t.
77291–77315 (Odd numbers). DTS(A). Dia. EE233. Lot No. 31022 BREL York
1987–88. –/82. 30.0 t.

319 001	CX	P	*TR*	SU	77291	62891	71772	77290
319 002	CX	P	*TR*	SU	77293	62892	71773	77292
319 003	CX	P	*TR*	SU	77295	62893	71774	77294

319 004	**CX**	P	*TR*	SU	77297	62894	71775	77296
319 005	**CX**	P	*TR*	SU	77299	62895	71776	77298
319 006	**CX**	P	*TR*	SU	77301	62896	71777	77300
319 007	**CX**	P	*TR*	SU	77303	62897	71778	77302
319 008	**CX**	P	*TR*	SU	77305	62898	71779	77304
319 009	**CX**	P	*TR*	SU	77307	62899	71780	77306
319 010	**CX**	P	*TR*	SU	77309	62900	71781	77308
319 011	**CX**	P	*TR*	SU	77311	62901	71782	77310
319 012	**CX**	P	*TR*	SU	77313	62902	71783	77312
319 013	**CX**	P	*TR*	SU	77315	62903	71784	77314

Names (carried on ATS):

319 005	Partnership For Progress	319 011	John Ruskin College
319 008	Cheriton	319 013	The Surrey Hills
319 009	Coquelles		

Class 319/2. DTS–PMB–ATS–DTC. 750 V d.c. third rail with provision for 25 kV a.c. 50 Hz overhead supply. 'Express' configuration units operated by Connex South Central on the London Victoria–Brighton route.

62904–62910. PMB. Dia. EN262. Lot No. 31023 BREL York 1987–88. Refurbished Railcare Wolverton 1996. –/60 2T. 51.0 t.
71785–71791. ATS. Dia. EH212. Lot No. 31024 BREL York 1987–88. Refurbished Railcare Wolverton 1996. –/52 1T 1TD. 31.0 t.
77316–77328 (Even numbers). DTC. Dia. EE374. Lot No. 31025 BREL York 1987–88. Refurbished Railcare Wolverton 1996. 18/36. 29.0 t.
77317–77329 (Odd numbers). DTS. Dia. EE244. Lot No. 31022 BREL York 1987–88. Refurbished Railcare Wolverton 1996. –/64. 29.7 t.

319 214	**CX**	P	*SC*	SU	77317	62904	71785	77316
319 215	**CX**	P	*SC*	SU	77319	62905	71786	77318
319 216	**CX**	P	*SC*	SU	77321	62906	71787	77320
319 217	**CX**	P	*SC*	SU	77323	62907	71788	77322
319 218	**CX**	P	*SC*	SU	77325	62908	71789	77324
319 219	**CX**	P	*SC*	SU	77327	62909	71790	77326
319 220	**CX**	P	*SC*	SU	77329	62910	71791	77328

Names (carried on ATS):

| 319 215 | London | 319 218 | Croydon |
| 319 217 | Brighton | | |

Class 319/3. DTS(A)–PMS–ATS–DTS(B). 25 kV 50 Hz a.c. overhead or 750 V d.c. third rail supply. Operated by Thameslink Rail on the 'City Metro' Luton–Sutton route.

63043–63062, 63098–63098. PMS. Dia. EC214. Lot No. 31064 BREL York 1990. –/79. 50.3 t.
71929–71948, 71979–71984. ATS. Dia. EH238. Lot No. 31065 BREL York 1990. –/74 2T. 33.1 t.
77458–77496, 77974–77984 (Even numbers). DTS(B). Dia. EE240. Lot No. 31066 BREL York 1990. –/78. 29.7 t.
77459–77497, 77973–77983 (Odd numbers). DTS(A). Dia. EE240. Lot No. 31063 BREL York 1990. –/70. 29.0 t.

Number	Former No.								
319 361	(319 161)	**TR**	P	*TR*	SU	77459	63043	71929	77458
319 362	(319 162)	**TR**	P	*TR*	SU	77461	63044	71930	77460
319 363	(319 163)	**TR**	P	*TR*	SU	77463	63045	71931	77462
319 364	(319 164)	**TR**	P	*TR*	SU	77465	63046	71932	77464
319 365	(319 165)	**TR**	P	*TR*	SU	77467	63047	71933	77466
319 366	(319 166)	**TR**	P	*TR*	SU	77469	63048	71934	77468
319 367	(319 167)	**TR**	P	*TR*	SU	77471	63049	71935	77470
319 368	(319 168)	**TR**	P	*TR*	SU	77473	63050	71936	77472
319 369	(319 169)	**TR**	P	*TR*	SU	77475	63051	71937	77474
319 370	(319 170)	**TR**	P	*TR*	SU	77477	63052	71938	77476
319 371	(319 171)	**TR**	P	*TR*	SU	77479	63053	71939	77478
319 372	(319 172)	**TR**	P	*TR*	SU	77481	63054	71940	77480
319 373	(319 173)	**TR**	P	*TR*	SU	77483	63055	71941	77482
319 374	(319 174)	**TR**	P	*TR*	SU	77485	63056	71942	77484
319 375	(319 175)	**TR**	P	*TR*	SU	77487	63057	71943	77486
319 376	(319 176)	**TR**	P	*TR*	SU	77489	63058	71944	77488
319 377	(319 177)	**TR**	P	*TR*	SU	77491	63059	71945	77490
319 378	(319 178)	**TR**	P	*TR*	SU	77493	63060	71946	77492
319 379	(319 179)	**TR**	P	*TR*	SU	77495	63061	71947	77494
319 380	(319 180)	**TR**	P	*TR*	SU	77497	63062	71948	77496
319 381	(319 181)	**TR**	P	*TR*	SU	77973	63093	71979	77974
319 382	(319 182)	**TR**	P	*TR*	SU	77975	63094	71980	77976
319 383	(319 183)	**TR**	P	*TR*	SU	77977	63095	71981	77978
319 384	(319 184)	**TR**	P	*TR*	SU	77979	63096	71982	77980
319 385	(319 185)	**TR**	P	*TR*	SU	77981	63097	71983	77982
319 386	(319 186)	**TR**	P	*TR*	SU	77983	63098	71984	77984

Class 319/4. DTC–PMS–ATS–DTS. 25 kV 50 Hz a.c. overhead or 750 V d.c. third rail supply. Operated by Thameslink Rail on the 'City Flyer' Bedford–Gatwick Airport–Brighton route.

Advertising Livery: •   319 422 'Luton Airport Parkway'.

62911–62936. PMS. Dia. EC209. Lot No. 31023 BREL York 1987–88. –/77 2T. 51.0 t.
62961–62974. PMS. Dia. EC209. Lot No. 31039 BREL York 1988. –/77 2T. 51.0 t.
71792–71817. ATS. Dia. EH234. Lot No. 31024 BREL York 1987–88. –/77 2T. 34.0 t.
71866–71879. ATS. Dia. EH234. Lot No. 31040 BREL York 1988. –/77 2T. 34.0 t.
77330–77380 (Even numbers). DTS. Dia. EE234. Lot No. 31025 BREL York 1987–88. –/78. 30.0 t.
77331–77381 (Odd numbers). DTC. Dia. EE314. Lot No. 31022 BREL York 1987–88. 12/54. 30.0 t.
77430–77456 (Even numbers). DTS. Dia. EE234. Lot No. 31041 BREL York 1988. –/74. 30.0 t.
77431–77457 (Odd numbers). DTC. Dia. EE314. Lot No. 31038 BREL York 1988. 12/54. 30.0 t.

319 421	**TR**	P	*TR*	SU	77331	62911	71792	77330
319 422	**AL**	P	*TR*	SU	77333	62912	71793	77332
319 423	**TR**	P	*TR*	SU	77335	62913	71794	77334
319 424	**TR**	P	*TR*	SU	77337	62914	71795	77336
319 425	**TR**	P	*TR*	SU	77339	62915	71796	77338
319 426	**TR**	P	*TR*	SU	77341	62916	71797	77340

319 427	**TR**	P	*TR*	SU	77343	62917	71798	77342
319 428	**TR**	P	*TR*	SU	77345	62918	71799	77344
319 429	**TR**	P	*TR*	SU	77347	62919	71800	77346
319 430	**TR**	P	*TR*	SU	77349	62920	71801	77348
319 431	**TR**	P	*TR*	SU	77351	62921	71802	77350
319 432	**TR**	P	*TR*	SU	77353	62922	71803	77352
319 433	**TR**	P	*TR*	SU	77355	62923	71804	77354
319 434	**TR**	P	*TR*	SU	77357	62924	71805	77356
319 435	**TR**	P	*TR*	SU	77359	62925	71806	77358
319 436	**TR**	P	*TR*	SU	77361	62926	71807	77360
319 437	**TR**	P	*TR*	SU	77363	62927	71808	77362
319 438	**TR**	P	*TR*	SU	77365	62928	71809	77364
319 439	**TR**	P	*TR*	SU	77367	62929	71810	77366
319 440	**TR**	P	*TR*	SU	77369	62930	71811	77368
319 441	**TR**	P	*TR*	SU	77371	62931	71812	77370
319 442	**TR**	P	*TR*	SU	77373	62932	71813	77372
319 443	**TR**	P	*TR*	SU	77375	62933	71814	77374
319 444	**TR**	P	*TR*	SU	77377	62934	71815	77376
319 445	**TR**	P	*TR*	SU	77379	62935	71816	77378
319 446	**TR**	P	*TR*	SU	77381	62936	71817	77380
319 447	**TR**	P	*TR*	SU	77431	62961	71866	77430
319 448	**TR**	P	*TR*	SU	77433	62962	71867	77432
319 449	**TR**	P	*TR*	SU	77435	62963	71868	77434
319 450	**TR**	P	*TR*	SU	77437	62964	71869	77436
319 451	**TR**	P	*TR*	SU	77439	62965	71870	77438
319 452	**TR**	P	*TR*	SU	77441	62966	71871	77440
319 453	**TR**	P	*TR*	SU	77443	62967	71872	77442
319 454	**TR**	P	*TR*	SU	77445	62968	71873	77444
319 455	**TR**	P	*TR*	SU	77447	62969	71874	77446
319 456	**TR**	P	*TR*	SU	77449	62970	71875	77448
319 457	**TR**	P	*TR*	SU	77451	62971	71876	77450
319 458	**TR**	P	*TR*	SU	77453	62972	71877	77452
319 459	**TR**	P	*TR*	SU	77455	62973	71878	77454
319 460	**TR**	P	*TR*	SU	77457	62974	71879	77456

CLASS 320   BREL OUTER SUBURBAN

DTS(A)–PMS–DTS(B). Gangwayed within unit. Disc brakes.
Construction: Steel.
Traction Motors: Four Brush TM2141B of 268 kW each.
Dimensions: 19.95 (DTS) or 19.92 (PMS) x 2.82 x 3.78 m.
Maximum Speed: 75 mph.   **Doors:** Power operated sliding.
Couplers: Tightlock.   **Bogies:** BREL P7-4/T3-7.
Multiple Working: Classes 313–323.

63021–63042. PMS. Dia. EC212. Lot No. 31062 BREL York 1990. –/77. 52.1 t.
77899–77920. DTS(A). Dia. EE238. Lot No. 31060 BREL York 1990. –/77. 30.7 t.
77921–77942. DTS(B). Dia. EE239. Lot No. 31061 BREL York 1990. –/76 31.7 t.

320 301	**S**	H	*SR*	GW	77899	63021	77921
320 302	**S**	H	*SR*	GW	77900	63022	77922

320 303	S	H	*SR*	GW	77901	63023	77923
320 304	S	H	*SR*	GW	77902	63024	77924
320 305	S	H	*SR*	GW	77903	63025	77925
320 306	CC	H	*SR*	GW	77904	63026	77926
320 307	CC	H	*SR*	GW	77905	63027	77927
320 308	CC	H	*SR*	GW	77906	63028	77928
320 309	CC	H	*SR*	GW	77907	63029	77929
320 310	CC	H	*SR*	GW	77908	63030	77930
320 311	CC	H	*SR*	GW	77909	63031	77931
320 312	CC	H	*SR*	GW	77910	63032	77932
320 313	CC	H	*SR*	GW	77911	63033	77933
320 314	CC	H	*SR*	GW	77912	63034	77934
320 315	CC	H	*SR*	GW	77913	63035	77935
320 316	CC	H	*SR*	GW	77914	63036	77936
320 317	CC	H	*SR*	GW	77915	63037	77937
320 318	CC	H	*SR*	GW	77916	63038	77938
320 319	CC	H	*SR*	GW	77917	63039	77939
320 320	CC	H	*SR*	GW	77918	63040	77940
320 321	CC	H	*SR*	GW	77919	63041	77941
320 322	CC	H	*SR*	GW	77920	63042	77942

Names (carried on PMS):

320 305	GLASGOW SCHOOL OF ART 1844–150–1994
320 306	Model Rail Scotland
320 309	Radio Clyde 25th Anniversary
320 311	The Royal College of Physicians and Surgeons of Glasgow
320 321	The Rt. Hon. John Smith, QC, MP
320 322	FESTIVE GLASGOW ORCHID

CLASS 321   BREL OUTER SUBURBAN

Various formations, see below. Gangwayed within unit. Disc brakes.
Construction: Steel.
Traction Motors: Four Brush TM2141B of 268 kW each.
Dimensions: 19.95 (DTC & DTS) or 19.92 (ATS & PMS) x 2.82 x 3.78 m.
Maximum Speed: 100 mph.   **Doors:** Power operated sliding.
Couplers: Tightlock.   **Bogies:** BREL P7-4/T3-7.
Multiple Working: Classes 313–323.

Advertising Livery:
• 321 319 'Braintree Freeport'.

Class 321/3. DTC–PMS–ATS–DTS. Small first class area.

62975–63020, 63105–63124. PMS. Dia. EC210. Lot No. 31054 BREL York
  1988–90. –/79 (* –/82). 51.5 t.
71880–71925, 71991–72010. ATS. Dia. EH235. Lot No. 31055 BREL York
  1988–90. –/74 (* –/75) 2T. 28.0 t.
77853–77898, 78280–78299. DTS. Dia. EE236. Lot No. 31056 BREL York
  1988–90. –/78. 29.1 t.
78049–78094, 78131–78150. DTC. Dia. EE308. Lot No. 31053 BREL York
  1988–90. 12/56 (* 16/57). 29.3 t.

321 301		**GE**	H	*GE*	IL	78049	62975	71880	77853
321 302		**GE**	H	*GE*	IL	78050	62976	71881	77854
321 303	*	**GE**	H	*GE*	IL	78051	62977	71882	77855
321 304	*	**GE**	H	*GE*	IL	78052	62978	71883	77856
321 305		**GE**	H	*GE*	IL	78053	62979	71884	77857
321 306		**GE**	H	*GE*	IL	78054	62980	71885	77858
321 307		**GE**	H	*GE*	IL	78055	62981	71886	77859
321 308		**GE**	H	*GE*	IL	78056	62982	71887	77860
321 309		**GE**	H	*GE*	IL	78057	62983	71888	77861
321 310		**GE**	H	*GE*	IL	78058	62984	71889	77862
321 311		**GE**	H	*GE*	IL	78059	62985	71890	77863
321 312		**GE**	H	*GE*	IL	78060	62986	71891	77864
321 313		**GE**	H	*GE*	IL	78061	62987	71892	77865
321 314		**GE**	H	*GE*	IL	78062	62988	71893	77866
321 315		**GE**	H	*GE*	IL	78063	62989	71894	77867
321 316		**GE**	H	*GE*	IL	78064	62990	71895	77868
321 317		**GE**	H	*GE*	IL	78065	62991	71896	77869
321 318		**GE**	H	*GE*	IL	78066	62992	71897	77870
321 319		**GE**	H	*GE*	IL	78067	62993	71898	77871
321 320		**GE**	H	*GE*	IL	78068	62994	71899	77872
321 321		**GE**	H	*GE*	IL	78069	62995	71900	77873
321 322		**GE**	H	*GE*	IL	78070	62996	71901	77874
321 323		**GE**	H	*GE*	IL	78071	62997	71902	77875
321 324		**GE**	H	*GE*	IL	78072	62998	71903	77876
321 325		**GE**	H	*GE*	IL	78073	62999	71904	77877
321 326		**GE**	H	*GE*	IL	78074	63000	71905	77878
321 327		**GE**	H	*GE*	IL	78075	63001	71906	77879
321 328		**GE**	H	*GE*	IL	78076	63002	71907	77880
321 329		**GE**	H	*GE*	IL	78077	63003	71908	77881
321 330		**GE**	H	*GE*	IL	78078	63004	71909	77882
321 331		**GE**	H	*GE*	IL	78079	63005	71910	77883
321 332		**GE**	H	*GE*	IL	78080	63006	71911	77884
321 333		**GE**	H	*GE*	IL	78081	63007	71912	77885
321 334		**GE**	H	*GE*	IL	78082	63008	71913	77886
321 335		**GE**	H	*GE*	IL	78083	63009	71914	77887
321 336		**GE**	H	*GE*	IL	78084	63010	71915	77888
321 337		**GE**	H	*GE*	IL	78085	63011	71916	77889
321 338		**GE**	H	*GE*	IL	78086	63012	71917	77890
321 339		**GE**	H	*GE*	IL	78087	63013	71918	77891
321 340		**GE**	H	*GE*	IL	78088	63014	71919	77892
321 341		**GE**	H	*GE*	IL	78089	63015	71920	77893
321 342		**GE**	H	*GE*	IL	78090	63016	71921	77894
321 343		**GE**	H	*GE*	IL	78091	63017	71922	77895
321 344		**GE**	H	*GE*	IL	78092	63018	71923	77896
321 345		**GE**	H	*GE*	IL	78093	63019	71924	77897
321 346		**GE**	H	*GE*	IL	78094	63020	71925	77898
321 347		**GE**	H	*GE*	IL	78131	63105	71991	78280
321 348		**GE**	H	*GE*	IL	78132	63106	71992	78281
321 349		**GE**	H	*GE*	IL	78133	63107	71993	78282
321 350		**GE**	H	*GE*	IL	78134	63108	71994	78283
321 351		**GE**	H	*GE*	IL	78135	63109	71995	78284

321 352	**GE**	H	*GE*	IL	78136	63110	71996	78285
321 353	**GE**	H	*GE*	IL	78137	63111	71997	78286
321 354	**GE**	H	*GE*	IL	78138	63112	71998	78287
321 355	**GE**	H	*GE*	IL	78139	63113	71999	78288
321 356	**GE**	H	*GE*	IL	78140	63114	72000	78289
321 357	**GE**	H	*GE*	IL	78141	63115	72001	78290
321 358	**GE**	H	*GE*	IL	78142	63116	72002	78291
321 359	**GE**	H	*GE*	IL	78143	63117	72003	78292
321 360	**GE**	H	*GE*	IL	78144	63118	72004	78293
321 361	**GE**	H	*GE*	IL	78145	63119	72005	78294
321 362	**GE**	H	*GE*	IL	78146	63120	72006	78295
321 363	**GE**	H	*GE*	IL	78147	63121	72007	78296
321 364	**GE**	H	*GE*	IL	78148	63122	72008	78297
321 365	**GE**	H	*GE*	IL	78149	63123	72009	78298
321 366	**GE**	H	*GE*	IL	78150	63124	72010	78299

Names (carried on ATS):

321 312	Southend-on-Sea		321 336	GEOFFREY FREEMAN ALLEN
321 334	Amsterdam		321 351	GURKHA

Class 321/4. DTC–PMS–ATS–DTS. Large first class area. All First Great Eastern operated DTC have 12 first class seats declassfied.

Advertising Livery:
• 321 428 'Birmingham Daytripper Ticket'.

63063–63092, 63099–63104, 63125–63136. PMS. Dia. EC210. Lot No. 31068 BREL York 1989–90. –/79. 51.5 t.
63082². PMS. Dia. EC210. Adtranz Crewe 1998. –/79. 51.5 t.
71949–71978, 71985–71990, 72011–72022. ATS. Dia. EH235. Lot No. 31069 BREL York 1989–90. –/74 2T. 28.0 t.
71966². ATS. Dia. EH235. Adtranz Crewe 1998. –/74 2T. 28.0 t.
77943–77972, 78274–78279, 78300–78311. DTS. Dia. EE236. Lot No. 31070 BREL York 1989–90. –/78. 29.1 t.
77960². DTS. Dia. EE236. Adtranz Crewe 1998. –/78. 29.1 t.
78095–78130/151–78162. DTC. Dia. EE309. Lot No. 31067 BREL York 1989–90. 28/40. 29.3 t.
78114². DTC. Dia. EE309. Adtranz Crewe 1998. 28/40. 29.3 t.

321 401	**N**	H	*SL*	BY	78095	63063	71949	77943
321 402	**N**	H	*SL*	BY	78096	63064	71950	77944
321 403	**N**	H	*SL*	BY	78097	63065	71951	77945
321 404	**N**	H	*SL*	BY	78098	63066	71952	77946
321 405	**N**	H	*SL*	BY	78099	63067	71953	77947
321 406	**N**	H	*SL*	BY	78100	63068	71954	77948
321 407	**N**	H	*SL*	BY	78101	63069	71955	77949
321 408	**N**	H	*SL*	BY	78102	63070	71956	77950
321 409	**N**	H	*SL*	BY	78103	63071	71957	77951
321 410	**N**	H	*SL*	BY	78104	63072	71958	77952
321 411	**N**	H	*SL*	BY	78105	63073	71959	77953
321 412	**N**	H	*SL*	BY	78106	63074	71960	77954
321 413	**N**	H	*SL*	BY	78107	63075	71961	77955
321 414	**N**	H	*SL*	BY	78108	63076	71962	77956

321 415	N	H	SL	BY	78109	63077	71963	77957
321 416	N	H	SL	BY	78110	63078	71964	77958
321 417	N	H	SL	BY	78111	63079	71965	77959
321 418	N	H	SL	BY	78112	63080	71968	77962
321 419	N	H	SL	BY	78113	63081	71967	77961
321 420	SL	H	SL	BY	78114^2	63082^2	71966^2	77960^2
321 421	N	H	SL	BY	78115	63083	71969	77963
321 422	N	H	SL	BY	78116	63084	71970	77964
321 423	N	H	SL	BY	78117	63085	71971	77965
321 424	N	H	SL	BY	78118	63086	71972	77966
321 425	N	H	SL	BY	78119	63087	71973	77967
321 426	N	H	SL	BY	78120	63088	71974	77968
321 427	N	H	SL	BY	78121	63089	71975	77969
321 428	AL	H	SL	BY	78122	63090	71976	77970
321 429	SL	H	SL	BY	78123	63091	71977	77971
321 430	SL	H	SL	BY	78124	63092	71978	77972
321 431	SL	H	SL	BY	78151	63125	72011	78300
321 432	SL	H	SL	BY	78152	63126	72012	78301
321 433	SL	H	SL	BY	78153	63127	72013	78302
321 434	SL	H	SL	BY	78154	63128	72014	78303
321 435	SL	H	SL	BY	78155	63129	72015	78304
321 436	SL	H	SL	BY	78156	63130	72016	78305
321 437	SL	H	SL	BY	78157	63131	72017	78306
321 438	GE	H	GE	IL	78158	63132	72018	78307
321 439	GE	H	GE	IL	78159	63133	72019	78308
321 440	GE	H	GE	IL	78160	63134	72020	78309
321 441	GE	H	GE	IL	78161	63135	72021	78310
321 442	GE	H	GE	IL	78162	63136	72022	78311
321 443	GE	H	GE	IL	78125	63099	71985	78274
321 444	GE	H	GE	IL	78126	63100	71986	78275
321 445	GE	H	GE	IL	78127	63101	71987	78276
321 446	GE	H	GE	IL	78128	63102	71988	78277
321 447	GE	H	GE	IL	78129	63103	71989	78278
321 448	GE	H	GE	IL	78130	63104	71990	78279

Names (carried on ATS):

321 407   HERTFORDSHIRE WRVS
321 439   Chelmsford Cathedral Festival
321 444   Essex Lifeboats

Class 321/9. DTS(A)–PMS–ATS–DTS(B). Leased by West Yorkshire PTE from International Bank of Scotland. Managed by Porterbrook Leasing Company.

63153–63155. PMS. Dia. EC216. Lot No. 31109 BREL York 1991. –/79. 51.5 t.
72128–72130. ATS. Dia. EH240. Lot No. 31110 BREL York 1991. –/74 2T. 28.0 t.
77990–77992. DTS(A). Dia. EE277. Lot No. 31108 BREL York 1991. –/78. 29.3 t.
77993–77995. DTS(B). Dia. EE277. Lot No. 31111 BREL York 1991. –/78. 29.1 t.

321 901	WY	P	NS	NL	77990	63153	72128	77993
321 902	WY	P	NS	NL	77991	63154	72129	77994
321 903	WY	P	NS	NL	77992	63155	72130	77995

CLASS 322   BREL OUTER SUBURBAN

DTC–PMS–ATS–DTS. Gangwayed within unit. Disc brakes.
Construction: Steel.
Traction Motors: Four Brush TM2141B of 268 kW each.
Dimensions: 19.95 (DTC & DTS) or 19.92 (ATS & PMS) x 2.82 x 3.78 m.
Maximum Speed: 100 mph.   **Doors:** Power operated sliding.
Couplers: Tightlock.   **Bogies:** BREL P7-4/T3-7.
Multiple Working: Classes 313–323.
Non-Standard Livery:
• 322 481–483 carry 'Stansted Skytrain' livery (grey with a yellow stripe).
Advertising Livery:
• 322 485 'Stansted Express'.

78163–78167. DTC. Dia. EE313. Lot No. 31094 BREL York 1990. 35/22. 30.4 t.
63137–63141. PMS. Dia. EC215. Lot No. 31092 BREL York 1990. –/70. 52.3 t.
72023–72027. ATS. Dia. EH239. Lot No. 31093 BREL York 1990. –/60 2T. 29.5 t.
77985–77989. DTS. Dia. EE242. Lot No. 31091 BREL York 1990. –/65. 29.8 t.

322 481	0	H	WN	HE	78163	72023	63137	77985
322 482	0	H	WN	HE	78164	72024	63138	77986
322 483	0	H	WN	HE	78165	72025	63139	77987
322 484	NW	H	WN	HE	78166	72026	63140	77988
322 485	AL	H	WN	HE	78167	72027	63141	77989

CLASS 323   HUNSLET-TPL OUTER SUBURBAN

DMS(A)–PTS–DMS(B). Gangwayed within unit. Disc brakes.
Construction: Welded aluminium alloy.
Traction Motors: Four Holec DMKT 52/24 of 146 kW per motor car.
Dimensions: 23.37 (DMS) or 23.44 (PTS) x 2.80 x . m.
Maximum Speed: 90 mph.   **Doors:** Power operated sliding plug.
Couplers: Tightlock.   **Bogies:** RFS BP62/BT52.
Multiple Working: Classes 313–323.

64001–64043. DMS(A). Dia. EA272. Lot No. 31112 Hunslet TPL 1992–93. –/98
(* –/82). 41.0 t.
72201–72243. PTS. Dia. EH296. Lot No. 31113 Hunslet TPL 1992–93. –/88
(* –/80) 1T. 39.4 t.
65001–65043. DMS(B). Dia. EA272. Lot No. 31114 Hunslet TPL 1992–93. –/98
(* –/82). 41.0 t.

323 201	CO	P	CT	SI	64001	72201	65001
323 202	CO	P	CT	SI	64002	72202	65002
323 203	CO	P	CT	SI	64003	72203	65005
323 204	CO	P	CT	SI	64004	72204	65004
323 205	CO	P	CT	SI	64005	72205	65003
323 206	CO	P	CT	SI	64006	72206	65006
323 207	CO	P	CT	SI	64007	72207	65007
323 208	CO	P	CT	SI	64008	72208	65008
323 209	CO	P	CT	SI	64009	72209	65009

323 210		CO	P	CT	SI	64010	72210	65010
323 211		CO	P	CT	SI	64011	72211	65011
323 212		CO	P	CT	SI	64012	72212	65012
323 213		CO	P	CT	SI	64013	72213	65013
323 214		CO	P	CT	SI	64014	72214	65014
323 215		CO	P	CT	SI	64015	72215	65015
323 216		CO	P	CT	SI	64016	72216	65016
323 217		CO	P	CT	SI	64017	72217	65017
323 218		CO	P	CT	SI	64018	72218	65018
323 219		CO	P	CT	SI	64019	72219	65019
323 220		CO	P	CT	SI	64020	72220	65020
323 221		CO	P	CT	SI	64021	72221	65021
323 222		CO	P	CT	SI	64022	72222	65022
323 223	*	GM	P	NW	LG	64023	72223	65023
323 224	*	NW	P	NW	LG	64024	72224	65024
323 225	*	GM	P	NW	LG	64025	72225	65025
323 226		GM	P	NW	LG	64026	72226	65026
323 227		GM	P	NW	LG	64027	72227	65027
323 228		GM	P	NW	LG	64028	72228	65028
323 229		GM	P.	NW	LG	64029	72229	65029
323 230		GM	P	NW	LG	64030	72230	65030
323 231		GM	P	NW	LG	64031	72231	65031
323 232		GM	P	NW	LG	64032	72232	65032
323 233		NW	P	NW	LG	64033	72233	65033
323 234		GM	P	NW	LG	64034	72234	65034
323 235		GM	P	NW	LG	64035	72235	65035
323 236		GM	P	NW	LG	64036	72236	65036
323 237		GM	P	NW	LG	64037	72237	65037
323 238		GM	P	NW	LG	64038	72238	65038
323 239		GM	P	NW	LG	64039	72239	65039
323 240		CO	P	CT	SI	64040	72340	65040
323 241		CO	P	CT	SI	64041	72341	65041
323 242		CO	P	CT	SI	64042	72342	65042
323 243		CO	P	CT	SI	64043	72343	65043

▲ 303 045 arrives at Glasgow Central on 12th October 1999 with a service from Gourock. This class is scheduled for replacement by Class 334 early in 2000.
Bob Sweet

▼ 310 089 passes Shadwell station of the Docklands Light Railway with the 10.10 London Fenchurch Street–Shoeburyness on 30th May 1998. **Kevin Conkey**

West Anglia Great Northern operated 313 060 wears an attractive advertising livery for the public transport initiative 'Intalink' as an alternative to the white undercoat livery worn by most other refurbished members of this class pending adoption of a new livery.

Brian Morrison

▲ 314 213 departs from Glasgow Central with a Cathcart Circle service on 12th October 1999.
Bob Sweet

▼ 315 816 nears Bow Junction, Stratford, with a service for London Liverpool Street on 9th September 1999.
Hugh Ballantyne

▲ Conversion of Class 317/2 to Class 317/6 was completed during 1999. 317 670 was photographed at Hackney Downs with the 13.42 Bishop's Stortford–London Liverpool Street on 26th May 1999. **Kevin Conkey**

▼ 318 253 passes Troon Golf Course, Ayrshire, with an Ayr–Glasgow Central working on 28th April 1999. **Paul Senior**

▲ The 10.08 London Victoria–Brighton service departs from Clapham Junction on 22nd March 1997 formed of 319 220 and 319 218. **Kevin Conkey**

▼ 320 319 arrives at Springburn with an empty working from Yoker SD on 13th August 1999. **Hugh Ballantyne**

321 436 passes Headstone Lane whilst working the 15.34 London Euston–Milton Keynes Central on 1st April 1999.

David Brown

▲ 322 483 passes through Bethnal Green with the 10.30 London Liverpool Street–Stansted Airport on 16th May 1999. These units are to be replaced on this service by Class 317/7 early in 2000. **Kevin Conkey**

▼ 323 223, one of three units with revised seating layout for use on services to/from Manchester Airport, leaves Stoke on Trent with the 09.08 to Manchester Piccadilly on 6th September 1999. **Colin J. Marsden**

▲ 325 005 passing Wandsworth Road with 1M44, 13.47 Tonbridge Royal Mail Terminal–Willesden Royal Mail Terminal on 6th August 1998.   **Hugh Ballantyne**

▼ Heathrow Express unit 332 007 approaches London Paddington on 16th June 1998.   **John G. Teasdale**

▲ 357 001 at Adtranz Derby, awaiting delivery to LTS Rail, on 26th August 1999.
Brian Morrison

▼ 365 001 formed the 13.52 Ramsgate–London Victoria service on 3rd February 1998.
Rodney Lissenden

▲ Class 483 units 002 and 004 near Ryde Esplanade with a Shanklin–Ryde Pier Head service on 21st August 1999. **Hugh Ballantyne**

▼ Class 438 trailer unit 417 was hired to Silverlink Train Services for use on the Gospel Oak–Barking line for a short period in the autumn of 1999. It is seen here propelled by 33103 passing Gospel Oak with a crew training run on 19th August 1999. **David Brown**

▲ Class 411/9 unit 1103 forms the 10.07 London Bridge–Tunbridge Wells service at Edenbridge Town on 27th March 1999.
Chris Wilson

▼ Class 411/5 unit 1534 shunts into the depot sidings at Fratton on 12th July 1999.
Chris Wilson

▲ Class 421/3 unit 1747 forms the 15.16 London Victoria–Bournemouth, seen passing St. Denys on 23rd July 1999.   **Brian Denton**

▼ Class 442 units 2406 and 2412 depart from Basingstoke with the 07.50 Poole–London Waterloo on 26th June 1999.   **David Brown**

▲ Class 423 units 3478 and 3501 head a 12-car empty train bound for Brighton on 17th June 1999. **Chris Wilson**

▼ Class 455/7 unit 5734 departs from Clapham Junction with a London Waterloo–Woking service on 22nd October 1997. **Rodney Lissenden**

▲ New Class 460 unit 8004 stands inside Wimbledon T&RSMD on 16th August 1999.   **Brian Morrison**

▼ Class 489 luggage van leads an 9-car 'Gatwick Express' formation on the 09.40 Gatwick Airport–London Victoria on 6th August 1999, with Class 73/2 locomotive, 73202 bringing up the rear.   **David Brown**

▲ 456 015 departs from London Bridge with the 09.59 London Bridge–Smitham on 11th November 1998. **Rodney Lissenden**

▼ 507 028 leaves Kirkdale with a Liverpool-bound service on 26th June 1999. **Hugh Ballantyne**

▲ Railtrack sandite laying unit 930 102 passes Millbrook on 23rd February 1999.
Brian Denton

▼ Eurostar units 3018 and 3017 pass Paddock Wood with a London Waterloo International–Paris Nord working on 28th August 1999.　　**Michael J. Collins**

CLASS 325   ABB ROYAL MAIL

DTV(A)–PMV–TAV–DTV(B). Non gangwayed. Disc brakes.
Construction: Steel.
Supply System: 25 kV 50 Hz a.c. overhead or 750 V d.c. third rail.
Traction Motors: Four GEC G315BZ of 247.5 kW each.
Dimensions: 20.35 x 2.82 x . m.   **Doors:** Roller shutter.
Maximum Speed: 100 mph.   **Bogies:** ABB P7-4/T3-7.
Couplers: Buckeye.   **Multiple Working:** Within class only.

68300–68330 (Even numbers). DTV(A). Dia. EE503. Lot No. 31144 ABB Derby
 1995. Load capacity 12.0 t. 29.2 t.
68340–68355. PMV. Dia. EC501. Lot No. 31145 ABB Derby 1995. Load capacity
 12.0 t. 49.5 t.
68360–68375. TAV. Dia. EH501. Lot No. 31146 ABB Derby 1995. Load capacity
 12.0 t. 30.7 t.
68301–68331 (Odd numbers). DTV(B). Dia. EE503. Lot No. 31144 ABB Derby
 1995. Load capacity 12.0 t. 29.1 t.

325 001	**RM**	RM	*E*	CE	68300	68340	68360	68301
325 002	**RM**	RM	*E*	CE	68302	68341	68361	68303
325 003	**RM**	RM	*E*	CE	68304	68342	68362	68305
325 004	**RM**	RM	*E*	CE	68306	68343	68363	68307
325 005	**RM**	RM	*E*	CE	68308	68344	68364	68309
325 006	**RM**	RM	*E*	CE	68310	68345	68365	68311
325 007	**RM**	RM	*E*	CE	68312	68346	68366	68313
325 008	**RM**	RM	*E*	CE	68314	68347	68367	68315
325 009	**RM**	RM	*E*	CE	68316	68348	68368	68317
325 010	**RM**	RM	*E*	CE	68318	68349	68369	68319
325 011	**RM**	RM	*E*	CE	68320	68350	68370	68321
325 012	**RM**	RM	*E*	CE	68322	68351	68371	68323
325 013	**RM**	RM	*E*	CE	68324	68352	68372	68325
325 014	**RM**	RM	*E*	CE	68326	68353	68373	68327
325 015	**RM**	RM	*E*	CE	68328	68354	68374	68329
325 016	**RM**	RM	*E*	CE	68330	68355	68375	68331

Names (carried on one DTV per side):

325 002   Royal Mail North Wales and North West
325 006   John Grierson
325 008   Peter Howarth C.B.E.

CLASS 332   SIEMENS EXPRESS

Various formations, see below. Gangwayed within unit. Disc brakes. Air
conditioned.
Construction: Steel.
Traction Motors: Two Siemens monomotors of 350 kW each per motor car.
Dimensions: 23.74 x 2.75 x . m.
Maximum Speed: 160 km/h.   **Doors:** Power operated sliding plug.
Couplers: Scharfenberg.   **Bogies:** CAF design.
Multiple Working: Within Class only.

Units 332 001–332 007. DMF–TS–PTS–DMS.

63400–63406. PTS. Dia. EH243. CAF 1997–98. –/44 1T 1W. 45.6 t.
72400–72413. TS. Dia. EH245. CAF 1997–98. –/56. 45.2 t.
78400–78412 (Even numbers). DMF. CAF 1997–98. Converted 1998 from DMS. 26/–. 48.8 t.
78401–78413 (Odd numbers). DMS. Dia. EA243. CAF 1997–98. –/48. 48.8 t.

332 001	**HX**	HX	*HX*	OH	78400	72412	63400	78401
332 002	**HX**	HX	*HX*	OH	78402	72409	63401	78403
332 003	**HX**	HX	*HX*	OH	78404	72407	63402	78405
332 004	**HX**	HX	*HX*	OH	78406	72405	63403	78407
332 005	**HX**	HX	*HX*	OH	78408	72411	63404	78409
332 006	**HX**	HX	*HX*	OH	78410	72410	63405	78411
332 007	**HX**	HX	*HX*	OH	78412	72401	63406	78413

Units 332 008–332 014. DMS–TS–PTS–DMF.

63407–63413. PTS. Dia. EH243. CAF 1997–98. –/44 1T 1W. 45.6 t.
72400–72413. TS. Dia. EH245. CAF 1997–98. –/56. 45.2 t.
78414–78426 (Even numbers). DMS. Dia. EA244. CAF 1997–98. –/48. 48.8 t.
78415–78427 (Odd numbers). DMF. Dia. EA1??. CAF 1997–98. Converted 1998 from DMS. 14/– 1W. 48.8 t.

332 008	**HX**	HX	*HX*	OH	78414	72413	63407	78415
332 009	**HX**	HX	*HX*	OH	78416	72400	63408	78417
332 010	**HX**	HX	*HX*	OH	78418	72402	63409	78419
332 011	**HX**	HX	*HX*	OH	78420	72403	63410	78421
332 012	**HX**	HX	*HX*	OH	78422	72404	63411	78423
332 013	**HX**	HX	*HX*	OH	78424	72408	63412	78425
332 014	**HX**	HX	*HX*	OH	78426	72406	63413	78427

CLASS 333   SIEMENS SUBURBAN

DMS(A)–TS–DMS(B). Gangwayed within unit. Disc brakes. Air conditioned.
Construction: Steel.
Traction Motors: Two Siemens monomotors of ??? kW each per motor car.
Dimensions: 23.74 x 2.75 x . m.
Maximum Speed: 160 km/h.   **Doors:** Power operated sliding plug.
Couplers: Scharfenberg.   **Bogies:** CAF design.
Multiple Working: Within Class only.

74461–74476. PTS. Dia. EH2??. CAF 2000.
78451–78481 (Odd numbers). DMS(A). Dia. EA2??. CAF 2000.
78452–78482 (Even numbers). DMS(B). Dia. EA2??. CAF 2000.

333 001	**NS**	A	*NS*	78451	74461	78452
333 002		A	*NS*	78453	74462	78454
333 003		A	*NS*	78455	74463	78456
333 004		A	*NS*	78457	74464	78458
333 005		A	*NS*	78459	74465	78460
333 006		A	*NS*	78461	74466	78462
333 007		A	*NS*	78463	74467	78464
333 008		A	*NS*	78465	74468	78466

333 009	A	NS	78467	74469	78468
333 010	A	NS	78469	74470	78470
333 011	A	NS	78471	74471	78472
333 012	A	NS	78473	74472	78474
333 013	A	NS	78475	74473	78476
333 014	A	NS	78477	74474	78478
333 015	A	NS	78479	74475	78480
333 016	A	NS	78481	74476	78482

CLASS 334   ALSTOM JUNIPER

DMS(A)–PTS–DMS(B). Gangwayed within unit. Disc brakes. Air conditioned.
Construction: Steel.
Traction Motors: Two Alstom ONIX 800 of 270 kW each per motor car.
Dimensions: 21.16 (DMS) or 19.94 (PTS) x 2.80 x . m.
Doors: Power operated sliding plug.
Maximum Speed: 100 mph.   **Bogies:** Alstom LTB3/TBP3.
Couplers: Scharfenberg.   **Multiple Working:** Within Class only.

64101–64140. DMS(A). Dia. EA215. Alstom Birmingham 1999–2000. –/64 1TD 2W. 42.6 t.
65101–65140. DMS(B). Dia. EA215. Alstom Birmingham 1999–2000. –/64. 42.6 t.
74301–74340. PTS. Dia.EH255. Alstom Birmingham 1999–2000. –/55. 39.4 t.

334 001	CC	H	SR	GW	64101	74301	65101
334 002	CC	H	SR	GW	64102	74302	65102
334 003		H	SR		64103	74303	65103
334 004		H	SR		64104	74304	65104
334 005		H	SR		64105	74305	65105
334 006		H	SR		64106	74306	65106
334 007		H	SR		64107	74307	65107
334 008		H	SR		64108	74308	65108
334 009		H	SR		64109	74309	65109
334 010		H	SR		64110	74310	65110
334 011		H	SR		64111	74311	65111
334 012		H	SR		64112	74312	65112
334 013		H	SR		64113	74313	65113
334 014		H	SR		64114	74314	65114
334 015		H	SR		64115	74315	65115
334 016		H	SR		64116	74316	65116
334 017		H	SR		64117	74317	65117
334 018		H	SR		64118	74318	65118
334 019		H	SR		64119	74319	65119
334 020		H	SR		64120	74320	65120
334 021		H	SR		64121	74321	65121
334 022		H	SR		64122	74322	65122
334 023		H	SR		64123	74323	65123
334 024		H	SR		64124	74324	65124
334 025		H	SR		64125	74325	65125
334 026		H	SR		64126	74326	65126

334 027	H	SR	64127	74327	65127
334 028	H	SR	64128	74328	65128
334 029	H	SR	64129	74329	65129
334 030	H	SR	64130	74330	65130
334 031	H	SR	64131	74331	65131
334 032	H	SR	64132	74332	65132
334 033	H	SR	64133	74333	65133
334 034	H	SR	64134	74334	65134
334 035	H	SR	64135	74335	65135
334 036	H	SR	64136	74336	65136
334 037	H	SR	64137	74337	65137
334 038	H	SR	64138	74338	65138
334 039	H	SR	64139	74339	65139
334 040	H	SR	64140	74340	65140

CLASS 357   ADTRANZ ELECTROSTAR

DMS(A)–PTS–MS–DMS(B). Gangwayed within unit. Disc and regenerative brakes. Air conditioning.
Construction: Welded aluminium alloy underframe, sides and roof. Steel ends. All sections bolted together.
Supply System: 25 kV a.c. 50Hz overhead (with provision for 750 V d.c. third rail supply).   **Bogies:** Adtranz P3-25/ T3-25.
Traction Motors: Two Adtranz of 250 kW each per motor car.
Dimensions: 20.40 (DMS) or 19.99 (MS & PTS) x 2.80 x 3.78 m.
Maximum Speed: 100 mph.   **Doors:** Power operated sliding plug.
Multiple Working: Within class.   **Couplers:** Tightlock.

67651–67696. DMS(A). Dia. EA273. Adtranz Derby 1999–2000. –/71. 40.7 t.
67751–67796. DMS(B). Dia. EA214. Adtranz Derby 1999–2000. –/71. 40.7 t.
74051–74096. PTS. Dia. EH215. Adtranz Derby 1999–2000. –/62 1TD 2W. 36.7 t.
74151–74196. MS. Dia. EC225. Adtranz Derby 1999–2000. –/78 . 39.5 t.

357 001	LS	P	LS	EM	67651	74051	74151	67751
357 002	LS	P	LS	EM	67652	74052	74152	67752
357 003	LS	P	LS	EM	67653	74053	74153	67753
357 004		P	LS		67654	74054	74154	67754
357 005		P	LS		67655	74055	74155	67755
357 006		P	LS		67656	74056	74156	67756
357 007		P	LS		67657	74057	74157	67757
357 008		P	LS		67658	74058	74158	67758
357 009		P	LS		67659	74059	74159	67759
357 010		P	LS		67660	74060	74160	67760
357 011	LS	P	LS	EM	67661	74061	74161	67761
357 012	LS	P	LS	EM	67662	74062	74162	67762
357 013	LS	P	LS	EM	67663	74063	74163	67763
357 014		P	LS		67664	74064	74164	67764
357 015		P	LS		67665	74065	74165	67765
357 016		P	LS		67666	74066	74166	67766
357 017		P	LS		67667	74067	74167	67767
357 018		P	LS		67668	74068	74168	67768

357 019	P	LS	67669	74069	74169	67769
357 020	P	LS	67670	74070	74170	67770
357 021	P	LS	67671	74071	74171	67771
357 022	P	LS	67672	74072	74172	67772
357 023	P	LS	67673	74073	74173	67773
357 024	P	LS	67674	74074	74174	67774
357 025	P	LS	67675	74075	74175	67775
357 026	P	LS	67676	74076	74176	67776
357 027	P	LS	67677	74077	74177	67777
357 028	P	LS	67678	74078	74178	67778
357 029	P	LS	67679	74079	74179	67779
357 030	P	LS	67680	74080	74180	67780
357 031	P	LS	67681	74081	74181	67781
357 032	P	LS	67682	74082	74182	67782
357 033	P	LS	67683	74083	74183	67783
357 034	P	LS	67684	74084	74184	67784
357 035	P	LS	67685	74085	74185	67785
357 036	P	LS	67686	74086	74186	67786
357 037	P	LS	67687	74087	74187	67787
357 038	P	LS	67688	74088	74188	67788
357 039	P	LS	67689	74089	74189	67789
357 040	P	LS	67690	74090	74190	67790
357 041	P	LS	67691	74091	74191	67791
357 042	P	LS	67692	74092	74192	67792
357 043	P	LS	67693	74093	74193	67793
357 044	P	LS	67694	74094	74194	67794
357 045	P	LS	67695	74095	74195	67795
357 046	P	LS	67696	74096	74196	67796

CLASS 365   ABB NETWORK EXPRESS

DMC(A)–TSD–TS–DMC(B) or DMC(A)–TSD–PTS–DMC(B). Gangwayed within unit. Disc, rheostatic and regenerative braking.
Construction: Welded aluminium alloy.
Supply System: 25 kV a.c. 50 Hz overhead with provision for 750 V d.c. third rail supply or 750 V d.c. third rail with provision for 25 kV a.c. 50 Hz overhead supply.
Traction Motors: Four GEC-Alsthom G354CX of 157 kW each per motor car.
Dimensions: 20.89 (DMC) or 20.06 (TS & TSD) x 2.81 x 3.77 m.
Maximum Speed: 100 mph.   **Doors:** Power operated sliding plug.
Couplers: Tightlock.   **Bogies:** ABB P3-16/T3-16.
Multiple Working: Classes 365, 465 and 466.

65894–65934. DMC(A). Dia. EA301. Lot No. 31133 ABB York 1994–95. 12/56. 41.7 t.
65935–65975. DMC(B). Dia, EA301. Lot No. 31136 ABB York 1994–95. 12/56. 41.7 t.
72240–72270 (Even numbers). TS. Dia. EH298. Lot No. 31135 ABB York 1994–95. –/68 1T. 34.6 t.
72272–72320 (Even numbers.). PTS. Dia. EH298. Lot No. 31135 ABB York 1994–95. –/68 1T. 34.6 t.
72241–72321 (Odd numbers). TSD. Dia. EH298. Lot No. 31134 ABB York 1994–95. –/59 1TD 1W. 32.9 t.

Units 365 001–365 516. Operated by Connex South Eastern. DMC(A)–TSD–TS–DMC(B). 750 V d.c. third rail with provision for 25 kV a.c. 50 Hz overhead supply.

365 501	**CS**	H	*SE*	SG	65894	72241	72240	65935
365 502	**CS**	H	*SE*	SG	65895	72243	72242	65936
365 503	**CS**	H	*SE*	SG	65896	72245	72244	65937
365 504	**CS**	H	*SE*	SG	65897	72247	72246	65938
365 505	**CS**	H	*SE*	SG	65898	72249	72248	65939
365 506	**CS**	H	*SE*	SG	65899	72251	72250	65940
365 507	**CS**	H	*SE*	SG	65900	72253	72252	65941
365 508	**CS**	H	*SE*	SG	65901	72255	72254	65942
365 509	**CS**	H	*SE*	SG	65902	72257	72256	65943
365 510	**CS**	H	*SE*	SG	65903	72259	72258	65944
365 511	**CS**	H	*SE*	SG	65904	72261	72260	65945
365 512	**CS**	H	*SE*	SG	65905	72263	72262	65946
365 513	**CS**	H	*SE*	SG	65906	72265	72264	65947
365 514	**CS**	H	*SE*	SG	65907	72267	72266	65948
365 515	**CS**	H	*SE*	SG	65908	72269	72268	65949
365 516	**CS**	H	*SE*	SG	65909	72271	72270	65950

Units 365 517–365 541. Operated by West Anglia Great Northern. DMC(A)–TSD–PTS–DMC(B). 25 kV a.c. 50 Hz overhead with provision for 750 V d.c. third rail supply.

365 517	**NT**	H	*WN*	HE	65910	72273	72272	65951
365 518	**NT**	H	*WN*	HE	65911	72275	72274	65952
365 519	**NT**	H	*WN*	HE	65912	72277	72276	65953
365 520	**NT**	H	*WN*	HE	65913	72279	72278	65954
365 521	**NT**	H	*WN*	HE	65914	72281	72280	65955
365 522	**NT**	H	*WN*	HE	65915	72283	72282	65956
365 523	**NT**	H	*WN*	HE	65916	72285	72284	65957
365 524	**NT**	H	*WN*	HE	65917	72287	72286	65958
365 525	**NT**	H	*WN*	HE	65918	72289	72288	65959
365 526	**NT**	H	*WN*	HE	65919	72291	72290	65960
365 527	**NT**	H	*WN*	HE	65920	72293	72292	65961
365 528	**NT**	H	*WN*	HE	65921	72295	72294	65962
365 529	**NT**	H	*WN*	HE	65922	72297	72296	65963
365 530	**NT**	H	*WN*	HE	65923	72299	72298	65964
365 531	**NT**	H	*WN*	HE	65924	72301	72300	65965
365 532	**NT**	H	*WN*	HE	65925	72303	72302	65966
365 533	**NT**	H	*WN*	HE	65926	72305	72304	65967
365 534	**NT**	H	*WN*	HE	65927	72307	72306	65968
365 535	**NT**	H	*WN*	HE	65928	72309	72308	65969
365 536	**NT**	H	*WN*	HE	65929	72311	72310	65970
365 537	**NT**	H	*WN*	HE	65930	72313	72312	65971
365 538	**NT**	H	*WN*	HE	65931	72315	72314	65972
365 539	**NT**	H	*WN*	HE	65932	72317	72316	65973
365 540	**NT**	H	*WN*	HE	65933	72319	72318	65974
365 541	**NT**	H	*WN*	HE	65934	72321	72320	65975

Names (carried on one side of each DMC):

365 505	Spirit of Ramsgate	365 515	Spirit of Dover

CLASS 375 ADTRANZ ELECTROSTAR

Various formations, see below. Gangwayed throughout. Disc and regenerative braking. Air conditioned.
Construction: Welded aluminium alloy underframe, sides and roof. Steel ends. All sections bolted together.
Supply System: 25 kV a.c. 50 Hz overhead and/or 750 V d.c. third rail. 750 V d.c only units also have provision for 25 kV a.c. 50 Hz overhead supply.
Traction Motors: Two Adtranz of 250 kW each per motor car.
Dimensions: 20.40 (DMS) or 19.99 (MS & PTS) x 2.80 x 3.78 m.
Maximum Speed: 100 mph.   **Doors:** Power operated sliding plug.
Couplers: Tightlock.   **Multiple Working:** Within class.
Bogies: Adtranz P3-25/T3-25.

Class 375/3. 750 V d.c. only 3-car units. DMS(A)–PTS–DMS(B).

67921–67930. DMS(A). Dia. EA277. Adtranz Derby 2000. –/64. . t.
67931–67940. DMS(B). Dia. EA277. Adtranz Derby 2000. –/64. . t.
74351–74360. PTS. Dia. EH254. Adtranz Derby 2000. –/56 1TD 2W. . t.

375 301	H	67921	74351	67931
375 302	H	67922	74352	67932
375 303	H	67923	74353	67933
375 304	H	67924	74354	67934
375 305	H	67925	74355	67935
375 306	H	67926	74356	67936
375 307	H	67927	74357	67937
375 308	H	67928	74358	67938
375 309	H	67929	74359	67939
375 310	H	67930	74360	67940

Class 375/6. Dual system 4-car units. DMS(A)–PTS–MS–DMS(B).

67801–67830. DMS(A). Dia. EA275. Adtranz Derby 1999–2000. –/60. 46.2 t.
67851–67880. DMS(B). Dia. EA275. Adtranz Derby 1999–2000. –/60. 46.2 t.
74201–74230. PTS. Dia. EH252. Adtranz Derby 1999–2000. –/56 1TD 2W. 40.7 t.
74251–74280. MS. Dia. EC230. Adtranz Derby 1999–2000. –/66 1T. 40.5 t.

375 601	U	H	AF	67801	74201	74251	67851
375 602	U	H		67802	74202	74252	67852
375 603		H		67803	74203	74253	67853
375 604		H		67804	74204	74254	67854
375 605		H		67805	74205	74255	67855
375 606		H		67806	74206	74256	67856
375 607		H		67807	74207	74257	67857
375 608		H		67808	74208	74258	67858
375 609		H		67809	74209	74259	67859
375 610		H		67810	74210	74260	67860
375 611		H		67811	74211	74261	67861
375 612		H		67812	74212	74262	67862
375 613		H		67813	74213	74263	67863
375 614		H		67814	74214	74264	67864
375 615		H		67815	74215	74265	67865

375 616	H	67816	74216	74266	67866
375 617	H	67817	74217	74267	67867
375 618	H	67818	74218	74268	67868
375 619	H	67819	74219	74269	67869
375 620	H	67820	74220	74270	67870
375 621	H	67821	74221	74271	67871
375 622	H	67822	74222	74272	67872
375 623	H	67823	74223	74273	67873
375 624	H	67824	74224	74274	67874
375 625	H	67825	74225	74275	67875
375 626	H	67826	74226	74276	67876
375 627	H	67827	74227	74277	67877
375 628	H	67828	74228	74278	67878
375 629	H	67829	74229	74279	67879
375 630	H	67830	74230	74280	67880

Class 375/7. 750 V d.c. only 4-car units. DMS(A)–PTS–MS–DMS(B).

67831–67845. DMS(A). Dia. EA276. Adtranz Derby 1999–2000. –/60. . t.
67881–67895. DMS(B). Dia. EA276. Adtranz Derby 1999–2000. –/60. t.
74231–74245. PTS. Dia. EH253. Adtranz Derby 1999–2000. –/56 1TD 2W. . t.
74281–74295. MS. Dia. EC231. Adtranz Derby 1999–2000. –/66 1T. . t.

375 701	H	67831	74281	74231	67881
375 702	H	67832	74282	74232	67882
375 703	H	67833	74283	74233	67883
375 704	H	67834	74284	74234	67884
375 705	H	67835	74285	74235	67885
375 706	H	67836	74281	74236	67886
375 707	H	67837	74287	74237	67887
375 708	H	67838	74288	74238	67888
375 709	H	67839	74289	74239	67889
375 710	H	67840	74290	74240	67890
375 711	H	67841	74291	74241	67891
375 712	H	67842	74292	74242	67892
375 713	H	67843	74293	74243	67893
375 714	H	67844	74294	74244	67894
375 715	H	67845	74295	74245	67895

CLASS 390   ALSTOM/FIAT PENDOLINO BRITANNICO

DMFRK–MFD–PTF–MF–MSD–PTSRMB–MSD–DMS or DMFRK–MFD–PTF–MF–TS–MSD–PTSRMB–MSD–DMS. Tilting units under construction for Virgin West Coast. Gangwayed within unit. Disc and regenerative braking. Air conditioned. A total of forty-four 8-car and nine 9-car units are on order, but only 2 units are scheduled for delivery during 2000.
Construction: Welded aluminium alloy.
Supply System: 25 kV a.c. 50 Hz overhead.
Traction Motors: Two Alstom ONIX 800 of 425 kW each per motor car.
Dimensions: 25.05 (driving cars) or 23.9 (non-driving cars) x 2.73 x 3.56 m.
Maximum Speed: 140 mph.   **Doors:** Power operated sliding plug.
Couplers: **Multiple Working:**
Bogies: Fiat-SIG

DMFRK. Dia. EA1 . Alstom Birmingham 2000–2002.
MFD. Dia. EC1 . Alstom Birmingham 2000–2002. 1TD 1W.
PTF. Dia. EH1 . Alstom Birmingham 2000–2002.
MF. Dia. EC1 . Alstom Birmingham 2000–2002.
MSD. Dia. EC2 . Alstom Birmingham 2000–2002. 1TD 1W.
PTSRMB. Dia. EN2 . Alstom Birmingham 2000–2002.
DMS. Dia. EA2 . Alstom Birmingham 2000–2002.
TS. Dia. EH2 . Alstom Birmingham 2000–2002. –/76.

390 001	GR	*VW*
390 002	GR	*VW*

4.2. 750 V d.c. THIRD RAIL EMUS

Supply System: 660–850 V d.c. third rail unless otherwise stated.

CLASS 483   METRO-CAMMELL

DMS(A)–DMS(B). Non gangwayed. End doors. Converted from vehicles purchased from London Transport in 1988.
Construction: Steel.
Traction Motors: Two Crompton Parkinson/GEC/BTH LT100 of 125 kW each per motor car.

Dimensions: 15.94 x 2.65 x 2.88 m.	**Doors**: Power operated sliding.
Maximum Speed: 45 mph.	**Bogies**: LT design.
Couplings: Wedgelock.	**Multiple Working**: Within class.

121–129. DMS(A). Dia. EA265. Metropolitan Cammell 1938. Rebuilt to Lot No. 31071 BRML Eastleigh 1989–92. –/42. 27.5 t.
221–229. DMS(B). Dia. EA266. Metropolitan Cammell 1938. Rebuilt to Lot No. 31072 BRML Eastleigh 1989–92. –/42. 27.5 t.

002	N	H	IL	RY	122	225
003	N	H		RY(S)	123	221
004	N	H	IL	RY	124	224
006	N	H	IL	RY	126	226
007	N	H	IL	RY	127	227
008	N	H	IL	RY	128	228
009	N	H	IL	RY	129	229

CLASS 438 (3-TC)   BR EXPRESS

DTS–TBS–DTS. Gangwayed throughout.
Construction: Steel.

Dimensions: 20.18 x 2.82 x 3.81 m.	**Doors**: Manually operated slam.
Maximum Speed: 90 mph.	**Bogies**: B5 (SR).
Couplings: Buckeye.	**Multiple Working**: SR type.

70812/826. TBS. Dia. EJ260. Lot No. 30765 York 1966–67. Rebuilt from loco-hauled BSK to Lot No. 30229 Metro Cammell 1955–57. –/32. 1T. 33.5 t.
76301–76302. DTS. Dia. EE266. Lot No. 30764 York 1966–67. Rebuilt from loco-hauled TSO to Lot No. 30219 Swindon 1955–57. –/64. 32.0 t.

417	B	CM	ON	TM	76301	70826	76302
Spare	B	CM	ON	TM		70812	

CLASSES 411 & 412 (3-or4-Cep/Bep)   **BR EXPRESS**

Various formations, see below. Gangwayed throughout.
Construction: Steel.
Traction Motors: Two English Electric 507 of 185 kW each per motor car.
Dimensions: 20.34 x 2.82 x 3.83 m.
Maximum Speed: 90 mph.   **Doors:** Manually operated slam.
Couplings: Buckeye.   **Multiple Working:** SR type.
Bogies: Mk. 4 (* Mk. 3B; † Mk. 6)/Commonwealth († B5 (SR)).

61229–61239 (Odd numbers). DMS(A). Dia. EA264. Lot No. 30449 Eastleigh
1958. –/64. 44.2 t.
61230–61240 (Even numbers). DMS(B). Dia. EA264. Lot No. 30449 Eastleigh
1958. –/64. 43.5 t.
61305–61409 (Odd numbers). DMS(A). Dia. EA264. Lot No. 30454 Eastleigh
1958–59. –/64. 44.2 t.
61304–61408 (Even numbers). DMS(B). Dia. EA264. Lot No. 30454 Eastleigh
1958–59. –/64. 43.5 t.
61694–61810 (Even numbers). DMS(A). Dia. EA264. Lot No. 30619 Eastleigh
1960–61. –/64. 44.2 t.
61695–61811 (Odd numbers). DMS(B). Dia. EA264. Lot No. 30619 Eastleigh
1960–61. –/64. 43.5 t.
61868–61870 (Even numbers). DMS(A). Dia. EA264. Lot No. 30638 Eastleigh
1961. –/64. 44.2 t.
61869–61871 (Odd numbers). DMS(B). Dia. EA264. Lot No. 30638 Eastleigh
1961. –/64. 43.5 t.
61948–61960 (Even numbers). DMS(A). Dia. EA264. Lot No. 30708 Eastleigh
1963. –/64. 44.2 t.
61949–61961 (Odd numbers). DMS(B). Dia. EA264. Lot No. 30708 Eastleigh
1963. –/64. 43.5 t.
69341–69347. TRBS. Dia. EN261. Built as TRB to Lot No. 30622 Eastleigh 1961.
Converted BREL Swindon 1982–84. –/24 plus 9 chairs 1T. 35.5 t.
70033–70036. TBC. Dia. EJ361. Lot No. 30109 Eastleigh 1956. 24/6 2T. 36.2 t.
70043–70044. TBC. Dia. EJ361. Lot No. 30639 Eastleigh 1961. 24/6 2T. 36.2 t.
70229–70234. TBC. Dia. EJ361. Lot No. 30450 Eastleigh 1958. 24/6 2T. 36.2 t.
70235–70240. TBC. Dia. EJ361. Lot No. 30451 Eastleigh 1958. 24/6 2T. 36.2 t.
70241–70242. TBC. Dia. EJ361. Lot No. 30640 Eastleigh 1961. 24/6 2T. 36.2 t.
70260–70302. TS. Dia. EH282. Lot No. 30455 Eastleigh 1958–59. –/64 2T. 31.5 t.
70303–70355. TS. Dia. EH282. Lot No. 30456 Eastleigh 1958–59. –/64 2T. 31.5 t.
70503–70551. TS. Dia. EH282. Lot No. 30620 Eastleigh 1960–61. –/64 2T. 31.5 t.
70552–70610. TS. Dia. EH282. Lot No. 30621 Eastleigh 1960–61. –/64 2T. 31.5 t.
70653–70659. TS. Dia. EH282. Lot No. 30709 Eastleigh 1963. –/64 2T. 31.5 t.
70660–70666. TS. Dia. EH282. Lot No. 30710 Eastleigh 1963. –/64 2T. 31.5 t.
71625–71636. TS. Dia. EH284. Converted BREL Swindon 1981–82 from
loco-hauled TSO of various lots. –/64 2T. 33.6 t.
71711–71712. TS. Dia. EH284. Converted BREL Swindon 1983–84 from
loco-hauled TSO of various lots. –/64 2T. 33.6 t.

Class 411/9 (3-Cep). DMS(A)–TBC–DMS(B).

No.	Former No.							
1101	(1530)	**N**	P	*SE*	RM	61331	70316	61330
1102	(1561)	**N**	P	*SE*	RM	61231	70604	61232
1103	(1610)	* **N**	P	*SE*	RM	61750	70580	61751
1104	(1613)	* **N**	P	*SE*	RM	61760	70585	61761
1105	(1619)	* **N**	P	*SE*	RM	61952	70655	61953
1106	(1510)	**N**	P	*SE*	RM	61365	70333	61364
1107	(1520)	**N**	P	*SE*	RM	61343	70327	61380
1108	(1536)	**N**	P	*SE*	RM	61399	70350	61398
1109	(1541)	**N**	P	*SE*	RM	61409	70355	61408
1110	(1543)	**N**	P	*SE*	RM	61323	70312	61322
1111	(1549)	**N**	P	*SE*	RM	61339	70320	61338
1112	(1554)	**N**	P	*SE*	RM	61369	70335	61368
1113	(1556)	**N**	P	*SE*	RM	61371	70336	61370
1114	(1559)	**N**	P	*SE*	RM	61377	70339	61376
1115	(1577)	* **N**	P	*SE*	RM	61718	70564	61719
1116	(1580)	* **N**	P	*SE*	RM	61756	70589	61757
1117	(1595)	* **N**	P	*SE*	RM	61704	70557	61705
1118	(1597)	* **N**	P	*SE*	RM	61708	70559	61709

(Class continued with 1507)

CLASSES 421 (4-Cig/3-Cop)   BR EXPRESS

Various formations, see below. Gangwayed throughout.
Construction: Steel.
Traction Motors: Four English Electric 507 of 185 kW each.
Dimensions: 20.19 x 2.82 x 3.86 m.
Maximum Speed: 90 mph.
Doors: Manually operated slam (d – central door locking).
Couplings: Buckeye.   **Multiple Working:** SR type.
Bogies: Mk. 4 or Mk. 6/B5 (SR).

62017–62070. MBS. Dia. ED264. Lot No. 30742 York 1964–65. –/56. 49.0 t.
62277–62286. MBS. Dia. ED264. Lot No. 30804 York 1970. –/56. (§ 1W) 49.0 t.
62287–62316. MBS. Dia. ED 264. Lot No. 30808 York 1970. –/56. (§ 1W) 49.0 t.
62355–62425. MBS. Dia. ED264. Lot No. 30816 York 1970. –/56. (§ 1W) 49.0 t.
62430. MBS. Dia. ED264. Lot No. 30829 York 1972. –/56. 49.0 t.
70260–70302. TS. Dia. EH282. Lot No. 30455 Eastleigh 1958–59. –/64 2T. 31.5 t. Class 411/5 cars.
70503–70551. TS. Dia. EH282. Lot No. 30620 Eastleigh 1960–61. –/64 2T. 31.5 t. Class 411/5 cars.
70695–70730. TS. Dia. EH287. Lot No. 30730 York 1964–65. –/72. 31.5 t.
70967–70996 TS. Dia. EH287. (• EH275). Lot No. 30809 York 1970–71. –/72. 31.5t.
71035–71105. TS. Dia. EH287. Lot No. 30817 York 1970. –/72. 31.5t.
71106. TS. Dia. EH287. Lot No. 30830 York 1972. –/72. 31.5t.
71766–71770. TS. Dia. EH287. Built as EMU TSRB to Lot No. 30744 York 1963–66. Converted BRML Eastleigh 1985–87. –/72. 31.5 t.

71926. TS. Dia. EH287. Built as EMU TSRB to Lot No. 30744 York 1963–66. Converted BRML Eastleigh 1988. –/72. 31.5t.

71927–71928. TS. Dia. EH287. Built as EMU TSRB to Lot No. 30805 York 1970. Converted BRML Eastleigh 1988. –/72. 31.5t.

76022–76075. DTC(B). Dia. EE369. Lot No. 30740 York 1964–65. 18/36 2T.

76076–76129. DTC(A) (†‡ DTS). Dia. EE369 (†‡ EE282). Lot No. 30741 York 1964–65. 18/36 († –/54; ‡ –/60) 2T. 35.5 t.

76561–76570. DTC(A) (†‡ DTS; § DTS(A)). Dia. EE369 (†‡ EE283; § EE245). Lot No. 30802 York 1970 (§ Rebuilt Wessex Traincare/Alstom Eastleigh 1997–98). 18/36 (*12/42; †–/54; ‡§ –/60) 2(§ 1)T. 35.5 t.

76571–76580. DTC(B) (§ DTS(B)). Dia. EE369 (§ EE246). Lot No. 30802 York 1970 (§ Rebuilt Wessex Traincare/Alstom Eastleigh 1997–98). 18/36 2(§1)T. 35.5 t.

76581–76610. DTC(A) (†‡ DTS; § DTS(A)). Dia. EE369 (§ EE245). Lot No. 30806 York 1970 (§ Rebuilt Wessex Traincare/Alstom Eastleigh 1997–98). 18/36 (*12/42; † –/54; ‡§ –/60) 2(§ 1)T. 35.5 t.

76611–76640. DTC(B) (§ DTS(B)). Dia. EE369 (§ EE246). Lot No. 30807 York 1970 (§ Rebuilt Wessex Traincare/Alstom Eastleigh 1997–98). 18/36 2(§1)T. 35.5 t.

76717–76787. DTC(A) (†‡ DTS; § DTS(A)). Dia. EE369 (†‡ EE282; § EE245). Lot No. 30814 York 1970–72 (§ Rebuilt Wessex Traincare/Alstom Eastleigh 1997–98). 18/36 (* 12/42; † –/54; ‡§ –/60) 2(§ 1)T. 35.5 t.

76788–76858. DTC(B) (§ DTS(B)). Dia. EE369 (§ EE246). Lot No. 30815 York 1970–72. (§ Rebuilt Wessex Traincare/Alstom Eastleigh 1997–98). 18/36 2T. 35.5 t.

76859. DTC(A). Dia. EE369. Lot No. 30827 York 1972. 12/42 2T. 35.5 t.

76860. DTC(B). Dia. EE369. Lot No. 30828 York 1972. 12/42 2T. 35.5 t.

Class 421/5 (4-Cig). DTC(A)–MBS-TS–DTC(B). 'Greyhound' units with additional stage of field weakening to improve the maximum attainable speed. Mk. 6 motor bogies.

1301	**ST**	H	*SW*	FR	76595	62301	70981	76625
1302	**ST**	H	*SW*	FR	76584	62290	70970	76614
1303	**ST**	H	*SW*	FR	76581	62287	70967	76611
1304	**ST**	H	*SW*	FR	76583	62289	70969	76613
1305	**ST**	H	*SW*	FR	76717	62355	71035	76788
1306	**ST**	H	*SW*	FR	76723	62361	71041	76794
1307	**ST**	H	*SW*	FR	76586	62292	70972	76616
1308	**ST**	H	*SW*	FR	76627	62298	70978	76622
1309	**ST**	H	*SW*	FR	76594	62300	70980	76624
1310	**ST**	H	*SW*	FR	76567	62283	71926	76577
1311	**ST**	H	*SW*	FR	76561	62277	71927	76571
1312	**ST**	H	*SW*	FR	76562	62278	71928	76572
1313	**ST**	H	*SW*	FR	76596	62302	70982	76626
1314	**ST**	H	*SW*	FR	76588	62294	70974	76618
1315	**ST**	H	*SW*	FR	76608	62314	70994	76638
1316	**ST**	H	*SW*	FR	76585	62291	70971	76615
1317	**ST**	H	*SW*	FR	76597	62303	70983	76592
1318	**ST**	H	*SW*	FR	76590	62296	70976	76620
1319	**ST**	H	*SW*	FR	76591	62297	70977	76621
1320	**ST**	H	*SW*	FR	76593	62299	70979	76623
1321	**ST**	H	*SW*	FR	76589	62295	70975	76619
1322	**ST**	H	*SW*	FR	76587	62293	70973	76617

Class 421/8 (4-Cig). DTC(A)–MBS–TS–DTC(B) 'Greyhound' units with additional stage of field weakening to improve the maximum attainable speed. Mk. 6 motor bogies. Former Class 422 units with TRBS replaced by Class 411/5 TS.

No.	Former No.								
1392	(2255)	**ST**	P	*SW*	FR	76811	62378	70273	76740
1393	(2258)	**ST**	P	*SW*	FR	76746	62384	70527	76817
1394	)2251)	**ST**	P	*SW*	FR	76726	62364	70663	76797
1395	(2262)	**ST**	P	*SW*	FR	76850	62417	70662	76779
1396	(2254)	**ST**	P	*SW*	FR	76803	62370	70531	76732
1397	(2260)	**ST**	P	*SW*	FR	76749	62387	70515	76820
1398	(2259)	**ST**	P	*SW*	FR	76819	62386	70292	76748
1399	(2256)	**ST**	P	*SW*	FR	76747	62385	70508	76818

Class 421/7 (3-Cop). DTS(A)–MBS–DTS(B). 3-car units for Connex South Central Brighton–Portsmouth 'Coastway' route. Mk. 6 motor bogies.

No.								
1401	§	**CX**	P	*SC*	BI	76568	62284	76578
1402	§	**CX**	P	*SC*	BI	76564	62280	76574
1403	§	**CX**	P	*SC*	BI	76563	62279	76573
1404	§	**CX**	P	*SC*	BI	76602	62308	76632
1405	§	**CX**	P	*SC*	BI	76565	62281	76575
1406	§	**CX**	P	*SC*	BI	76728	62366	76799
1407	§	**CX**	P	*SC*	BI	76729	62367	76800
1408	§	**CX**	P	*SC*	BI	76750	62388	76821
1409	§	**CX**	P	*SC*	BI	76569	62285	76579
1410	§	**CX**	P	*SC*	BI	76734	62372	76805
1411	§	**CX**	P	*SC*	BI	76570	62286	76580

Name (Carried on MBS):

1409   Operation Perseus

(Class continued with 1701)

CLASS 411 (4-Cep)   BR EXPRESS

For details see page 299.

Class 411/5 (4-Cep). 4-car units. DMS(A)–TBC–TS–DMS(B).

No.								
1507	**ST**	P	*SW*	FR	61363	70332	70289	61362
1509	**N**	P	*SE*	RM	61335	70318	70275	61334
1511	**N**	P	*SE*	RM	61367	70334	70291	61366
1512	**ST**	P	*SW*	FR	61321	70311	70268	61320
1517	**N**	P	*SW*	FR	61317	70309	70266	61316
1518	**N**	P		ZG(S)	61333	70317	70274	61332
1519	**ST**	P	*SW*	FR	61403	70352	70516	61402
1527	**N**	P	*SW*	FR	61237	70239	70233	61238
1531	**ST**	P	*SW*	FR	61233	70237	70231	61234
1532	**N**	P		FR(S)	61391	70346	71628	61390
1533	**ST**	P	*SW*	FR	61393	70347	71627	61385
1534	**ST**	P	*SW*	FR	61405	70353	71626	61404
1535	**ST**	P	*SW*	FR	61397	70349	71629	61396

1537		**ST**	P	*SW*	FR	61229	70235	70229	61230
1538		**ST**	P	*SW*	FR	61307	70304	70261	61306
1539		**ST**	P	*SW*	FR	61401	70351	71632	61400
1544		**ST**	P	*SW*	FR	61315	70308	70265	61349
1547		**ST**	P	*SW*	FR	61329	70578	70272	61328
1548		**ST**	P	*SW*	FR	61375	70338	70295	61374
1550		**N**	P	*SW*	FR	61313	70307	70264	61312
1551		**N**	P	*SE*	RM	61325	70313	70270	61324
1553		**N**	P	*SW*	FR	61728	70306	70263	61350
1555		**N**	P	*SW*	FR	61311	70326	70283	61310
1557		**N**	P		CJ(S)	61337	70331	70288	61360
1560		**N**	P	*SE*	RM	61387	70344	70301	61386
1562		**N**	P	*SE*	RM	61407	70236	70241	61406
1563	*	**ST**	P	*SW*	FR	61740	70575	70526	61741
1564	*	**N**	P	*SE*	RM	61788	70599	70550	61789
1565	*	**ST**	P	*SW*	FR	61762	70586	71711	61763
1566	*	**ST**	P	*SW*	FR	61722	70566	70517	61723
1568	*	**ST**	P	*SW*	FR	61766	70588	70539	61767
1570	*	**N**	P	*SE*	RM	61738	70574	70525	61739
1571	*	**N**	P	*SW*	FR	61806	70608	71636	61807
1572	*	**N**	P	*SW*	FR	61734	70572	70523	61735
1573	*	**ST**	P	*SW*	FR	61726	70568	70519	61727
1574	*	**N**	P	*SE*	RM	61792	70601	71635	61793
1575	*	**N**	P	*SE*	RM	61768	70583	70540	61769
1576	*	**N**	P	*SE*	RM	61770	70590	70541	61771
1578	*	**ST**	P	*SW*	FR	61700	70555	70506	61701
1581	*	**ST**	P	*SW*	FR	61784	70597	70548	61785
1582	*	**N**	P	*SE*	RM	61748	70603	71630	61797
1584	*	**N**	P	*SE*	RM	61752	70581	70532	61753
1585	*	**N**	P	*SE*	RM	61710	70560	70511	61711
1586	*	**N**	P	*SE*	RM	61714	70562	70513	61715
1587	*	**N**	P	*SE*	RM	61764	70587	71625	61765
1588	*	**N**	P	*SE*	RM	61720	70044	70520	61721
1589	*	**N**	P		ZG(S)	61742	70576		
1590	*	**N**	P	*SE*	RM	61696	70553	70504	61697
1591	*	**N**	P	*SE*	RM	61790	70600	70551	61791
1592	*	**N**	P	*SE*	RM	61778	70594	70545	61779
1593	*	**N**	P	*SE*	RM	61730	70570	70521	61731
1594	*	**N**	P	*SE*	RM	61754	70582	70533	61755
1599	*	**N**	P	*SE*	RM	61706	70558	70509	61707
1602	*	**CX**	P	*SE*	RM	61958	70565	70279	61959
1606	*	**N**	P		AF(S)	61694	70552		61695
1607	*	**N**	P	*SE*	RM	61698	70554	70505	61699
1609	*	**N**	P	*SE*	RM	61744	70577	70528	61745
1611	*	**N**	P	*SE*	RM	61758	70584	70537	61759
1612	*	**ST**	P	*SW*	FR	61794	70602	70535	61795
1614	*	**N**	P	*SE*	RM	61702	70556	70507	61703
1615	*	**N**	P	*SE*	RM	61956	70657	70664	61957
1616	*	**N**	P	*SE*	RM	61950	70654	70543	61951
1617	*	**N**	P		CJ(S)	61800	70605	70661	61801
1618	*	**N**	P		RM(S)	61868	70043	70230	61869

1697	†	**N**	P	*SW*	FR	61373	70337	70294	61372
1698	†	**N**	P	*SW*	FR	61355	70343	70300	61384
1699	†	**N**	P	*SW*	FR	61712	70561	70512	61713
Spare		**N**	P		ZD(S)	61383			

Spare TS.

Spare		**N**	P		SU(S)	70035			
Spare		**N**	P		ZG(S)	70503	70536		
Spare		**N**	P		CJ(S)	70277	70284	70290	70293
Spare		**N**	P		CJ(S)	70296	70297	70510	70534
Spare		**N**	P		CJ(S)	71631	71633		

CLASS 421 (4-Cig)   BR EXPRESS

For details see pages 300–301.

Class 421/3 (4-Cig). DTC(A)/(†‡DTS)–MBS–TS–DTC(B). Mk. 4 motor bogies.

1701		**U**	A	*SE*	RM	76087	62028	70706	76033
1702	†	**CX**	A	*SC*	BI	76101	62042	70720	76047
1703	†	**CX**	A	*SC*	BI	76097	62038	70716	76043
1704	†	**CX**	A	*SC*	BI	76092	62033	70711	76038
1705	†	**CX**	A	*SC*	BI	76076	62017	70695	76022
1706	†	**CX**	A	*SC*	BI	76094	62035	70713	76040
1707	†	**CX**	A	*SC*	BI	76084	62025	70703	76030
1708	†	**N**	A	*SC*	BI	76110	62051	70729	76056
1709	†	**N**	A	*SC*	BI	76103	62044	70722	76049
1710	†	**CX**	A	*SC*	BI	76078	62019	70697	76024
1711	‡	**N**	A	*SC*	BI	76114	62055	71766	76060
1712	†	**N**	A	*SC*	BI	76079	62020	70698	76025
1713	†	**N**	A	*SC*	BI	76128	62069	71767	76074
1714	†	**N**	A	*SC*	BI	76077	62018	70696	76023
1717	†	**N**	A	*SC*	BI	76083	62024	70702	76029
1719	†	**CX**	A	*SC*	BI	76116	62057	70719	76062
1720	†	**N**	A	*SC*	BI	76098	62039	71769	76044
1721	†	**CX**	A	*SC*	BI	76090	62031	70709	76036
1722	‡	**CX**	A	*SC*	BI	76106	62047	70725	76052
1724	†	**CX**	A	*SC*	BI	76120	62061	71770	76066
1725	†	**CX**	A	*SC*	BI	76088	62029	70707	76034
1726	†	**CX**	A	*SC*	BI	76109	62050	70728	76055
1727	†	**CX**	A	*SC*	BI	76111	62052	70730	76057
1731	†	**CX**	A	*SC*	BI	76095	62036	70714	76041
1733	†	**CX**	A	*SC*	BI	76112	62063	71047	76068
1734	†	**CX**	A	*SC*	BI	76063	62054	71044	76059
1735	†	**CX**	A	*SC*	BI	76117	62058	71050	76051
1736	†	**U**	A	*SC*	BI	76124	62065	71052	76070
1737	†	**U**	A	*SC*	BI	76121	62062	71058	76067
1738	†	**CX**	A	*SC*	BI	76129	62064	71046	76069
1739	†	**CX**	A	*SC*	BI	76123	62070	71066	76075
1740	†	**CX**	A	*SC*	BI	76126	62067	71097	76072
1741	†	**CX**	A	*SC*	BI	76089	62030	70708	76035

1742		**U**	A	*SE*	RM	76086	62027	70705	76032
1743	†	**CX**	A	*SC*	BI	76118	62059	71065	76064
1744	†	**CX**	A	*SC*	BI	76127	62068	71064	76073
1745	†	**CX**	A	*SC*	BI	76085	62026	70704	76031
1746	‡	**CX**	A	*SC*	BI	76091	62032	70710	76037
1747	†	**CX**	A	*SC*	BI	76093	62034	70712	76026
1748		**U**	A	*SE*	RM	76115	62056	71067	76061
1750	†	**CX**	A	*SC*	BI	76080	62021	70699	76039
1751	†	**CX**	A	*SC*	BI	76125	62066	71051	76071
1752	†	**CX**	A	*SC*	BI	76119	62060	70717	76065
1753	†	**CX**	A	*SC*	BI	76102	62043	70721	76048
Spare		**N**		AF(S)			62053	71068	76058

Class 421/4 (4-Cig). DTC(A)/(†‡DTS)–MBS–TS–DTC(B). Mk. 6 motor bogies.

1801	†	**N**	P	*SC*	BI	76848	71095	62415	76777
1802	†	**N**	P	*SC*	BI	76754	62392	71072	76825
1803	†	**N**	A	*SC*	BI	76780	62418	71098	76851
1804	†	**N**	A	*SC*	BI	76778	62416	71096	76849
1805	†	**N**	A	*SC*	BI	76782	62420	71100	76853
1806	*	**N**	H	*SE*	RM	76783	62421	71101	76854
1807	*	**N**	H	*SE*	RM	76784	62422	71102	76855
1808	*	**N**	H	*SE*	RM	76785	62423	71103	76856
1809	*	**N**	H	*SE*	RM	76786	62424	71104	76857
1810	*	**N**	H	*SE*	RM	76787	62425	71105	76858
1811	*	**N**	H	*SE*	RM	76781	62419	71099	76852
1812	*d	**N**	H	*SE*	RM	76757	62395	71075	76828
1813	*	**N**	H	*SE*	RM	76859	62430	71106	76860
1831	†	**CX**	A	*SC*	BI	76598	62304	70984	76628
1832	†	**CX**	A	*SC*	BI	76719	62357	71037	76790
1833	†	**CX**	A	*SC*	BI	76582	62288	70968	76612
1834	†	**CX**	A	*SC*	BI	76566	62282	70988	76576
1835	†	**CX**	A	*SC*	BI	76601	62307	70987	76631
1837	†	**CX**	A	*SC*	BI	76722	62360	71040	76793
1839	*	**N**	H	*SE*	RM	76607	62313	70993	76637
1840	*	**N**	H	*SE*	RM	76724	62362	71042	76795
1841	*	**N**	H	*SE*	RM	76603	62309	70989	76633
1842	*	**N**	H	*SE*	RM	76725	62363	71043	76796
1843	*	**N**	H	*SE*	RM	76731	62369	71049	76802
1845	†	**CX**	A	*SC*	BI	76599	62305	70985	76718
1846	†	**CX**	A	*SC*	BI	76737	62375	71055	76808
1847	†	**CX**	A	*SC*	BI	76600	62306	70986	76630
1848	†	**CX**	A	*SC*	BI	76605	62311	70991	76635
1850	†	**CX**	A	*SC*	BI	76629	62356	71036	76789
1851	†	**CX**	A	*SC*	BI	76721	62359	71039	76792
1853	†	**CX**	A	*SC*	BI	76606	62312	70992	76636
1854	†	**CX**	A	*SC*	BI	76738	62376	71056	76809
1855	†	**CX**	A	*SC*	BI	76720	62358	71038	76791
1856	†	**CX**	A	*SC*	BI	76739	62377	71057	76810
1857	†	**CX**	A	*SC*	BI	76610	62316	70996	76640
1858	‡	**CX**	A	*SC*	BI	76604	62310	70990	76634
1859	‡	**CX**	A	*SC*	BI	76727	62365	71045	76798

1860	‡	**CX**	A	*SC*	BI	76752	62390	71070	76823
1861	‡	**CX**	A	*SC*	BI	76735	62373	71053	76806
1862	†	**CX**	A	*SC*	BI	76736	62374	71054	76807
1863	†	**CX**	A	*SC*	BI	76742	62380	71060	76813
1864	†	**CX**	A	*SC*	BI	76741	62379	71059	76812
1865	†	**CX**	A	*SC*	BI	76745	62383	71063	76639
1866	†	**CX**	A	*SC*	BI	76743	62381	71061	76814
1867	†	**CX**	A	*SC*	BI	76744	62382	71062	76815
1868	†	**CX**	A	*SC*	BI	76751	62389	71069	76822
1869	†	**CX**	A	*SC*	BI	76753	62391	71071	76804
1870	*	**CX**	H	*SE*	RM	76108	62409	71089	76842
1871	*	**N**	H	*SE*	RM	76756	62394	71074	76827
1872	*	**N**	H	*SE*	RM	76771	62396	71076	76829
1873	*	**N**	H	*SE*	RM	76759	62397	71077	76830
1874	†	**CX**	A	*SC*	BI	76755	62393	71073	76826
1876	*	**N**	H	*SE*	RM	76761	62399	71079	76832
1877	*	**N**	H	*SE*	RM	76763	62401	71081	76834
1878	*	**N**	H	*SE*	RM	76768	62406	71086	76839
1879	*	**N**	H	*SE*	RM	76760	62398	71078	76831
1880		**ST**	H	*SW*	FR	76770	62408	71088	76841
1881		**ST**	H	*SW*	FR	76762	62400	71080	76833
1882		**ST**	H	*SW*	FR	76765	62403	71083	76836
1883		**ST**	H	*SW*	FR	76764	62402	71082	76835
1884		**N**	H	*SW*	FR	76767	62405	71085	76838
1885		**N**	H	*SW*	FR	76769	62407	71087	76840
1886		**N**	H	*SW*	FR	76772	62410	71090	76843
1887		**N**	H	*SW*	FR	76766	62404	71084	76837
1888		**N**	H	*SW*	FR	76773	62411	71091	76844
1889		**N**	H	*SW*	FR	76774	62412	71092	76845
1890		**N**	H	*SW*	FR	76775	62413	71093	76846
1891		**N**	H	*SW*	FR	76776	62414	71094	76847
Spare	•	**BG**	A		ZG(S)			70995	

Class 421/6 (4-Cig). DTS–MBS–TS–DTC(B). Mk. 6 motor bogies.

1901	†	**CX**	P	*SC*	BI	76082	62023	70701	76028
1902	†	**CX**	P	*SC*	BI	76100	62041	71768	76046
1903	†	**CX**	A	*SC*	BI	76081	62022	70700	76027
1904	†	**CX**	A	*SC*	BI	76107	62048	70726	76053
1905	‡	**CX**	A	*SC*	BI	76099	62040	70718	76045
1906	†	**CX**	A	*SC*	BI	76105	62046	70724	76113
1907	†	**CX**	A	*SC*	BI	76104	62045	70723	76050
1908	†	**CX**	A	*SC*	BI	76096	62037	70715	76042

CLASS 412 (4-Bep)   BR EXPRESS

For details see page 299.

Class 412 (4-Bep). DMS(A)–TBC–TRBS–DMS(B).

| 2301 | † | **ST** | P | *SW* | FR | 61804 | 70607 | 69341 | 61805 |
| 2302 | † | **ST** | P | *SW* | FR | 61774 | 70592 | 69342 | 61809 |

2303	†	**ST**	P	*SW*	FR	61954	70656	69343	61955
2304	†	**ST**	P	*SW*	FR	61736	70573	69344	61737
2305	†	**ST**	P	*SW*	FR	61798	70354	69345	61799
2306	†	**ST**	P	*SW*	FR	61808	70609	69346	61775
2307	†	**ST**	P	*SW*	FR	61802	70606	69347	61803

CLASS 442 (5-Wes)   BREL EXPRESS

DTF–TS–MBLS–TSW–DTS. Gangwayed throughout. Air conditioned.
Construction: Steel.
Traction Motors: Four English Electric 546 of 300 kW each.
Dimensions: 23.15 (DTF & DTS) or 23.00 (MBLS, TS & TSW) x 2.74 x 3.81m.
Doors: Power operated sliding plug.
Maximum Speed: 100 mph.   **Bogies:** BR Mk. 6/BREL T4.
Couplings: Buckeye.   **Multiple Working:** SR type.

62937–62960. MBLS. Dia. ED268. Lot No. 31034 BREL Derby 1988–89. Modified
  Adtranz Crewe 1998. –/30 1W. 55.2 t.
71818–71841. TS. Dia. EH288. Lot No. 31032 BREL Derby 1988–89. –/80 2T.
  35.3 t.
71842–71865. TSW. Dia. EH289. Lot No. 31033 BREL Derby 1988–89. –/76 1W
  2T. 35.4 t.
77382–77405. DTF. Dia. EE160. Lot No. 31030 BREL Derby 1988–89. 50/– 1T.
  39.1 t.
77406–77429. DTS. Dia. EE273. Lot No. 31031 BREL Derby 1988–89. –/78 1T.
  39.1 t.

2401	**SW**	A	*SW*	BM	77382	71818	62937	71842	77406
2402	**SW**	A	*SW*	BM	77383	71819	62938	71843	77407
2403	**SW**	A	*SW*	BM	77384	71820	62941	71844	77408
2404	**SW**	A	*SW*	BM	77385	71821	62939	71845	77409
2405	**SW**	A	*SW*	BM	77386	71822	62944	71846	77410
2406	**SW**	A	*SW*	BM	77389	71823	62942	71847	77411
2407	**SW**	A	*SW*	BM	77388	71824	62943	71848	77412
2408	**SW**	A	*SW*	BM	77387	71825	62945	71849	77413
2409	**SW**	A	*SW*	BM	77390	71826	62946	71850	77414
2410	**SW**	A	*SW*	BM	77391	71827	62948	71851	77415
2411	**SW**	A	*SW*	BM	77392	71828	62940	71858	77422
2412	**SW**	A	*SW*	BM	77393	71829	62947	71853	77417
2413	**SW**	A	*SW*	BM	77394	71830	62949	71854	77418
2414	**SW**	A	*SW*	BM	77395	71831	62950	71855	77419
2415	**SW**	A	*SW*	BM	77396	71832	62951	71856	77420
2416	**SW**	A	*SW*	BM	77397	71833	62952	71857	77421
2417	**SW**	A	*SW*	BM	77398	71834	62953	71852	77416
2418	**SW**	A	*SW*	BM	77399	71835	62954	71859	77423
2419	**SW**	A	*SW*	BM	77400	71836	62955	71860	77424
2420	**SW**	A	*SW* ·	BM	77401	71837	62956	71861	77425
2421	**SW**	A	*SW*	BM	77402	71838	62957	71862	77426
2422	**SW**	A	*SW*	BM	77403	71839	62958	71863	77427
2423	**SW**	A	*SW*	BM	77404	71840	62959	71864	77428
2424	**SW**	A	*SW*	BM	77405	71841	62960	71865	77429

Names (carried on MBLS):

2401	BEAULIEU	2412	SPECIAL OLYMPICS
2402	COUNTY OF HAMPSHIRE	2415	MARY ROSE
2403	THE NEW FOREST	2416	MUM IN A MILLION 1997 –
2404	BOROUGH OF WOKING		DOREEN SCANLON
2405	CITY OF PORTSMOUTH	2418	WESSEX CANCER TRUST
2406	VICTORY	2419	BBC SOUTH TODAY
2407	THOMAS HARDY	2420	CITY SOUTHAMPTON
2408	COUNTY OF DORSET	2423	COUNTY OF SURREY
2409	BOURNEMOUTH ORCHESTRAS	2422	OPERATION OVERLORD
2410	MERIDIAN TONIGHT		

CLASS 423 (4-Vep/4-Vop)   BR OUTER SUBURBAN

Various formations, see below. Gangwayed throughout.
Construction: Steel.
Traction Motors: Four English Electric 507 of 185 kW each.
Dimensions: 20.18 x 2.82 x 3.84 m.   **Doors:** Manually operated slam.
Maximum Speed: 90 mph.   **Multiple Working:** SR type.
Couplings: Buckeye.   **Bogies:** Mk. 4/B5 (SR).
Note: 70904" is actually 70954.

62121–62140. MBS. Dia. ED266. Lot No. 30760 Derby 1967. –/76. 49.0 t.
62182–62216. MBS. Dia. ED266. Lot No. 30773 York 1967–68. –/76. 49.0 t.
62217–62266. MBS. Dia. ED266. Lot No. 30794 York 1968–69. –/76. 49.0 t.
62267–62276. MBS. Dia. ED266. Lot No. 30800 York 1970. –/76. 49.0 t.
62317–62354. MBS. Dia. ED266. Lot No. 30813 York 1970–73. –/76. 49.0 t.
62435–62475. MBS. Dia. ED266. Lot No. 30853 York 1973–74. –/76. 49.0 t.
70781–70800. TS. Dia. EH291. Lot No. 30759 Derby 1967. –/98. 31.5 t.
70872–70906. TS. Dia. EH291. Lot No. 30772 York 1967–68. –/98. 31.5 t.
70907–70956. TS. Dia. EH291. Lot No. 30793 York 1968–69. –/98. 31.5 t.
70957–70966. TS. Dia. EH291. Lot No. 30801 York 1970. –/98. 31.5 t.
70997–71034. TS. Dia. EH291. Lot No. 30812 York 1970–73. –/98. 31.5 t.
71115–71155. TS. Dia. EH291. Lot No. 30852 York 1973–74. –/98. 31.5 t.
76230–76269. DTC. Dia. EE373. Lot No. 30758 York 1967. 18/46 (†§ 12/52)1T. 35.0 t.
76275. DTS. Dia. EE266. Built as loco-hauled vehicle to Lot No. 30086 Eastleigh 1953–55. Converted to Lot No. 30764 York 1966. –/64. 32.0 t.
76333–76402. DTC (*‡ DTS). Dia. EE373 (* EE281; ‡ EE278). Lot No. 30771 York 1967–68. (*Converted Adtranz, Chart Leacon 1999). 18/46 († 12/52)1T ; (* –/70; ‡ –/88 0T). 32.5 t.
76441–76540. DTC. Dia. EE373. Lot No. 30792 York 1968–69. 18/46 (†‡ 12/52) 1T. 32.5 t.
76541–76560. DTC. Dia. EE373. Lot No. 30799 York 1970. 18/46 († 12/52) 1T. 32.5 t.
76641–76716. DTC. Dia. EE373. Lot No. 30811 York 1970–73. 18/46 († 12/52) 1T. 32.5 t.
76861–76942. DTC. Dia. EE368. Lot No. 30853 York 1973–74. 18/46 († 12/52) 1T. 32.5 t.

Class 423/1 (4-Vep). DTC–MBS–TS–DTC.

3401	**ST**	H	*SW*	WD	76230	62276	70781	76231
3402	**ST**	H	*SW*	WD	76233	62123	70782	76232
3403	**CX**	H	*SC*	BI	76234	62254	70783	76235
3404	**ST**	H	*SW*	WD	76378	62261	70894	76236
3405	**ST**	H	*SW*	WD	76239	62271	70785	76238
3406	**ST**	H	*SW*	WD	76241	62130	70786	76240
3407	**ST**	H	*SW*	WD	76243	62348	70787	76242
3408	**ST**	H	*SW*	WD	76244	62435	70788	76245
3409	**ST**	H	*SW*	WD	76246	62239	70789	76247
3410	**ST**	H	*SW*	WD	76369	62442	70790	76249
3411	**ST**	H	*SW*	WD	76250	62342	70791	76251
3412 †	**N**	A	*SE*	RM	76252	62340	70792	76253
3413	**ST**	H	*SW*	WD	76255	62441	70793	76254
3414	**ST**	H	*SW*	WD	76257	62446	70794	76248
3415	**N**	H	*SW*	WD	76258	62462	70795	76259
3416 †	**N**	A	*SE*	RM	76261	62451	70796	76260
3417	**ST**	H	*SW*	WD	76262	62236	70797	76263
3418	**ST**	H	*SW*	WD	76265	62133	70875	76264
3419	**ST**	H	*SW*	WD	76267	62354	70799	76266
3420	**ST**	H	*SW*	WD	76269	62349	70800	76268
3421 †	**CX**	A	*SE*	RM	76889	62449	71129	76890
3422 †	**CX**	A	*SE*	RM	76372	62201	70891	76371
3423 †	**CX**	A	*SE*	RM	76452	62222	70912	76451
3424 †	**CX**	A	*SE*	RM	76354	62185	70882	76353
3425	**ST**	H	*SW*	WD	76338	62192	70874	76358
3426	**ST**	H	*SW*	WD	76386	62208	70898	76385
3427	**ST**	H	*SW*	WD	76374	62184	70892	76373
3428	**ST**	H	*SW*	WD	76454	62223	70913	76453
3429	**ST**	H	*SW*	WD	76334	62202	70872	76333
3430	**ST**	H	*SW*	WD	76348	62189	70879	76347
3431	**ST**	H	*SW*	WD	76458	62182	70915	76457
3432	**ST**	H	*SW*	WD	76400	62225	70905	76399
3433	**ST**	H	*SW*	WD	76444	62215	70908	76443
3434	**ST**	H	*SW*	WD	76462	62218	70917	76461
3435	**CX**	P	*SC*	BI	76342	62228	70876	76341
3436	**CX**	P	*SC*	BI	76350	62190	70880	76349
3437	**CX**	P	*SC*	BI	76346	62186	70878	76345
3445 †	**CX**	A	*SE*	RM	76450	62242	70911	76449
3446 †	**CX**	A	*SE*	RM	76532	62243	70952	76531
3447 †	**CX**	A	*SE*	RM	76380	62199	70895	76379
3448 †	**CX**	A	*SE*	RM	76376	62221	70886	76375
3449 †	**CX**	A	*SE*	RM	76336	62205	70873	76335
3450 †	**CX**	A	*SE*	RM	76460	62203	70916	76459
3451 †	**N**	A	*SE*	RM	76488	62240	70930	76487
3452 †	**CX**	A	*SE*	RM	76340	62183	71021	76690
3453 †	**CX**	A	*SE*	RM	76382	62226	70896	76381
3454 †	**CX**	A	*SE*	RM	76390	62200	70798	76389
3455	**ST**	H	*SW*	WD	76388	62206	70899	76387
3456	**ST**	H	*SW*	WD	76456	62210	70914	76455

3457		ST	H	*SW*	WD	76392	62197	70901	76391
3458		ST	H	*SW*	WD	76394	62209	70902	76393
3459		ST	H	*SW*	WD	76396	62224	70903	76395
3466		ST	H	*SW*	WD	76464	62214	70918	76463
3467		ST	H	*SW*	WD	76446	62217	70909	76445
3468		ST	H	*SW*	WD	76448	62267	70910	76447
3469		N	H	*SW*	WD	76546	62219	70959	76545
3470		CX	H	*SW*	WD	76496	62220	70934	76495
3471	†	CX	A	*SE*	RM	76498	62269	70935	76497
3472	†	N	A	*SE*	RM	76500	62244	70936	76499
3473	‡	CX	A	*SE*	RM	76502	62245	70937	76339
3474	†	N	A	*SE*	RM	76504	62246	70938	76503
3475	†	N	A	*SE*	RM	76552	62270	70962	76551
3479		CX	H	*SC*	BI	76655	62272	71004	76656
3480		ST	H	*SC*	WD	76474	62323	70923	76473
3481		ST	H	*SW*	WD	76647	62324	70900	76648
3482		CX	H	*SC*	BI	76657	62320	71005	76658
3483		CX	H	*SC*	BI	76661	62233	71007	76662
3484		CX	H	*SC*	BI	76476	62325	70924	76475
3485		CX	H	*SC*	BI	76508	62327	70940	76507
3486		CX	H	*SC*	BI	76478	62234	70925	76477
3487	†	CX	A	*SE*	RM	76645	62250	70941	76509
3488		CX	H	*SC*	BI	76663	62235	71008	76664
3489		CX	H	*SC*	BI	76665	62251	71009	76666
3490		CX	H	*SC*	BI	76695	62228	71024	76696
3491	†	N	A	*SE*	RM	76337	62436	70927	76481
3492	†	N	A	*SE*	RM	76667	62344	71010	76668
3493	†	N	A	*SE*	RM	76669	62237	71011	76670
3494	†	N	A	*SE*	RM	76675	62330	71014	76676
3495	†	N	A	*SE*	RM	76699	62331	71026	76700
3496	†	N	A	*SE*	RM	76673	62334	71013	76674
3497	†	N	A	*SE*	RM	76671	62346	71012	76672
3498	†	N	A	*SE*	RM	76701	62333	71027	76702
3499	†	N	A	*SE*	RM	76901	62347	71135	76902
3500	†	N	A	*SE*	RM	76470	62455	70921	76469
3501		CX	P	*SC*	BI	76512	62332	70942	76511
3503		CX	P	*SC*	BI	76681	62231	71017	76682
3504		CX	P	*SC*	BI	76711	62351	71032	76712
3505		CX	P	*SC*	BI	76472	62352	70922	76471
3508		ST	H	*SW*	WD	76643	62273	70998	76644
3509		ST	H	*SW*	WD	76560	62275	70966	76559
3510		ST	H	*SW*	WD	76641	62318	70997	76642
3511	†	CX	A	*SE*	RM	76893	62135	70999	76648
3512		CX	P	*SC*	BI	76679	62337	71016	76680
3514		CX	P	*SC*	BI	76683	62136	71018	76684
3515		CX	P	*SC*	BI	76544	62319	70958	76543
3516		ST	H	*SW*	WD	76693	62268	71023	76694
3517		CX	P	*SC*	BI	76685	62338	71019	76686
3518		CX	P	*SC*	BI	76689	62343	70887	76363
3519		ST	H	*SW*	WD	76556	62274	70964	76555
3520		ST	H	*SW*	WD	76697	62131	71025	76698

3521	†	**N**	A	*SE*	RM	76484	62345	70928	76483
3523		**CX**	H	*SC*	BI	76651	62139	71002	76652
3524		**CX**	H	*SC*	BI	76466	62322	70919	76370
3529		**CX**	H	*SC*	BI	76659	62257	71006	76660
3530		**CX**	H	*SC*	BI	76468	62256	70920	76467
3531		**CX**	H	*SC*	BI	76649	62230	71001	76650
3535		**CX**	P	*SC*	BI	76677	62335	71015	76678
3536		**N**	H	*SW*	WD	76384	62207	70897	76383
3539		**N**	H	*SW*	WD	76861	62122	71115	76862
3540		**N**	H	*SW*	WD	76863	62128	71116	76864
3542		**ST**	H	*SW*	WD	76480	62127	70926	76479
3543	†	**N**	A	*SE*	RM	76899	62137	71134	76900
3544	†	**N**	A	*SE*	RM	76892	62454	71131	76894
3545	†	**N**	A	*SE*	RM	76875	62121	71122	76876
3546		**CX**	P	*SC*	BI	76687	62339	71020	76688
3547	†	**N**	A	*SE*	RM	76895	62126	71132	76896
3548	†	**N**	A	*SE*	RM	76903	62452	71136	76904
3549		**CX**	P	*SC*	BI	76707	62132	71030	76708
3551		**CX**	P	*SC*	BI	76465	62456	71033	76714
3552		**ST**	H	*SW*	WD	76715	62353	71034	76716
3553	†	**N**	A	*SE*	RM	76913	62241	71141	76914
3554	†	**CX**	A	*SE*	RM	76905	62461	71137	76906
3555		**ST**	H	*SW*	WD	76865	62140	71117	76866
3556	†	**CX**	A	*SE*	RM	76885	62457	71127	76886
3557		**ST**	H	*SW*	WD	76869	62437	71119	76870
3558		**ST**	H	*SW*	WD	76352	62447	70881	76351
3559		**ST**	H	*SW*	WD	76486	62439	70929	76485
3560	†	**CX**	A	*SE*	RM	76897	62191	71133	76898
3561		**ST**	H	*SW*	WD	76867	62453	71118	76868
3562	†	**CX**	A	*SE*	RM	76907	62129	71138	76908
3563		**ST**	H	*SW*	WD	76873	62438	71121	76874
3564	†	**CX**	A	*SE*	RM	76883	62458	71126	76884
3565	†	**CX**	A	*SE*	RM	76877	62134	71123	76878
3566	†	**CX**	A	*SE*	RM	76915	62443	71142	76916
3567		**ST**	H	*SW*	WD	76871	62138	71120	76872
3568	†	**CX**	A	*SE*	RM	76887	62440	71128	76888
3569		**ST**	H	*SW*	WD	76344	62448	70877	76343
3570	†	**CX**	A	*SE*	RM	76909	62187	71139	76910
3571	†	**CX**	A	*SE*	RM	76927	62463	71148	76928
3572	†	**CX**	A	*SE*	RM	76879	62468	71124	76880
3573	†	**CX**	A	*SE*	RM	76919	62444	71144	76920
3574	†	**CX**	A	*SE*	RM	76929	62464	71149	76930
3575	†	**CX**	A	*SE*	RM	76931	62469	71150	76932
3576		**ST**	H	*SW*	WD	76362	62196	70890	76361
3577	†	**CX**	A	*SE*	RM	76933	62459	71151	76934
3578		**ST**	H	*SW*	WD	76356	62193	70883	76355
3579	†	**CX**	A	*SE*	RM	76935	62471	71152	76936
3580		**ST**	H	*SW*	WD	76360	62195	70885	76359
3581		**ST**	H	*SW*	WD	76366	62198	70888	76365
3582	†	**CX**	A	*SE*	RM	76891	62472	71130	76275
3583	†	**CX**	A	*SE*	RM	76937	62450	71153	76938

3584	†	CX	A	SE	RM	76881	62473	71125	76882
3585	†	CX	A	SE	RM	76939	62445	71154	76940
3586	†	CX	A	SE	RM	76921	62474	71145	76922
3587	†	CX	A	SE	RM	76925	62465	71147	76926
3588	†	CX	A	SE	RM	76923	62467	71146	76924
3589	†	CX	A	SE	RM	76911	62466	71140	76912
3590	†	CX	A	SE	RM	76941	62460	71155	76942
3591	†	CX	A	SE	RM	76917	62475	71143	76918
3801	†	CX	P	SE	RM	76522	62229	70947	76521
3802	†	CX	P	SE	RM	76534	62188	70953	76533
3803	†	CX	P	SE	RM	76494	62263	70933	76493
3804	†	CX	P	SE	RM	76368	62204	70889	76367
3805	†	CX	P	SE	RM	76540	62211	70956	76539
3806	†	CX	P	SE	RM	76538	62212	70955	76537
3807	†	CX	P	SE	RM	76542	62264	70957	76541
3808	†	CX	P	SE	RM	76550	62248	70961	76549
3809		N	P	SW	WD	76516	62253	70944	76515
3810		N	P	SW	WD	76709	62252	71031	76710
3811		N	P	SW	WD	76514	62249	70943	76513
3812		ST	P	SW	WD	76703	62238	71028	76704
Spare		N	H		WD(S)		62470		

Class 423/2 (4-Vop). DTS–MBS–TS–DTS. Declassified units for Connex South Central 'South London Metro' services.

No.	Former No.								
3901	3439	*	CX	P	SC	BI	76402	62227	70906	76401
3902	3533	*	CX	P	SC	BI	76364	62260	70949	76525
3903	3462	*	CX	P	SC	BI	76536	62213	70904[ii]	76535
3904	3513	*	CX	P	SC	BI	76691	62336	71022	76692
3905	3463	*	CX	P	SC	BI	76398	62266	70904	76397
3906	3550	*	CX	P	SC	BI	76490	62350	70931	76489
3907	3534	*	CX	P	SC	BI	76506	62259	70939	76505
3908	3464	*	CX	P	SC	BI	76442	62265	70907	76441
3909	3522	*	CX	P	SC	BI	76705	62341	71029	76706
3910	3438	*	CX	P	SC	BI	76530	62262	70951	76529
3911	3476	*	CX	P	SC	BI	76548	62247	70960	76547
3912	3442	*	CX	P	SC	BI	76492	62216	70932	76491
3913	3478	*	CX	P	SC	BI	76653	62125	71003	76654
3914	3527	*	CX	P	SC	BI	76520	62326	70946	76519
3915	3526	*	CX	P	SC	BI	76524	62255	70948	76523
3916	3528	*	CX	P	SC	BI	76518	62258	70945	76517
3917	3507	*	CX	P	SC	BI	76558	62232	70965	76557
3918	3532	*	CX	P	SC	BI	76528	62321	70950	76527
3919	3506	*	CX	P	SC	BI	76554	62317	70963	76553

CLASS 455   BREL SUBURBAN

DTS–MS–TS–DTS. Gangwayed throughout. Disc brakes (5913–15 have tread brakes).
Construction: Steel (MS & DTS); Steel underframe, aluminium alloy body and roof (TS).
Traction Motors: Four GEC507-20J of 185 kW each.
Dimensions: 19.92 x 2.82 x 3.77 (3.58 Class 455/7 TSO) m.
Maximum Speed: 75 mph.   **Couplers:** Tightlock.
Doors: Power operated sliding.
Bogies: BP27/BT13 (Classes 455/8 and 455/9) or BX1 (Class 455/7).
Multiple Working: Classes 455–457.

Class 455/7. Built as 3-car units, augmented with ex-Class 508 TS. Pressure heating & ventilation.

62783–62825. MS. Dia. EC203. Lot No. 30975 BREL York 1984–85. –/84. 45.0 t.
71526–71568. TS. Dia. EH219. Lot No. 30944 BREL York 1977–80. –/86. 25.5 t.
77727–77812. DTS. Dia. EE218. Lot No. 30976 BREL York 1984–85. –/74. 29.5 t.

5701	N	P	SW	WD	77727	62783	71545	77728
5702	N	P	SW	WD	77729	62784	71547	77730
5703	N	P	SW	WD	77731	62785	71540	77732
5704	N	P	SW	WD	77733	62786	71548	77734
5705	N	P	SW	WD	77735	62787	71565	77736
5706	N	P	SW	WD	77737	62788	71534	77738
5707	N	P	SW	WD	77739	62789	71536	77740
5708	N	P	SW	WD	77741	62790	71560	77742
5709	N	P	SW	WD	77743	62791	71532	77744
5710	N	P	SW	WD	77745	62792	71566	77746
5711	N	P	SW	WD	77747	62793	71542	77748
5712	N	P	SW	WD	77749	62794	71546	77750
5713	N	P	SW	WD	77751	62795	71567	77752
5714	ST	P	SW	WD	77753	62796	71539	77754
5715	ST	P	SW	WD	77755	62797	71535	77756
5716	ST	P	SW	WD	77757	62798	71564	77758
5717	N	P	SW	WD	77759	62799	71528	77760
5718	N	P	SW	WD	77761	62800	71557	77762
5719	ST	P	SW	WD	77763	62801	71558	77764
5720	ST	P	SW	WD	77765	62802	71568	77766
5721	ST	P	SW	WD	77767	62803	71553	77768
5722	ST	P	SW	WD	77769	62804	71533	77770
5723	ST	P	SW	WD	77771	62805	71526	77772
5724	ST	P	SW	WD	77773	62806	71561	77774
5725	ST	P	SW	WD	77775	62807	71541	77776
5726	ST	P	SW	WD	77777	62808	71556	77778
5727	ST	P	SW	WD	77779	62809	71562	77780
5728	ST	P	SW	WD	77781	62810	71527	77782
5729	ST	P	SW	WD	77783	62811	71550	77784
5730	ST	P	SW	WD	77785	62812	71551	77786
5731	ST	P	SW	WD	77787	62813	71555	77788
5732	ST	P	SW	WD	77789	62814	71552	77790

5733	**ST**	P	*SW*	WD	77791	62815	71549	77792
5734	**ST**	P	*SW*	WD	77793	62816	71531	77794
5735	**ST**	P	*SW*	WD	77795	62817	71563	77796
5736	**ST**	P	*SW*	WD	77797	62818	71554	77798
5737	**ST**	P	*SW*	WD	77799	62819	71544	77800
5738	**ST**	P	*SW*	WD	77801	62820	71529	77802
5739	**ST**	P	*SW*	WD	77803	62821	71537	77804
5740	**ST**	P	*SW*	WD	77805	62822	71530	77806
5741	**ST**	P	*SW*	WD	77807	62823	71559	77808
5742	**ST**	P	*SW*	WD	77809	62824	71543	77810
5750	**ST**	P	*SW*	WD	77811	62825	71538	77812

Names:

5711	SPIRIT OF RUGBY
5731	VARIETY CLUB
5735	The Royal Borough of Kingston
5750	Wimbledon Train Care

Class 455/8. Pressure heating & ventilation.

62709–62782. MS. Dia. EC203. Lot No. 30973 BREL York 1982–84. –/84. 45.6 t.
71637–71710. TS. Dia. EH221. Lot No. 30974 BREL York 1982–84. –/84. 27.1 t.
77579–77726. DTS. Dia. EE218. Lot No. 30972 BREL York 1982–84. –/74. 29.5 t.

5801	**N**	H	*SC*	SU	77579	62709	71637	77580
5802	**N**	H	*SC*	SU	77581	62710	71664	77582
5803	**N**	H	*SC*	SU	77583	62711	71639	77584
5804	**CX**	H	*SC*	SU	77585	62712	71640	77586
5805	**N**	H	*SC*	SU	77587	62713	71641	77588
5806	**N**	H	*SC*	SU	77589	62714	71642	77590
5807	**N**	H	*SC*	SU	77591	62715	71643	77592
5808	**N**	H	*SC*	SU	77593	62716	71644	77594
5809	**N**	H	*SC*	SU	77595	62717	71645	77596
5810	**N**	H	*SC*	SU	77597	62718	71646	77598
5811	**N**	H	*SC*	SU	77599	62719	71647	77600
5812	**N**	H	*SC*	SU	77601	62720	71648	77602
5813	**N**	H	*SC*	SU	77603	62721	71649	77604
5814	**N**	H	*SC*	SU	77605	62722	71650	77606
5815	**CX**	H	*SC*	SU	77607	62723	71651	77608
5816	**N**	H	*SC*	SU	77609	62724	71652	77633
5817	**N**	H	*SC*	SU	77611	62725	71653	77612
5818	**N**	H	*SC*	SU	77613	62726	71654	77614
5819	**N**	H	*SC*	SU	77615	62727	71655	77616
5820	**N**	H	*SC*	SU	77617	62728	71656	77618
5821	**N**	H	*SC*	SU	77619	62729	71657	77620
5822	**N**	H	*SC*	SU	77621	62730	71658	77622
5823	**N**	H	*SC*	SU	77623	62731	71659	77624
5824	**N**	H	*SC*	SU	77637	62732	71660	77626
5825	**N**	H	*SC*	SU	77627	62733	71661	77628
5826	**N**	H	*SC*	SU	77629	62734	71662	77630
5827	**N**	H	*SC*	SU	77610	62735	71663	77632
5828	**N**	H	*SC*	SU	77631	62736	71638	77634

5829	N	H	SC	SU	77635	62737	71665	77636
5830	N	H	SC	SU	77625	62743	71666	77638
5831	N	H	SC	SU	77639	62739	71667	77640
5832	N	H	SC	SU	77641	62740	71668	77642
5833	N	H	SC	SU	77643	62741	71669	77644
5834	N	H	SC	SU	77645	62742	71670	77646
5835	N	H	SC	SU	77647	62738	71671	77648
5836	N	H	SC	SU	77649	62744	71672	77650
5837	N	H	SC	SU	77651	62745	71673	77652
5838	N	H	SC	SU	77653	62746	71674	77654
5839	N	H	SC	SU	77655	62747	71675	77656
5840	N	H	SC	SU	77657	62748	71676	77658
5841	N	H	SC	SU	77659	62749	71677	77660
5842	N	H	SC	SU	77661	62750	71678	77662
5843	N	H	SC	SU	77663	62751	71679	77664
5844	N	H	SC	SU	77665	62752	71680	77666
5845	N	H	SC	SU	77667	62753	71681	77668
5846	N	H	SC	SU	77669	62754	71682	77670
5847	N	P	SW	WD	77671	62755	71683	77672
5848	N	P	SW	WD	77673	62756	71684	77674
5849	N	P	SW	WD	77675	62757	71685	77676
5850	N	P	SW	WD	77677	62758	71686	77678
5851	N	P	SW	WD	77679	62759	71687	77680
5852	N	P	SW	WD	77681	62760	71688	77682
5853	N	P	SW	WD	77683	62761	71689	77684
5854	N	P	SW	WD	77685	62762	71690	77686
5855	N	P	SW	WD	77687	62763	71691	77688
5856	N	P	SW	WD	77689	62764	71692	77690
5857	N	P	SW	WD	77691	62765	71693	77692
5858	N	P	SW	WD	77693	62766	71694	77694
5859	N	P	SW	WD	77695	62767	71695	77696
5860	N	P	SW	WD	77697	62768	71696	77698
5861	N	P	SW	WD	77699	62769	71697	77700
5862	N	P	SW	WD	77701	62770	71698	77702
5863	N	P	SW	WD	77703	62771	71699	77704
5864	N	P	SW	WD	77705	62772	71700	77706
5865	N	P	SW	WD	77707	62773	71701	77708
5866	N	P	SW	WD	77709	62774	71702	77710
5867	N	P	SW	WD	77711	62775	71703	77712
5868	N	P	SW	WD	77713	62776	71704	77714
5869	N	P	SW	WD	77715	62777	71705	77716
5870	N	P	SW	WD	77717	62778	71706	77718
5871	N	P	SW	WD	77719	62779	71707	77720
5872	N	P	SW	WD	77721	62780	71708	77722
5873	N	P	SW	WD	77723	62781	71709	77724
5874	N	P	SW	WD	77725	62782	71710	77726

Class 455/9. Convection heating.

62826–62845. MS. Dia. EC206. Lot No. 30992 BREL York 1985. –/84. 45.6
(† 48.0) t.
67400. TS. Dia. EH236. Built as a Class 210 DEMU vehicle to Lot No. 30932
BREL Derby 1981. Subsequently converted to EMU vehicle. –/84. 26.8 t.
71714–71733. TS. Dia. EH224. Lot No. 30993 BREL York 1985. –/84. 27.1 t.
77813–77852. DTS. Dia. EE226. Lot No. 30991 BREL York 1985. –/74. 29.5 t.

5901		**ST**	P	*SW*	WD	77813	62826	71714	77814
5902		**ST**	P	*SW*	WD	77815	62827	71715	77816
5903		**ST**	P	*SW*	WD	77817	62828	71716	77818
5904		**ST**	P	*SW*	WD	77819	62829	71717	77820
5905		**ST**	P	*SW*	WD	77821	62830	71725	77822
5906		**ST**	P	*SW*	WD	77823	62831	71719	77824
5907		**ST**	P	*SW*	WD	77825	62832	71720	77826
5908		**ST**	P	*SW*	WD	77827	62833	71721	77828
5909		**ST**	P	*SW*	WD	77829	62834	71722	77830
5910		**ST**	P	*SW*	WD	77831	62835	71723	77832
5911		**ST**	P	*SW*	WD	77833	62836	71724	77834
5912	†	**ST**	P		ZG(S)	77835	62837	71731	77836
5913		**ST**	P	*SW*	WD	77837	62838	71726	77838
5914		**ST**	P	*SW*	WD	77839	62839	71727	77840
5915		**ST**	P	*SW*	WD	77841	62840	71728	77842
5916		**ST**	P	*SW*	WD	77843	62841	71729	77844
5917		**ST**	P	*SW*	WD	77845	62842	71730	77846
5918		**ST**	P	*SW*	WD	77847	62843	71732	77848
5919		**ST**	P	*SW*	WD	77849	62844	71718	77850
5920		**N**	P	*SW*	WD	77851	62845	71733	77852
Spare		**N**	P		WD(S)		67400		

CLASS 458 (4-Jop)   ALSTOM JUNIPER

DMC(A)–PTS–MS–DMC(B). Gangwayed throughout. Disc and regenerative
brakes. Air conditioned.
Construction: Steel.
Supply System: 750 V d.c. third rail with provision for 25 kV a.c. 50 Hz
overhead.
Traction Motors: Two Alstom ONIX 800 of 270 kW each per motor car.
Dimensions: 21.16 (DMC) or 19.94 (MS & PTS) x 2.80 x . m.
Maximum Speed: 100 mph.   **Doors:** Power operated sliding plug.
Couplers: Tightlock.   **Bogies:** ACR.
Multiple Working: Within Class.

67601–67630. DMC(A). Dia. EA302. Alstom Birmingham 1998–2000. 12/63.
45.2 t.
67701–67730. DMC(B). Dia. EA303. Alstom Birmingham 1998–2000. 12/63.
45.2 t.
74001–74030. PTS. Dia. EH250. Alstom Birmingham 1998–2000. –/49 1TD 2W.
33.3 t.
74101–74130. MS. Dia. EC226. Alstom Birmingham 1998–2000. –/75 1T. 40.6 t.

8001	**U**	P	*SW*	WD	67601	74001	74101	67701
8002	**SW**	P	*SW*	WD	67602	74002	74102	67702
8003	**SW**	P	*SW*	WD	67603	74003	74103	67703
8004	**SW**	P	*SW*	WD	67604	74004	74104	67704
8005		P			67605	74005	74105	67705
8006		P			67606	74006	74106	67706
8007		P			67607	74007	74107	67707
8008		P			67608	74008	74108	67708
8009		P			67609	74009	74109	67709
8010		P			67610	74010	74110	67710
8011		P			67611	74011	74111	67711
8012		P			67612	74012	74112	67712
8013		P			67613	74013	74113	67713
8014		P			67614	74014	74114	67714
8015		P			67615	74015	74115	67715
8016		P			67616	74016	74116	67716
8017		P			67617	74017	74117	67717
8018		P			67618	74018	74118	67718
8019		P			67619	74019	74119	67719
8020		P			67620	74020	74120	67720
8021		P			67621	74021	74121	67721
8022		P			67622	74022	74122	67722
8023		P			67623	74023	74123	67723
8024		P			67624	74024	74124	67724
8025		P			67625	74025	74125	67724
8026		P			67626	74026	74126	67726
8027		P			67627	74027	74127	67727
8028		P			67628	74028	74128	67728
8029		P			67629	74029	74129	67729
8030		P			67630	74030	74130	67730

CLASS 488   BR EXPRESS

Various formations, see below. Gangwayed throughout. Air conditioned.
Construction: Steel.   **Dimensions:** 20.38 x 2.84 x 3.79 m.
Maximum Speed: 90 mph.   **Doors:** Manually operated slam.
Couplings: Buckeye.   **Bogies:** B4.
Multiple Working: SR type.
Advertising Livery:
•   Continental Airlines.

72500–72509. TFH. Dia. EP101. Built as loco-hauled vehicles to Lot No. 30859
    Derby 1973–74. Converted BREL Eastleigh 1983–84. 41/– 1T. 35.0 t.
72602–14/6–8/20–44/6/7. TSH. Dia. EP201. Built as loco-hauled vehicles to
    Lot No. 30860 Derby 1973–74. Converted BREL Eastleigh 1983–84. –/48 1T.
    35.0 t.
72615/19/45. TSH. Dia. EP201. Built as loco-hauled vehicles to Lot No. 30846
    Derby 1973. Converted BREL Eastleigh 1983–84. –/48 1T. 35.0 t.
72701–72718. TS. Dia. EH290. Built as loco-hauled vehicles to Lot No. 30860
    Derby 1973–74. Converted BREL Eastleigh 1983–84. –/48 1T. 35.0 t.

CLASS 488/2. 2-car units. TFH–TSH.

8201	**GX**	P	*GX*	SL	72500	72638
8202	**GX**	P	*GX*	SL	72501	72617
8203	**AL**	P	*GX*	SL	72502	72640
8204	**AL**	P	*GX*	SL	72503	72641
8205	**GX**	P	*GX*	SL	72504	72628
8206	**GX**	P	*GX*	SL	72505	72629
8207	**AL**	P	*GX*	SL	72506	72642
8208	**AL**	P	*GX*	SL	72507	72643
8209	**GX**	P	*GX*	SL	72508	72644
8210	**AL**	P	*GX*	SL	72509	72635

CLASS 488/3. 3-car units. TFH–TS–TSH.

8302	**GX**	P	*GX*	SL	72602	72701	72604
8303	**GX**	P	*GX*	SL	72603	72702	72608
8304	**AL**	P	*GX*	SL	72606	72703	72611
8305	**AL**	P	*GX*	SL	72605	72704	72609
8306	**GX**	P	*GX*	SL	72607	72705	72610
8307	**GX**	P	*GX*	SL	72612	72706	72613
8308	**GX**	P	*GX*	SL	72614	72707	72615
8309	**GX**	P	*GX*	SL	72616	72708	72639
8310	**AL**	P	*GX*	SL	72618	72709	72619
8311	**GX**	P	*GX*	SL	72620	72710	72621
8312	**GX**	P	*GX*	SL	72622	72711	72623
8313	**GX**	P	*GX*	SL	72624	72712	72625
8314	**AL**	P	*GX*	SL	72626	72713	72627
8315	**GX**	P	*GX*	SL	72636	72714	72645
8316	**GX**	P	*GX*	SL	72630	72715	72631
8317	**GX**	P	*GX*	SL	72632	72716	72633
8318	**GX**	P	*GX*	SL	72634	72717	72637
8319	**AL**	P	*GX*	SL	72646	72718	72647

CLASS 489   BR LUGGAGE VAN

DMLV. Gangwayed at non-driving end only. Operate with Class 488.
Construction: Steel.
Traction Motors: Two English Electric 507 of 185 kW each.
Dimensions: 20.45 x 2.82 x 3.86 m.   **Doors:** Manually operated slam.
Maximum Speed: 90 mph.   **Bogies:** B4.
Couplings: Buckeye.   **Multiple Working:** SR type.

68500–68509. DMLV. Dia. EB501. Built as DMBS to Lot No. 30452 Eastleigh
1959. Converted BREL Eastleigh 1983–84. 40.5 t.

9101	**GX**	P	*GX*	SL	68500
9102	**GX**	P	*GX*	SL	68501
9103	**GX**	P	*GX*	SL	68502
9104	**GX**	P	*GX*	SL	68503
9105	**GX**	P	*GX*	SL	68504
9106	**GX**	P	*GX*	SL	68505
9107	**GX**	P	*GX*	SL	68506

9108	GX	P	GX	SL	68507
9109	GX	P	GX	SL	68508
9110	GX	P	GX	SL	68509

CLASS 424   ADTRANZ CLASSIC PROTOTYPE

DTS. Gangwayed within unit.
Construction: Steel.
Dimensions:
Maximum Speed: 90 mph.
Couplers: Tightlock.
Non Standard Livery:
Doors: Power operated sliding.
Bogies: B5 (SR).
Multiple Working:
• Silver with black window surrounds.

76112. DTS. Dia. EE280. Built as DTCso to Lot No. 30741 York 1963–66. Rebuilt Adtranz Derby 1997. –/77. 34.0 t.

| 424 001 | 0 | A | | ZD(S) | 76112 |

CLASS 456   BREL SUBURBAN

DMS–DTS. Gangwayed within unit. Disc brakes.
Construction: Steel.
Traction Motors: Two GEC507-20J of 185 kW each.
Dimensions: 19.95 x 2.82 x . m.
Maximum Speed: 75 mph.
Couplers: Tightlock.
Doors: Power operated sliding.
Bogies: BREL P7/T3.
Multiple Working: Classes 455–457, 507 & 508.

64735–64758. DMS. Dia. EA267. Lot No. 31073 BREL York 1990–91. –/79. 41.1 t.
78250–78273. DTS. Dia. EE276. Lot No. 31074 BREL York 1990–91. –/73. 31.4 t.

456 001	N	P	SC	SU	64735	78250
456 002	N	P	SC	SU	64736	78251
456 003	N	P	SC	SU	64737	78252
456 004	N	P	SC	SU	64738	78253
456 005	N	P	SC	SU	64739	78254
456 006	N	P	SC	SU	64740	78255
456 007	N	P	SC	SU	64741	78256
456 008	N	P	SC	SU	64742	78257
456 009	N	P	SC	SU	64743	78258
456 010	N	P	SC	SU	64744	78259
456 011	N	P	SC	SU	64745	78260
456 012	N	P	SC	SU	64746	78261
456 013	N	P	SC	SU	64747	78262
456 014	N	P	SC	SU	64748	78263
456 015	N	P	SC	SU	64749	78264
456 016	N	P	SC	SU	64750	78265
456 017	N	P	SC	SU	64751	78266
456 018	N	P	SC	SU	64752	78267
456 019	N	P	SC	SU	64753	78268
456 020	N	P	SC	SU	64754	78269

456 021	**N**	P	*SC*	SU	64755	78270
456 022	**N**	P	*SC*	SU	64756	78271
456 023	**N**	P	*SC*	SU	64757	78272
456 024	**CX**	P	*SC*	SU	64758	78273

Name (carried on DTS):

456 024   Sir Cosmo Bonsor

CLASS 460   ALSTOM JUNIPER

DMF–TF–TC–MS(A)–MS(B)–TS–MS(C)–DMS. Gangwayed within unit. Disc and
regenerative brakes.
Construction: Steel.
Traction Motors: Two Alstom ONIX 800 of 270 kW each per motor car.
Dimensions: 21.01 (DMF & DMS) or 19.94 (other cars) x 2.80 x . m.
Maximum Speed: 100 mph.   **Doors:** Power operated sliding plug.
Couplers: Scharfenberg.   **Bogies:** ACR.
Multiple Working:

67901–67908. DMF. Dia. EA101. Alstom Birmingham. 1999–2000. 10/– . 42.6 t.
67911–67918. DMS. Dia. EA274. Alstom Birmingham 1999–2000. –/56. 45.3 t.
74401–74408. TF. Dia. EH161. Alstom Birmingham 1999–2000. 28/– 1TD 1W.
33.5 t.
74411–74418. TC. Dia. EH364. Alstom Birmingham 1999–2000. 9/42 1T. 34.9 t.
74421–74428. MS(A). Dia. EC227. Alstom Birmingham 1999–2000. –/60. 42.5 t.
74431–74438. MS(B). Dia. EC228 . Alstom Birmingham 1999–2000. –/60. 42.5 t.
74441–74448. TS. Dia. EH251. Alstom Birmingham 1999–2000. –/38 1TD 1W.
35.2 t.
74451–74458. MS(C). Dia. EC229 . Alstom Birmingham 1999–2000. –/60. 40.5 t.

460 001	**U**	P	*GX*	SL	67901 74401 74411 74421 74431 74441 74451 67911
460 002	**U**	P	*GX*	SL	67902 74402 74412 74422 74432 74442 74452 67912
460 003	**GX**	P	*GX*	SL	67903 74403 74413 74423 74433 74443 74453 67913
460 004	**GX**	P	*GX*	SL	67904 74404 74414 74424 74434 74444 74454 67914
460 005		P			67905 74405 74415 74425 74435 74445 74455 67915
460 006		P			67906 74406 74416 74426 74436 74446 74456 67916
460 007		P			67907 74407 74417 74427 74437 74447 74457 67917
460 008		P			67908 74408 74418 74428 74438 74448 74458 67918

CLASS 465   BREL NETWORKER

DMS–TS(A)–TS(B)–DMS. Gangwayed within unit. Disc, rheostatic and
regenerative brakes.
Construction: Welded aluminium alloy.
Traction Motors: Four Brush TIM 970 or GEC-Alsthom G352BY of 280 kW
each per motor car.
Dimensions: 20.89 (DMS) or 20.06 (other cars) x 2.81 x 3.77 m.
Maximum Speed: 75 mph.   **Doors:** Power operated sliding plug.
Couplers: Tightlock.   **Bogies:** BREL P3-16/T3-16.
Multiple Working: Classes 365, 465 & 466. Couplers within units on Class
465/2 cars are not compatible with Classes 465/0 and 465/1.

64759–64858. DMS. Dia. EA268. Lot No. 31100 BREL York 1992–93. –/86. 39.2 t.
65700–65799. DMS. Dia. EA269. Lot No. 31103 GEC-Alsthom Birmingham 1992–93. –/86. 38.9 t.
65800–65893. DMS. Dia. EA268. Lot No. 31130 ABB York 1993–94. –/86. 39.0 t.
72028–72126 (Even numbers). TS(A). Dia. EH293. Lot No. 31102 BREL York 1992–93. –/86. 30.4 t.
72029–72127 (Odd numbers). TS(B). Dia. EH292. Lot No. 31101 BREL York 1992–93. –/86. 30.5 t.
72719–72817 (Even numbers). TS(A). Dia. EH294. Lot No. 31104 GEC-Alsthom Birmingham 1992–93. –/86. 30.2 t.
72720–72818 (Even numbers). TS(B). Dia. EH295. Lot No. 31105 GEC-Alsthom Birmingham 1992–93. –/90. 29.1 t.
72900–72992 (Even numbers). TS(A). Dia. EH293. Lot No. 31132 ABB York 1993–94. –/90. 29.5 t.
72901–72993 (Odd numbers). TS(B). Dia. EH294. Lot No. 31131 ABB York 1993–94. –/86. 30.2 t.

Class 465/0. Built by ABB. Brush traction motors.

465 001	**CS**	H	*SE*	SG	64759	72028	72029	64809
465 002	**CS**	H	*SE*	SG	64760	72030	72031	64810
465 003	**CS**	H	*SE*	SG	64761	72032	72033	64811
465 004	**NT**	H	*SE*	SG	64762	72034	72035	64812
465 005	**NT**	H	*SE*	SG	64763	72036	72037	64813
465 006	**CS**	H	*SE*	SG	64764	72038	72039	64814
465 007	**CS**	H	*SE*	SG	64765	72040	72041	64815
465 008	**CS**	H	*SE*	SG	64766	72042	72043	64816
465 009	**CS**	H	*SE*	SG	64767	72044	72045	64817
465 010	**CS**	H	*SE*	SG	64768	72046	72047	64818
465 011	**CS**	H	*SE*	SG	64769	72048	72049	64819
465 012	**CS**	H	*SE*	SG	64770	72050	72051	64820
465 013	**CS**	H	*SE*	SG	64771	72052	72053	64821
465 014	**CS**	H	*SE*	SG	64772	72054	72055	64822
465 015	**CS**	H	*SE*	SG	64773	72056	72057	64823
465 016	**CS**	H	*SE*	SG	64774	72058	72059	64824
465 017	**CS**	H	*SE*	SG	64775	72060	72061	64825
465 018	**CS**	H	*SE*	SG	64776	72062	72063	64826
465 019	**CS**	H	*SE*	SG	64777	72064	72065	64827
465 020	**CS**	H	*SE*	SG	64778	72066	72067	64828
465 021	**NT**	H	*SE*	SG	64779	72068	72069	64829
465 022	**NT**	H	*SE*	SG	64780	72070	72071	64830
465 023	**NT**	H	*SE*	SG	64781	72072	72073	64831
465 024	**NT**	H	*SE*	SG	64782	72074	72075	64832
465 025	**NT**	H	*SE*	SG	64783	72076	72077	64833
465 026	**NT**	H	*SE*	SG	64784	72078	72079	64834
465 027	**NT**	H	*SE*	SG	64785	72080	72081	64835
465 028	**NT**	H	*SE*	SG	64786	72082	72083	64836
465 029	**NT**	H	*SE*	SG	64787	72084	72085	64837
465 030	**NT**	H	*SE*	SG	64788	72086	72087	64838
465 031	**NT**	H	*SE*	SG	64789	72088	72089	64839
465 032	**NT**	H	*SE*	SG	64790	72090	72091	64840
465 033	**NT**	H	*SE*	SG	64791	72092	72093	64841

465 034	**NT**	H	*SE*	SG	64792	72094	72095	64842
465 035	**NT**	H	*SE*	SG	64793	72096	72097	64843
465 036	**NT**	H	*SE*	SG	64794	72098	72099	64844
465 037	**NT**	H	*SE*	SG	64795	72100	72101	64845
465 038	**NT**	H	*SE*	SG	64796	72102	72103	64846
465 039	**NT**	H	*SE*	SG	64797	72104	72105	64847
465 040	**NT**	H	*SE*	SG	64798	72106	72107	64848
465 041	**NT**	H	*SE*	SG	64799	72108	72109	64849
465 042	**NT**	H	*SE*	SG	64800	72110	72111	64850
465 043	**NT**	H	*SE*	SG	64801	72112	72113	64851
465 044	**NT**	H	*SE*	SG	64802	72114	72115	64852
465 045	**NT**	H	*SE*	SG	64803	72116	72117	64853
465 046	**NT**	H	*SE*	SG	64804	72118	72119	64854
465 047	**NT**	H	*SE*	SG	64805	72120	72121	64855
465 048	**NT**	H	*SE*	SG	64806	72122	72123	64856
465 049	**NT**	H	*SE*	SG	64807	72124	72125	64857
465 050	**NT**	H	*SE*	SG	64808	72126	72127	64858

Class 465/1. Built by ABB. Brush traction motors.

465 151	**NT**	H	*SE*	SG	65800	72900	72901	65847
465 152	**NT**	H	*SE*	SG	65801	72902	72903	65848
465 153	**NT**	H	*SE*	SG	65802	72904	72905	65849
465 154	**NT**	H	*SE*	SG	65803	72906	72907	65850
465 155	**NT**	H	*SE*	SG	65804	72908	72909	65851
465 156	**NT**	H	*SE*	SG	65805	72910	72911	65852
465 157	**NT**	H	*SE*	SG	65806	72912	72913	65853
465 158	**NT**	H	*SE*	SG	65807	72914	72915	65854
465 159	**NT**	H	*SE*	SG	65808	72916	72917	65855
465 160	**NT**	H	*SE*	SG	65809	72918	72919	65856
465 161	**NT**	H	*SE*	SG	65810	72920	72921	65857
465 162	**NT**	H	*SE*	SG	65811	72922	72923	65858
465 163	**NT**	H	*SE*	SG	65812	72924	72925	65859
465 164	**NT**	H	*SE*	SG	65813	72926	72927	65860
465 165	**NT**	H	*SE*	SG	65814	72928	72929	65861
465 166	**NT**	H	*SE*	SG	65815	72930	72931	65862
465 167	**NT**	H	*SE*	SG	65816	72932	72933	65863
465 168	**NT**	H	*SE*	SG	65817	72934	72935	65864
465 169	**NT**	H	*SE*	SG	65818	72936	72937	65865
465 170	**NT**	H	*SE*	SG	65819	72938	72939	65866
465 171	**NT**	H	*SE*	SG	65820	72940	72941	65867
465 172	**NT**	H	*SE*	SG	65821	72942	72943	65868
465 173	**NT**	H	*SE*	SG	65822	72944	72945	65869
465 174	**NT**	H	*SE*	SG	65823	72946	72947	65870
465 175	**NT**	H	*SE*	SG	65824	72948	72949	65871
465 176	**NT**	H	*SE*	SG	65825	72950	72951	65872
465 177	**NT**	H	*SE*	SG	65826	72952	72953	65873
465 178	**NT**	H	*SE*	SG	65827	72954	72955	65874
465 179	**NT**	H	*SE*	SG	65828	72956	72957	65875
465 180	**NT**	H	*SE*	SG	65829	72958	72959	65876
465 181	**NT**	H	*SE*	SG	65830	72960	72961	65877
465 182	**NT**	H	*SE*	SG	65831	72962	72963	65878

465 183	**NT**	H	*SE*	SG	65832	72964	72965	65879
465 184	**NT**	H	*SE*	SG	65833	72966	72967	65880
465 185	**NT**	H	*SE*	SG	65834	72968	72969	65881
465 186	**NT**	H	*SE*	SG	65835	72970	72971	65882
465 187	**NT**	H	*SE*	SG	65836	72972	72973	65883
465 188	**NT**	H	*SE*	SG	65837	72974	72975	65884
465 189	**NT**	H	*SE*	SG	65838	72976	72977	65885
465 190	**NT**	H	*SE*	SG	65839	72978	72979	65886
465 191	**NT**	H	*SE*	SG	65840	72980	72981	65887
465 192	**NT**	H	*SE*	SG	65841	72982	72983	65888
465 193	**NT**	H	*SE*	SG	65842	72984	72985	65889
465 194	**NT**	H	*SE*	SG	65843	72986	72987	65890
465 195	**NT**	H	*SE*	SG	65844	72988	72989	65891
465 196	**NT**	H	*SE*	SG	65845	72990	72991	65892
465 197	**NT**	H	*SE*	SG	65846	72992	72993	65893

Class 465/2. Built by GEC-Alsthom. GEC-Alsthom traction motors.

465 201	**NT**	A	*SE*	SG	65700	72719	72720	65750
465 202	**NT**	A	*SE*	SG	65701	72721	72722	65751
465 203	**NT**	A	*SE*	SG	65702	72723	72724	65752
465 204	**NT**	A	*SE*	SG	65703	72725	72726	65753
465 205	**NT**	A	*SE*	SG	65704	72727	72728	65754
465 206	**NT**	A	*SE*	SG	65705	72729	72730	65755
465 207	**NT**	A	*SE*	SG	65706	72731	72732	65756
465 208	**NT**	A	*SE*	SG	65707	72733	72734	65757
465 209	**NT**	A	*SE*	SG	65708	72735	72736	65758
465 210	**NT**	A	*SE*	SG	65709	72737	72738	65759
465 211	**NT**	A	*SE*	SG	65710	72739	72740	65760
465 212	**NT**	A	*SE*	SG	65711	72741	72742	65761
465 213	**NT**	A	*SE*	SG	65712	72743	72744	65762
465 214	**NT**	A	*SE*	SG	65713	72745	72746	65763
465 215	**NT**	A	*SE*	SG	65714	72747	72748	65764
465 216	**NT**	A	*SE*	SG	65715	72749	72750	65765
465 217	**NT**	A	*SE*	SG	65716	72751	72752	65766
465 218	**NT**	A	*SE*	SG	65717	72753	72754	65767
465 219	**NT**	A	*SE*	SG	65718	72755	72756	65768
465 220	**NT**	A	*SE*	SG	65719	72757	72758	65769
465 221	**NT**	A	*SE*	SG	65720	72759	72760	65770
465 222	**NT**	A	*SE*	SG	65721	72761	72762	65771
465 223	**NT**	A	*SE*	SG	65722	72763	72764	65772
465 224	**NT**	A	*SE*	SG	65723	72765	72766	65773
465 225	**NT**	A	*SE*	SG	65724	72767	72768	65774
465 226	**NT**	A	*SE*	SG	65725	72769	72770	65775
465 227	**NT**	A	*SE*	SG	65726	72771	72772	65776
465 228	**NT**	A	*SE*	SG	65727	72773	72774	65777
465 229	**NT**	A	*SE*	SG	65728	72775	72776	65778
465 230	**NT**	A	*SE*	SG	65729	72777	72778	65779
465 231	**NT**	A	*SE*	SG	65730	72779	72780	65780
465 232	**NT**	A	*SE*	SG	65731	72781	72782	65781
465 233	**NT**	A	*SE*	SG	65732	72783	72784	65782
465 234	**NT**	A	*SE*	SG	65733	72785	72786	65783

465 235	**NT**	A	*SE*	SG	65734	72787	72788	65784
465 236	**NT**	A	*SE*	SG	65735	72789	72790	65785
465 237	**NT**	A	*SE*	SG	65736	72791	72792	65786
465 238	**NT**	A	*SE*	SG	65737	72793	72794	65787
465 239	**NT**	A	*SE*	SG	65738	72795	72796	65788
465 240	**NT**	A	*SE*	SG	65739	72797	72798	65789
465 241	**NT**	A	*SE*	SG	65740	72799	72800	65790
465 242	**NT**	A	*SE*	SG	65741	72801	72802	65791
465 243	**NT**	A	*SE*	SG	65742	72803	72804	65792
465 244	**NT**	A	*SE*	SG	65743	72805	72806	65793
465 245	**NT**	A	*SE*	SG	65744	72807	72808	65794
465 246	**NT**	A	*SE*	SG	65745	72809	72810	65795
465 247	**NT**	A	*SE*	SG	65746	72811	72812	65796
465 248	**NT**	A	*SE*	SG	65747	72813	72814	65797
465 249	**NT**	A	*SE*	SG	65748	72815	72816	65798
465 250	**NT**	A	*SE*	SG	65749	72817	72818	65799

CLASS 466   BREL NETWORKER

DMS–DTS. Gangwayed within unit. Disc, rheostatic and regenerative brakes. 466 017 has experimental 2 + 2 seating.
Construction: Welded aluminium alloy.
Traction Motors: Four GEC-Alsthom G352BY of 280 kW each.
Dimensions: 20.89 (DMS) or 20.06 (DTS) x 2.81 x 3.77 m.
Maximum Speed: 75 mph.   **Doors:** Power operated sliding plug.
Couplers: Tightlock.   **Bogies:** BREL P3-16/T3-16.
Multiple Working: Classes 365, 465 & 466.

64860–64902. DMS. Dia. EA271. Lot No. 31128 GEC-Alsthom Birmingham 1993–94. –/86 (* –/72). 38.8 t.
78312–78354. DTS. Dia. EE279. Lot No. 31129 GEC-Alsthom Birmingham 1993–94. –/82 (* –/68). 33.2 t.

466 001		**NT**	A	*SE*	SG	64860	78312
466 002		**NT**	A	*SE*	SG	64861	78313
466 003		**NT**	A	*SE*	SG	64862	78314
466 004		**NT**	A	*SE*	SG	64863	78315
466 005		**NT**	A	*SE*	SG	64864	78316
466 006		**NT**	A	*SE*	SG	64865	78317
466 007		**NT**	A	*SE*	SG	64866	78318
466 008		**NT**	A	*SE*	SG	64867	78319
466 009		**NT**	A	*SE*	SG	64868	78320
466 010		**NT**	A	*SE*	SG	64869	78321
466 011		**NT**	A	*SE*	SG	64870	78322
466 012		**NT**	A	*SE*	SG	64871	78323
466 013		**NT**	A	*SE*	SG	64872	78324
466 014		**NT**	A	*SE*	SG	64873	78325
466 015		**NT**	A	*SE*	SG	64874	78326
466 016		**NT**	A	*SE*	SG	64875	78327
466 017	*	**NT**	A	*SE*	SG	64876	78328
466 018		**NT**	A	*SE*	SG	64877	78329

466 019	**NT**	A	*SE*	SG	64878	78330
466 020	**NT**	A	*SE*	SG	64879	78331
466 021	**NT**	A	*SE*	SG	64880	78332
466 022	**NT**	A	*SE*	SG	64881	78333
466 023	**NT**	A	*SE*	SG	64882	78334
466 024	**NT**	A	*SE*	SG	64883	78335
466 025	**NT**	A	*SE*	SG	64884	78336
466 026	**NT**	A	*SE*	SG	64885	78337
466 027	**NT**	A	*SE*	SG	64886	78338
466 028	**NT**	A	*SE*	SG	64887	78339
466 029	**NT**	A	*SE*	SG	64888	78340
466 030	**NT**	A	*SE*	SG	64889	78341
466 031	**NT**	A	*SE*	SG	64890	78342
466 032	**NT**	A	*SE*	SG	64891	78343
466 033	**NT**	A	*SE*	SG	64892	78344
466 034	**NT**	A	*SE*	SG	64893	78345
466 035	**NT**	A	*SE*	SG	64894	78346
466 036	**NT**	A	*SE*	SG	64895	78347
466 037	**NT**	A	*SE*	SG	64896	78348
466 038	**NT**	A	*SE*	SG	64897	78349
466 039	**NT**	A	*SE*	SG	64898	78350
466 040	**NT**	A	*SE*	SG	64899	78351
466 041	**NT**	A	*SE*	SG	64900	78352
466 042	**NT**	A	*SE*	SG	64901	78353
466 043	**NT**	A	*SE*	SG	64902	78354

CLASS 507   BR SUBURBAN

BDMS–TS–DMS. Gangwayed within unit. End doors. Disc & rheostatic brakes.
Construction: Steel underframe, aluminium alloy body and roof.
Traction Motors: Four GEC G310AZ of 82.125 kW per motor car.
Dimensions: 20.02 (BDMS & DMS) or 19.92 (TS) x 2.82 x 3.58 m.
Maximum Speed: 75 mph.   **Doors:** Power operated sliding.
Couplers: Tightlock.   **Bogies:** BREL BX1.
Multiple Working: Classes 507 & 508.
Note: Fitted with de-icing equipment.

64367–64399. BDMS. Dia. EI202. Lot No. 30906 York 1978–80. –/74. 37.1 t.
64405–64437. DMS. Dia. EA201. Lot No. 30908 York 1978–80. –/74. 35.6 t.
71342–71374. TS. Dia. EH205. Lot No. 30907 York 1978–80. –/82. 25.6 t.

507 001	**MT**	A	*ME*	BD	64367	71342	64405
507 002	**MT**	A	*ME*	BD	64368	71343	64406
507 003	**MT**	A	*ME*	BD	64369	71344	64407
507 004	**MT**	A	*ME*	BD	64388	71345	64408
507 005	**MT**	A	*ME*	BD	64371	71346	64409
507 006	**MT**	A	*ME*	BD	64372	71347	64410
507 007	**MT**	A	*ME*	BD	64373	71348	64411
507 008	**MT**	A	*ME*	BD	64374	71349	64412
507 009	**MT**	A	*ME*	BD	64375	71350	64413
507 010	**MT**	A	*ME*	BD	64376	71351	64414

507 011	**MT**	A	*ME*	BD	64377	71352	64415
507 012	**MT**	A	*ME*	BD	64378	71353	64416
507 013	**MT**	A	*ME*	BD	64379	71354	64417
507 014	**MT**	A	*ME*	BD	64380	71355	64418
507 015	**MT**	A	*ME*	BD	64381	71356	64419
507 016	**MT**	A	*ME*	BD	64382	71357	64420
507 017	**MT**	A	*ME*	BD	64383	71358	64421
507 018	**MT**	A	*ME*	BD	64384	71359	64422
507 019	**MT**	A	*ME*	BD	64385	71360	64423
507 020	**MT**	A	*ME*	BD	64386	71361	64424
507 021	**MT**	A	*ME*	BD	64387	71362	64425
507 023	**MT**	A	*ME*	BD	64389	71364	64427
507 024	**MT**	A	*ME*	BD	64390	71365	64428
507 025	**MT**	A	*ME*	BD	64391	71366	64429
507 026	**MT**	A	*ME*	BD	64392	71367	64430
507 027	**MT**	A	*ME*	BD	64393	71368	64431
507 028	**MT**	A	*ME*	BD	64394	71369	64432
507 029	**MT**	A	*ME*	BD	64395	71370	64433
507 030	**MT**	A	*ME*	BD	64396	71371	64434
507 031	**MT**	A	*ME*	BD	64397	71372	64435
507 032	**MT**	A	*ME*	BD	64398	71373	64436
507 033	**MT**	A	*ME*	BD	64399	71374	64437

CLASS 508   BREL SUBURBAN

DMS–TS–BDMS. Gangwayed within unit. End doors. Disc & rheostatic brakes.
Construction: Steel underframe, aluminium alloy body and roof.
Traction Motors: Four GEC G310AZ of 82.125 kW per motor car.
Dimensions: 20.02 (DMS & BDMS) or 19.92 (TS) x 2.82 x 3.58 m.
Maximum Speed: 75 mph.   **Doors:** Power operated sliding.
Couplers: Tightlock.   **Bogies:** BREL BX1.
Multiple Working: Classes 507 & 508.

64649–64691. DMS. Dia. EA208 (*EA211). Lot No. 30979 BREL York 1979–80
(* Facelifted 1998–99 by Wessex Traincare/Alstom Eastleigh). –/68 (*–/66).
36.2 t.
64692–64734. BDMS. Dia. EI203 (*EI204). Lot No. 30981 BREL York 1979–80
(Facelifted 1998–99 by Wessex Traincare/Alstom Eastleigh). –/68 (*–/74).
36.6 t.
71483–71525. TS. Dia. EH218 (*EH246). Lot No. 30980 BREL York 1979–80
(Facelifted 1998–99 by Wessex Traincare/Alstom Eastleigh). –/86 (*–/79).
26.7 t.

Class 508/1. Standard design.

508 102	**MT**	A	*ME*	WK(S)	64650	71484	64693
508 103	**MT**	A	*ME*	BD	64651	71485	64694
508 104	**MT**	A	*ME*	BD	64652	71486	64695
508 108	**MT**	A	*ME*	NB(S)	64656	71490	64699
508 110	**MT**	A	*ME*	KK(S)	64658	71492	64701
508 111	**MT**	A	*ME*	BD	64659	71493	64702
508 112	**MT**	A	*ME*	BD	64660	71494	64703

508 114	**MT**	A	*ME*	BD	64662	71496	64705
508 115	**MT**	A	*ME*	BD	64663	71497	64706
508 117	**MT**	A	*ME*	BD	64665	71499	64708
508 118	**MT**	A	*ME*	BD(S)	64666	71500	64709
508 120	**MT**	A	*ME*	KK(S)	64668	71502	64711
508 122	**MT**	A	*ME*	KK(S)	64670	71504	64713
508 123	**MT**	A	*ME*	NB(S)	64671	71505	64714
508 124	**MT**	A	*ME*	BD	64672	71506	64715
508 125	**MT**	A	*ME*	BD	64673	71507	64716
508 126	**MT**	A	*ME*	BD	64674	71508	64717
508 127	**MT**	A	*ME*	BD	64675	71509	64718
508 128	**MT**	A	*ME*	BD	64676	71510	64719
508 130	**MT**	A	*ME*	BD	64678	71512	64721
508 131	**MT**	A	*ME*	KK(S)	64679	71513	64722
508 134	**MT**	A	*ME*	BD	64682	71516	64725
508 135	**MT**	A	*ME*	NB(S)	64683	71517	64726
508 136	**MT**	A	*ME*	BD	64684	71518	64727
508 137	**MT**	A	*ME*	BD	64685	71519	64728
508 138	**MT**	A	*ME*	BD	64686	71520	64729
508 139	**MT**	A	*ME*	BD	64687	71521	64730
508 140	**MT**	A	*ME*	BD	64688	71522	64731
508 141	**MT**	A	*ME*	BD	64689	71523	64732
508 142	**MT**	A	*ME*	WK(S)	64690	71524	64733
508 143	**MT**	A	*ME*	BD	64691	71525	64734

Class 508/2. Facelifted units for Connex South Eastern.

508 201	*	**CX**	A	*SE*	GI	64649	71483	64692
508 202	*	**CX**	A	*SE*	GI	64653	71487	64696
508 203	*	**CX**	A	*SE*	GI	64654	71488	64697
508 204	*	**CX**	A	*SE*	GI	64655	71489	64698
508 205	*	**CX**	A	*SE*	GI	64657	71491	64700
508 206	*	**CX**	A	*SE*	GI	64661	71495	64714
508 207	*	**CX**	A	*SE*	GI	64664	71498	64707
508 208	*	**CX**	A	*SE*	GI	64667	71501	64710
508 209	*	**CX**	A	*SE*	GI	64669	71503	64712
508 210	*	**CX**	A	*SE*	GI	64677	71511	64720
508 211	*	**CX**	A	*SE*	GI	64680	71514	64723
508 212	*	**CX**	A	*SE*	GI	64681	71515	64724

4.3. EUROSTAR UNITS (CLASS 373)

Eurostar units were built for use on services between Britain and Continental Europe via the Channel Tunnel. They have largely been used for this purpose, but with the following exceptions:

*   Four SNCF-owned units (3203/04/27/28) were removed from the Eurostar pool as surplus during 1999 and are now used on services within Continental Europe only.
*   From May 2000, six 8-car sets will be hired to Great North Eastern Railway for use on services between London King's Cross and York.
*   Regional Eurostar services have yet to commence.

Each train consists of two Eurostar units coupled, with a motor car at each driving end. Services starting from/terminating at London Waterloo International are formed of two 9-car units coupled, whilst those to/from other British destinations will be formed of two 8-car units coupled. All units are articulated with an extra motor bogie on the coach adjacent to the motor car.

DM–MS–4TS–RB–2TF–TBF or DM–MS–3TS–RB–TF–TBF. Gangwayed within pair of units. Air conditioned.
Construction: Steel.
Supply Systems: 25 kV a.c. 50 Hz overhead or 3000 V d.c. overhead or 750 V d.c. third rail (* also equipped for 1500 V d.c. overhead operation).
Wheel Arrangement: Bo–Bo + Bo–2–2–2–2–2–2–2–2.
Length: 22.15 m (DM), 21.85 m (MSOL & TBFOL), 18.70 m (other cars).
Maximum Speed: 300 km/h.
Built: 1992-93 by GEC-Alsthom/Brush/ANF/De Dietrich/BN Construction/ACEC.
Note: DM vehicles carry the set numbers indicated below.

10-Car Sets. Built for services starting from/terminating at London Waterloo. Individual vehicles in each set are allocated numbers 7xxxx0 + 7xxxx1 + 7xxxx2 + 7xxxx3 + 7xxxx4 + 7xxxx5 + 7xxxx6 + 7xxxx8 + 7xxxx9, where xxxx denotes the set number.

Advertising Liveries:
*   3005/06 'The Beatles Yellow Submarine'.

73xxx0 series. DM. Dia. LA501. Lot No. 31118 1992–95. 68.5 t.
73xxx1 series. MS. Dia. LB202. Lot No. 31119 1992–95. –/48 2T. 44.6 t.
73xxx2 series. TS. Dia. LC202. Lot No. 31120 1992–95. –/58 1T. 28.1 t.
73xxx3 series. TS. Dia. LD202. Lot No. 31121 1992–95. –/58 2T. 29.7 t.
73xxx4 series. TS. Dia. LE202. Lot No. 31122 1992–95. –/58 1T. 28.3 t.
73xxx5 series. TS. Dia. LF202. Lot No. 31123 1992–95. –/58 2T. 29.2 t.
73xxx6 series. RB. Dia. LG502. Lot No. 31124 1992–95. 31.1 t.
73xxx7 series. TF. Dia. LH102. Lot No. 31125 1992–95. 39/– 1T. 29.6 t.
73xxx8 series. TF. Dia. LJ102. Lot No. 31126 1992–95. 39/– 1T. 32.2 t.
73xxx9 series.TBF. Dia. LK102. Lot No. 31127 1992–95. 25/– 1TD. 39.4 t.

3001	**EU**	EU	*EU*	NP
3002	**EU**	EU	*EU*	NP
3003	**EU**	EU	*EU*	NP
3004	**EU**	EU	*EU*	NP

3005	**EU**	EU	*EU*	NP
3006	**EU**	EU	*EU*	NP
3007	**EU**	EU	*EU*	NP
3008	**EU**	EU	*EU*	NP

3009	**AL**	EU	*EU*	NP	3206	**EU**	SF	*EU*	LY
3010	**AL**	EU	*EU*	NP	3207*	**EU**	SF	*EU*	LY
3011	**EU**	EU	*EU*	NP	3208*	**EU**	SF	*EU*	LY
3012	**EU**	EU	*EU*	NP	3209	**EU**	SF	*EU*	LY
3013	**EU**	EU	*EU*	NP	3210	**EU**	SF	*EU*	LY
3014	**EU**	EU	*EU*	NP	3211	**EU**	SF	*EU*	LY
3015	**EU**	EU	*EU*	NP	3212	**EU**	SF	*EU*	LY
3016	**EU**	EU	*EU*	NP	3213	**EU**	SF	*EU*	LY
3017	**EU**	EU	*EU*	NP	3214	**EU**	SF	*EU*	LY
3018	**EU**	EU	*EU*	NP	3215*	**EU**	SF	*EU*	LY
3019	**EU**	EU	*EU*	NP	3216*	**EU**	SF	*EU*	LY
3020	**EU**	EU	*EU*	NP	3217	**EU**	SF	*EU*	LY
3021	**EU**	EU	*EU*	NP	3218	**EU**	SF	*EU*	LY
3022	**EU**	EU	*EU*	NP	3219	**EU**	SF	*EU*	LY
3101	**EU**	SB	*EU*	FF	3220	**EU**	SF	*EU*	LY
3102	**EU**	SB	*EU*	FF	3221	**EU**	SF	*EU*	LY
3103	**EU**	SB	*EU*	FF	3222	**EU**	SF	*EU*	LY
3104	**EU**	SB	*EU*	FF	3223*	**EU**	SF	*EU*	LY
3105	**EU**	SB	*EU*	FF	3224*	**EU**	SF	*EU*	LY
3106	**EU**	SB	*EU*	FF	3225*	**EU**	SF	*EU*	LY
3107	**EU**	SB	*EU*	FF	3226*	**EU**	SF	*EU*	LY
3108	**EU**	SB	*EU*	FF	3229*	**EU**	SF	*EU*	LY
3201	* **EU**	SF	*EU*	LY	3230*	**EU**	SF	*EU*	LY
3202	* **EU**	SF	*EU*	LY	3231	**EU**	SF	*EU*	LY
3205	**EU**	SF	*EU*	LY	3232	**EU**	SF	*EU*	LY

8-Car Sets. Built for Regional Eurostar services. Individual vehicles in each set are allocated numbers 7xxxx0 + 7xxxx1 + 7xxxx3 + 7xxxx2 + 7xxxx5 + 7xxxx6 + 7xxxx7 + 7xxxx9, where xxxx denotes the set number.

733xx0 series. DM. Dia. LA502. 68.5 t.
733xx1 series. MS. Dia. LB203. –/48 1T. 44.6 t.
733xx3 series. TS. Dia. LD203. –/58 2T. 29.7 t.
733xx2 series. TS. Dia. LC203. –/58 1T. 28.1 t.
733xx5 series. TS. Dia. LF203. –/58 1T. 29.2 t.
733xx6 series. RB. Dia. LG503. 31.1 t.
733xx7 series. TF. Dia. LH103. 39/– 1T. 29.6 t.
733xx9 series. TBF. Dia. LK103. 18/– 1TD. 39.4 t.

3301	**EU**	EU	*EU*	NP	3308	**EU**	EU	*EU*	NP(S)
3302	**EU**	EU	*EU*	NP	3309	**EU**	EU	*EU*	NP
3303	**EU**	EU	*EU*	NP	3310	**EU**	EU	*EU*	NP
3304	**EU**	EU	*EU*	NP	3311	**EU**	EU	*EU*	NP
3305	**EU**	EU	*EU*	NP	3312	**EU**	EU	*EU*	NP
3306	**EU**	EU	*EU*	NP	3313	**EU**	EU	*EU*	NP(S)
3307	**EU**	EU	*EU*	NP(S)	3314	**EU**	EU	*EU*	NP(S)

Spare DM:

3999	**EU**	EU	*EU*	NP	

4.4. SERVICE EMUS

CLASS 316   TEST UNIT

BDB–M–DT. Gangwayed within unit. Converted from Class 307. Test bed for
Class 323 electrical equipment.
Construction: Steel.
Supply System: 25 kV a.c. 50 Hz overhead or 750 V d.c. third rail.
Traction Motors: Four Holec DMKT52/24 of 146 kW each.
Dimensions: 20.31 (BDB & DT) or 20.18 (M) x 2.82 x 3.86 m.
Maximum Speed: 75 mph.   **Doors:** Manually operated slam.
Couplings: Buckeye.   **Bogies:** Gresley ED7/B4.
Multiple Working:

61018. M. Dia. EZ   . Lot No. 30203 Eastleigh 1954–56. Converted BR, Derby
    1992. . t.
75018. DT. Dia. EZ   . Lot No. 30206 Eastleigh 1954–56. Converted BR, Derby
    1992. . t.
75118. BDB. Dia. EZ   . Lot No. 30205 Eastleigh 1954–56. Converted BR, Derby
    1992. . t.

316 997	**BG**	SO		EH(S)	75118 61018 75018

CLASS 930/0   SANDITE & DE-ICING UNITS

DMB–DMB. Gangwayed within unit. Converted from Class 405.
Construction: Steel.   **Supply System:** 750 V d.c. third rail.
Traction Motors: Two English Electric 507 of 185 kW each per car.
Maximum Speed: 75 mph.   **Doors:** Manually operated slam.
Couplings: Buckeye.   **Bogies:** Central 43 inch.
Multiple Working: SR type.   **Dimensions:** 19.05 x 2.74 x 3.99 m.

977586/587/604/605. DMB. Dia. EZ512. Lot No. 3231 SR Eastleigh 1947. 39.0 t.
975588/589/592/595/597–600/602/603. DMB. Dia. EZ512 Lot No. 1060. SR
    Eastleigh 1941. 39.0 t.
975590/591/596/601. DMB. Dia. EZ512. Lot No. 3384 Eastleigh 1948. 39.0 t.
975593/594. DMB. Dia. EZ512. Lot No. 3618 Eastleigh 1950. 39.0 t.
975896/897. DMB. Dia. EZ512. Lot No. 3506 Eastleigh 1950. 39.0 t.

930 001	**RO**	RK		AF(S)	975596	975605
930 002	**RO**	RK	*RK*	RM	975896	975897
930 003	**RO**	RK	*RK*	SU	975594	975595
930 004	**RO**	RK	*RK*	WD	975586	975587
930 005	**RK**	RK	*RK*	WD	975588	975589
930 006	**RO**	RK	*RK*	WD	975590	975591
930 007	**RO**	RK	*RK*	GI	975592	975593
930 008	**RK**	RK	*RK*	GI	975604	975597
930 009	**N**	RK	*RK*	BI	975598	975599
930 010	**RK**	RK	*RK*	BI	975600	975601
930 011	**RO**	RK	*RK*	SU	975602	975603

CLASS 930/1   TRACTOR UNIT

DMB–DMB. Gangwayed within unit.
Construction: Steel.
Supply System: 750 V d.c. third rail.
Traction Motors: Two English Electric 507 of 185 kW each per motor car.
Dimensions: 20.42 x 2.82 x 3.86 m.
Maximum Speed: 90 mph.   **Doors:** Manually operated slam.
Couplings: Buckeye.   **Multiple Working:** SR type.
Bogies: Mk. 4 or Mk. 3B/Commonwealth.
Note: Official RSL unit number is 930 101.

977207. DMB. Dia. EZ522. Lot No. 30388 Eastleigh 1958. 40.5 t.
977609. DMB. Dia. EZ522. Lot No. 30617 Eastleigh 1961. 40.5 t.

930 014   **N**   R K   AF(S)   977207 977609

CLASS 930/0   SANDITE & DE-ICING TRAILERS

DT. Non gangwayed. Converted from Class 416/2.
Construction: Steel.
Dimensions: 20.44 x 2.82 x 3.86 m.   **Bogies:** Mark 3D.
Maximum Speed: 75 mph.   **Doors:** Manually operated slam.
Couplings: Buckeye with additional Tightlock at non driving ends only.
Multiple Working: With Classes 317 and 319.

975578/579. DT. Dia. EZ526. Lot No. 30117 Eastleigh 1954. 32.5 t.

930 078   **RO**   R K   *RK*   HE   977578
930 079   **N**   R K   *RK*   SU   977579

CLASS 930/0   ROUTE LEARNING UNIT

DM–TB–DM. Gangwayed within unit. Converted from Class 411/4.
Construction: Steel.
Supply System: 750 V d.c. third rail.
Traction Motors: Two English Electric 507 of 185 kW each per motor car.
Dimensions: 20.34 x 2.82 x 3.83 m.
Maximum Speed: 90 mph.   **Doors:** Manually operated slam.
Couplings: Buckeye.   **Bogies:** Mk. 4/Commonwealth.
Multiple Working: SR type.

977861. DM. Dia. EZ536. Lot No. 30111 Eastleigh 1956. 44.2 t.
977862. TB. Dia. EZ542. Lot No. 30110 Eastleigh 1956. 36.2 t.
977863. DM. Dia. EZ536. Lot No. 30108 Eastleigh 1956. 43.5 t.

930 082   **CX**   SC   *OT*   SU   977861 977862 977863

CLASS 930/1   SANDITE UNIT

DMB–DMB. Gangwayed within unit. Converted from Class 416.
Construction: Steel.   **Supply System:** 750 V d.c. third rail.
Traction Motors: Two English Electric 507 of 185 kW each per motor car.
Dimensions: 19.23 x 2.74 x 3.99 m.   **Doors:** Manually operated slam.
Maximum Speed: 75 mph.   **Bogies:** Central 40 inch.
Couplings: Buckeye.   **Multiple Working:** SR type.

977533. DMB. Dia. EZ512. Lot No. 4016 Eastleigh 1954–55. 40.5 t.
977534. DMB. Dia. EZ512. Lot No. 4099 Eastleigh 1955–56. 40.5 t.

930 102	**RO**	RK	*RK*	FR	977533 977534

CLASS 930/2   SANDITE & DE-ICING UNITS

DMB–DMB. Gangwayed within unit. Converted from Class 416/2.
Construction: Steel.   **Supply System:** 750 V d.c. third rail.
Traction Motors: Two English Electric 507 of 185 kW each per motor car.
Dimensions: 20.44 x 2.82 x 3.86 m.   **Doors:** Manually operated slam.
Maximum Speed: 75 mph.   **Bogies:** Mk. 3B.
Couplings: Buckeye.   **Multiple Working:** SR type.

977566/567. DMB. Dia. EZ525. Lot No. 30116 Eastleigh 1954–55. 40.5 t.
977804/864. DMB. Dia. EZ522. Lot No. 30119 Eastleigh 1954. 40.5 t.
977805/865/871. DMB. Dia. EZ522. Lot No. 30167 Eastleigh 1955. 40.5 t.
977872/924/925. DMB. Dia. EZ522. Lot. No. 30314. Eastleigh 1956–58. 40.5 t.
977874/875. DMB. Dia. EZ522. Lot No. 30114 Eastleigh 1954. 40.5 t.

930 201	**RO**	RK	*RK*	FR	977566 977567
930 202	**RK**	RK	*RK*	FR	977804 977805
930 203	**RO**	RK	*RK*	RM	977864 977865
930 204	**N**	RK	*RK*	RM	977874 977875
930 205	**RO**	RK	*RK*	RM	977871 977872
930 206	**RO**	RK	*RK*	WD	977924 977925

CLASS 931   ROUTE LEARNING UNITS

DT–DMB or DMB–DT. Gangwayed within unit. Converted from Class 416/2.
Construction: Steel.   **Supply System:** 750 V d.c. third rail.
Traction Motors: Two English Electric 507 of 185 kW each.
Dimensions: 20.44 x 2.82 x 3.86 m.   **Doors:** Manually operated slam.
Maximum Speed: 75 mph.   **Bogies:** Mk. 3B.
Couplings: Buckeye.   **Multiple Working:** SR type.

977856. DT. Dia. EZ541. Lot No. 30168 Eastleigh 1955. 30.5 t.
977857. DMB. Dia. EZ522. Lot No. 30167 Eastleigh 1955. 40.5 t.
977917. DMB. Dia. EZ522. Lot No. 30119 Eastleigh 1954. 40.5 t.
977918. DT. Dia. EZ541. Lot No. 30120 Eastleigh 1954. 30.5 t.

931 001	**N**	SE	*OT*	RM	977856 977857
931 002	**N**	SE	*OT*	RM	977917 977918

CLASS 931 TRACTOR UNIT

DMB–DMB. Gangwayed within unit. Converted from Class 416/2.
Construction: Steel.   **Supply System:** 750 V d.c. third rail.
Traction Motors: Two English Electric 507 of 185 kW each per motor car.
Dimensions: 20.44 x 2.82 x 3.86 m.   **Doors:** Manually operated slam.
Maximum Speed: 75 mph.   **Bogies:** Mk. 3B.
Couplings: Buckeye.   **Multiple Working:** SR type.

977559/560. DMB. Dia. EZ525. Lot No. 30116 Eastleigh 1954-55. 40.5 t.

931 062	**N**	SE	*OT*	RM	977559	977560	The Sprinkler

CLASS 932 TEST UNITS

DM–TB–T–DM. Gangwayed throughout. Converted from Class 411. Test units
for manufacturers' traction packages.
Construction: Steel.
Supply System: 750 V d.c. third rail or 25 kV a.c. 50 Hz overhead (* 15 kV a.c.
16.7 Hz overhead).
Traction Motors: Adtranz. († Two EE 507 of 185 kW each (61948); Alstom (61949).
Maximum Speed: **Doors:** Manually operated slam.
Couplings: Buckeye.   **Multiple Working:** SR type.
Bogies: Mk. 4 /Commonwealth.   **Dimensions:** 20.34 x 2.82 x 3.83 m.
Non Standard Liveries:
* 932 545 is Adtranz blue with a white stripe.
* 932 620 has one side of each car painted in GEC-Alsthom white and orange livery and the other side of each car painted in livery **P**.
Note: 932 545 is currently based at the Adtranz works at Västerås, Sweden.

61358/359. DM. Dia. EZ5   . Lot No. 30454 Eastleigh 1958–59.
61948/949. DM. Dia. EZ5   . Lot No. 30708 Eastleigh 1963.
70330. TB. Dia. EZ5   . Lot No. 30456 Eastleigh 1958–59.
70653. TB. Dia. EZ5   . Lot No. 30709 Eastleigh 1963.
70660. PT. Dia. EZ   . Lot No. 30710 Eastleigh 1963.

| 932 545 | * | **0** | P | *AD* | Sweden | 61359 | 70330 | | 61358 |
| 932 620 | † | **0** | P | *AM* | IL | 61948 | 70653 | 70660 | 61949 |

CLASS 936/0 SANDITE UNIT

DM–DTB. Gangwayed throughout. Converted from Class 501.
Construction: Steel.   **Supply System:** 750 V d.c. third rail.
Traction Motors: Four GEC of 137 kW each.
Dimensions: 18.47 x 2.90 x 3.86 m.   **Doors:** Manually operated slam.
Maximum Speed: 70 mph.   **Bogies:** BR2.
Couplings: Buckeye.   **Multiple Working:** SR type.

977349. DM. Dia. EZ504. Lot No. 30326 Eastleigh 1957–58. 48.0 t.
977350. DTB. Dia. EZ506. Lot No. 30328 Eastleigh 1957–58. 30.5 t.

936 003	**MD**	RK	*RK*	BD	977349	977350

CLASS 937   SANDITE UNIT

BDT–MB–DT. Gangwayed within unit. Converted from Class 308.
Construction: Steel.
Supply System: 25 kV a.c. 50 Hz overhead.
Traction Motors: Four English Electric 536A of 143.5 kW each.
Dimensions: 19.88 (BDT & DT) or 19.35 (MB) x 2.82 x 3.86 m.
Maximum Speed: 75 mph.   **Doors:** Manually operated slam.
Couplings: Buckeye.   **Bogies:** Gresley ED5/ET5.
Multiple Working: Classes 303–312 only.

977876/926. BDT. Dia. EZ545. Lot No. 30656 York 1961. 36.3 t.
977877/927. MB. Dia. EZ546. Lot No. 30657 York 1961. 55.0 t.
977878/928. DT. Dia. EZ547. Lot No. 30659 York 1961. 33.0 t.

| 937 990 | **N** | RK | *RK* | EM | 977876 | 977877 | 977878 |
| 937 991 | **N** | RK | *RK* | IL | 977926 | 977927 | 977928 |

UNCLASSIFIED   GENERATOR COACH

QXA. Gangwayed throughout. Converted from Class 438. Operates with
999550.
Construction: Steel.   **Dimensions:** 20.18 x 2.82 x 3.81 m.
Maximum Speed: 90 mph.   **Doors:** Manually operated slam.
Couplings: Buckeye.   **Bogies:** B5 (SR).

977335. QXA. Dia. QX174. Lot No. 30764 York 1966–67. 32.0 t.

| – | **SO** | SO | *SO* | ZA | 977335 |

UNCLASSIFIED   LUL TRACK RECORDING CAR

T. LUL Track Recording Car. Converted from 1973 tube stock.
Construction: Steel.   **Dimensions:**
Maximum Speed: 70 mph.   **Doors:** Power operated sliding.
Couplings: Buckeye.   **Bogies:** LT design.
Non Standard Livery: White with blue lower body stripe and red doors.
Note: Also carries LUL number TRC666.

999666. T. Dia. EZ548. Metropolitan Cammell 1974. Converted BREL Derby
1987. 23.8 t.

| – | **0** | LU | *OT* | WR | 999666 |

4.5. VEHICLES AWAITING DISPOSAL

25 kV a.c. 50 Hz OVERHEAD EMUS

Complete Units:

302 201	**N**	H	PY(S)	75085	61060	70060	75033
302 204	**N**	H	PY(S)	75088	61063	70063	75036
302 213	**N**	H	PY(S)	75097	61072	70072	75060
302 216	**N**	H	PY(S)	75100	61075	70075	75063
302 218	**N**	H	PY(S)	75191	61077	70077	75065
302 221	**N**	H	PY(S)	75194	61080	70080	75068
302 224	**N**	H	PY(S)	75197	61083	70083	75071
302 225	**N**	H	PY(S)	75198	61084	70084	75072
302 226	**N**	H	PY(S)	75199	61085	70085	75073
302 227	**N**	H	PY(S)	75325	61193	70193	75250
302 228	**N**	H	PY(S)	75201	61087	70087	75075
302 230	**N**	H	PY(S)	75205	61091	70091	75079
936 103	**RO**	RK	GW(S)	977844	977845	977846	
936 104	**RO**	RK	YO(S)	977847	977848	977849	

Spare Cars:

Cl. 307	**BG**	E		KN(S)	75023

750 V d.c. THIRD RAIL EMUS

Complete Units:

4308	**N**	H	PY(S)	61275	75395		
5001	**G**	H	KN(S)	14001	15207	15101	14002
5176	**B**	H	KN(S)	14352	15396	15354	14351
6213	**BG**	H	PY(S)	65327	77512		
6308	**N**	H	PY(S)	14564	16108		
6309	**N**	H	PY(S)	14562	16106		
6402	**N**	H	PY(S)	65362	77547		
7001	**N**	P	ZG(S)	67300	67301		
9003	**B**	P	BM(S)	68003			
9007	**J**	P	BM(S)	68007			
9009	**J**	P	BM(S)	68009			
931 090	**J**	P	BM(S)	68010			
931 092	**N**	P	BM(S)	68002			
931 094	**N**	P	BM(S)	68004			
931 095	**J**	P	BM(S)	68005			
931 098	**N**	P	BM(S)	68008			

Spare Cars:

Cl. 422	**N**	P	ZG(S)	69302	69304	69306	69307
Cl. 422	**N**	P	ZG(S)	69316	69318	69333	69335

5. LOCO-HAULED NON-PASSENGER-CARRYING COACHING STOCK

The notes shown for locomotive-hauled passenger stock generally apply also to non-passenger-carrying coaching stock (often abbreviated to NPCCS).

TOPS TYPE CODES

TOPS type codes for NPCCS are made up as follows:

(1) Two letters denoting the type of the vehicle:

AX	Nightstar generator van
AY	Eurostar barrier Vehicle
NA	Propelling control vehicle.
NB	High security brake van (100 m.p.h.).
NC	Gangwayed brake van modified for newspaper conveyance (100 m.p.h.).
ND	Gangwayed brake van (90 m.p.h.).
NE	Gangwayed brake van (100 m.p.h.).
NF	Gangwayed brake van with guard's safety equipment removed.
NG	Motorail loading wagon.
NH	Gangwayed brake van (110 m.p.h.).
NI	High security brake van (110 m.p.h.).
NJ	General utility van (90 m.p.h.).
NK	High security general utility van (100 m.p.h.).
NL	Newspaper van.
NN	Courier vehicle.
NO	General utility van (100 m.p.h. e.t.h. wired).
NP	General utility van for post office use or Motorail van (110 m.p.h.).
NR	BAA container van (100 m.p.h.).
NS	Post office sorting van.
NT	Post office stowage van.
NU	Brake post office stowage van.
NV	Motorail van (side loading).
NX	Motorail van (100 m.p.h.).
NY	Exhibition van.
NZ	Driving brake van (also known as driving van trailer).
QS	EMU translator vehicle.
YR	Ferry van (special Southern Region version of NJ with two pairs of side doors instead of three).

(2) A third letter denoting the brake type:

A	Air braked
V	Vacuum braked
X	Dual braked

OPERATING CODES

The normal operating codes are given in parentheses after the TOPS type codes. These are as follows:

BG	Gangwayed brake van.

BPOT   Brake post office stowage van.
DLV   Driving brake van (also known as driving van trailer – DVT).
GUV   General utility van.
PCV   Propelling control van.
POS   Post office sorting van.
POT   Post office stowage van.

AK51 (RK)   KITCHEN CAR

Dia. AK503. Mark 1. Converted 1989 from RBR. Fluorescent lighting. Commonwealth bogies. ETH 2X.

Lot No. 30628 Pressed Steel 1960–61. 39 t.

Note: Kitchen cars have traditionally been numbered in the NPCCS series, but have passenger coach diagram numbers!

80041	(1690)	x	CC	RS	*ON*	BN

NN   COURIER VEHICLE

Dia. NN504. Mark 1. Converted 1986–7 from BSKs. One compartment retained for courier use. Roller shutter doors. ETH 2.

80207. Lot No. 30721 Wolverton 1963. Commonwealth bogies. 37 t.
80211–7/23. Lot No. 30699 Wolverton 1962. Commonwealth bogies. 37 t.
80220. Lot No. 30573 Gloucester 1960. B4 bogies. 33 t.

Non-Standard Livery: 80211 is purple.

80207	(35466)	x	PC	VS	*ON*	SL
80211	(35296)		O	CN		FK
80212	(35307)	x	RM	E		OM
80213	(35316)	x	CH	RV	*ON*	CP
80217	(35299)	x	M	14	*OS*	NY
80220	(35276)	x	G	WT		BQ
80223	(35331)	x	RY	CN		DY

Name: 80207 is branded 'BAGGAGE CAR No.11'.

NP   POST OFFICE GUV

Dia. NP502. Mark 1. Converted 1991–93 from newspaper vans. Short frames (57'). Originally converted from GUV. Fluorescent lighting, toilet and gangways fitted. Load 14 t. B5 bogies. ETH 3X.

Lot No. 30922 Wolverton or Doncaster 1977–78. 31 t.

80251	(86467, 94017)	x	RM	E	TE
80252	(86718, 94022)		RM	E	TE
80253	(86170, 94018)		RM	E	OM
80254	(86082, 94012)	x	RM	E	OM
80255	(86098, 94019)	x	RM	E	OM
80256	(86408, 94013)	x	RM	E	OM
80258	(86651, 94002)		RM	E	OM
80259	(86845, 94005)	x	RM	E	OM

NS (POS)   POST OFFICE SORTING VAN

Used in travelling post office (TPO) trains. Mark 1. Various diagrams.

The following lots have BR Mark 1 bogies except * B5 bogies. (subtract 2 t from weight).

80303–80305. Lot No. 30486 Wolverton 1959. Dia. NS501. Originally built with nets for collecting mail bags in motion. Equipment now removed. ETH 3X. 36 t.
80306–80308. Lot No. 30487 Wolverton 1959. Dia. NS502. ETH 3. 36 t.
80309–80314. Lot No. 30661 Wolverton 1961. Dia. NS501. ETH 3. 37 t.
80315–80316. Lot No. 30662 Wolverton 1961. Dia. NS501. ETH 3X. 36 t.

80303	x*	**RM**	E		OM	80310	v	**RM** E	OM
80305	v	**RM**	E		OM	80312	v	**RM** E	OM
80306	v	**RM**	E		OM	80314	x*	**RM** E	OM
80308	x*	**RM**	E		OM	80315	v	**RM** E	OM
80309	x*	**RM**	E		OM	80316	x*	**RM** E	OM

The following lots are pressure ventilated and have B5 bogies.

80319–80327. Dia. NS504. Lot No. 30778 York 1968–69. ETH 4. 35 t.
80328–80338. Dia. NS505. Lot No. 30779 York 1968–69. ETH 4. 35 t.
80339–80355. Dia. NS506. Lot No. 30780 York 1968–69. ETH 4. 35 t.

80319		**RM**	E	*E*	EN	80338	**RM**	E		Bristol E. Yd.
80320		**RM**	E	*E*	EN	80339	**RM**	E	*E*	BK
80321		**RM**	E	*E*	BK	80340	**RM**	E	*E*	BK
80322		**RM**	E	*E*	EN	80341	**RM**	E	*E*	EN
80323		**RM**	E	*E*	EN	80342	**RM**	E	*E*	BK
80324		**RM**	E	*E*	EN	80343	**RM**	E	*E*	BK
80325		**RM**	E	*E*	EN	80344	**RM**	E	*E*	BK
80326		**RM**	E	*E*	EN	80345	**RM**	E	*E*	EN
80327		**RM**	E	*E*	BK	80346	**RM**	E	*E*	EN
80328		**RM**	E		OM	80347	**RM**	E	*E*	EN
80329		**RM**	E		OM	80348	**RM**	E	*E*	BZ
80330		**RM**	E		Bristol Pylle Hill	80349	**RM**	E	*E*	EN
80331		**RM**	E	*E*	EN	80350	**RM**	E	*E*	BK
80332		**RM**	E	*E*	EN	80351	**RM**	E	*E*	EN
80333		**RM**	E	*E*	EN	80352	**RM**	E	*E*	BK
80334		**RM**	E	*E*	BK	80353	**RM**	E	*E*	EN
80335	x	**RM**	E		OM	80354	**RM**	E	*E*	BK
80336		**RM**	E		Bristol E. Yd.	80355	**RM**	E	*E*	EN
80337		**RM**	E	*E*	NC					

Names:

80320	The Borders Mail	80339	Brian Quinn
80327	George James		

80356–80380. Lot No. 30839 York 1972–73. Dia. NS501. Pressure ventilated. Fluorescent lighting. B5 bogies. ETH 4X. 37 t.

80356	**RM** E	*E*		BK	80357	**RM** E	*E*		BK

80358	RM	E	*E*	EN	80370	RM	E	*E*	BK
80359	RM	E	*E*	BK	80371	RM	E	*E*	BZ
80360	RM	E	*E*	EN	80372	RM	E	*E*	EN
80361	RM	E	*E*	EN	80373	RM	E	*E*	EN
80362	RM	E	*E*	EN	80374	RM	E	*E*	EN
80363	RM	E	*E*	BK	80375	RM	E	*E*	BK
80364	RM	E	*E*	BK	80376	RM	E	*E*	BK
80365	RM	E	*E*	EN	80377	RM	E	*E*	EN
80366	RM	E	*E*	EN	80378	RM	E	*E*	EN
80367	RM	E	*E*	EN	80379	RM	E	*E*	EN
80368	RM	E	*E*	BK	80380	RM	E	*E*	BZ
80369	RM	E	*E*	EN					

Names:

80360	Derek Carter		80367	M.G. Berry

80381–80395. Lot No. 30900 Wolverton 1977. Dia NS531. Converted from SK. Pressure ventilated. Fluorescent lighting. B5 bogies. ETH 4X. 38 t.

80381	(25112)	RM E	*E*	EN	80389	(25103)	RM E			ZG
80382	(25109)	RM E	*E*	EN	80390	(25047)	RM E	*E*	EN
80383	(25033)	RM E	*E*	EN	80392	(25082)	RM E	*E*	EN
80384	(25078)	RM E	*E*	EN	80393	(25118)	RM E	*E*	EN
80385	(25083)	RM E	*E*	EN	80394	(25156)	RM E	*E*	EN
80386	(25099)	RM E	*E*	EN	80395	(25056)	RM E	*E*	EN
80387	(25045)	RM E	*E*	EN					

Name: 80390 Ernie Gosling

NT (POT)   POST OFFICE STOWAGE VAN

Mark 1. Open vans used for stowage of mail bags in conjunction with POS.

Lot No. 30488 Wolverton 1959. Dia. NT502. Originally built with nets for collecting mail bags in motion. Equipment now removed. B5 bogies. ETH 3. 35 t.

80400	RM	E	*E*	BK	80402	RM	E	*E*	BK
80401	RM	E	*E*	EN					

The following eight vehicles were converted at York from BSK to lot 30143 (80403) and 30229 (80404–80414). No new lot number was issued. Dia. NT503. B5 bogies. 35 t. (* Dia. NT501 BR2 bogies 38 t. ETH 3 (3X*).

80403	(34361)	RM E	*E*	BZ	80411	(35003)	*	RM E	*E*	BZ
80404	(35014)	RM E	*E*	BZ	80412	(35002)	*	RM E	*E*	EN
80405	(35009)	RM E	*E*	BZ	80413	(35004)	*	RM E	*E*	EN
80406	(35022)	RM E	*E*	EN	80414	(35005)	*	RM E	*E*	EN

Lot No. 30781 York 1968. Dia. NT505. Pressure ventilated. B5 bogies. ETH 4. 34 t.

80415	RM	E	*E*	EN	80419	RM	E	*E*	EN
80416	RM	E	*E*	EN	80420	RM	E	*E*	BK
80417	RM	E	*E*	EN	80421	RM	E	*E*	EN

| 80422 | | **RM** E | *E* | EN | | 80424 | | **RM** E | *E* | EN |
| 80423 | | **RM** E | *E* | EN | | | | | | |

Lot No. 30840 York 1973. Dia. NT504. Pressure ventilated. fluorescent lighting. B5 bogies. ETH 4X. 35 t.

80425		**RM** E	*E*	BK		80428		**RM** E	*E*	EN
80426		**RM** E	*E*	EN		80429		**RM** E	*E*	BK
80427		**RM** E	*E*	EN		80430		**RM** E	*E*	EN

Lot No. 30901 Wolverton 1977. converted from SK. Dia. NT521. Pressure ventilated. Fluorescent lighting. B5 bogies. ETH 4X. 35 t.

80431	(25104)	**RM** E	*E*	EN		80436	(25077)	**RM** E	*E*	EN
80432	(25071)	**RM** E	*E*	EN		80437	(25068)	**RM** E	*E*	EN
80433	(25150)	**RM** E	*E*	BK		80438	(25139)	**RM** E	*E*	BK
80434	(25119)	**RM** E	*E*	EN		80439	(25127)	**RM** E	*E*	BK
80435	(25117)	**RM** E	*E*	EN						

NU (BPOT)   BRAKE POST OFFICE STOWAGE VAN

Dia. NU502. Mark 1. As NT but with brake compartment. Pressure ventilated. B5 bogies. ETH4.

Lot No. 30782 York 1968. 36 t.

| 80456 | | **RM** E | *E* | EN | | 80458 | | **RM** E | *E* | EN |
| 80457 | | **RM** E | *E* | EN | | | | | | |

NZ (DLV)   DRIVING BRAKE VAN (110 m.p.h.)

Dia. NZ501. Mark 3B. Air conditioned. T4 bogies. dg. ETH 5X.

Lot No. 31042 Derby 1988. 45.18 t.

82101	**V**	P	*VW*	OY		82121	**V**	P	*VW*	PC
82102		P	*VW*	OY		82122	**V**	P	*VW*	MA
82103	**V**	P	*VW*	OY		82123	**V**	P	*VW*	PC
82104	**V**	P	*VW*	PC		82124	**V**	P	*VW*	PC
82105	**V**	P	*VW*	PC		82125	**V**	P	*VW*	PC
82106	**V**	P	*VW*	OY		82126	**V**	P	*VW*	OY
82107		P	*VW*	PC		82127	**V**	P	*VW*	OY
82108	**V**	P	*VW*	PC		82128	**V**	P	*VW*	OY
82109	**V**	P	*VW*	PC		82129	**V**	P	*VW*	OY
82110	**V**	P	*VW*	PC		82130	**V**	P	*VW*	MA
82111	**V**	P	*VW*	PC		82131	**V**	P	*VW*	OY
82112	**V**	P	*VW*	PC		82132	**V**	P	*VW*	OY
82113	**V**	P	*VW*	OY		82133	**V**	P	*VW*	OY
82114		P	*VW*	MA		82134	**V**	P	*VW*	OY
82115	**V**	P	*VW*	MA		82135	**V**	P	*VW*	MA
82116	**V**	P	*VW*	PC		82136		P	*VW*	MA
82117	**V**	P	*VW*	PC		82137	**V**	P	*VW*	MA
82118	**V**	P	*VW*	OY		82138	**V**	P	*VW*	PC
82119	**V**	P	*VW*	MA		82139	**V**	P	*VW*	PC
82120	**V**	P	*VW*	MA		82140	**V**	P	*VW*	MA

82141	V	P	*VW*	MA	82147	V	P	*VW*	MA
82142	V	P	*VW*	MA	82148	V	P	*VW*	PC
82143	V	P	*VW*	OY	82149	V	P	*VW*	PC
82144	V	P	*VW*	OY	82150	V	P	*VW*	PC
82145	V	P	*VW*	MA	82151		P	*VW*	OY
82146	V	P	*VW*	MA	82152	V	P	*VW*	MA

Names:

82115	Liverpool John Moores University
82120	Liverpool Chamber of Commerce
82121	Carlisle Cathedral
82124	The Girls' Brigade
82126	G8 Summit Birmingham 1998
82127	Abraham Darby
82132	INDUSTRY 96 West Midlands
82134	Sir Henry Doulton 1820–1897
82135	Spirit of Cumbria
82147	The Red Devils
82148	International Spring Fair
82149	101 Squadron

NZ (DLV)   DRIVING BRAKE VAN (140 m.p.h.)

Dia. NZ502. Mark 4. Air conditioned. Swiss-built (SIG) bogies. dg. ETH 6X.

Lot No. 31043 Metro-Cammell 1988. 45.18 t.

82200	GN	H	*GN*	BN	82216	GN	H	*GN*	BN
82201	GN	H	*GN*	BN	82217	GN	H	*GN*	BN
82202	GN	H	*GN*	BN	82218	GN	H	*GN*	BN
82203	GN	H	*GN*	BN	82219	GN	H	*GN*	BN
82204	GN	H	*GN*	BN	82220	GN	H	*GN*	BN
82205	GN	H	*GN*	BN	82221	GN	H	*GN*	BN
82206	GN	H	*GN*	BN	82222	GN	H	*GN*	BN
82207	GN	H	*GN*	BN	82223	GN	H	*GN*	BN
82208	GN	H	*GN*	BN	82224	GN	H	*GN*	BN
82209	GN	H	*GN*	BN	82225	GN	H	*GN*	BN
82210	GN	H	*GN*	BN	82226	GN	H	*GN*	BN
82211	GN	H	*GN*	BN	82227	GN	H	*GN*	BN
82212	GN	H	*GN*	BN	82228	GN	H	*GN*	BN
82213	GN	H	*GN*	BN	82229	GN	H	*GN*	BN
82214	GN	H	*GN*	BN	82230	GN	H	*GN*	BN
82215	GN	H	*GN*	BN	82231	GN	H	*GN*	BN

ND (BG)   GANGWAYED BRAKE VAN (90 m.p.h.)

Dia. ND501. Mark 1. Short-frames (57'). Load 10t. All vehicles were built with BR Mark 1 bogies. ETH 1. Vehicles numbered 81xxx had 3000 added to the original numbers to avoid confusion with Class 81 locomotives. The full lot number list is listed here for reference purposes with renumbered vehicles. No unmodified vehicles remain in service.

80525. Lot No. 30009 Derby 1952–53. 31 t.
80621. Lot No. 30046 York 1954. 31.5 t.
80700. Lot No. 30136 Metro-Cammell 1955. 31.5 t.
80731–80791. Lot No. 30140 BRCW 1955–56. 31.5 t.
80826–80848. Lot No. 30144 Cravens 1955. 31.5 t.
80855–80960. Lot No. 30162 Pressed Steel 1956–57. 32 t.
80971–81014. Lot No. 30173 York 1956. 31.5 t.
81025–81051. Lot No. 30224 Cravens 1956. 31.5 t.
81055–81175. Lot No. 30228 Metro-Cammell 1957–58. 31.5 t.
81182–81188. Lot No. 30234 Cravens 1956–57. 31.5 t.
81205–81265. Lot No. 30163 Pressed Steel 1957. 31.5 t.
81266–81309. Lot No. 30323 Pressed Steel 1957. 32 t.
81316–81497. Lot No. 30400 Pressed Steel 1957–58. 32 t.
81498–81568. Lot No. 30484 Pressed Steel 1958. 32 t.
81590. Lot No. 30715 Gloucester 1962. 31 t.
81604–81606. Lot No. 30716 Gloucester 1962. 31 t.

The following converted NDs are in service:

84025. ND rebogied with Commonwealth bogies (add 1.5 t to weight) and adapted
for use as exhibition van 1998 at Lancastrian Carriage & Wagon Co. Ltd.
84382/7/477. Dia. NB501. High security brake van. Converted 1985 at Wembley Heavy Repair Depot from ND. Gangways removed. B4 bogies.

84025	(81025)	v	**M**	RA	CP
84382	(81382, 80460)	x	**RX**	E	Cambridge Coalfields Sdgs.
84387	(81387, 80461)	x	**B**	E	CW
84477	(81477, 80463)	x	**B**	E	CW

NJ (GUV)   GENERAL UTILITY VAN

Dia. NJ501. Mark 1. Short frames. Load 14 t. Screw couplings. These vehicles
had 7000 added to the original numbers to avoid confusion with Class 86
locomotives. The full lot number list is listed here for reference purposes with
renumbered vehicles. No unmodified vehicles remain in service. All vehicles
were built with BR Mark 2 bogies. ETH 0 or 0X*.

86081–86499. Lot No. 30417 Pressed Steel 1958–59. 30 t.
86508–86518. Lot No. 30343 York 1957. 30 t.
86521–86651. Lot No. 30403 York/Glasgow 1958–60. 30 t.
86656–86834. Lot No. 30565 Pressed Steel 1959. 30 t.
86836–86978. Lot No. 30616 Pressed Steel 1959–60. 30 t.

NE/NH (BG)   GANGWAYED BRAKE VAN (100/110 m.p.h.)

NE are ND but rebogied with B4 bogies suitable for 100 m.p.h. NH are identical but are allowed to run at 110 m.p.h. with special maintenance of the bogies. For lot numbers refer to original number series. Deduct 1.5t from weights.
All NHA are *pg. ETH 1 (1X*).

Non-standard Livery: 92116 is purple.

92100	(81391)	to	RV	CP
92111	(81432)	NHA	H	CP

92114	(81443)		NHA		H		LT
92116	(81450)		to	0	CN		FK
92125	(81470)		to		DR		SD
92146	(81498)		NHA		H		LT
92159	(81534)		NHA		H	SR	IS
92174	(81567)		NHA		H	SR	IS
92175	(81568)		pg		H		CP
92193	(81604)		pg		E		Preston Station
92194	(81606)		to		H	SR	IS
92234	(81336, 84336)	*		RX	E		DY
92238	(81563, 84563)			RY	E		DY
92252	(80959)	x*		RY	E		BK
92261	(80988)	x*		RY	E		BK
92267	(81404, 84404)	x			E		BK

NE (BG)   GANGWAYED BRAKE VAN (100 m.p.h.)

As ND but rebogied with Commonwealth bogies suitable for 100 m.p.h. ETH 1 (1X*). For lot numbers refer to original number series. Add 1.5 t to weights to allow for the increased weight of the Commonwealth bogies.

92302	(81501, 84501)		RX	E	KM
92303	(81427, 84427)		RX	E	DY
92306	(81217, 84217)	*	RY	E	KM
92309	(81043, 84043)	x*	RX	E	Arpley Yard
92311	(81453, 84453)	x	RY	E	CW
92312	(81548, 84548)		RX	E	KM
92314	(80777)	x*	RY	E	CW
92316	(80980)	x*	RY	E	KM
92319	(81055, 84055)	*	RY	E	KM
92321	(81566, 84566)		RY	E	FK
92323	(80832)	*	R	E	KM
92324	(81087, 84087)		RY	E	KM
92325	(80791)		RY	E	KM
92328	(80999)	x*	RY	E	KM
92329	(81001, 84001)	*	RY	E	KM
92330	(80995)	x*	RY	E	KM
92332	(80845)	*	RX	E	KM
92333	(80982)	*	RY	E	KM
92337	(81140, 84140)	*	RX	E	KM
92340	(81059, 84059)	*	RY	E	KM
92341	(81316, 84316)	x	RY	E	KM
92343	(81505, 84505)	x	R	E	KM
92344	(81154, 84154)	*	RY	E	KM
92345	(81083, 84083)	x*	RY	E	KM
92346	(81091, 84091)		RY	E	KM
92347	(81326, 84326)		RX	E	DY
92348	(81075, 84075)	x*	R	E	KM
92350	(81049, 84049)	*	RY	E	DY
92353	(81323, 84323)		R	E	KM
92355	(81517, 84517)	x	RX	E	DY

92356	(81535, 84535)	x		E	KM
92357	(81136, 84136)		RX	E	KM
92362	(81188, 84188)	x	RY	E	KM
92363	(81294, 84294)	x	RY	E	CW
92364	(81030, 84030)	x*	R	E	KM
92365	(81122, 84122)		RX	E	KM
92366	(81551, 84551)		RX	E	KM
92369	(80960)	x*		E	Doncaster Dock Siding
92370	(81324, 84324)		RX	E	KM
92377	(80928)	*	RX	E	DY
92379	(80914)	*	RX	E	KM
92380	(81247, 84247)	*	R	E	KM
92381	(81476, 84476)		RX	E	KM
92382	(81561, 84561)		RX	E	DY
92384	(80893)		RY	E	CW
92385	(81261, 84261)	x*	RY	E	KM
92389	(81026, 84026)	*	RY	E	KM
92390	(80834)	*		E	KM
92392	(80861)	*	RY	E	KM
92395	(81274, 84274)			E	KM
92398	(80859)	x*	RY	E	KM
92400	(81211, 84211)	*		E	CW
92401	(81280, 84280)	x	RX	E	KM
92402	(81099, 84099)	*	RY	E	KM
92404	(81051, 84051)	x		E	KM
92409	(81370, 84370)	x		E	OM
92410	(81469, 84469)	x		E	CW
92412	(81354, 84354)	*	RY	E	CW
92413	(81472, 84472)	x	RY	E	CW
92414	(81458, 84458)	x		E	OM
92415	(81388, 84388)		RX	E	KM
92416	(81250, 84250)	*	RY	E	KM
92417	(80885)	*	RX	E	KM
92418	(81512, 84512)	*	RX	E	OM

NF (BG)   GANGWAYED BRAKE VAN (100 m.p.h.)

As NE but with emergency equipment removed. For details and lot numbers
refer to original number series. 92518–92728 have B4 bogies whilst 92804–
92897 have Commonwealth bogies.

b (Dia. NB501). High security brake van. Converted at Wembley Heavy Repair
Depot from ND 1985. Gangways removed. Now used for movement of materials between EWS maintenance depots.

92530	(81461, 84461)	xb	RX	E	*E*	EN
92542	(81207, 92942)		RX	E		KM
92562	(81232, 92962)		RX	E		OM
92568	(81244, 92968)		RX	E		OM
92607	(81410, 92107)		RX	E		OM
92804	(81339, 92304)	x	RX	E		KM

92805	(81590, 92305)	x	RX	E		KM
92810	(81105, 92310)		RX	E		KM
92815	(80848, 92315)	*	RX	E		CU
92817	(80836, 92317)	x	RX	E		KM
92822	(80771, 92322)	x	RX	E		Arpley Yard
92827	(80842, 92327)	x	RX	E		KM
92831	(81365, 92331)	x	RX	E		KM
92842	(81397, 92342)	x	RY	E		KM
92852	(81182, 92352)	*	RX	E		DY
92854	(81353, 92354)	x	RX	E		Arpley Yard
92859	(81275, 92359)	*	RX	E		DY
92860	(81431, 92360)		RX	E		OM
92861	(81463, 92361)		R	E		KM
92867	(81293, 92367)	x	RX	E		CU
92872	(81362, 92372)	x	RY	E		CW
92873	(81528, 92373)		RX	E		KM
92876	(81374, 92376)	*	RX	E		KM
92883	(81429, 92383)	*	RX	E		OM
92886	(80843, 92386)	x	RX	E		KM
92897	(80700, 92397)	x*	RY	E		KM

NE/NH (BG)   GANGWAYED BRAKE VAN (100/110 m.p.h.)

Renumbered from 920xx series by adding 900 to number to avoid conflict with Class 92 locos. Class continued from 92267.

92901	(80855, 92001)	NHA		H	SR	IS
92904	(80867, 92004)	*pg	G	VS		SL
92908	(80895, 92008)	NHA		H	SR	IS
92912	(80910, 92012)	*pg		H		KN
92916	(80930, 92016)	x*pg	RY	E		BK
92923	(80971, 92023)	*pg		H		LT
92927	(81061, 92027)	NHA		H		LT
92928	(81064, 92028)	NHA		H		LT
92929	(81077, 92029)	NHA		H	GW	OO
92931	(81102, 92031)	NHA		H	SR	IS
92933	(81123, 92033)	NHA		H		ZC
92934	(81142, 92034)	NHA		H		LT
92935	(81150, 92035)	*pg		H		ZN
92936	(81158, 92036)	NHA		H	SR	IS
92937	(81165, 92037)	NHA		H		ZH
92938	(81173, 92038)	NHA		H	SR	IS
92939	(81175, 92039)	NHA		H		ZH
92940	(81186, 92040)	pg		H	SR	IS
92946	(81214, 92046)	NHA		H	SR	IS
92948	(81218, 92048)	NHA		H		ZC
92961	(81231, 92061)			H		LT
92986	(81282, 92086)	to		H		CP
92988	(81284, 92088)	to		H		LT
92991	(81308, 92091)	to		H		LT
92998	(81381, 92098)	NHA		H		LT

NL   NEWSPAPER VAN

Dia. NL501. Mark 1. Short frames (57'). Converted from NJ (GUV). Fluorescent lighting, toilets and gangways fitted. Load 14 t. As EWS does not now carry newspaper traffic these are now all out of use. B5 Bogies. ETH 3X.

Lot No. 30922 Wolverton or Doncaster 1977–78. 31 t.

94003	(86281, 93999)	x	RX	E	OM
94004	(86156, 85504)		RY	E	OM
94006	(86202, 85506)		RX	E	OM
94007	(86572, 85507)		B	E	OM
94009	(86144, 85509)		RY	E	OM
94010	(86151, 85510)	x	RX	E	OM
94011	(86437, 85511)		RX	E	OM
94016	(86317, 85516)	x	B	E	OM
94020	(86220, 85520)	x	RY	E	OM
94021	(86204, 85521)	x	B	E	OM
94024	(86106, 85524)		B	E	OM
94025	(86377, 85525)		RY	E	TE
94026	(86703, 85526)	x	RY	E	OM
94027	(86732, 85527)		R	E	FK
94028	(86733, 85528)	x	RX	E	TE
94029	(86740, 85529)	x	RY	E	OM
94030	(86746, 85530)	x	B	E	OM
94032	(86730, 85532)		RX	E	OM

NKA   HIGH SECURITY GENERAL UTILITY VAN

Dia. NK501. Mark 1. These vehicles are GUVs further modified with new floors, three roller shutter doors per side and the end doors removed. For lot Nos. see original number series. Commonwealth bogies. Add 2 t to weight. ETH0X.

94100	(86668, 95100)	RX	E	E	BK
94101	(86142, 95101)	RX	E	E	BK
94102	(86762, 95102)	RX	E	E	BK
94103	(86956, 95103)	RX	E	E	BK
94104	(86942, 95104)	RX	E	E	EN
94106	(86353, 95106)	RX	E	E	BK
94107	(86576, 95107)	RX	E	E	EN
94108	(86600, 95108)	RX	E	E	BK
94110	(86393, 95110)	RX	E	E	BK
94111	(86578, 95111)	RX	E	E	EN
94112	(86673, 95112)	RX	E	E	EN
94113	(86235, 95113)	RX	E	E	BK
94114	(86081, 95114)	RX	E	E	BK
94116	(86426, 95116)	RX	E	E	BK
94117	(86534, 95117)	RX	E	E	BK
94118	(86675, 95118)	RX	E	E	EN
94119	(86167, 95119)	RX	E	E	EN
94121	(86518, 95121)	RX	E	E	BK
94123	(86376, 95123)	RX	E	E	BK

94126	(86692, 95126)	**RX**	E *E*	BK
94132	(86607, 95132)	**RX**	E *E*	EN
94133	(86604, 95133)	**RX**	E *E*	BK
94137	(86610, 95137)	**RX**	E *E*	EN
94138	(86212, 95138)	**RX**	E *E*	EN
94140	(86571, 95140)	**RX**	E *E*	BK
94146	(86648, 95146)	**RX**	E *E*	BK
94147	(86091, 95147)	**RX**	E *E*	BK
94148	(86416, 95148)	**RX**	E *E*	EN
94150	(86560, 95150)	**RX**	E *E*	BK
94153	(86798, 95153)	**RX**	E *E*	EN
94155	(86820, 95155)	**RX**	E *E*	EN
94157	(86523, 95157)	**RX**	E *E*	EN
94160	(86581, 95160)	**RX**	E *E*	BK
94164	(86104, 95164)	**RX**	E *E*	EN
94166	(86112, 95166)	**RX**	E *E*	BK
94168	(86914, 95168)	**RX**	E *E*	BK
94170	(86395, 95170)	**RX**	E *E*	BK
94172	(86429, 95172)	**RX**	E *E*	EN
94174	(86852, 95174)	**RX**	E *E*	EN
94175	(86521, 95175)	**RX**	E *E*	BK
94176	(86210, 95176)	**RX**	E *E*	EN
94177	(86411, 95177)	**RX**	E *E*	BK
94180	(86362, 95141)	**RX**	E *E*	EN
94182	(86710, 95182)	**RX**	E *E*	BK
94190	(86624, 95350)	**RX**	E *E*	EN
94191	(86596, 95351)	**RX**	E *E*	BK
94192	(86727, 95352)	**RX**	E *E*	EN
94193	(86514, 95353)	**RX**	E *E*	EN
94195	(86375, 95355)	**RX**	E *E*	BK
94196	(86478, 95356)	**RX**	E *E*	BK
94197	(86508, 95357)	**RX**	E *E*	BK
94198	(86195, 95358)	**RX**	E *E*	BK
94199	(86854, 95359)	**RX**	E *E*	BK
94200	(86207, 95360)	**RX**	E *E*	EN
94202	(86563, 95362)	**RX**	E *E*	BK
94203	(86345, 95363)	**RX**	E *E*	BK
94204	(86715, 95364)	**RX**	E *E*	BK
94205	(86857, 95365)	**RX**	E *E*	BK
94207	(86529, 95367)	**RX**	E *E*	BK
94208	(86656, 95368)	**RX**	E *E*	EN
94209	(86390, 95369)	**RX**	E *E*	BK
94211	(86713, 95371)	**RX**	E *E*	EN
94212	(86728, 95372)	**RX**	E *E*	EN
94213	(86258, 95373)	**RX**	E *E*	EN
94214	(86367, 95374)	**RX**	E *E*	BK
94215	(86862, 94077)	**RX**	E *E*	BK
94216	(86711, 93711)	**RX**	E *E*	EN
94217	(86131, 93131)	**RX**	E *E*	BK
94218	(86541, 93541)	**RX**	E *E*	BK
94221	(86905, 93905)	**RX**	E *E*	BK

94222	(86474, 93474)	**RX**	E	*E*	EN
94223	(86660, 93660)	**RX**	E	*E*	BK
94224	(86273, 93273)	**RX**	E	*E*	BK
94225	(86849, 93849)	**RX**	E	*E*	BK
94226	(86525, 93525)	**RX**	E	*E*	BK
94227	(86585, 93585)	**RX**	E	*E*	BK
94228	(86511, 93511)	**RX**	E	*E*	BK
94229	(86720, 93720)	**RX**	E	*E*	BK

NAA   PROPELLING CONTROL VEHICLE

Dia. NA508. Mark 1. Class 307 driving trailers converted for use in propelling mail trains out of termini. Fitted with roller shutter doors. Equipment fitted for communication between cab of PCV and locomotive. B5 bogies. ETH 2X.

Lot No. 30206 Eastleigh 1954–556. Converted at Hunslet-Barclay, Kilmarnock 1994–6.

94302	(75124)	**RX** E *E*	BK	94323	(75110)	**RX** E *E*	EN
94303	(75131)	**RX** E *E*	EN	94324	(75103)	**RX** E *E*	EN
94304	(75107)	**RX** E *E*	EN	94325	(75113)	**RX** E *E*	EN
94305	(75104)	**RX** E *E*	EN	94326	(75123)	**RX** E *E*	BK
94306	(75112)	**RX** E *E*	BK	94327	(75116)	**RX** E *E*	EN
94307	(75127)	**RX** E *E*	EN	94331	(75022)	**RX** E *E*	BK
94308	(75125)	**RX** E *E*	EN	94332	(75011)	**RX** E *E*	EN
94309	(75130)	**RX** E *E*	EN	94333	(75016)	**RX** E *E*	EN
94310	(75119)	**RX** E *E*	EN	94334	(75017)	**RX** E *E*	EN
94311	(75105)	**RX** E *E*	EN	94335	(75032)	**RX** E *E*	BK
94312	(75126)	**RX** E *E*	BK	94336	(75031)	**RX** E *E*	EN
94313	(75129)	**RX** E *E*	BK	94337	(75029)	**RX** E *E*	EN
94314	(75109)	**RX** E *E*	BK	94338	(75008)	**RX** E *E*	EN
94315	(75132)	**RX** E *E*	EN	94339	(75024)	**RX** E *E*	BK
94316	(75108)	**RX** E *E*	EN	94340	(75012)	**RX** E *E*	BK
94317	(75117)	**RX** E *E*	EN	94341	(75007)	**RX** E *E*	BK
94318	(75115)	**RX** E *E*	EN	94342	(75005)	**RX** E *E*	BK
94319	(75128)	**RX** E *E*	EN	94343	(75027)	**RX** E *E*	EN
94320	(75120)	**RX** E *E*	EN	94344	(75014)	**RX** E *E*	BK
94321	(75122)	**RX** E *E*	EN	94345	(75004)	**RX** E *E*	EN
94322	(75111)	**RX** E *E*	BK				

NBA   HIGH SECURITY BRAKE VAN (100 m.p.h.)

Dia. NB501. Mark 1. These vehicles are NEs further modified with sealed gangways, new floors, built-in tail lights and roller shutter doors. For lot Nos. see original number series. B4 bogies. 31.4 t. ETH 1X.

94400	(81224, 92954)	**RX**	E	*E*	BK
94401	(81277, 92224)	**RX**	E	*E*	EN
94403	(81479, 92629)	**RX**	E	*E*	BK
94404	(81486, 92135)	**RX**	E	*E*	BK
94405	(80890, 92233)	**RX**	E	*E*	EN
94406	(81226, 92956)	**RX**	E	*E*	BK

94407	(81223, 92553)	**RX**	E	*E*	BK
94408	(81264, 92981)	**RX**	E	*E*	BK
94410	(81205, 92941)	**RX**	E	*E*	EN
94411	(81378, 92997)	**RX**	E	*E*	EN
94412	(81210, 92945)	**RX**	E	*E*	EN
94413	(80909, 92236)	**RX**	E	*E*	NC
94414	(81377, 92996)	**RX**	E	*E*	BK
94415	(81309, 92992)	**RX**	E	*E*	EN
94416	(80929, 92746)	**RX**	E	*E*	BK
94418	(81248, 92244)	**RX**	E	*E*	BK
94420	(81325, 92263)	**RX**	E	*E*	BK
94421	(81230, 92960)	**RX**	E	*E*	EN
94422	(81516, 92651)	**RX**	E	*E*	BK
94423	(80923, 92914)	**RX**	E	*E*	BK
94424	(81400, 92103)	**RX**	E	*E*	EN
94426	(81283, 92987)	**RX**	E	*E*	BK
94427	(80894, 92754)	**RX**	E	*E*	BK
94428	(81550, 92166)	**RX**	E	*E*	BK
94429	(80870, 92232)	**RX**	E	*E*	EN
94431	(81401, 92604)	**RX**	E	*E*	BK
94432	(81383, 92999)	**RX**	E	*E*	EN
94433	(81495, 92643)	**RX**	E	*E*	EN
94434	(81268, 92584)	**RX**	E	*E*	NC
94435	(81485, 92134)	**RX**	E	*E*	EN
94436	(81237, 92565)	**RX**	E	*E*	BK
94437	(81403, 92208)	**RX**	E	*E*	EN
94438	(81425, 92251)	**RX**	E	*E*	BK
94439	(81480, 92130)	**RX**	E	*E*	BK
94440	(81497, 92645)	**RX**	E	*E*	BK
94441	(81492, 92140)	**RX**	E	*E*	BK
94442	(80932, 92723)	**RX**	E	*E*	BZ
94443	(81473, 92127)	**RX**	E	*E*	BK
94444	(81484, 92133)	**RX**	E	*E*	BK
94445	(81444, 92615)	**RX**	E	*E*	EN
94446	(80857, 92242)	**RX**	E	*E*	EN
94447	(81515, 92266)	**RX**	E	*E*	EN
94448	(81541, 92664)	**RX**	E	*E*	BK
94449	(81536, 92747)	**RX**	E	*E*	BK
94450	(80927, 92915)	**RX**	E	*E*	BK
94451	(80955, 92257)	**RX**	E	*E*	EN
94452	(81394, 92602)	**RX**	E	*E*	BK
94453	(81170, 92239)	**RX**	E	*E*	EN
94454	(81465, 92124)	**RX**	E	*E*	EN
94455	(81239, 92264)	**RX**	E	*E*	BK
94457	(81454, 92119)	**RX**	E	*E*	BK
94458	(81255, 92974)	**RX**	E	*E*	BK
94459	(81490, 92138)	**RX**	E	*E*	BK
94460	(81266, 92983)	**RX**	E	*E*	EN
94461	(81487, 92136)	**RX**	E	*E*	EN
94462	(81289, 92270)	**RX**	E	*E*	EN
94463	(81375, 92995)	**RX**	E	*E*	EN

94464	(81240, 92262)		RX	E	*E*	EN
94465	(81481, 92131)		RX	E	*E*	BK
94466	(81236, 92964)		RX	E	*E*	EN
94467	(81245, 92969)		RX	E	*E*	BK
94468	(81259, 92978)		RX	E	*E*	BK
94469	(81260, 92979)		RX	E	*E*	BK
94470	(81442, 92113)		RX	E	*E*	NC
94471	(81518, 92152)		RX	E	*E*	BK
94472	(81256, 92975)		RX	E	*E*	BK
94473	(81262, 92272)		RX	E	*E*	EN
94474	(81452, 92618)		RX	E	*E*	EN
94475	(81208, 92943)		RX	E	*E*	EN
94476	(81209, 92944)		RX	E	*E*	BK
94477	(81494, 92642)		RX	E	*E*	BK
94478	(81488, 92637)		RX	E	*E*	EN
94479	(81482, 92132)		RX	E	*E*	BK
94480	(81411, 92608)		RX	E	*E*	EN
94481	(81493, 92641)		RX	E	*E*	BK
94482	(81491, 92639)		RX	E	*E*	NC
94483	(81500, 92647)		RX	E	*E*	EN
94484	(81426, 92110)		RX	E	*E*	BK
94485	(81496, 92644)		RX	E	*E*	EN
94486	(81254, 92973)		RX	E	*E*	BK
94487	(81413, 92609)		RX	E	*E*	BK
94488	(81405, 92105)		RX	E	*E*	BK
94490	(81409, 92606)		RX	E	*E*	EN
94491	(80936, 92753)		RX	E	*E*	BK
94492	(80888, 92721)		RX	E	*E*	BK
94493	(80944, 92919)		RX	E	*E*	BK
94494	(81451, 92617)		RX	E	*E*	BK
94495	(80871, 92755)		RX	E	*E*	BK
94496	(81514, 92650)		RX	E	*E*	BK
94497	(80877, 92717)		RX	E	*E*	BK
94498	(81225, 92555)		RX	E	*E*	BK
94499	(81258, 92577)		RX	E	*E*	BK

NBA/NIA HIGH SECURITY BRAKE VAN (100/110 m.p.h.)

Dia. NB501 or NI501. Mark 1. These vehicles are NEs further modified with sealed gangways, new floors, built-in tail lights and roller shutter doors. For lot Nos. see original number series. B4 bogies. 31.4 t. ETH 1X.

These vehicles are identical to the 94400–94499 series. Certain vehicles are being given a special maintenance regime whereby tyres are reprofiled more frequently than normal and are then allowed to run at 110 m.p.h. Vehicles from the 94400 series upgraded to 110 m.p.h. are being renumbered in this series. Vehicles are NBA (100 m.p.h.) unless marked NIA (110 m.p.h.)

94500	(81457, 92121)	NIA	RX	E	*E*	BK
94501	(80891, 92725)		RX	E	*E*	BK
94502	(80924, 92720)	NIA	RX	E	*E*	BK
94503	(80873, 92709)	NIA	RX	E	*E*	ML

94504	(80935, 92748)		**RX**	E	*E*	BK	
94505	(81235, 92750)	NIA	**RX**	E	*E*	ML	
94506	(80958, 92922)	NIA	**RX**	E	*E*	ML	
94507	(80876, 92505)	NIA	**RX**	E	*E*	BK	
94508	(80887, 92722)	NIA	**RX**	E	*E*	BK	
94509	(80897, 92509)	NIA	**RX**	E	*E*	BK	
94510	(80945, 92265)		**RX**	E	*E*	BK	
94511	(81504, 92714)	NIA	**RX**	E	*E*	ML	
94512	(81265, 92582)		**RX**	E	*E*	BK	
94513	(81257, 92576)		**RX**	E	*E*	BK	
94514	(81459, 92122)	NIA	**RX**	E	*E*	ML	
94515	(80916, 92513)	NIA	**RX**	E	*E*	ML	
94516	(81267, 92211)	NIA	**RX**	E	*E*	BK	
94517	(81489, 92243)	NIA	**RX**	E	*E*	ML	
94518	(81346, 92258)		**RX**	E	*E*	BK	
94519	(,)		**RX**	E			
94520	(80940, 92917)	NIA	**RX**	E	*E*	ML	
94521	(80900, 92510)	NIA	**RX**	E	*E*	ML	
94522	(80880, 92907)	NIA	**RX**	E	*E*	ML	
94523	(81509, 92649)	NIA	**RX**	E	*E*	BK	
94524	(,)		**RX**	E			
94525	(80902, 92229)	NIA	**RX**	E	*E*	BK	
94526	(80941, 92518)	NIA	**RX**	E	*E*	BK	
94527	(80921, 92728)	NIA	**RX**	E	*E*	BK	
94528	(,)		**RX**	E			
94529	(,)		**RX**	E			
94530	(81511, 94409)	NIA	**RX**	E	*E*	ML	
94531	(80879, 94456)	NIA	**RX**	E	*E*	ML	
94532	(81423, 94489)	NIA	**RX**	E	*E*	BK	
94533	(80937, 94425)	NIA	**RX**	E	*E*	BK	
94534	(80908, 94430)	NIA	**RX**	E	*E*	BK	
94535	(80858, 94419)	NIA	**RX**	E	*E*	BK	
94536	(,)		**RX**	E			
94537	(,)		**RX**	E			

NO (GUV) GENERAL UTILITY VAN (100 m.p.h.)

Dia. NO513. Mark 1. For lot Nos. see original number series. Commonwealth bogies except where shown otherwise. Add 2 t to weight (Subtract 1 t for B4). ETH 0X.

95105	(86126, 93126)		**RX**	E		CU
95109	(86269, 93269)	x	**B**	E		CU
95120	(86468, 93468)	x	**RY**	E		CU
95124	(86836, 93836)	x	**R**	E		CU
95125	(86143, 93143)	x	**B**	E		CU
95128	(86764, 93764)	x	**RY**	E		CW
95129	(86347, 93347)	x	**RY**	E		CW
95131	(86860, 93860)		**RX**	E		OM
95135	(86249, 93249)	x	**RY**	E		CU
95136	(86396, 93396)	x	**RX**	E		OM

95144	(86165, 93165)	x	**RY**	E	OM
95145	(86293, 93293)	x	**RX**	E	CU
95151	(86606, 93606)	x	**RX**	E	OM
95152	(86969, 93969)	x	**RY**	E	CU
95156	(86160, 93160)	x	**RX**	E	OM
95165	(86262, 93262)	x	**RX**	E	CU
95167	(86255, 93255)		**RX**	E	OM
95171	(86110, 93110)	x	**RX**	E	OM
95190	(86643, 95393)	B4	**RY**	E	OM
95194	(86192, 93192)	x B4	**RX**	E	OM
95196	(86775, 93775)	x B4	**RX**	E	OM
95198	(86134, 93134)	x B4	**RX**	E	OM
95199	(86141, 93141)	x B4	**RX**	E	OM

NCX   NEWSPAPER VAN (100 m.p.h.)

Dia. NC501. Mark 1. BGs modified to carry newspapers. As EWS does not now carry newspaper traffic these are now all out of use. For lot Nos. refer to original number series. Commonwealth bogies. Add 2 t to weight. ETH3 (3X*).

95201	(80875)	x	**RX**	E	KM
95204	(80947)	x*	**RX**	E	OM
95211	(80949)	x	**RY**	E	KM
95217	(81385, 84385)	x	**B**	E	OM
95227	(81292, 95310)	x	**RX**	E	KM
95228	(81014, 95332)	x	**RX**	E	NC
95230	(80525, 95321)	x	**RX**	E	DY

NAA   PROPELLING CONTROL VEHICLE

Dia. NA508. Mark 1. Class 307 driving trailers converted for use in propelling mail trains out of termini. Fitted with roller shutter doors. Equipment was fitted for communication between cab of PCV and locomotive but this is now isolated and the vehicles are in use as normal vans. B5 bogies. ETH 2X.

Lot No. 30206 Eastleigh 1954–556. Converted at RTC, Derby 1993.

95300	(75114, 94300)	**RX**	E	*E* EN
95301	(75102, 94301)	**RX**	E	*E* EN

NOV   GENERAL UTILITY VAN (100 m.p.h.)

Dia. NO513. Mark 1. For lot No. refer to original number series. Commonwealth bogies. Add 2 t to weight. ETH0X.

95366	(86251, 93251)	v	**B**	E	Bristol Pylle Hill

NRX   BAA CONTAINER VAN (100 m.p.h.)

Dia. NR503. Mark 1. Modified for carriage of British Airports Authority containers with roller shutter doors and roller floors and gangways removed. For lot Nos. see original number series. Now used for movement of materials between EWS maintenance depots. Commonwealth bogies. Add 2 t to weight.. ETH3.

| 95400 | (80621, 95203) | x | **RX** | E | *E* | CD |
| 95410 | (80826, 95213) | x | **E** | E | *E* | EN |

NKA   HIGH SECURITY GENERAL UTILITY VAN

Dia. NK502. Mark 1. These vehicles are GUVs further modified with new floors, two roller shutter doors per side, middle doors sealed and end doors removed. For lot Nos. see original number series. Commonwealth bogies. Add 2 t to weight. ETH 0X.

95715	(86174, 95115)	**R**	E	*E*	EN
95727	(86323, 95127)	**R**	E	*E*	EN
95734	(86462, 95134)	**RX**	E	*E*	EN
95739	(86172, 95139)	**R**	E	*E*	EN
95743	(86485, 95143)	**RX**	E	*E*	EN
95749	(86265, 95149)	**R**	E	*E*	EN
95754	(86897, 95154)	**R**	E	*E*	EN
95758	(86499, 95158)	**RX**	E	*E*	EN
95759	(86084, 95159)	**RX**	E	*E*	EN
95761	(86205, 95161)	**RX**	E	*E*	EN
95762	(86122, 95162)	**RX**	E	*E*	EN
95763	(86407, 95163)	**R**	E	*E*	EN

NX (GUV)   MOTORAIL VAN (100 m.p.h.)

Dia. NX501. Mark 1. For details and lot numbers see original number series. ETH 0 (0X*).

96100	(86734, 93734)	*B5		H		KN
96110	(86738, 93738)	*C		H		KN
96112	(86750, 93750)	*C		H		LT
96130	(86736, 93736)	*C		H		KN
96131	(86737, 93737)	*C		H		KN
96132	(86754, 93754)	*C		H		LT
96133	(86685, 93685)	C		H		LT
96134	(86691, 93691)	C		H		LT
96135	(86755, 93755)	C		H		CP
96136	(86735, 93735)	C		H		LT
96137	(86748, 93748)	C	**B**	H		ZN
96138	(86749, 93749)	C		H		LT
96139	(86751, 93751)	C		H	*VW*	MA
96141	(86753, 93753)	C	**B**	H		LT
96162	(86647, 93647)	*C		H		LT
96163	(86646, 93646)	*C		H		KN
96164	(86880, 93880)	*C		H		LT
96165	(86784, 93784)	*C		H		KN
96166	(86834, 93834)	*C		H		KN
96167	(86756, 93756)	*C		H		KN
96168	(86978, 93978)	*C		H		LT
96170	(86159, 93159)	x*C		H		KN
96171	(86326, 93326)	x*C		H		LT
96172	(86363, 93363)	x*C		H		KN

96173	(86440, 93440)	x*C	H	KN
96174	(86453, 93453)	x*C	H	LT
96175	(86628, 93628)	x*C	H	KN
96176	(86641, 93641)	x*C	H	KN
96178	(86782, 93782)	*C	H	KN
96179	(86910, 93910)	*C	H	LT
96181	(86875, 93875)	*C	H	LT
96182	(86944, 93944)	*C	H	CP
96185	(86083, 93083)	x*C	H	LT
96186	(86087, 93087)	x*C	H	LT
96187	(86168, 93168)	x*C	H	LT
96188	(86320, 93320)	x*C	H	KN
96189	(86447, 93447)	x*C	H	LT
96190	(86448, 93448)	x*C	H	LT
96191	(86665, 93665)	x*C	H	KN
96192	(86669, 93669)	x*C	H	KN
96193	(86874, 93874)	x*C	H	LT
96194	(86949, 93949)	x*C	H	LT
96195	(86958, 93958)	x*C	H	LT

NP (GUV)   MOTORAIL VAN (110 m.p.h.)

Dia. NP503. Mark 1. Vehicles modified with concertina end doors. For details and lot numbers see original number series. B5 Bogies. ETH 0X.

96210	(86355, 96159)	H	LT
96212	(86443, 96161)	H	LT
96218	(86286, 96151)	H	LT

AX5G   NIGHTSTAR GENERATOR VAN

Dia. AX502. Mark 3A. Generator vans converted from sleeping cars for use on 'Nightstar' services. Designed to operate between two Class 37/6 locomotives. Gangways removed. Two Cummins diesel generator groups providing a 1500 V train supply. Hydraulic parking brake. 61-way ENS interface jumpers. BT10 bogies.

Lot No. 30960 Derby 1981–83. 46.01 t.

96371	(10545, 6371)	**EP**	EU	*EU*	NP
96372	(10564, 6372)	**EP**	EU	*EU*	NP
96373	(10568, 6373)	**EP**	EU	*EU*	NP
96374	(10585, 6374)	**EP**	EU	*EU*	NP
96375	(10587, 6375)	**EP**	EU	*EU*	NP

AY5 (BV)   EUROSTAR BARRIER VEHICLE

Dia. AY501. Mark 1. Converted from GUVs. Bodies removed. B4 bogies.

96380–96382/9. Lot No. 30417 Pressed Steel 1958–59. 40 t.
96383. Lot No. 30565 Pressed Steel 1959. 40 t.
96384/6/7. Lot No. 30616 Pressed Steel 1959–60. 40 t.
96385. Lot No. 30343 York 1957. 40 t.

96388. Lot No. 30403 Glasgow 1958–60. 40 t.

96380	(86386, 6380)	**B**	EU	*EU*	NP
96381	(86187, 6381)	**B**	EU	*EU*	NP
96382	(86295, 6382)	**B**	EU	*EU*	NP
96383	(86664, 6383)	**B**	EU	*EU*	NP
96384	(86955, 6384)	**B**	EU	*EU*	NP
96385	(86515, 6385)	**B**	EU	*EU*	NP
96386	(86859, 6386)	**B**	EU	*EU*	NP
96387	(86973, 6387)	**B**	EU	*EU*	NP
96388	(86562, 6388)	**B**	EU	*EU*	NP
96389	(86135, 6389)	**B**	EU	*EU*	NP

NG   MOTORAIL LOADING WAGON

Dia. NG 503. These vehicles have been converted and renumbered from weltrol wagons and were used for loading purposes.

Built Swindon 1960. Wagon Lot No. 3102 (3192*).

96452	(B900917)		H	LT
96453	(B900926)	*	H	LT

NVA   MOTORAIL VAN (100 m.p.h.)

Dia. NV502. Mark 1. Built 1998–9 by Marcroft Engineering using underframe and running gear from Motorail GUVs. Side loading with one end sealed. The vehicles run in pairs and access is available to the adjacent vehicle. For details and lot numbers see original number series. B5 bogies. ETH 0X.

* Prototype vehicle. Dia NV501. End doors. Now out of use.

96601	(86741, 96101)	*	**FT**	H		PY
96602	(86097, 96150)		**GW**	H	*GW*	PZ
96603	(86334, 96155)		**GW**	H	*GW*	PZ
96604	(86337, 96156)		**GW**	H	*GW*	PZ
96605	(86344, 96157)		**GW**	H	*GW*	PZ
96606	(86324, 96213)		**GW**	H	*GW*	PZ
96607	(86351, 96215)		**GW**	H	*GW*	PZ
96608	(86385, 96216)		**GW**	H	*GW*	PZ
96609	(86327, 96217)		**GW**	H	*GW*	PZ

NY   EXHIBITION VAN

Various interiors. Converted from various vehicle types. Electric heating from shore supply. Livery varies according to job being undertaken.

Converted Salisbury 1981 from RBs of Lot No. 30636 Pressed Steel 1962. Club cars. Dia NY523/4 respectively. Commonwealth bogies.

99645	(1765)	v	**0**	E	FK.
99646	(1766)	v	**0**	E	FK.

Converted Railway Age, Crewe 1996 from TSO to Lot No. 30822 Derby 1971. B4 bogies.

99662   (5689)   **0**   CN   FK

Converted Railway Age, Crewe 1996 from SO to Lot No. 30821 Derby 1971.
Originally FO. B4 bogies.

99663   (3194, 6223)   **0**   CN   FK
99664   (3189, 6231)   **0**   CN   FK

Converted Railway Age, Crewe 1996 from TSO to Lot No. 30837 Derby 1972.
B4 bogies.

99665   (5755)   **0**   CN   FK

Converted Railway Age, Crewe 1996 from FO to Lot No. 30843 Derby 1972–73.
B4 bogies.

99666   (3250)   **0**   CN   FK

YR   FERRY VAN

Dia. YR025. This vehicle was built to a wagon lot although the design closely
resembles that of NJ except it only has two sets of doors per side. Short
Frames (57'). Load 14 t. Commonwealth bogies.

Built Eastleigh 1958. Wagon Lot. No. 2849. 30 t.

889202   **PC**   VS   *ON*   SL

Name: 889202 is branded 'BAGGAGE CAR No.8'.

QSA   EMU TRANSLATOR VEHICLES

These vehicles are numbered in the former BR departmental number series
but are included here as they are owned by leasing companies and used by
them for moving their vehicles around the national system in the same way
as other vehicles included in this book. Various diagrams. Converted from
Mark 1 RSOs, RUOs and BSKs.

975864. Lot No. 30054 Eastleigh 1951–54. BR Mark 1 bogies.
975867. Lot No. 30014 York 1950–51. BR Mark 1 bogies.
975875. Lot No. 30143 Charles Roberts 1954–55. BR Mark 1 bogies.
975871–975978. Lot No. 30647 Wolverton 1959–61. Commonwealth bogies.
977087. Lot No. 30229 Metro–Cammell 1955–57. Commonwealth bogies.

975864	(3849)		H	*H*	IL
975867	(1006)		H	*H*	IL
975878	(34643)		H	*H*	IL
975971	(1054)	**P**	P	*P*	CJ
975972	(1039)	**P**	P	*P*	CJ
975973	(1021)	**P**	P	*P*	CJ
975974	(1030)	**N**	A	*A*	IL
975975	(1042)	**P**	P	*P*	CJ
975976	(1033)		A		KN
975977	(1023)		A		KN
975978	(1025)	**N**	A	*A*	IL
977087	(34971)		H	*H*	IL

5.2. NPCCS AWAITING DISPOSAL

This list contains the last known locations of NPCCS vehicles awaiting disposal. The definition of which vehicles are "awaiting disposal" is somewhat vague, but generally speaking these are vehicles of types not now in normal service or vehicles which have been damaged by fire, vandalism or collision.

80735	Perth Holding Sidings
80865	Hornsey Sand Terminal
84197	Worksop
84361	Cambridge Station Yard
84364	Doncaster West Yard
84519	Crewe Coal Sidings
92067	ZB
92198	ZB
92199	ZB
93180	Derby South Dock Siding
93234	Hayes & Harlington
93358	Mossend Yard
93446	Crewe South Yard
93457	Cricklewood Rubbish Terminal
93482	Bedford Civil Engineers Sidings
93542	Hayes & Harlington
93579	DY
93723	BY
93930	Crewe South Yard
93952	Willesden Brent Sidings
93979	Willesden Brent Sidings
96250	Oxford Hinksey Yard
96256	Oxford Hinksey Yard
96260	Oxford Hinksey Yard
96265	Oxford Hinksey Yard
99648	Eastleigh Locomotive Holding Sidings

6. CODES

6.1 LIVERY CODES

* denotes an obsolete livery style no longer used for repaints.

Code	Description
AE	AEA Technology *(Blue with white stripes)*.
AL	Advertising livery *(See class heading)*.
AR	Anglia Railways *(Turquoise blue with white stripe)*.
B*	BR *(Blue)*.
BG	BR *(Blue and grey lined out in white)*.
BL*	BR *(Blue with yellow cabs, grey roof, large numbers)*.
BR*	BR *(Blue with red solebar stripe)*.
CC	BR/Strathclyde PTE *(Carmine & cream lined out in black and straw – not lined out on Class 334)*.
CE*	BR Civil Engineers *(Yellow & grey with black cab doors and window surrounds)*.
CH	BR or GWR style *(Chocolate and cream)*.
CO	Centro *(Grey/green with light blue, white & yellow stripes)*.
CP	ScotRail Caledonian Sleepers *(Two-tone purple with silver stripe)*.
CR	Chiltern Railways *(Blue and white with a thin red stripe)*.
CS	Connex *(Blue with yellow lower body and blue solebar)*.
CT	Central Trains *(Light green with dark green lower body and yellow doors. Blue flash at vehicle ends and at cantrail level)*.
CX	Connex *(White with yellow lower body and blue solebar)*.
DG*	BR Departmental *(Plain dark grey with black cab doors and window surrounds)*.
DR	Direct Rail Services *(Dark blue with light blue roof)*.
DS*	Danske Statsbaner *(Blue and red with moon and star motifs)*.
E	English Welsh & Scottish Railway *(Maroon bodyside & roof with gold stripe, gold reflective stripe at solebar level)*.
EP	European Passenger Services *(Two-tone grey with dark blue roof)*.
ET	Eurotunnel *(Two-tone grey and white with green and blue bands)*.
EU	Eurostar. *(White with dark blue & yellow stripes)*.
F*	BR Trainload Freight *(Two-tone grey with black cab doors and window surrounds. No logos)*.
FA*	BR Trainload Construction *(Two-tone grey with black cab doors and window surrounds. Yellow & blue chequered logo)*.
FC*	BR Trainload Coal *(Two-tone grey with black cab doors and window surrounds. Black & yellow logo)*.
FD*	BR Railfreight Distribution *(Two-tone grey with black cab doors and window surrounds. Yellow & red logo)*.
FE*	Railfreight Distribution International *(Two tone-grey with black cab doors and dark blue roof. Red & yellow logo)*.
FF*	Freightliner *(Two-tone grey with black cab doors and window surrounds. Freightliner logo)*.
FL	Freightliner *(Dark green with yellow cabs)*.
FM*	BR Trainload Metals *(Two-tone grey with black cab doors and window surrounds. Yellow & blue chevrons logo)*.

FN* Foster Yeoman *(Blue/silver/blue. Cast numberplates)*.
FO* BR Railfreight *(Grey bodyside, yellow cabs, red buffer beam, large double-arrow logo)*.
FP* BR Trainload Petroleum *(Two-tone grey with black cab doors and window surrounds. Yellow & blue waves logo)*.
FQ* BR Railfreight *(Grey bodyside, yellow cabs, red buffer beam/stripe at solebar level, large double-arrow logo)*.
FR Fragonset Railways *(Black with silver roof and a red bodyside band lined out in white)*.
FT* Forward Trust Rail *(Blue and white lined out in straw)*.
FY Foster Yeoman *(Blue/silver. Cast numberplates)*.
G* BR *(Plain or two-tone green)*.
GE First Great Eastern *(Grey, green, blue and white)*.
GL First Great Western *(Green with gold decals)*.
GM Greater Manchester PTE *(Light grey/dark grey with red and white stripes)*.
GN Great North Eastern Railway *(Dark blue with a red stripe)*.
GS Great Scottish & Western Railway *(Maroon)*.
GW First Great Western *(Green & Ivory with gold stripe)*.
GX Gatwick Express *(Dark grey/white/burgundy/white)*.
GY Eurotunnel *(Grey and yellow)*.
HA Hanson Quarry Products *(Dark blue and silver)*.
HB* Hunslet-Barclay *(Two-tone grey with red solebar)*.
HX Heathrow Express *(Silver with black window surrounds)*.
I* BR InterCity *(Dark grey/white/red//light grey and – on locos – yellow lower cabsides)*.
IM* BR Mainline *(Dark grey/white/red/light grey)*.
IS* BR InterCity Swallow *(Dark grey/white/red/white)*.
J* London & South East sector *(Two tone brown with orange stripe)*.
LH* BR Loadhaul *(Black with orange cabsides)*.
LS LTS Rail *(Grey/white/green/white/blue/white)*.
LN LNER *(Green and cream)*.
M BR *(Maroon, lined out in straw and black)*.
MA Maintrain *(Light blue)*.
MB West Coast Railway Company *(Maroon and Beige)*.
MD Mersey Travel departmental *(Yellow/black)*.
MG* BR Mainline Freight *(Two-tone grey with black cab doors and window surrounds)*.
ML* BR Mainline Freight *(Aircraft blue with silver stripe)*.
MM Midland Main Line *(Teal green with cream lower body sides and three orange stripes)*.
MT Mersey Travel *(Yellow/white with grey and black stripes)*.
N BR Network South East *(Grey/white/red/white/blue/white)*.
NB* North West Regional Railways *(Grey/white/blue/white/blue/white)*.
NS Northern Spirit *(Turquoise blue with lime green N)*.
NT Network South East *(Grey/red/white/blue/white)*.
NW North West Trains *(Blue with gold cant rail stripe and star)*.
O Non standard liveries *(see notes in class headings for details)*.
P Porterbrook Leasing Company *(Purple & grey)*.
PC Pullman Car Company *(Umber & cream with gold lettering)*.
PM* Provincial Midline *(Dark blue/grey with dark blue and grey stripes)*.
PS* Provincial Services *(Dark blue/grey with light blue & white stripes)*.

R*	Plain red.
RB	Regency Rail Cruises *(Oxford blue and cream)*.
RE*	Provincial Express *(Light grey/buff/dark grey with white, dark blue & light blue stripes)*.
RF*	RFS (E) *(Light grey with yellow and blue stripes)*.
RG*	BR Parcels *(Dark grey and red)*.
RK	Railtrack *(Green and blue)*.
RM	Royal Mail *(Red with yellow stripes)*.
RN*	North West Regional Railways *(Dark blue/grey with green & white stripes)*.
RO*	Railtrack *(Orange with white and grey stripes)*.
RP	Royal Train *(Claret, lined out in red and black)*.
RR*	Regional Railways *(Dark Blue/Grey with light blue & white stripes, three narrow dark blue stripes at cab ends)*.
RX*	Rail Express Systems *(Dark grey and red with blue markings)*.
RY*	Parcels Sector *(Red with yellow stripes)*.
S*	Strathclyde PTE *(Orange/black lined out in white)*.
SL	Silverlink *(Indigo blue with white stripe, green lower body & yellow doors)*.
SO	Serco Railtest *(Red/grey)*.
SR	ScotRail *(White, terracotta, purple and aquamarine)*.
SS	ScotRail Caledonian Sleepers *(Two-tone purple with silver stripe)*.
ST	Stagecoach South West Trains *(White/orange/white/red/white/blue/white)*.
SW	South West Trains *(White/black/orange/red/blue, with red doors)*.
T*	Transrail *(Two-tone grey with Transrail logos)*.
TC*	BR Civil Engineers/Transrail. *(Yellow & grey with black cab doors and window surrounds. Transrail logo)*.
TR	Thameslink Rail *(Dark blue with a broad orange stripe and two narrower white bodyside stripes plus white cantrail stripe)*.
TW	Tyne & Wear PTE *(White/yellow with blue stripe)*.
TX	Northern Spirit Transpennine Express *(Plum with yellow N)*.
U	Undercoat *(White or grey undercoat)*.
V	Virgin Trains *(Red & grey with three white stripes)*.
VN	VSOE 'Northern Belle' *(Crimson lake and cream)*.
WL*	Waterman Railways *(Black with cream and red lining)*.
WO*	Great Western Trains *(Green and ivory)*.
WN	West Anglia Great Northern Railway *(White with blue, grey and orange stripes)*.
WR*	Waterman Railways *(Maroon with cream stripes)*.
WV*	Waterman Railways *(West Coast Joint Stock style lined purple lake)*.
WW	Wales & West Alphaline *(Silver grey, yellow and white, with dark blue doors)*.
WY*	West Yorkshire PTE *(Red/cream with thin yellow stripe)*.
Y*	Plain yellow.
YN	West Yorkshire PTE *(Red with light grey N)*.
YO*	Foster Yeoman *(Blue/silver/blue. Cast numberplate)*.

6.2 OWNER CODES

Code	Owner
14	75014 Locomotive Operators Group.
24	6024 Preservation Society Ltd.
50	The Fifty Fund.
62	The Princess Royal Class Locomotive Trust Ltd.
70	Clun Castle Ltd.
90	Deltic 9000 Locomotives Ltd.
A	Angel Train Contracts Ltd.
A4	The A4 Locomotive Society Ltd.
AD	Adtranz (DaimlerChrysler Rail Systems UK).
AE	AEA Technology PLC.
AM	Alstom Ltd.
AR	Anglia Railways Train Services Ltd.
AY	Amey Fleet Services Ltd.
BM	Birmingham Railway Museum Trust Ltd.
CA	Cardiff Railway Company Ltd.
CM	Cambrian Trains Ltd.
CN	The Carriage & Traction Company Ltd.
DP	The Deltic Preservation Society Ltd.
DR	Direct Rail Services Ltd.
E	English Welsh & Scottish Railway Ltd.
EF	EWS Finance Ltd.
EL	East Lancashire Railway Trust Ltd.
EN	Enron Teesside Operations Ltd.
ER	Eastleigh Railway Preservation Society Ltd.
ET	Eurotunnel PLC.
EU	Eurostar (UK) Ltd.
FL	Freightliner Ltd.
FR	Fragonset Railways Ltd.
FS	Flying Scotsman Railways Ltd.
FX	The Felixstowe Dock and Railway Company Ltd.
FY	Foster Yeoman Ltd.
GR	GL Railease Ltd.
GS	The Great Scottish & Western Railway Company Ltd.
GW	Great Western Trains Company Ltd.
H	HSBC Rail (UK) Ltd.
HA	The Hanson Group Ltd.
HD	Hastings Diesels Ltd.
HN	Harry Needle Railroad Company Ltd.
HS	Harry Schneider.
HT	Heritage Traction Leasing Ltd.
HX	British Airports Authority PLC.
IE	Ian Storey Engineering.
JK	Dr. John Kennedy.
LU	London Underground Ltd.
LW	London & North Western Railway Company Ltd.
MA	Maintrain Ltd.

MD	Ministry of Defence.
ME	Merseyrail Electrics Ltd.
MH	Mid-Hants Railway PLC.
MN	Merchant Navy Locomotive Preservation Society Ltd.
NE	North Eastern Locomotive Preservation Group Ltd.
NR	National Railway Museum.
NS	Northern Spirit Ltd.
NY	North Yorkshire Moors Railway.
O	Other owners (see class heading).
P	Porterbrook Leasing Company Ltd.
PE	Princess Elizabeth Locomotive Society.
RA	Railfilms Ltd.
RC	Railcare Ltd.
RF	RFS (E) Ltd.
RI	Rail Assets Investments Ltd.
RK	Railtrack PLC.
RL	RMS Locotech.
RM	Royal Mail.
RS	Rail Charter Services Ltd.
RT	RT Rail Tours Ltd.
RV	Riviera Trains Ltd.
SB	SNCB/NMBS (Société Nationale des Chemins de fer Belges/ Nationale Maatschapij der belgische Spoorwegen).
SC	Connex South Central.
SE	Connex South Eastern.
SF	SNCF (Société Nationale des Chemins de fer Français).
SH	Scottish Highland Railway Company Ltd.
SO	Serco Railtest Ltd.
SP	The Scottish Railway Preservation Society Ltd.
SR	ScotRail Railways Ltd.
SS	Sea Containers Railway Services Ltd.
SV	Severn Valley Railway Company Ltd.
SW	South West Trains Ltd.
VS	Venice Simplon-Orient-Express Ltd.
VW	West Coast Trains Ltd.
WC	West Coast Railway Co.
WF	Western Falcon Rail.
WN	West Anglia Great Northern Railway Ltd.
WT	Wessex Trains Ltd.

6.3 LOCOMOTIVE POOL CODES

Code	Pool
CDJD	Serco Railtest. Class 08.
CTLO	Cambrian Trains. Operational Fleet
DFFT	Freightliner. Class 47 (with sanding equipment).
DFGM	Freightliner. Class 66.
DFHZ	Freightliner. Class 57.
DFLC	Freightliner. Class 90.
DFLM	Freightliner. Class 47 (with multiple working equipment).
DFLS	Freightliner. Class 08.
DFLT	Freightliner. Classes 37 & 47.
DFNC	Freightliner. Class 86.
DHLT	Freightliner. Locomotives awaiting maintenance/repair.
DNLL	Deltic 9000 Locomotives. Hire Locomotives.
GPSN	Eurostar (UK). Class 73.
GPSS	Eurostar (UK). Class 08.
GPSV	Eurostar (UK). Class 37.
HASS	ScotRail Railways. Class 08.
HEBD	Merseyrail Electrics. Class 73.
HFSL	Virgin Cross Country. Class 08.
HFSN	Virgin West Coast. Class 08.
HGSS	Maintrain. Class 08 (Tyseley).
HISE	Maintrain. Class 08 (Derby).
HISL	Maintrain. Class 08 (Neville Hill).
HJSE	First Great Western. Class 08 (Landore).
HJSL	First Great Western. Class 08 (Laira).
HJXX	First Great Western. Class 08 (Old Oak HST & St. Phillips Marsh).
HLSV	Cardiff Railway Co. Class 08. Hire locomotive.
HNRL	Harry Needle Railroad Company. Hire locomotives.
HQXX	West Anglia Great Northern Railway. Class 03.
HSSN	Anglia Railways. Class 08.
HWSU	Connex South Central. Class 09.
HYSB	South West Trains. Class 73.
IANA	Anglia Railways. Classes 47 & 86.
ICCA	Virgin Cross Country. Class 86.
ICCP	Virgin Cross Country. Class 43.
IECA	Great North Eastern Railway. Class 91.
IECB	Great North Eastern Railway. Class 89.
IECP	Great North Eastern Railway. Class 43.
ILRA	Virgin Cross Country. Class 47.
IMLP	Midland Mainline. Class 43.
IVGA	Gatwick Express. Class 73.
IWCA	Virgin West Coast. Classes 87 & 90.
IWCP	Virgin West Coast. Class 43.
IWLA	First Great Western. Class 47.
IWPA	Virgin West Coast. Class 86.
IWRP	First Great Western. Class 43.
KCSI	Adtranz. Class 08 (Ilford).

KDSD	Adtranz. Class 08 (Doncaster).
KESE	Alstom. Class 08 (Eastleigh).
KGSS	Railcare. Class 08 (Glasgow).
KWSW	Railcare. Class 08 (Wolverton).
MBDL	Non TOC owned diesel locomotives.
MBEL	Non TOC owned electric locomotives.
SAXL	HSBC Rail (UK). Off lease.
SBXL	Porterbrook Leasing. Off lease.
SCXL	Angel Train Contracts. Off lease.
SDFR	Fragonset Railways. Operational locomotives.
WAAN	EWS. Class 67.
WBAN	EWS. Class 66.
WCAN	EWS. Class 60.
WDAN	EWS. Class 59/2.
WEMF	EWS. Class 90 (locomotives not suitable for 110 mph running with NIA vehicles).
WEMP	EWS. Class 86, plus Class 90 locomotives suitable for 110 mph running with NIA vehicles.
WFAN	EWS. Class 58.
WGAN	EWS. Class 56.
WHCN	EWS. Class 47 (Non-Railnet).
WHDA	EWS. Class 47 (VIP & Charter traffic).
WHDC	EWS. Class 47 (On hire to ScotRail).
WHDP	EWS. Class 47 (Rail Express Services – Railnet).
WHDT	EWS. Class 47 (On hire to Serco Railtest).
WHPT	EWS. New locomotives (pre-acceptance).
WHZX	EWS. Locomotives awaiting disposal.
WKBN	EWS. Classes 37/0, 37/3 and 37/5.
WKCD	EWS. Class 37/4 (On hire to First North Western).
WKCN	EWS. Class 37/4.
WKGN	EWS. Class 37/7.
WKMB	EWS. Class 37 (RETB equipped).
WKMF	EWS. Class 37 (Special projects – France).
WKMS	EWS. Class 37 (Temporarily retained for infrastructure duties).
WMAN	EWS. Class 31.
WNWX	EWS. Main line locomotives – strategic reserve.
WNXX	EWS. Main line locomotives – stored.
WNYX	EWS. Main line locomotives – for component recovery.
WNZX	EWS. Locomotives awaiting disposal.
WPAN	EWS. Class 73.
WSAC	EWS. Class 33. Aberdeen area shunting/trip locomotives.
WSAW	EWS. Shunting locomotives (on hire to Allied Steel & Wire).
WSEM	EWS. Shunting locomotives (East Midlands).
WSNE	EWS. Shunting locomotives (North East England).
WSNW	EWS. Shunting locomotives (North West England).
WSSC	EWS. Shunting locomotives (Scotland).
WSSE	EWS. Shunting locomotives (London & South East England).
WSSW	EWS. Shunting locomotives (South Wales).
WSWM	EWS. Shunting locomotives (West Midlands).
WSWS	EWS. Shunting locomotives (Wessex).
WSWX	EWS. Shunting locomotives – strategic reserve.

WSXX	EWS. Shunting locomotives – stored.
WSYH	EWS. Shunting locomotives (South Yorkshire & Humberside).
WSYX	EWS. Shunting locomotives – component recovery only.
WTAN	EWS. Class 92 (Wembley–Fréthun route).
WTEN	EWS. Class 92 (Dollands Moor–Wembley–Mossend–Doncaster & Crewe–Trafford Park routes).
WTWN	Class 92 (Eurotunnel only).
XHSD	Direct Rail Services. Operational locomotives.
XHSS	Direct Rail Services. Stored locomotives.
XYPA	Mendip Rail. Class 59/0.
XYPO	Mendip Rail. Class 59/1.
XYPS	Mendip Rail. Shunting locomotives.

PLATFORM 5 EUROPEAN HANDBOOKS

Since the opening of the Channel Tunnel, more and more enthusiasts
have turned their attentions to the immmense variety of railways which
exist on the continent. The Platform 5 European Handbooks are the
most comprehesive guides to the rolling stock of selected European
railway administrations available. Each book in the series is similar in
layout to this book and includes the following:

* **Locomotives**
* **Railcars and Multiple Units**
* **Depot Allocations (where allocated)**
* **Technical Data**

* **Preserved Locomotives, Museums and Museum Lines**
* **Lists of Depots and Workshops**

Each book is A5 size, thread sewn and includes 32 pages of colour
photographs (16 pages in Irish Railways). Irish Railways also include
details of hauled coaching stock. The following are currently available:

No.1: Benelux Railways 4th edition (SPRING) £14.50

No.3: Austrian Railways 3rd edition £10.50

No.4: French Railways 3rd ed. £14.50

No.5: Swiss Railways 2nd edition £13.50

No.6: Italian Railways 1st edition £13.50

No.7: Irish Railways 1st edition £9.95

Available from the Platform 5 Mail Order Department.
To place an order, please follow the instructions on the last page
of this book.

6.4 OPERATION CODES

Code	Operator
A	Angel Train Contracts.
AD	Adtranz.
AM	Alstom.
AR	Anglia Railways.
AY	Amey Railways.
CA	Cardiff Railways.
CR	Chiltern Railways.
CT	Central Trains.
DR	Direct Rail Services
E	English Welsh & Scottish Railway.
EU	Eurostar (UK).
H	HSBC Rail (UK).
GE	First Great Eastern.
GN	Great North Eastern Railway.
GW	First Great Western.
GX	Gatwick Express.
HX	Heathrow Express.
IL	Island Line.
LS	LTS Rail.
ME	Merseyrail Electrics.
MM	Midland Main Line.
NS	Northern Spirit.
NW	First North Western.
ON	Used normally on special or charter passenger services.
OS	Support Coach.
OT	Non revenue earning (e.g. Test Trains, Research, Route Learning).
P	Porterbrook Leasing.
RK	Railtrack.
RP	Royal Train.
SC	Connex South Central.
SE	Connex South Eastern.
SL	Silverlink.
SO	Serco Railtest.
SR	ScotRail.
SW	South West Trains.
TR	Thameslink Rail.
TT	Thames Trains.
VW	Virgin West Coast
VX	Virgin Cross Country.
WC	West Coast Railway
WN	West Anglia Great Northern.
WW	Wales & West Passenger Trains

6.5 DEPOT & LOCATION CODES

* denotes unofficial code.

Code	Location	Operator
AF	Chart Leacon T&RSMD (Ashford, Kent)	Adtranz
AL	Aylesbury TMD	Adtranz (on behalf of Chiltern Railways)
AN	Allerton T&RSMD	EWS
AY	Ayr SD	EWS
BD	Birkenhead North T&RSMD	Merseyrail Electrics
BH	Barrow Hill T&RSMD	Barrow Hill Engine Shed Society
BI	Brighton T&RSMD	Connex South Central
BK	Barton Hill T&RSMD (Bristol)	EWS
BL*	Billingham TMD	Enron Teesside Operations
BM	Bournemouth T&RSMD	South West Trains
BN	Bounds Green T&RSMD (London)	Great North Eastern Railway
BP	Blackpool North CS	Storage location only
BQ	Bury	East Lancashire Railway
BS	Bescot TMD (Walsall)	EWS
BT	Bo'Ness CARMD	Bo'Ness & Kinneil Railway
BY	Bletchley T&RSMD	Silverlink
BZ	St. Blazey T&RSMD (Par)	EWS
CB*	Crewe Brook Sidings	Storage location only
CC*	Cambridge Coalfields Sidings	Storage location only
CD	Crewe Diesel TMD	EWS
CE	Crewe International Electric T&RSMD	EWS
CF	Cardiff Canton (Loco) TMD	EWS
CF	Cardiff Canton (DMU/LHCS) T&RSMD	Wales & West; Cardiff Railways
CH	Chester T&RSMD	First North Western
CJ	Clapham Yard SD	Storage location only
CK	Corkerhill TMD	ScotRail
CL	Carlisle Upperby (closed)	Storage location only
CP	Crewe Carriage Depot T&RSMD	London & North Western Railway
CQ	Crewe (The Railway Age) T&RSMD	Carriage & Traction Company
CS	Carnforth T&RSMD	West Coast Railway
CU*	Carlisle Currock WRD (closed)	Storage location only
CW*	Crewe South Yard	Storage location only
DE*	Dewsbury	RMS Locotech
DI*	Didcot Railway Centre	Great Western Society
DR	Doncaster TMD	EWS
DS*	Doncaster Station	Storage location only
DW	Doncaster West Yard	Storage location only
DY	Derby Etches Park T&RSMD	Maintrain (on behalf of Midland Mainline)
EC	Edinburgh Craigentinny T&RSMD	Great North Eastern Railway
EH	Eastleigh TMD	EWS

EM	East Ham T&RSMD	LTS Rail
EN	Euston Downside CARMD	EWS
FB	Ferrybridge T&RSMD	EWS
FD	Unallocated	Freightliner
FE	Unallocated	Freightliner
FF	Forest (Brussels) T&RSMD	SNCB/NMBS
FH	Frodingham (Scunthorpe)(closed)	Storage location only
FK*	Ferme Park CSD	Storage location only
FR	Fratton T&RSMD	South West Trains
FS	Unallocated	Freightliner
FW	Fort William SD	EWS
FX*	Felixstowe	Felixstowe Dock & Railway Co.
GD	Gateshead WRD (closed)	Storage location only
GI	Gillingham T&RSMD	Connex South Eastern
GW	Shields Road (Glasgow) T&RSMD	ScotRail/Alstom
HA	Haymarket (Edinburgh) TMD	ScotRail
HE	Hornsey T&RSMD	West Anglia Great Northern Railway
HG	Hither Green TMD	EWS
HM	Healey Mills (Wakefield)	Storage location only
HT	Heaton (Newcastle upon Tyne) T&RSMD	Northern Spirit
HY*	Hinksey Yard (Oxford)	Storage location only
IL	Ilford T&RSMD	First Great Eastern
IM	Immingham TMD	EWS
IS	Inverness T&RSMD	ScotRail
IS	Inverness CARMD	ScotRail
KD	Carlisle Kingmoor TMD	Direct Rail Services
KK	Kirkdale SD	Merseyrail Electrics
KM*	Carlisle Kingmoor Yard	Storage location only
KN*	MOD Kineton	Storage location only
KR	Kidderminster	Severn Valley Railway
KY	Knottingley T&RSMD	EWS
LA	Laira (Plymouth) T&RSMD	First Great Western
LB	Loughborough	Brush Traction
LE	Landore (Swansea) T&RSMD	First Great Western
LG	Longsight Electric (Manchester) T&RSMD	Crossfleet Maintenance (On behalf of Virgin Cross Country)
LL	Liverpool Downhill CSD	West Coast Traincare (On behalf of Virgin West Coast)
LO	Longsight Diesel (Manchester) TMD	First North Western
LR	Leicester SD	EWS
LT*	MOD Longtown	Storage location only
LY	Le Landy (Paris) T&RSMD	SNCF
MA	Longsight (Manchester) CARMD	West Coast Traincare (On behalf of Virgin West Coast)
MD	Merehead T&RSMD	Mendip Rail
MG	Margam (Port Talbot) SD	EWS
MH	Millerhill (Edinburgh) SD	EWS
ML	Motherwell T&RSMD	EWS
MM	Moreton-in-Marsh	Storage location only

NATO	On loan to North Atlantic Treaty Organisation in Kosovo.	
NB*	New Brighton EMU Sidings	Storage location only
NC	Norwich Crown Point T&RSMD	Anglia Railways
NH	Newton Heath T&RSMD	First North Western
NL	Neville Hill InterCity T&RSMD (Leeds)	Maintrain (On behalf of Midland Mainline)
NL	Neville Hill DMU/EMU T&RSMD (Leeds)	Northern Spirit
NP	North Pole International T&RSMD (London)	Eurostar (UK)
NY	Grosmont T&RSMD	North Yorkshire Moors Railway
OC	Old Oak Common TMD (London)	EWS
OH	Old Oak Common Electric T&RSMD (London)	Siemens (on behalf of British Airports Authority)
OM	Old Oak Common CARMD (London)	Storage location only
OO	Old Oak Common HST T&RSMD (London)	First Great Western
OY	Oxley T&RSMD (Wolverhampton)	West Coast Traincare (On behalf of Virgin West Coast)
PB	Peterborough SD	EWS
PC	Polmadie T&RSMD	West Coast Traincare (On behalf of Virgin West Coast)
PH	Perth SD	ScotRail
PM	St. Phillips Marsh T&RSMD (Bristol)	First Great Western
PN*	Preston Station	Storage location only
PQ*	Parkeston Yard	Storage location only
PY*	MOD Pig's Bay (Shoeburyness)	Storage location only
PZ	Penzance	First Great Western
RG	Reading TMD	Thames Trains
RL	Ropley	Mid Hants Railway
RM	Ramsgate T&RSMD	Connex South Eastern
RY	Ryde T&RSMD (Isle of Wight)	Island Line
SA	Salisbury TMD	South West Trains
SD	Sellafield TMD	Direct Rail Services
SE	St. Leonards T&RSMD	St. Leonards Railway Engineering
SF	Stratford SD (London)	EWS
SG	Slade Green T&RSMD	Connex South Eastern
SI	Soho T&RSMD	Maintrain (On behalf of Central Trains)
SK	Swanwick Junction T&RSMD	Midland Railway
SL	Stewarts Lane T&RSMD (London)	Gatwick Express
SNCF	On loan to Société Nationale des Chemins de fer Français in France	
SO	Southport EMU Sidings	Storage location only
SP	Springs Branch CRDC (Wigan)	EWS
SU	Selhurst T&RSMD (Croydon)	Connex South Central
SZ	Southall T&RSMD	Flying Scotsman Railways
TE	Thornaby T&RSMD	EWS
TL*	Temple Mills Yard (London)	Storage location only
TM	Birmingham Railway Museum	Birmingham Railway Museum/ Fragonset Railways
TO	Toton TMD (Nottinghamshire)	EWS

TS	Tyseley T&RSMD	Maintrain (On behalf of Central Trains)
TT*	Toton Training School (Nottinghamshire)	Storage location only
WA	Warrington Arpley SD	EWS
WB	Wembley CSD	West Coast Traincare (On behalf of Virgin West Coast)
WD	Wimbledon T&RSMD	South West Trains
WI*	Willesden Brent Sidings	Storage location only
WK*	West Kirkby	Storage location only
WN	Willesden TMD (London)	West Coast Traincare (On behalf of Virgin West Coast)
WR*	West Ruislip	London Underground
YK	York SD	Northern Spirit
YM	National Railway Museum, York	Science Museum
YO*	Yoker SD	ScotRail
ZA	Railway Technical Centre, Derby	Serco Railtest/AEA Technology/ Fragonset Railways
ZB	Doncaster	RFS (E)
ZC	Crewe	Adtranz
ZD	Derby Litchurch Lane	Adtranz
ZE*	Birmingham	Alstom
ZF	Doncaster	Adtranz
ZG	Eastleigh	Alstom
ZH	Glasgow	Railcare
ZI	Ilford	Adtranz
ZN	Wolverton	Railcare
ZP	Horbury (Wakefield)	Bombardier-Prorail

6.6 DEPOT TYPE CODES

CARMD	Carriage Maintenance Depot
CRDC	Component Recovery & Distribution Centre
CSD	Carriage Servicing Depot
CS	Carriage Sidings
SD	Servicing Depot
TMD	Traction Maintenance depot
T&RSMD	Traction & Rolling Stock depot
WRD	Wagon Repair Depot

6.7 GENERAL ABBREVIATIONS

a.c.	alternating current
BR	British Railways
BSI	Bergische Stahl Industrie
d.c.	direct current
DEMU	Diesel-electric multiple unit
Dia.	Diagram
DMU	Diesel multiple unit (general term)
EMU	Electric multiple unit.
FLT	Freightliner Terminal
ft.	feet
GNER	Great North Eastern Railway
GNR	Great Northern Railway
GWR	Great Western Railway.
h.p.	horsepower
HST	High Speed Train
Hz	Hertz
in.	inches
kN	kilonewtons
km/h	kilometres per hour
kW	kilowatts
lbf	pounds force
LMR	British Railways, London Midland Region
LMS	London Midland & Scottish Railway
LNER	London & North Eastern Railway
LNWR	London & North Western Railway
LT	London Transport
LUL	London Underground Limited
m.	metres
mm.	millimetres
m.p.h.	miles per hour
NPCCS	Non-Passenger-Carrying Coaching Stock
No.	number
RCH	Railway Clearing House
r.p.m.	revolutions per minute
RSL	Rolling Stock Library
SR	British Railways, Southern Region
T	Toilets
t.	tonnes
TD	Toilets suitable for disabled passengers
TOPS	Total Operations Processing System
V	Volts
W	Wheelchair spaces

6.8 BUILDER DETAILS

These are shown in class headings, the following abbreviations being used:

ABB Derby	ABB, Derby Carriage Works (now Adtranz Derby).
ABB Doncaster	ABB, Doncaster Works (now Adtranz Doncaster).
ABB York	ABB, York.
Adtranz Derby	Adtranz, Derby Carriage Works.
Alexander	Walter Alexander, Falkirk.
Alstom Birmingham	Alstom, Saltley, Birmingham.
Alstom Eastleigh	Alstom, Eastleigh Works.
Ashford	BR, Ashford Works.
Barclay	Andrew Barclay, Caledonia Works, Kilmarnock (now Hunslet-Barclay).
Bombardier BN	Bombardier BN, Brugge, Belgium.
Bombardier Prorail	Bombardier Prorail, Horbury Junction, Wakefield.
BRCW	Birmingham Railway Carriage & Wagon, Smethwick.
BREL Derby	BREL, Derby Carriage Works.
BREL Eastleigh	BREL, Eastleigh Works (later Wessex Traincare, now Alstom Eastleigh).
BREL Swindon	BREL, Swindon Works.
BREL Wolverton	BREL, Wolverton Works (now Railcare, Wolverton).
BREL York	BREL, York Works (later ABB York).
CAF	Construcciones y Auxiliar de Ferrocarriles, Zaragosa, Spain.
Cowlairs	BR, Cowlairs Works.
Cravens	Cravens, Sheffield.
Derby	BR, Derby Carriage Works (later BREL Derby, then ABB Derby, now Adtranz Derby).
Doncaster	BR, Doncaster Works (later BREL Doncaster, then BRML Doncaster, then ABB Doncaster, now Adtranz Doncaster).
Eastleigh	BR, Eastleigh Works (later BREL Eastleigh, then Wessex Traincare, now Alstom Eastleigh).
GEC-A Birmingham	GEC-Alsthom, Saltley, Birmingham.
Gloucester	Gloucester Railway Carriage & Wagon, Gloucester.
Hunslet-Barclay	Hunslet-Barclay, Caledonia Works, Kilmarnock.
Hunslet TPL	Hunslet Transportation Projects, Leeds.
Lancing	SR, Lancing Works (later BR, Lancing Works).
Leyland Bus	Leyland Bus, Workington.
Metro-Cammell	Metropolitan-Cammell, Saltley, Birmingham (later GEC-A Birmingham, now Alstom Birmingham).
Pressed Steel	Pressed Steel, Linwood.
Railcare Glasgow	Railcare, Springburn Works, Glasgow.
Railcare Wolverton	Railcare, Wolverton.
Charles Roberts	Charles Roberts, Horbury Junction, Wakefield (later Procor, now BombardierProrail).
RTC	BR, Railway Technical Centre, Derby.
Swindon	BR, Swindon Works.
Wessex Traincare	Wessex Traincare, Eastleigh (now Alstom Eastleigh).
York	BR, York Carriage Works (later BREL York, then ABB York).

7. UK LIGHT RAIL SYSTEMS & METROS

7.1. BLACKPOOL & FLEETWOOD TRAMWAY

Until the opening of Manchester Metrolink, the Blackpool & Fleetwood Tramway was the only urban/inter-urban tramway system left in Britain. The infrastructure is owned by the local authorities and the tramway operated by Blackpool Transport Services Ltd.

System: 660 V d.c. overhead.
Depot & Workshops: Rigby Road, Blackpool.
Livery: Cream and green. (many in advertising livery).

Notes: Numbers in brackets are pre-1968 numbers. All cars are single-deck unless stated otherwise.

OPEN BOAT CARS   A1-1A

Built: 1934–5 by English Electric. 12 built (225–236).
Traction Motors: Two EE327 of 30 kW.
Seats: 56.

600 (225)	604 (230)	606 (235)
602 (227)	605 (233)	607 (236)

REPLICA VANGUARD   A1-1A

Built: 1987 by Blackpool & Fleetwood Tramway, Blackpool on underframe of one man car No. 7 which was itself converted from English Electric Railcoach 619 (282).
Traction Motors: Two EE327 of 30 kW.
Seats:

619

BRUSH RAILCOACHES   A1-1A

Built: 1937 by Brush. 20 built (284–303).
Traction Motors: Two EE305 of 40 kW (*EE327 of 30 kW).
Seats: 48.

Note: 635 carries its original number 298.

621 (284)		627 (290)	634 (297)
622 (285)	*	630 (293)	635 (298)
623 (286)		631 (294)	636 (299)
625 (288)		632 (295)	637 (300)
626 (289)		633 (296)	

CENTENARY CLASS   A1-1A

Built: 1984–7. Body by East Lancs. Coachbuilders, Blackburn. One man operated.
Traction Motors: Two EE305 of 40 kW.
Seats: 52.

* Rebuilt from GEC car 651.

641	643	645	647
642	644	646	648 *

CORONATION CLASS   Bo-Bo

Built: 1953 by Charles Roberts & Co., Wakefield. Resilient wheels. 25 built (304–328).
Traction motors: Four Crompton-Parkinson 92 of 34 kW.
Seats: 56.

660 (324)

PROGRESS TWIN CARS   A1-1A + 2-2

Built: Motor cars (671–677) rebuilt 1958–60 from English Electric railcoaches by Blackpool Corporation Transport. Driving trailers (681–687) built 1960 by Metro-Cammell.
Traction Motors: Two EE305 of 40 kW.
Seats: 53 + 53.

671+681 (281+T1)	674+684 (284+T4)	676+686 (286+T6)
672+682 (282+T2)	675+685 (285+T5)	677+687 (287+T7)
673+683 (283+T1)		

ENGLISH ELECTRIC RAILCOACHES   A1-1A

Built: Rebuilt 1958–60 from English Electric railcoaches. Originally ran with trailers.
Traction Motors: Two EE305 of 40 kW.
Seats: 48.

678 (278)	679 (279)	680 (280)

"BALLOON" DOUBLE DECKERS   A1-1A

Built: 1934–5 by English Electric. 700–712 were originally built with open tops, and 706 has now reverted to that condition and is named 'PRINCESS ALICE'.
Traction Motors: Two EE305 of 40 kW.
Seats: 94.

* Rebuilt with new front end design and air-conditioned cabs.
§ Converted to ice cream tram seating 64 with an ice cream sales area in one of the lower saloons.
R Red and white livery.

700	(237)		709	(246)	
701	(238)	**R**	710	(247)	
702	(239)		711	(248)	
703	(240)		712	(249)	
704	(241)		713	(250)	
706	(243)		715	(252)	
707	(244)	*	716	(253)	
708	(245)		717	(254)	

718	(255)	
719	(256)	§
720	(257)	
721	(258)	
722	(259)	
723	(260)	
724	(261)	
726	(263)	

ILLUMINATED CARS

732	(168)	Rocket	Built: 1961	Seats: 47
733	(209)	Western Train loco. & tender	Built: 1962	Seats: 35
734	(174)	Western Train coach	Built: 1962	Seats: 60
735	(222)	Hovertram	Built: 1963	Seats: 99
736	(170)	HMS Blackpool	Built: 1965	Seats: 71

WORKS CARS

259	(748, 624)	Permanent way car	Converted: 1971
260	(751, 628, 291)	Crane car and rail carrier	Converted: 1973
752	(2, 1)	Rail grinder and snowplough	Converted: 19
753	(S)	Overhead line car	Converted: 1958
754		New works car (unnumbered)	Built: 1993

JUBILEE CLASS DOUBLE DECKERS

Built: Rebuilt 1979/82 from Balloon cars. Standard bus ends, thyristor control and stairs at each end. 761 has one door per side whereas 762 has two.
Traction Motors: Two EE305 of 40 kW.
Seats: 100.

761	(725, 262)		762	(714, 251)

VINTAGE CARS

Blackpool & Fleetwood 2	Crossbench	Built: 1898
Blackpool & Fleetwood 31	"Marton box car"	Built: 1901
Blackpool & Fleetwood 40	Box car	Built: 1914
Blackpool & Fleetwood 167	"Pantograph car"	Built: 1928
Bolton 66	Bogie double-decker	Built: 1901

7.2 CROYDON TRAMLINK

This new system runs through central Croydon with lines to Wimbledon, Addington and Beckenham Junction/Elmers End. It is not yet open for passenger service, but is expected to open early in 2000. Operated by Tramlink Croydon Ltd.

System: 750 V d.c. overhead.
Depot & Workshops: Therapia Lane, Croydon.
Livery: Red and white.

SIX AXLE ARTICULATED CARS   Bo–2–Bo

Built: 1998-99 by Bombardier-Wien Schienenfahrzeuge, Austria.
Traction Motors: Four of 120 kW each.
Seats: 70.
Dimensions: 30.10 x 2.65 m.
Couplers: Scharfenberg.
Doors: Sliding plug.
Weight: 36.3 t.
Braking: Disc, regenerative and magnetic track.
Max. Speed: 80 km/h.

A Advertising livery.

2530	2534	2538	2542 **A**	2546 **A**	2550
2531 **A**	2535	2539	2543	2547	2551
2532	2536	2540	2544	2548	2552
2533 **A**	2537	2541	2545	2549	2553

7.3. DOCKLANDS LIGHT RAILWAY

This is a light rail line running in London's East End between Bank, Tower Gateway and Stratford to Lewisham and Beckton. Originally owned by London Transport, it is now owned by DLR Ltd. and operated by DLR Management Ltd. Cars normally operate automatically using the Alcatel "Seltrack" moving block signalling system.

System: 750 V d.c. third rail (bottom contact).
Depots: Poplar, Beckton.
Workshops: Poplar
Livery: Red and blue.

CLASS B90   B–2–B

Built: 1991–2 by BN Construction, Brugge, Belgium. (now Bombardier BN).
Chopper control.
Traction Motors: Two Brush of 140 kW.

Seats: 66.
Dimensions: 28.80 x 2.65 m.
Couplers: Scharfenberg.
Doors: Sliding. End doors for staff use.
Weight: 36 t.
Braking: Rheostatic.
Max. Speed: 80 km/h.

22	26	30	34	38	42
23	27	31	35	39	43
24	28	32	36	40	44
25	29	33	37	41	

CLASS B92   B–2–B

Built: 1992–5 by BN Construction, Brugge, Belgium. (now Bombardier BN).
Chopper control.
Traction Motors: Two Brush of 140 kW.
Seats: 66.
Dimensions: 28.80 x 2.65 m.
Couplers: Scharfenberg.
Doors: Sliding. End doors for staff use.
Weight: 36 t.
Braking: Rheostatic.
Max. Speed: 80 km/h.

A Advertising livery.

45	**A**	53	61	69		77	85
46	**A**	54	62	70		78	86
47	**A**	55	63	71		79	87
48	**A**	56	64	72	**A**	80	88
49	**A**	57	65	73		81	89
50	**A**	58	66	74		82	90
51	**A**	59	67	**A**	75	83	91
52		60	68	**A**	76	84	

BATTERY/ELECTRIC WORKS LOCO   B

Built: 1991 by RFS Engineering, Kilnhurst.
Electrical Equipment:

Unnumbered

DIESEL SHUNTER   B

Built: 1962 by Ruston & Hornsby, Lincoln.
Engine:
Transmission: Mechanical.

Unnumbered

7.4. MANCHESTER METROLINK

This light rail system runs from Bury to Altrincham through the streets of Manchester, with a spur to Piccadilly. A new line has been built to Salford Quays and Eccles. The system is franchised to the Altram consortium and the operation is subcontracted to Serco Metrolink.

System: 750 V d.c. overhead.
Depot & Workshops: Queens Road, Manchester.
Livery: White, dark grey and blue.

SIX-AXLE ARTICULATED CARS   Bo–2–Bo

Built: 1991–2 by Firema, Italy. Chopper control.
Traction Motors: Four GEC of 130 kW.
Seats: 84.
Dimensions: 29.00 x 2.65 m.
Couplers: Scharfenberg.
Doors: Sliding.
Weight: 45 t.
Braking: Rheostatic, regenerative, disc and emergency track.
Max. Speed: 80 km/h.

* Fitted with front valances, retractible couplers and controllable magnetic track brakes for running to Eccles.

1001		1014	THE CITY OF DRAMA
1002		1015	* SPARKY
1003		1016	
1004	THE ROBERT OWEN	1017	
1005	*	1018	SIR MATT BUSBY
1006		1019	
1007		1020	THE DAVID GRAHAM CBE
1008	MANCHESTER AIRPORT	1021	THE GREATER MANCHESTER RADIO
1009		1022	THE GRAHAM ASHWORTH
1010	MANCHESTER CHAMPION	1023	
1011		1024	THE JOHN GREENWOOD
1012		1025	
1013	THE FUSILIER	1026	THE POWER

SIX-AXLE ARTICULATED CARS   Bo–2–Bo

Built: 1999 by Ansaldo, Italy. Chopper control. Fitted with front valances, retractible couplers and controllable magnetic track brakes for running to Eccles.
Traction Motors: Four GEC of 130 kW.
Seats: 82.
Dimensions: 29.00 x 2.65 m.
Couplers: Scharfenberg.
Doors: Power operated sliding.

Weight: 45 t.
Braking: Rheostatic, regenerative, disc and magnetic track.
Max. Speed: 80 km/h.

2001	2004
2002	2005
2003	2006

SPECIAL PURPOSE VEHICLE

Built: 1991 by RFS Industries, Kilnhurst.
Engine: Caterpillar 3306 PCT of 170 kW.
Transmission: Mechanical. Rockwell T280.
Couplers: Scharfenberg.
Max. Speed: 40 km/h.

Unnumbered

7.5 MIDLAND METRO

This new operation runs from Birmingham Snow Hill to Wolverhampton along the former GWR line to Wolverhampton Low Level. On the approach to Wolverhampton it deviates from the former railway alignment to run on-street to the St. George's terminus. Operated by Travel West Midlands Ltd.

System: 750 V d.c. overhead.
Depot & Workshops: Wednesbury.
Livery: Dark blue and light grey with green stripe, yellow doors and red front end and roof.

SIX AXLE ARTICULATED CARS   Bo–2–Bo

Built: 1998–99 by Ansaldo Transporti, Italy.
Traction Motors: Four.
Seats: 58.
Dimensions: 24.00 x 2.65 m.
Couplers: Not equipped.
Doors: Power operated sliding plug.
Weight: 35.6 t.
Braking: Rheostatic, regenerative, disc and magnetic track.
Max. Speed: 75 km/h.

01	04	07	10	13	15
02	05	08	11	14	16
03	06	09	12		

7.6. STAGECOACH SUPERTRAM

This light rail system has three lines, to Halfway in the south east of Sheffield with a spur from Gleadless Townend to Herdings, to Middlewood in the north west with a spur from Hillsborough to Malin Bridge and to Meadowhall Interchange in the north east adjacent to the large shopping complex. Because of the severe gradients in Sheffield (up to 1 in 10), all axles are powered on the vehicles which are owned by South Yorkshire Light Rail Ltd., a subsidiary of South Yorkshire Passenger Transport Executive, but are mortgaged to Lloyd's Bank, whilst the operating company, South Yorkshire Supertram Ltd. has been leased to Stagecoach Holdings Ltd. for 27 years and is now known as Stagecoach Supertram.

System: 750 V d.c. overhead.
Depot & Workshops: Nunnery.
Livery: White with orange, red and blue stripes.

A Advertising livery.

EIGHT-AXLE ARTICULATED UNITS   B–B–B–B

Built: 1993–4 by Duewag, Düsseldorf, Germany.
Traction Motors: Four monomotors.
Seats: 88.
Dimensions: 34.75 x 2.65 m.
Couplers: Not equipped.
Doors: Sliding plug.
Weight: 52 t.
Braking: Rheostatic, regenerative, disc and emergency track.
Max. Speed: 50 m.p.h.

101	106	110	114	118	122
102	107	111	115	119	123
103	108	112	116	120 **A**	124
104	109	113	117	121	125
105					

FOUR WHEELED WORKS CAR   B

Built: 1968 by Reichsbahn Ausbesserungswerke Schöneweide, Berlin, East Germany as single-ended passenger car with electrical equipment by LEW Henningsdorf. Converted 1980 to double-ended works car. Delivered to Sheffield on 7th November 1996.
Traction Motors: Two.

721 039-4   (5104, 217 303-7)   out of use

7.7. STRATHCLYDE PTE UNDERGROUND

This circular 4 foot gauge underground line in Glasgow is generally referred to as the "Subway" or the "Clockwork Orange". It is operated by Strathclyde PTE.

System: 600 V d.c. third rail.
Depot & Workshops: Broomloan.
Livery: Orange and black.

SINGLE POWER CARS   Bo–Bo

Built: 1977–79 by Metropolitan Cammell, Birmingham. Refurbished 1993–95 by ABB Derby.
Traction Motors: Four GEC G312AZ of 35.6 kW each.
Seats: 36.
Dimensions: 12.81 x 2.34 m.
Couplers: Wedglock.
Doors: Sliding.
Weight: 19.62 t.
Maximum Speed: 54 km/h.

101	107	113	119	124	129
102	108	114	120	125	130
103	109	115	121	126	131
104	110	116	122	127	132
105	111	117	123	128	133
106	112	118			

INTERMEDIATE TRAILERS   2–2

Built: 1992 by Hunslet-Barclay, Kilmarnock.
Seats: 40.
Dimensions: 12.70 x 2.34 m.   **Doors:** Sliding.
Couplers: Wedglock.   **Weight:** 17.25 t.
Maximum Speed: 54 km/h.

201	203	205	206	207	208
202	204				

BATTERY ELECTRIC WORKS LOCOS   Bo

Built: 1977 by Clayton Equipment, Hatton.
Battery: 96 cell Chloride lead acid.
Traction Motors: Two GEC G312AZ of 35.6 kW each.
Dimensions: 4.65 x ?.?? m.
Couplers: Wedglock.
Weight: 14.8 tonnes.

L2	LOBEY DOSSER
L3	RANK BAJIN

BATTERY ELECTRIC WORKS LOCO   Bo

Built: 1974 by Clayton Equipment, Hatton. One of a pair of 3 ft. gauge locomotives for use on the Channel Tunnel construction project. Both were converted to 4 ft. gauge in 1976 or 1977 and used by contractors Taylor Woodrow on the Strathclyde Underground modernisation between 1977 and 1980 before being stored at Taylor Woodrow, Southall. Both were purchased in a derelict condition by Strathclyde PTE in 1987, and one loco, L4, was rebuilt by Clayton in 1988 from the parts recovered from these two locomotives. L4 was further rebuilt by Hunslet-Barclay, Kilmarnock, in 1990 to make it compatible with L2 and L3.
Battery: 96 cell Chloride lead acid.
Traction Motors: Two GEC G312AZ of 35.6 kW each.
Couplers: Wedglock.

L4   EL FIDELDO

7.8. TYNE AND WEAR METRO

System: 1500 V d.c. overhead.
Depot & Workshops: South Gosforth.
Livery: Yellow and white unless otherwise indicated.

SIX-AXLE ARTICULATED UNITS   B–2–B

Built: 1978–81 by Metropolitan Cammell, Birmingham (4001/2 were built by Metropolitan Cammell in 1976 and rebuilt 1984–87 by Hunslet TPL, Leeds).
Traction Motors: Two Siemens of 187 kW each.
Seats: 68 (* 84; § 70).   **Dimensions:** 27.80 x 2.65 x 3.15 m.
Couplers: BSI.   **Doors:** Sliding plug.
Weight: 39.0 t.   **Maximum Speed:** 80 km/h.

A Advertising livery; **B** Blue and yellow; **G** Green and yellow; **R** Red and yellow.
0 Original 1975 livery with red stripe as used on test track.
§ Red Triangle coupling code. Can only couple to other Red Triangle Cars.

4001	0	4019	R	4037	R	4055	R	4073	R
4002	A	4020	R	4038	R	4056 *	A	4074	R
4003	R	4021	R	4039	A	4057	A	4075	B
4004 ▲	G	4022	R	4040	R	4058 *		4076 *	
4005	R	4023 *		4041	R	4059	R	4077	R
4006	R	4024 *▲		4042	A	4060	R	4078	R
4007	R	4025 *		4043	R	4061 ▲	G	4079	R
4008	B	4026	R	4044	R	4062	R	4080	R
4009	R	4027	R	4045	A	4063 *	A	4081 *	
4010	R	4028	R	4046	R	4064	R	4082	G
4011	R	4029 *▲		4047 *▲		4065	R	4083 *	A
4012	R	4030	R	4048	B	4066	B	4084	R
4013	R	4031 *		4049	A	4067	R	4085	B
4014	R	4032	R	4050	R	4068	R	4086	B
4015	R	4033	R	4051	R	4069	R	4087 §	A
4016	B	4034	R	4052	R	4070	R	4088	R
4017	R	4035	B	4053 *		4071 *		4089	R
4018 *		4036	G	4054 *		4072 *▲		4090	R

Names:

4026	George Stephenson	4065	Dame Catherine Cookson
4041	HARRY COWANS	4077	Robert Stephenson
4060	Thomas Bewick	4078	ELLEN WILKINSON

BATTERY/ELECTRIC WORKS LOCOS

Built: 1989–90 by Hunslet TPL, Leeds.
Traction Motors: Two Hunslet-Greenbat T9-4P of 67 kW each.
Dimensions: 9.00 x ?.?? m.   **Couplers:** BSI.
Weight: 26.25 t.   **Maximum Speed:** 50 km/h.
Livery: Green, with red solebar and black & yellow striped ends.

BL1	BL2	BL3

Front Cover Photograph: Class 86 25 kV 50 Hz a.c. overhead electric locomotive 86215, wearing Anglia Railways livery, heads a rake of largely likewise liveried carriages forming a Harwich International–London Liverpool Street 'Boat Train' service at Kelvedon on 15th August 1999.   **Michael J. Collins**

Back Cover Photograph: The oldest complete train in regular passenger service on the first day of the millennium was Class 101 2-car unit 101 685. It has been restored to original BR green livery and was photographed approaching Sheffield on 4th April 1999 with the 08.46 stopping service from Manchester.   **Les Nixon**